Toward a Democratic Science

Toward a
Democratic Science

Scientific Narration and

Civic Communication

Richard Harvey Brown

Yale University Press

New Haven and London

Printed in the United States of America.

Library of Congress Cataloging-in-Publication Data
Brown, Richard Harvey.
Toward a democratic science : scientific narration and civic communication /
Richard Harvey Brown.
p. cm.
Includes bibliographical references and index.
ISBN 0-300-06707-0 (cloth : alk. paper)
1. Science—Social aspects.   2. Science—Philosophy.   3. Communication
in science.   4. Science—Moral and ethical aspects.   5. Narration
(Rhetoric)   I. Title.
Q175.5.B76   1998
303.48′3—dc21   97-14234

A catalogue record for this book is available from the British Library.

The paper in this book meets the guidelines for permanence and durability of the Committee on Production Guidelines for Book Longevity of the Council on Library Resources.

10   9   8   7   6   5   4   3   2   1

For Jason Walter Brown,
scientist, brother, and friend,
whose love, and whose intellectual passion,
moved me to seek a language
common to our differing pursuits.

Contents

Preface

Science has become a dominant form of thinking and of justifying and organizing social arrangements in modern societies. Science also offers a language for communication between differing cultural groups, and it is a crucial factor in advanced economic production. Despite this centrality, however, science does not adequately provide value and dignity to our existence. Instead, it is through public narrations that we give meaning to our world and to our lives.

Thus science and narration seem to exclude each other. In this separation we are forced to choose between the amoral rationality of science and the seemingly irrational moralism of storytelling, with little confluence of the two in reasoned public moral action. This segregation of reason and ethics engenders crises of citizenship and of legitimacy. To be a citizen means to act publicly as a whole person, that is, as a rational moral agent. But when moral discourse and action become exclusively emotive or private, and when actions taken in the public arena are governed purely by functional efficiency or irrational stories, then the space for reasoned public moral action is drastically reduced. Even private actions become less morally significant when they are removed from their larger institutional contexts, and privatization of ethics also undermines personal dignity, integrity, and identity. As less and less public space is available for the exercise of citizenship, the moral basis of the public sphere is subverted, bringing on a crisis of legitimacy.

Many thinkers have analyzed these contradictions and suggested ways to overcome them. Certainly any adequate intervention entails an understanding of how the discourses of reason and narration interact and are infused with power. One would hope, also, to foster an alternative public discourse that conjoined efficiency in techno-administrative systems with meaning and morality in our lifeworlds. Indeed, if we are to have integrity and self-direction in both our personal and our civic lives, we must integrate these two ways of knowing and being. Such an integration is the larger telos of this book.

One move in such a project is to construe science as a kind of narration and to understand narration as a form of reason. Scientific and moral discourses are two ways to navigate the stream of language. And once we understand science as a rhetorical practice—a kind of storytelling—science is subsumed within narration, which is a capacity possessed by members of all human communities. Science as narration thereby becomes available in principle to ordinary citizens in the rational, ethical construction of their common life.

This central argument is developed in several stages. In the beginning of the book I argue that human experience in general has a rhetorical or textual character. Then I apply this perspective to the social sciences, arguing that they too are discursive constructions. My next moves are to expand this imagery and reasoning to the natural and experimental sciences. Finally I offer a practical example of how a narrative view of science can help integrate science within an ethical political discourse of citizens. This example is generalized in the volume's conclusion.

Through this strategy of argument, this book seeks to address several questions that are central to public knowledge and civic communication. How might the public space be reclaimed from scientistic experts and irrational storytellers and expanded for citizen self-direction? How can we redeem science from absolutist pretensions of positivist ideologues, on the one hand, and liberate it from the political and economic opportunism of the corporate state, on the other? How can we move beyond the naive or cynical technicism of positivist planners and the sterile moralism or implicit nihilism of their romantic or reactionary critics? What is the role in such a project for narratives of scientific and ethical traditions? How can more embracing narratives be created that subsume scientific-technical knowledge within a broader reasoned ethical public life?

Adequate responses to such questions require alternative visions of science and democracy that are more utopian than ideological. One such vision is that of a "democratic science" that is cognitively accessible and politically accountable to nonprofessional publics. This involves not only a reconceptualization of science as narrative practice but also the democratization of the apparatus for making science policy and for doing and using science. Another necessary element is social movements that provide political will and civic intelligence for such transformations. The civic discourse that emerges in such utopian changes is one in which science and ethics are fused in prudent judgment by citizens reasoning and deciding together as they create themselves and their civic culture.

Acknowledgments

Writers who draw on disciplines not their own are akin to ethnographers who depend on native informants in order to get it right, or even to stay alive. I am likewise indebted to scholars and friends in the disciplines that I discuss or use as resources. Without them this project would not have survived. Chapter 1, "Scientific Knowledge, Rhetorical Criticism, and Civic Communication," emerged from discussions with Herbert Simons, and part of it appeared in the collection he edited with Michael Billig, *After Postmodernism* (Sage, 1994). Chapter 2, "Textuality, Social Science, and Society," benefited greatly from criticism received from Steven Seidman and David G. Wagner, who co-edited *Postmodernism and Social Theory* (Basil Blackwell, 1992), in which sections of the chapter appeared.

Chapter 3, "Social Science and the Poetics of Public Truth," emerged from stories told variously to the Colloquium on Social Ontology, co-sponsored by the Swedish Academy of Sciences and Linacre College at Oxford in March 1988, and to the audience at the inauguration of the Perelman Professorship at the University of Maryland in October 1988. I thank my critics at these gatherings—

especially Tom Burns and Rom Harré—for their instructive comments. I am also greatly indebted to George Ritzer and to the anonymous reviewers of *Sociological Forum,* in which an earlier version of this chapter appeared (vol. 5, no. 1 [March 1990]).

Chapter 4, "Science and Storytelling," owes much to critical comments of the members of the Symposium on Narrative and the Human Sciences, especially Allen Scult and Mitchell Ash, and the symposium organizers, Michael Calvin McGee and Bruce Gronbeck. The work in this chapter was also graciously supported by University House, the University of Iowa's Center for Advanced Studies, which hosted the symposium. An earlier version of this chapter appeared in *Philosophy and Rhetoric* 27, no. 1 (1994). My discussion of ethnographic discourse in this chapter and the next is greatly informed by discussions with practitioners, such as Jon W. Anderson and especially Lydia Nakashima Degarrod.

I am also grateful to Norman Denzin, Paul Roth, and Brian Fry for helpful suggestions on the essay that became chapter 5, "Narrative and Truth in Scientific Practice." My initial ideas were first presented at the Institute for Humanities, Wesleyan University, September 1988. A somewhat more advanced version appeared in *Current Perspectives in Social Theory* 11 (1990).

Parts of chapter 6, "Modern Science," benefited from the advice of Norman Denzin and anonymous reviewers of the *Sociological Quarterly,* in which an earlier version of the chapter appeared (vol. 34, no. 1 [1993]). Parts of chapter 7, "Poetics, Politics, and Professionalization in the Rise of American Psychology," appeared in *History of the Human Sciences* 5, no. 1 (1992). I thank the editor, Irving Velody, for his suggestion for improving my earlier draft. Chapter 8, "Toward a Field Theory of Knowledge/Power in Science and Civic Life," owes much to the comments and writings of Dick Pels, Ralph Kuhn, and Daniel Schubert. Chapter 9, "Democratic Science in Practice," is mostly written by Robert Brulle. Much of chapter 10, "Science and Citizenship in a Technicist Culture," emerged from conversations with Manfred Stanley, Walter Jost, Herbert Simons, Bruce Gronbeck, James Klumpp, Scott Baker, and Allen Scult. An overview of this project was presented to the Poroi Group at the University of Iowa, where it received helpful criticism from Ken Cmiel, Robert Boynton, and especially Donald McCloskey.

Colleagues at the University of Maryland contributed to this book, sometimes with specific insights and always through an ambiance of cordial intellectual discourse. My students, such as Robert Brulle, Ralph Kuhn, Daniel Schubert, Joan Vecchia, and Robert Wagmiller, played an even larger role in challenging my ideas—especially those ideas advanced in seminars on critical theory, postmodernism, and sociology of science. I am happy to thank Cynthia Mewborn, Geraldine Todd, Nancy W. Crawford, and Susan Bilek for their cheerful efficiency in typing many drafts of this book.

Toward a Democratic Science

Chapter 1 Scientific Knowledge, Rhetorical Criticism, and Civic Communication

The meaning of real human lives, whether of individuals or collectives, is the meaning of the plots, quasiplots, paraplots, or failed plots by which the events that those lives comprise are endowed with the aspect of stories. . . . A meaningful life is one that aspires to the cogency of a story with a plot.
Hayden White (1987:173)

It has become a general faith . . . that [science] and technical organization are a necessary and sufficient condition for arriving at truth; that they encompass all truth; and that they will be sufficient, if not at the moment, then shortly, to answer the questions that life thrusts upon us.
William Barret (1977)

There is a profound chasm between science and ethics in our public life. Science guarantees that we live in a shared external world that can be known through reason. It provides an apparently neutral discourse through which peoples of different interests or values can speak. It has also become a driving force in economic and social production. As such, science permits us to create and maintain our complex social and technical systems. But identity, morality, community, and tradition are achieved through narration. It is through public narrations that we give meaning to our worlds and to our lives.

The discourses of science and narration seem to exclude each other. In this separation, a narrowly conceived technical rationality is accepted as the objective language of public life, and ethical reflection is reduced to subjective or purely private realms. Thus we have amoral scientism in one sphere and irrational moralism in the other, with little confluence of the two in reasoned public moral action.

This separation of reason and ethics is historically recent. In classical thought, moral and scientific questions were both parts of philosophy, and calculations of efficiency pertained to the private sphere, to the *economia* or household. Politics, in turn, was a matter of prudence, of exercising seasoned judgment on practical cases. With the rise of positive science in the modern period, however, theoretical inquiry was joined with empirical research, but only at the cost of separating scientific from moral inquiry. The effect of this separation was to advance science by retarding ethics. Early modern thinkers equated God with Nature, Nature with Reason, Reason with science, and science with efficient control. By rejecting discourse on social ends, science was to provide a means for mastering nature, eventually including human nature and conduct as well.

The Enlightenment *philosophes* extended the scope of science from nature to human affairs in the hope of redesigning society on the basis of Reason. But only with the joint advent of social science and industrial society did this hope approach its realization. In the twentieth century, scientific calculation has been applied not only to matters of natural philosophy but also to social policies, programs, organizations, and human beings. In the process, moral discourse was banished from the kingdom of truth and relegated to the spheres of will, emotion, or subjective opinion. Public knowledge finally came to be understood as scientific knowledge, and science eventually became the most generally legitimate discourse on matters of public concern. Positivism became the legitimating epistemology for morally neutral science, and a vulgar, practical interpretation of science became a legitimating rhetoric of domination by government agencies, corporations, and experts. As scientific rationality took the form of *social* technologies for the guidance of human affairs, however, the earlier optimism about reason's ethical role in life and society diminished, and the alliance of science and freedom, and of reason and democracy, began to dissolve.

The privileged status of scientific and technical knowledge gives privileged status to experts who possess it. This empowerment of experts yields a depowerment of citizens. The criterion for the new knowledge is certitude, which entails a skepticism toward intuition, persuasion, judgment, and tradition. The new knowledge also requires a reductive approach to its topics in the name of objectivity and precision, and a specialized, partial vision in the name of competence. In contrast to the specialized value-neutral expert, however, the citizen ideally acts in the public sphere as a moral agent, judges the ends of policies as well their instruments, and exercises prudence and persuasion to make decisions in a field of uncertainty. As public policy and organizational direction become the domains of experts, however, there is a corresponding reduction of social space for action by citizens. Experts' knowledge comes to oppose citizens' actions and vice-versa. Persons may assert their own needs or interests, but any claim on public credence in the name of collective values is seen as either fundamentalist dogma or elitist manipulation. Value positions that infuse one's world with meaning and elicit committed action are devalued because they cannot have a basis in public (that is, scientific) rationality. Values are thought to be either self-evident or posited arbitrarily or manipulatively, rather than arrived at through reasoning and evidence. Justice, freedom, dignity, or any other general public interest is thereby redefined and re-allocated into the scientistic conceptual scheme. No longer culturally taken for granted, no longer even the ends that all means are expected to serve, democratic values now become utilities, costs, benefits, and risks.

The crisis of moral reason in public life is also existential: it concerns the erosion of the pretheoretical conviction that there is a moral sense to the world from which the self derives significance, and that the person's action in some ways can affect this world. The practice of citizenship is the political and institutional expression of these cultural convictions in democratic societies. But when this pretheoretical faith in the meaningfulness of one's world and the efficacy of one's actions is shattered, a crisis of freedom, dignity, and citizenship emerges. An exemplar situation might be "that of a person who despite appropriate motivation, reasonable education, and freedom from political tyranny nonetheless comes to feel that what goes on in the world has no coherent relationship to his morally intended actions. . . . If, for such a person, there is a sharp discontinuity between 'self' and 'world,' among moral intentions, actions, and outcomes, then it is both the meaning of the world and that of his own agency in it that are at stake" (Stanley 1981:158).

Such a situation occurs when moral traditions are rendered private or nonrational and the shared public reality appears in scientistic, ethically neutral garb.

But such values as justice, dignity, or freedom, like the value of science itself, can never be justified by scientific theories or technical calculations of utility alone, however rational these may be. This is because such values presuppose the possibility of an ethically intelligible world—a world that is not governed by scientific calculation. Yet such a world is explicitly removed from the scientistic discourse that has invaded public life and has come to define the nature of reason. The habits of objectivity, value neutrality, and rational calculation, when expanded to all spheres of human praxis, eliminate the practical and ideational bases of a shared ethical ontology, vocabulary, or tradition, the existence of or at least the search for which is central to democratic culture.

Thus, the conquest of ends by means is also a conquest of democracy by rationality. This is because the central humanistic value of the inherent dignity and freedom of each person is also a central legitimating principle of democracy and, reciprocally, because democracy is a major institutional expression of the cultural value of personal agency. But governance through social engineering, scientific techniques, and expert calculation construes persons as means or utilities, not ends or agents. Such rational governance thus undermines the cultural integument of democracy—the pretheoretical belief in the ethical significance of human agents in a world that is meaningful.

In such a system, administrative rationality becomes the definition of legality in a procedural democracy that is without any necessary ethical content. Self-determination is no longer an end in itself under which all particular interests are justly subordinated. Instead, democracy is seen as a method for allocating resources among groups, for selecting leaders, or for legitimating elites, a mechanism for distributing those rewards that the official system chooses to provide (Habermas 1970a:124; Gross 1980). Such a democracy makes it possible to have mastery of nature, the maintenance of health, and even happiness, all without freedom or dignity, for these are now rendered matters of subjective or personal opinion, redefined to serve elitist interests, and irrelevant if not obstacles to the efficient operation of the system.

This instrumental view of public discourse is illustrated by Narveson's (1967:185) discussion of the value of dignity. "Our account of utility," he writes, "implies that a person's dignity, in the irreducible sense, should count for roughly as much as the person having it wants it to count for, relative to his other desires." In other words, the "irreducible sense" of dignity *is* reducible to whatever anyone wants. In the same spirit, Lazlo (1971:178) reduces dignity to biocybernetic transactions: "Human dignity signifies the being . . . as well as the well-being . . . of the person. . . . Both the biological being and the cultural well-being of the individual represent normative organism-environment trans-actional states, in which the individual's needs and demands are matched by the appropriate environmental states and events."

Such writing and practice—in decision science, operations research, and other forms of social engineering—posit the absence of a public capable of reasoning about values. Beyond its obtuse philistinism, such technicist dis-course reverses the democratic impulse by encouraging citizens to occupy themselves with private matters while remaining beholden to their expert representatives in public affairs. Technicists are successful in cultivating such civic incompetence to the extent that ordinary citizens come to regard, say, foreign policy or scientific research as remote from their own daily concerns. "Yet the felt abstractness or remoteness of these activities, which the [technicist] promotes as grounds for rule by experts, does not necessarily reflect any causal detachment from everyday life. After all, the price of consumer goods at home, as well as their access, could easily be affected by either a breakdown in interna-tional relations or a scientific redefinition of product safety standards. What *is* detached from everyday life, however, is a rhetoric for talking about the causal connections," through which various constituencies could realize what is at stake for them in the conduct of public affairs (Fuller 1993:xix). Indeed, the technicist rhetoric of policy sciences explicitly eschews the deliberative rhetoric through which, since Aristotle, citizens were said to prudently conduct their civic life.

This sort of anti-democratic rationality infuses much contemporary prac-tice. Today various forms of scientific management have become the primary means of coordinating complex human activities in advanced societies. Knowl-edge of psychology guides and justifies the instrumental management of per-sonnel or propaganda. Economic knowledge guides and legitimates fiscal pol-icy and industrial planning. Sociology of organizations informs and legitimates executive practice. Applied knowledge of the natural sciences guides policies, regulations, and product development in myriad areas of contemporary gov-ernment and business. Knowledge of demographics, social survey methods, and electronic communication is crucial in political campaigns.

These new social technologies have forced us to reconsider the historic relation between knowledge and practice. Indeed, in the fast capitalism of today (Agger 1989), reflective, civic, aesthetic, or moral intelligence has become inexpedient. A technological society needs trained scientists, experts, and func-tionaries who react appropriately, but these persons do not need to understand either the functional connections of the system as a whole or the existential

consequences of their actions for society's members. As the path from knowledge to practice becomes shorter and more direct, action shrinks to reaction,
and fewer people know what they are doing in the sense that they know *why*
they do it that way (Blumenberg 1987:446–47).

The requirement of "performativity" (Lyotard 1988) makes it unnecessary
and often inefficient for functionaries or directors of contemporary systems to
act deliberatively and knowledgeably. Indeed, as knowledge becomes reduced
to information, and as human action is supplanted by systems behavior, the
older relation between contingent knowledge and prudent action is unhinged.
Along with this, the traditional role of rhetoric as the mediator between theory
and practice is brought into question. Unlike earlier periods when rhetoric
helped citizens make reasonable decisions in a field of uncertainty, today rhetoric has a new civic function: to criticize, to make visible the opaque, and to
demystify mystified relations. Still, we have to act even when we do not know
what to do or why we should do it. This transparent incongruence creates an
aporia of skepticism that cannot be filled either by rational planning or by the
momentum of sheer urgency. And it is within that aporia, between the absolutisms of scientific realism and ethical dogmatism, that critical rhetoric can regain
a dialectical, deliberative function.

The Greeks of Plato's Athens, like the Puritans of colonial America, operated
within a moral universe without invidious distinctions between politics and
ethics. By contrast, most contemporary discussions of ethics take as obvious the
need to distinguish talk of efficacy and talk of ethics. Moreover, such discussions generally assume that efficacy is the domain of reason, science, and
expertise, whereas ethics is a matter of revelation, opinion, or emotion. This
bifurcation has a number of dimensions. One of them is an assumption central
to the positivist habitus—that scientific rationality is independent of its social
contexts. That is, it is thought that the standards used to evaluate representations of truth (theories, facts), and our symbolic resources for constructing
them (logic, language, instrumentation), are autonomous of the historically
local discourses by which they are generated. Conversely, it is held that when
representations rest within more local processes of social and linguistic construction they do not warrant the status of truth.

These views often are held by both proponents and critics of positivism. Take
Paul Feyerabend. Even this self-declared anarchist accepts the antinomies that
emerge from the positivist view of reason. Feyerabend argued persuasively that

science would be irrational were it in fact to follow the rules of neo-positivists and critical rationalists. Yet Feyerabend's very criticism accepts without challenge, and apparently without awareness, the same fundamental assumption of his adversaries—that to be rational is to follow some specified universal method. And by assuming that scientific method must be constrictive and absolutist, he was led to advocate an epistemological anarchy in which "what remains are aesthetic judgments, judgments of taste, metaphysical prejudices, religious desires, in short, *what remains are our subjective wishes*" (Feyerabend 1978:385). This position does violence to formal rationality as well as to judgments of taste.

In the same spirit, much of the ethnographic sociology of science (e.g., Latour 1987; Knorr-Cetina and Mulkay 1983; Pickering 1992) shows science to be made up through locally embedded practices. On this account, pretensions to objectivity, universalism, and value freedom are debunked and science is unmasked as the social and rhetorical construction of a fragile and always partial and temporary consensus. "Actual science," argue such sociologists, does not and could not correspond to the "ideal science" imagined by positivist philosophers. Some researchers then assumed, with Pickering (1984a:413–14), that because "world-views are cultural products, . . . there is no obligation upon anyone framing a view of the world to take account of what twentieth century science has to say."

The ironic force of such debunking statements, however, depends on the reader's accepting an assumption that certain social constructionists share with their positivist adversaries: that science does indeed require a global philosophic justification for its veracity and, hence, that the absence of one subverts both the validity of claims of scientific truth and the significance of science in the modern world (Rouse 1988:6). But there is no warrant for the view that scientific beliefs must be absolute or universal in order to be valid or useful.

Rather than focusing on the impossibility of total objectivity or truth, then, it may be more fruitful to understand the conditions in which statements or actions are nonetheless accepted as objective, valid, or legitimate. That everything is a sign for some other sign can be made to have practical import if we shift Ferdinand de Saussure's question, What stands for what? toward Lenin's question, Who stands for whom? And from there, to the question, What scientific and social discourses would support each person standing for himself and each standing for each other?

I believe that a rhetoric of scientific and civic narration, if practiced in a critical ironic mode, engages such questions, not to resolve them but to live with and exploit their conflicts. Such a discourse is one of both resistance and affirmation, with the space of fruitful tensions between them always shifting. This need not and should not keep us from making moral or scientific judgments. But such judgments can occur neither on an absolute foundation nor in the dissolving emperium of language; instead, they occur in the space between the two. Indeed, the place of judgment is precisely in the aporias between data and explanation or action and reflection—between the world and the word.

Scientific realists and language relativists themselves seem to be aware of this. Although each tends to be imperialistic, they rarely advocate strong comprehensive programs. Instead, the play between realists and relativists usually is about where to draw the (bottom) line—what shall be considered actual and what symbolic. For most realists, the line that is drawn defines certain ontological and ethical absolutes—beliefs in things or values the abandonment or even the questioning of which seems too awful to think about. For realists, "stones," "nature," or "this table" are factual realities that common sense tells us are unshakable; the evil of human suffering or the Holocaust likewise are moral facts. But even relativists often seek a fortress of facticity to defend what they see as the corrosive effects of their own otherwise relativistic thinking. One example is the usually relativistic ethnographer of science Harry Collins (1990:41, 50), who distinguishes animals and rocks as part of the natural world in contrast to human beings who exist through culture: "A rock instructs everyone equally, without needing to be recognized. As we stumble against a rock, our actions are directly caused by the rock rather than our interpretations of what the rock is." Similarly, Hikins and Zagacki (1988:208) draw a moral line between realism and relativism at genocide: "There are numerous truths in which we can reasonably place our confidence, such as 'The Mi Lai Massacre is morally abhorrent,' and 'Adolph Hitler was a wicked man.'"

A number of remarks can be made about such line-drawing, which, building on Edwards, Ashmore, and Potter (1992), I will call respectively the unwitting concession, the misguided attack, the epistemic-judgmental conflation, the gesture child morality, and the joyless unwisdom of false dichotomies. First, those who take a realist stance on some ultimate category like stones or suffering are making large, though usually unwitting, concessions to the relativist position. That is, in resorting to such cases, "realists appear to be setting aside, even conceding, a huge amount of more contentious stuff to relativism—language, madness, the social order, cognition, even science" (Edwards, Ashmore, and

Potter 1992:3). In building a wall around certain core verities, realists confine themselves to the castle keep. Instead of continuing to attack this apparent stronghold, relativists might do well to cavort in their command of everything else.

Second, when realists insist on some absolute truths or essences of the real, they believe they are striking a blow against relativists. They are not. Their argument: "But what about this table, rock, etc.? (Thump, kick). You're not going to tell me that *that's* not real?!" But if this is an argument, it is against a caricatured *inversion of realism,* not of relativism. The thoughtful relativist does not assert the nonreality of things or values, but only challenges their self-evidentness. He or she asks always "How do you know?" "How is it made evident or true, by whom, to whom, where and for what practical purposes?" This is not a denial of the reality of anything but only a inquiry into methods by which such assertions are socially, historically, and rhetorically manifested. But many realists don't make this distinction. For example, Larry Laudan (1990:74) distorts the relativist's position that *nature* does not choose theories into the assertion that *evidence* does not shape them. Thus Laudan inverts the relativist position that matter-doesn't-reason into the "argument" that reason-doesn't-matter, and the relativist is presented as a self-refuting irrationalist (Fuller 1993:329). This is a misguided attack.

In the same spirit, Collins asserts that rocks instruct without needing to be recognized. But how could one stumble on Collins' rock without recognizing it? How could a rock "cause" "actions"? How does his "rock" become a rock for the stumbler and not a Gibraltar for the British or ore for the miner or a gem for the jeweler? Why does the realist invoke stones or suffering at that moment, in that discussion, for that audience? And to what effect, and why? These are the interesting questions for relativists, and they are not necessarily inconsistent with, nor should they be overcome or silenced by, commonsense or morally cherished truths.

Rhetorical criticism, then, relativizes truth by showing different versions of it to be alternative constructions, none of which corresponds absolutely and universally to an external reality that is knowable without symbolic mediation. Rhetoric is not only the technique that realists use in producing cognitive or moral effects; as used by relativists, it is also a means of keeping the production of such effects transparent and thus more open to challenge or refinement. Indeed, relativists show us what prices we pay for our absolutisms. Absolutists retort that such rhetorical accounts cannot themselves be credited because they are subject to the same deconstruction that was applied to the initial assertion. But this is an attack of the *realist's* version of truth, not on the *relativist's* position.

Put slightly differently, anti-relativists argue that relativists refute themselves by asserting universally the principle that there are no universal principles of truth. This attack is misguided for two reasons. First, its presupposition is false because relativists claim only local, situated truthfulness for their assertions; and second, local truth is not equivalent to falsity. Again, what is attacked are absolutist positions, not relativist ones. Indeed, relativists can elaborate Gadamer's and MacIntyre's thinking to argue that absolute relativism, like complete universalism or any other absolutism, is impossible because complete independence of a tradition of argumentation is impossible, even for radical relativists.

Thus such attacks make sense only if one assumes that relativists are inverted clones of realists and that rhetoricians are attempting to provide a universally true account of science, ethics, or reality. If this is not the rhetoricians' purpose, the attack is without consequence. And, as Kenneth Gergen (1990:297) stated, "Why should truth be the point of rhetorical analysis? The concept [of] truth, as commonly employed during the present century (e.g., correspondence with fact), is already saturated with empiricist foundationalism. Thus, the point of such analysis is not to be truthful (or untruthful), because this concept presupposes the very structure that is under attack. Rather, the point is to invite the reader into linguistic space that, once understood, enables one to transcend the ontology into which he or she was previously locked" and to ask about the context, the consequences, the animus, and the effects of the story being told.

It also seems useful to distinguish between epistemic relativism and judgmental relativism, which usually are conflated by anti-relativists and sometimes by relativists themselves (Bhasker 1979; Rorty 1988, 1989). Epistemic relativism asserts that all knowledge emerges from and is shaped by particular historical and social circumstances and that, therefore, there is no realm of "pure data" describable either extralinguistically or in a nonindexical language (Barnes and Law 1976; Collins 1983:102). By contrast, judgmental relativism makes the further claim that because all forms of knowledge are epistemically relative they therefore are all equally valid (or invalid). They all are embedded in local historical, social, and linguistic practices, and, therefore, we cannot compare different forms of knowledge and discriminate among them. But these latter assertions of judgmental relativism are not in the least entailed by the position of epistemological relativism. Indeed, in some ways the two are opposite. First, judgmental relativists assume that standards must be absolute or universal to be valid, whereas epistemological relativists identify alternative forms of valid knowledge and, more important, of knowledge production. Second, epistemological relativism is a stance one may assume when talking about forms of knowledge. But it usually is quite inappropriate when actually using one of them. Thus, for example, the fact that any explanatory category can be analyzed rhetorically does not count, by itself, as a criticism of the usability of that category (Collins 1983:101). Nor could we easily analyze the category rhetorically and simultaneously deploy it as an explanation within its specific domain. Concepts can be treated as topics *of* research or as resources *for* research. The epistemological relativism implied in the first does not warrant a judgmental relativism about the second.

Accordingly, epistemological relativism appears to be a precondition for the need and possibility of making determinations about the validity of knowledge systems. This is far from the disavowal by judgmental relativists of such determinations. As Knorr-Cetina and Mulkay (1983:6) put it, "The belief that scientific knowledge does not merely replicate nature *in no way* commits the epistemic relativist to the view that therefore all forms of knowledge will be equally successful in solving a practical problem, equally adequate in explaining a puzzling phenomenon or, in general, equally acceptable to all participants. Nor does it follow that we cannot discriminate between different forms of knowledge with a view to their relevance or adequacy in regard to a specific goal." Of course I have distinguished epistemological relativism from an absolutist type of judgmental relativism. But, as we have seen, such absolutism is a caricature of relativist thinking. More precisely expressed, a nonabsolutist form of judgmental relativism is perfectly consistent with epistemological relativism. Judgmental relativism does not flatten or negate all judgments; it only advises that they are unlikely to be universally adequate. We might take copies of both *Moby Dick* and *Celestial Navigation* on our sailboat, respecting the relative validity of each for their specific purposes, both of which we may judge useful for the larger purpose of our voyage.

This leads to a fourth observation—the gesture child morality of absolutist assertions. The gesture child, remember, is that thwarted and abused creature who will be satisfied by the mere appearance of caring without anything of substance being delivered. Realists who invoke such evils as torture as a stop on relativizing analyses seem to think they are engaged in moral conduct simply by censuring others for inquiring into the argumentative devises inherent in their (or any other) moral position. But moral truths, like facts of nature, do not come already labeled and categorized in language. They need to be articulated in order to become public moral facts—the way that slavery-is-evil became a moral fact for Western humanity only in the past century or so. To forbid inquiry into this process does not contribute to its advancement. Indeed, such a strategy prohibits the very discursive practices of which democratic communities are made. And, by itself, it does nothing whatever to help the enslaved or tortured, etc. Instead, it treats them as gesture children.

Some realists argue that the promise of a realist ontology "lies in encouraging social scientists to engage in critical social theory" (Wendt and Shapiro 1993:3; see Harvey 1989; Nussbaum 1992, 1993). Other realists insist that Truth is the regulative principle that distinguishes science from opinion and saves theory from intellectual and, ultimately, moral disorder. Without the constraints of Truth or Reality, they say, anything goes, and science and ethics collapse into will, emotion, or incoherence (Tomlinson 1989:52). Indeed, some insist that "what is really at stake is nothing less than the future progress of our civilization" (Theocharis and Psimopoulos 1987:597; see Popper 1966:369). Here the realist invites the relativist to get back on the seesaw of absolutism, to argue against Reality or Truth or to defend the ultimate arbitrariness of everything. But this misunderstands a rhetorically self-conscious relativism, which is not an alternative theory of truth but rather a method for persuading absolutists to abandon their obsessions. Again, the question for relativists is not whether Truth or Realty exist but how certain statements acquire that status, how "Truth" or "Reality" serve as regulative tropes of discourse.

Moreover, even on its own terms, the assertion of essential values, social forces, or human needs on realist grounds is a weak move rhetorically, because realist language can be readily invoked (and often is) to justify immoral conditions. The disasters of nationalist realpolitik or biologies of racism of past and present centuries should teach us that. Fewer atrocities in the history of the world have been the result of excessive tolerance than the result of absolutism. Which is worse, the possibility that evil will be tolerated in the name of cultural relativism, or the promise that future atrocities will be justified by some group's assurance that they are absolutely right? Whereas tyranny is or depends on absolutism, in a democratic polity we are and must be relativists in practice because we exercise judgment as citizens in shaping or finding ethical truth. Democratic practice requires prudent judgment, and such judgment presupposes critical, even deconstructive, reflection on political experience that is inherently contingent. Hence, our best defense, relativists would argue, is always to insist on knowing the reasons and methods of persuasion in such matters and how they may be justified.

David Hume examined this question in the final section of *An Inquiry Concerning Human Understanding,* where he reflected on the academical or skeptical philosophy, which was also his own method. After evaluating various arguments of relativists, he concluded that "the chief and most confounding objection to *excessive* skepticism" is that it produces no durable benefit to society: "We need only ask such a skeptic, What his meaning is? And what he proposes by all these curious researches? He is immediately at a loss, and knows not what to answer. A *Copernican* or *Ptolemaic,* who supports each his different system of astronomy, may hope to produce a conviction, which will remain constant and durable, with his audience. . . . But a *Pyrhonian* cannot expect that his philosophy will have any constant influence on the mind: or if it has, that its influence would be beneficial to society" (Hume 1975:159–60).

Hume's attack here is against an absolutist kind of skepticism, which he distinguished from what he called mitigated skepticism. This latter kind of skepticism aims neither to define an absolute truth nor to refute all argument of philosophers. It is less a doctrine or method than an ethical outlook and practice. As Hume said, "The greater part of mankind are naturally apt to be affirmative and dogmatical in their opinions." But if they could be shown the infirmities of their own understanding, "such a reflection would naturally inspire them with more modesty and reserve" and reduce their tendency "to haughtiness and obstinacy." Seen this way, a relativizing rhetorical stance is not another absolutism. Instead, it aims to cultivate specific intellectual and civic virtues (Chabot 1993:8).

There is also a certain joyless unwisdom in the framing of the choice as one between realistic descriptions and relativistic constructions. The unwisdom for the realist is in the elimination of the imagination, the refusal to consider how facts are manufactured, the reluctance to stretch the mind beyond what can be "concretely" known. The joylessness is in refusing the creative delight of intellectual and aesthetic play. Conversely, if the relativist dogmatically ignores recalcitrance in experience, as Kenneth Burke called it, he or she diminishes the heroic and tragic dimensions of life that deepen our joy and wisdom. By contrast, a serious playfulness is available to those who exploit the tension between opposing dogmatisms and extremes. In the spirit of Kierkegaard's mastered irony, this could be the relativist libertine donning the garb of the realist monk, or the realist playing the relativist, each to make her moral or intellectual point. Why, after all, should we let the opposing players have all the good parts? For example, in this chapter I have relativized realism and essentialized a kind of rhetorical practice for the purpose of framing the rest of this book. But I might well take an opposite stance when speaking to other publics for other ends. Thus relativists are not so much against realists as they are against heavy-spirited absolutists.

The point is not simply to blast realists for dogmatic foundationalism but to explore the various rhetorics of foundationalism. In a time when such foundationalisms proliferate in deadly competition, rhetoricians need to assess the practices that flow from them (Nelson 1990:259). Indeed, relativists can become realists for particular occasions of persuasion, and they can also affirm with many realists that humane values must be supported by just social conditions and defended with good reasons. Like most realists, relativists want discussion to lead somewhere worth going. But they also want always to keep the discussion of *ends* open through critique of discourse, for they know that our strategies of discourse shape what we will find when we get there. This is especially true of scientific discourse, which has shaped a world in which its makers feel less and less at home.

The very debate between realists and relativists suggests that today our sense of reality is far from stable, that we are seekers of certitude at the graveside of God. This metaphysical unease marks both our personal alienation from the Eden of absolutism and the dynamism of our culture and of science itself. The surplus of signification that generates our doubt also provides a vast potential for destructive creation, from the Big Bang to the death of the author. In this context, realism and relativism may denote less the nature of Nature than they express differing desires and conditions of certitude. For example, "the constructivist image of science as flexible negotiation and pragmatic tinkering reflects scientific work that is highly uncertain and constantly changing through permanent discoveries. The positivist image of science as rule-following is more accurate for more routinized work with low uncertainty" (Fuchs 1992:32; see Douglas 1985:19; Collins 1992; Rorty 1979:321). Flexible, polycentric, loosely coupled disciplines or societies tend to be relativistic. More hierarchic, tightly knit organizations tend to be realistic. But because of this social contextualization of perspectives, relativisms are constantly in danger of becoming realisms, and the reverse. In 1969, for example, "quark" was a convenient symbol, according to physicist J. J. Kokkedee, "not to be taken for more than what it is, namely the tentative and simplistic expression of an as yet obscure dynamics." Yet for quantum physicists quarks soon would become real and quark theory true. "The quark model gives an excellent description of half the world," said George Zweig. Said Richard Fenyman, "Let us assume it is true" (quotations from Pickering 1984a:91, 114, 147; see Gross 1989:201; Fine 1986:125–26).

Is there, then, much difference between the willing suspension of disbelief required for fictions and the willing extension of belief given to facts? Indeed, usually we are realists about our own certitudes and relativists about those of others. Perhaps this apparent arbitrariness is instead a necessary feature of discourse itself, because to make any assertion or critique requires us to privilege the position from which we are making it. Thus Pfohl (1977) relativized the term "discovery" in his analysis "The 'Discovery' of Child Abuse," but he invested realism in the concept "child abuse," although this term and the terms "child" and "abuse" could easily be relativized by examining their "discovery" (that is, their rhetorical invention) earlier in our history (Simons 1990:11). Woolgar and Pawluch (1985) call this process of manipulating the boundary between relativism and realism "ontological gerrymandering," but as Trevor Pinch noted, they and other social constructionists regularly gerrymander themselves: "In order for any claim to be made, some areas of discourse must be privileged. . . . Bloor in effect privileges his own discourse, of discourse, Collins privileges social science discourse, and Mulkay, Woolgar, and Ashmore claim to privilege nothing at all, and thereby as far as I can see can claim nothing at all" (Pinch 1987).

In this book I privilege a rhetorical sociological view, not merely to relativize science or its philosophies but more to show how the realities of nature and the truths of science are realized narratologically and, thereby, how they might be subsumed within a larger civic discourse. The major source of uncertainty for scientists, after all, is not how the world is but how it will be described in the future—how it will be described and who will get to describe it (Fuchs 1992). These temporal questions of how and who are put in the foreground by a socio-narratological approach. I believe that such an approach, rather than under-mining science, as some positivists *and* postmodernists have assumed it does, offers two crucial advantages for the practice and acceptance of science, one epistemological, the other ideological. First, a social rhetorical understanding of scientific practice claims the epistemic privilege "of being able to reinvest in scientific practice its own scientific gains, in the form of a sociological increase in epistemological vigilance" (Bourdieu 1981:xiii; see Fuller 1988). Between the linguistically precise reifications of rationalist philosophers and the practical but imprecise articulations of working scientists, social scientists can objectify the process of scientific objectification and render it available for inspection to philosophers and scientists alike. That is, sociologists can make explicitly evident the logics-in-use that usually are not articulated by those whose sole perspective is either logical universals or practical know-how. Sociological objectifications of scientific objectification show that the cognitive utopias of apologists of science neither describe successful scientific activity nor serve as feasible norms of scientific judgment. Because "norms" imply enforcement, and "should" presupposes "can," such epistemological ideals as inspecting the logical adequacy of proposed hypotheses or replicating the experiments of colleagues would have to be practicable for these cognitive norms to make sense (Fuller 1988:268; H. Collins 1989). However, in Big Science, which is often the model of good science, such inspecting and replicating is usually not feasible, thereby rendering idealized versions of science irrational as either descriptions or legitimations. Conversely, if we recast the realist norms as rhetorical practices, such contradictions can be overcome. For example, instead of imagining a correspondence between mind and reality or theories and theory-independent data, we can understand "correspondence" as the concordance of theoretical utterances and observational utterances "on which all speakers of the language give the same verdict" (Quine 1969:86–87; see Gross 1989:203). Seen this way, science is a complex, developing network of such agreements on the coherence of different kinds of statements. Far from denigrating science, this view pays tribute to an extraordinary cultural achievement: the institutionalization of practices for gaining consensus on immensely complex issues.

It thus would seem that science is being undermined not so much by relativist criticisms as by the inadequacy of the very philosophies of science used to defend it. If these philosophies can be easily challenged, they clearly are no bulwark against the deligitimation of science (Collins 1983:99–101; Chalmers 1990:3–8). By contrast, the rhetorical, sociological perspective, with its focus on legitimation, becomes more salient than the classical philosophic concern with justification. Of course, the relative decline of legitimacy of science has less to do with philosophy than with the politics and economics of science. Scientists traditionally have justified their privilege and autonomy in terms of the disinterestedness of their personal motives and the social and technical utility of their findings. Moreover, by discursively and institutionally dichotomizing means from ends and the cognitive from the moral, scientists also exempted themselves from responsibility for possible negative consequences of technical applications of scientific knowledge. Today, however, science has become a central force in capitalist production—it drives various industries and is a major industry itself. In addition, science consumes large public investments, scientific discourse has become a dominant language of public life, the "externalities" of applications of science (as in nuclear power or petrochemical plants) have become ecologically dangerous, and persons themselves have become the objects of technical manipulation through applied genetics, psychopharmaceutical control of moods and behaviors, and other forms of human and social engineering. In this context, the segregation of science and ethics becomes untenable, and the presumed value neutrality and privileged autonomy of scientists and their patrons is delegitimated not only as irrational but also as immoral.

In these conditions, we need less of rationalistic designs of scientific utopias and more of a reconstruction of our scientistic culture; less of prideful attempts to master nature and more of a democratic control of science and technology; less of a scientification of the world to the exclusion of ethical judgment and more of a relegitimization of scientific knowledge in terms of democratic practice. I believe that the rhetorical practice appropriate for such a project should be open ended, dialectical, and ironic (Brown 1989a:ch. 5). That is, it should acknowledge the contradictions between the reflection of reality *in* language and the constitution of reality *by* language. It recognizes that the very debate over whether language makes or fakes reality is itself foundationalist (Fish 1989:482). It accepts that the literal and the metaphoric are reciprocally defining and mutually transforming. Indeed, the very effectiveness of such a practice as irony depends on its constituting at least part of the world as literally true in order to unmask false versions. Such an irony also builds solidarity between speaker and audience because the audience is presumed, unlike naive outsiders, to be capable of noting the irony. This irony also fosters agency and enlightenment, because it never states absolutely which of the terms of opposition is intended to be the truer or better one. This must be decided by the auditors. Contrary to François Lyotard, the ironicist plays two language games at once, making opposites perhaps commensurable. But unlike Jürgen Habermas, the ironicist does not want to be universally understood (Capel 1965:32). In deploying the dialectics of irony, in *seeing* the irony or in *being* ironic, we take more seriously the deep ambiguities of all representations, all quests, all truths.

Thus, although this book is intensely informed by moral intentions, I hope it is not moralistic in propounding any specific doctrine, except perhaps the "doctrine" of reflexivity itself. But this kind of relativity must be endorsed by all persons who call themselves scholars and, ideally, all who are citizens as well. Further, a reflexive, consciously rhetorical mode of discourse is arguably itself an ethical practice. In a period of deep moral disorder, Alasdair MacIntyre insisted, it is not possible to do ethics by argument because the parties in conflict do not share commensurate intellectual traditions in which persuasive discourse could be rationally framed. In response, "MacIntyre suggests the neo-Aristotelian concept of historically continuous traditions as the locus of both meaning and ethics which will stave off the specter of chaotic relativism" (Pearce and Chen 1989:129). In a similar move, in this book I turn toward rhetoric in order to create a rational ethical *community,* not just produce a critique of science or a list of moral percepts. The *practices* of decoding and re-encoding, of translation and interlocution, and of rhetorical deconstruction and constitution, are acts of social and moral creation, closer to an initiation ritual than a philosophic treatise. By engaging in such practices we produce communities in which felicitous conditions for enacting an open democratic discourse are fostered.

Finally, I believe that this book invites deconstruction of its own judgments by the very rhetorical, relativizing methods that it directs to its topic. As Edwards, Ashmore, and Potter (1992:30–31) summarize them, the criteria of reflexive judgment are three: First, "*Provisionality.* That is the principle that for common sense, science, and textual analysis alike, any version or presentation of the world is to be understood as provisional, as susceptible to deconstruction or doubt, disproof or cancellation. . . . Second, *Shorthand.* This is the principle that any version or demonstration of reality is held to be a kind of shorthand for all the processes of construction that produce it, or would have to be produced to warrant it if challenged." Finally, *Irony.* This is the notion that, since claims and demonstrations of the real are rhetorical devises, they are available to everyone and are potentially contestable and even convertible.

The practice of such an open discourse encourages us to put our own cherished views at risk and to recognize the rationality and humanity of persons whose ideas and values may be radically different from our own. We are also encouraged to recognize the paradoxical nature of our own pursuit—that the truth (or justice or community) that we seek is shaped in our own quest to discover it. However, this realization of truth (or justice, and so on) in discourse seems to require that we posit Truth outside of discourse itself. To figuratively manifest truth we take it to be literally existent. Why should this be so? Why have people so wanted the notion of a certain Truth? Why has it been a central and continuing desire of philosophers, theologians, and scientists, not to speak of lay believers, for millennia, at least in the West? I believe this is largely because the creation of truths locally, historically, and provisionally responds to particular practical or disciplinary needs that the concept of one universal

Truth seeks to unify in the interest of cognitive and social order. Thus the creation of local, relative truths and the belief in a universal, absolute, or essential Truth are both complementary and incompatible. Each contradicts but is logically implied by the other.

We might conclude that there is no such thing as *the* concept of Truth or Reality, and that there are only highly regionalized, unsystematically connected functions that seemed, erroneously, to be subsumable in a structured concept. Or we might conclude that although the various functions of the concept are sometimes at odds, the concept of Truth still provides procedures for resolving conflicts among competing claims for cognitive (and political) rights and obligations even though it partially embeds and expresses just those conflicts.

Or we may conclude, as I do for the moment, that we need not take a definitive position on such issues. Instead, we can hold that literal grounds are necessary for metaphoric flights, and that the solidarity and cohesion fostered by universal Truth presuppose the openness and innovation fostered by many local truths. The interesting space for civically minded scholars is the aporia between such conflicting necessities. Indeed, if we are modernist in our ethical commitments (to truth, freedom, or justice) and postmodern in our criticality, that aporia will be precisely our location—a location that is also the starting place for the remaining chapters of this book.

Chapter 2 Textuality, Social Science, and Society: Toward a Scientific Discourse for Civic Competence

The creation of the world did not take place once and for all time, but takes place every day. Habit then is the generic term for the countless treaties concluded between the countless subjects that constitute the individual and their countless correlative objects.
Samuel Beckett, Proust

So the real issue is not between people who think one view is as good as another and people who do not. It is between those who think our culture, or purpose, or institutions cannot be supported except conversationally, and people who still hope for other sorts of support.
Richard Rorty (1982:167)

The conflict in our culture between science and ethics can also be stated as an incompatibility of cognition and identity. Cognition through science yields a shared external world that provides a framework for our common life. But identity depends on constancy of human agency and intentions, and this cannot be achieved through scientific cognition. Instead it is through narration that we form our identities and give our lives their meanings.[1] Thus there is a contradiction: persons and peoples are constructed rhetorically through narration (Rorty 1987; Bruner 1987), but life or history as narration has no epistemological passport to enter the kingdom of legitimate knowledge. As Pierre Bourdieu suggested (1987a:2): "To produce a life history or to consider life as a history, that is, a coherent narrative of a significant and directed sequence of events, is perhaps to conform to a rhetorical illusion, to the common representation of existence that a whole literary tradition has always and continues to reinforce."

On this account, science yields truths from nature without meaning, whereas narrative gives moral meaning to history and persons, but these are mere illusions. In this bifurcated way of thinking, narrative discourse is associated with the fictional and subjective realms, whereas scientific discourse employs an ostensibly nonmoral, objectivist vocabulary. The conflict between these vocabularies has grown sterile mainly because we need them both—scientific discourse to understand and direct our complex systems, narrations of self and society to give moral meaning to our lifeworlds and our polities. If we are to have integrity and self-direction in our personal and civic lives, we must integrate these two ways of knowing and being. To do this we need to be able to judge the truth of narratives and to have poetic criteria for science.

One perspective that invites such a synthesizing poetics of truth is the view of science and society as texts. In this view, language is not a reflection either of the world or of the mind. Instead, it is a social historical *practice*. And however polluted this communicative practice may be, it is the only river on which truth can ride. In this perspective, the meanings of words are not taken from things or intentions but arise from socially coordinated actions (Mills 1974:677). Words help constitute and mediate social behaviors, they provide legitimating or stigmatizing vocabularies of motive, and they mask or reveal structures of domination.

Science, especially social science, is also a civic discourse, a language in which public policies are established or contested. As such, scientific theories may be judged for their ideological or practical effects. This political function of theory is not independent of its intellectual content. Theories operate within, and implicitly project, a basic image of the world—a root metaphor of nature, persons, or society. Positivist social theory elaborates the metaphors of society as an organism or a machine, thereby generating theories and data that support social doctoring or social engineering. Because these root metaphors do not provide a language for describing human agency, however, logical and moral contradictions arise when positivists seek to extend their theories to include the lifeworlds of persons.

By contrast, this chapter outlines an alternative to positivist general theory, an alternative based on the metaphor of society and conduct as discourse, text, or language. The root metaphor of society as discourse may be more adequate than positivism logically, morally, and politically. Logically, this metaphor can describe both social structure and personal consciousness, both *langue* and *parole,* in an integrated and consistent fashion. Morally, the textualist approach begins and ends in the conception of personal agency and the human author-ship of the world, thereby providing a theoretical resource for any possible ethics. Politically, it serves to reveal the ideological encoding of any discourse, thereby encouraging criticality and openness in public debate.

THE RHETORICAL CONSTITUTION OF THE SOCIAL AND POLITICAL TEXT

Textual analysis of society not only shows that received forms of knowledge are structured like language; it also reveals how these structures are invented through acts of speech.[2] Thus the textual metaphor invites us to investigate our linguistic constraints and capacities because it sees persons as carriers of pre-formed linguistic structures as well as agents who perform culture and speech. By simultaneously addressing both structure and agency, such an approach not only can unmask overdetermined encodings; it also offers hope for developing practical definitions of morally and politically competent discourse. Thus tex-tual analysis of society is central to what Habermas (1979) and Stanley (1981) regard as the next stage in the moral development of reason: the creation of a rational ethic of civic communication.

The textualist approach also illuminates how selves and societies are con-structed and deconstructed through rhetorical practices. In this view, the cre-ation of a meaningful reality involves the intersubjective use of symbols through which happenings are organized into events and experience. That is, experience is expressed and achieved through persuasive and convincing com-munication, through rhetoric. People establish a repertoire of categories by which aspects of what-is-to-be-the-case are fixed, focused, or forbidden. These aspects are foregrounded and become articulated or conscious experience against a background of unspoken or silenced existence. Happenings and things may thereby be made objective and ordered in temporal series. The knowledge that emerges from this process takes a narrative form (Greimas 1987:ch. 6; Brown 1990). Reciprocally, the ordering of a past, present, and future enables the structuring of perceptual experience, the organization of memory, and the construction of the events, identities, and lives that they express (Bruner 1987:15). Stories about wayward uncles or successful cousins not only enforce family values but also help constitute the order and meaning of family itself (Langellier and Peterson 1993). Football teams, businesses, and government bureaus also elicit compliance and thereby re-create themselves through stories (Witten 1993). Through narratives of life and loss, business achievement or failure, we "do" family, we "do" organization, and we thereby construct culture and ourselves (Ewick and Sibley 1995:213). Such rhetorically constructed narrative unity provides models of identity for people in particular symbolic settings or lifeworlds. It also guides people in knowing what is real and what is illusion, what is permissible and what is forbidden, what goes without saying and what must not be said. The construction of a worldview is thus a practical, rhetorical accomplishment of a human community over time.

In this construction of a world, other worlds are foreclosed. This process can be likened to Henri Michaux's description of a "schizophrenic table" recounted by Gilles Deleuze and Félix Guattari (1983). This table, built by a schizophrenic patient, had no usable surface; it was all framework, legs, angles, additions, and accumulations. To produce a surface out of such a table would require that irregularities be removed and accretions be cleared away. Politics and theories too (no less than the subject) require a similar process of clearing away, of smoothing and leveling. Only such a process allows clarity and coherence to emerge and enables the politics and theories to become smooth and useful.

The production of things, meanings, disciplines, or persons requires the suppression of the unruly materials from which they are made. This process of repression is itself repressed, as are the costs that are incurred in creating unitary orders and meanings. Thus there is always a "surplus reality" because existence (potential experience) is always larger than any lived experience that is socially, symbolically produced. Moreover, as shown in Laurence Sterne's *Tristram Shandy*, there is always a "surplus of the signified," because we experience more than we know, and we know tacitly more than we can state. Hence, the unreflected, signified world is always larger than whatever versions of it that become canonized into formal knowledge. The territories of existence are always larger than any particular map, and by mapping in one official way we narrow awareness of alternative ways of experiencing the terrain of possible experience. Theories, models, paradigms, and disciplines also, perforce, are complicit in this process of exclusion.

In articulating experience through categories, discursive practices realize differences and distinctions, defining what is normal and deviant and, hence, expressing and enacting forms of domination. Thus the processes of definition

and exclusion not only are logical properties of discourse; they are also preconditions of intelligibility, sociation, social order, and social control. To ensure
mutual intelligibility, to form intersubjective groups, and to regularize symbolically guided social behavior, some (versions of) reality must be legitimized at
the expense of competitors. Such legitimation is an operation of closure. That
is, it discounts the value of pursuing further implications and protects established interpretations by means of social sanctions that marginalize or silence
dissident voices. Thus legitimation is achieved rhetorically (Brulle 1994:4; Stanley 1981:131). In Michel Foucault's (1970, 1972) phrase, it establishes a "regime of
truth," a meta-narrative by which the society lives.

Orthodox political theories hold that human nature generates social order;
for example, for Thomas Hobbes brutish human nature necessitated a Leviathan state. But both organizations and persons can also be understood as co-
generated through discursive practices. Different dominant discursive practices
reflect different collective habits of mind and action. In Bourdieu's (1977:73)
usage, the habitus is a system of durable, transposable dispositions that help
generate and structure practices and representations. The habitus guides
people's improvisations as they respond to changing situations. By helping to
routinize actions and accounts, the habitus secures a commonsense world
endowed with objectivity that is based on tacit agreements about the meanings
of practice and the nature of reality (Brulle 1988:4). These shared onto-opera-
tional assumptions make intelligibility and predictability possible and therefore
require and permit the coordination of the actions of members of a given group
as well as resistance to that coordination.

Reciprocally, from such routinized coordinated actions emerge institutions,
social structures, and ontological assumptions. Likewise, social organizations
can be seen as the practical realizations of discourses that are historically developed through communicative interaction. Such discourses are built up through
past actions and reproduced as they are unreflectively deployed by contemporary actors who themselves have been partly constituted through that discourse.
These ways of being and acting are also relationships of power that have been
disguised as natural; they have become sedimented into institutions and within
the actors themselves. This interactional, organizational, and political paradigm (or, to use Bourdieu's term, the objectified habitus), provides

 roles to be enacted in particular ways, in particular settings, and in particular relations to
 other roles. These roles need not be specified by explicit rules for enactment, though
 often, as in manuals of etiquette, job descriptions, and constitutions, they are. This tacit
 intersubjective property of paradigms constitutes in effect the "agreement" between

members that enables the orderly production of role enactment. That is, the structuring of interaction requires members to rely upon shared but largely tacit background knowledge that is embodied in implicit paradigms of social order. Paradigms involve political organization, and with this the imposition of sanctions against violators of the paradigms' tacit rules. (Brown 1978:373–74)

Thus, much of the knowledge offered by social (and scientific) paradigms is knowledge about role enactment, or practical social know-how, including not only rules but informal knowledge of how to *apply* the rules—when, by whom, and in what situations.

Temporally stable patterned and coordinated actions—that is, institutions—may realize "emergent properties" in the sense that their operations cannot be fully understood in terms of the intentions of their members. Moreover, for members such institutions may become icons, artifacts thought to have a life of their own, independent of the volition of actors within them. Yet such institutions, cognitive structures, and other collective phenomena cannot be realized except in and through the system of dispositions and discursive practices of the agents who constitute them.

Closure and legitimation also involve the repression or marginalization of alternative realities. The establishment of an orthodoxy thus creates heterodoxies—subjugated discourses that stand outside the regime of truth. Foucault characterizes these discourses as "a whole set of knowledges that have been disqualified as inadequate to their task or insufficiently elaborated; naive knowledge, located low down on the hierarchy, beneath the required level of cognition or scientificity" (Foucault 1980:82; see Kristeva 1973). In modern Western societies, such alternative realities are different and deviant from the dominant scientific habitus. They include dreamtime, carnal wisdom, mystic experience, feminine intuition, primitive thought, aesthetic perception, hand intelligence, street smarts, lower-class lore, folkways, dopeways, old wives' tales, grace, and other forms of knowing.

These alternative realities are delegitimated by marginalizing the discursive practices through which they are constructed. Such practices become unofficial, extra-institutional, and "backstage," expressed in a "restricted" rather than "elaborated" code (see Goffman 1959; Bernstein 1971; Brown 1987:ch. 1). From the viewpoint of the dominant habitus, these discourses are linguistically deprived. Their delegitimation also delegitimates the lifeworlds of their users and the users themselves. The official discourse becomes the only one that provides "symbolic capital" that could be fruitfully invested in institutional relations. This limits the power and autonomy of speakers of marginalized discourses and forces them to adopt the dominant definition of reality and its regime of truth if they are to participate as full members in the collective institutional life. Indeed, compliance and full membership are expressed practically through adequate performance of the dominant speech behavior.

Thus relations of domination are produced through practice and reified for members as things given by God, Nature, Tradition, History, or Reason. This movement from creative agency to reified structure is enacted through various rhetorical strategies that conceal from social members their own rhetorical construction of social reality. Society, and science too, come to be seen as given in nature rather than made in culture. Reification thus allows relations of domination and authority to be seen as given instead of made; it thereby facilitates conformity and continued reproduction of the social order. This ascription of naturalness inclines agents to accommodate to the social order as it is. It becomes a "realized morality" to its members (Bourdieu 1977:163–64).

Because society and others appear as moral entities, individuals design their actions to maintain their esteem and avoid shame and exclusion. Everyday interactions therefore usually are polite interactions, aimed at avoiding embarrassment. Should the social fabric and persons' moral regard be temporarily torn, these may be mended with excuses and justifications (Goffman 1959; Schudson and Crellanin 1984; Gamson 1985; Rawls-Warfield 1987; Lyman and Scott 1970; Williams 1991). In everyday life, Goffman (1974:14) tells us, we are occupied with "maintaining the definition of the situation" in order to "cope with the bizarre potentials of social life." "Definitional disruptions . . . would occur much more frequently were not constant precaution taken" (Goffman 1959:13). The social order, in other words, requires that "others" are "forced to accept some events as conventional or natural signs of something not directly available to the senses" (Goffman 1959:2). Thus, the realized morality of everyday interactions makes challenges to authority seem undesirable and unnecessary, at best risky and difficult, and sometimes literally unimaginable.

The metaphor of society as rhetorical or textual construction allows us to sublate the views both of social structures as objective entities acting on individuals, and of subjective agents inventing their worlds out of conscious intentions. Structuralists are unable to explain the genesis and function of structures in everyday practice. Conversely, hermeneutically informed observation of structures-in-use reveals that members have practical knowledge of and mastery over them, even though they may be unable to articulate what the structures are and may even refuse to acknowledge they exist. Thus, the central aspect of structures is not their functions (à la Emile Durkheim) nor their internal logic (à la Claude Lévi-Strauss) but their fetishism (à la Karl Marx). Structures are linguistically encoded forms of domination that close off critical reflection by members and often by social analysts as well. Thus, in the rhetorical view, both structures and consciousness are seen as practical, historic accomplishments, brought about through everyday communicative action, the result of rhetorical (poetic and political) struggles over the nature and meaning of the real. This is no less true of science than it is of other realms of social life.

SOME DISCURSIVE THEORIES OF THE SOCIAL

Discursive analysis of society reveals that social science is itself a discursive practice. Like all human experience, science is a conversation that takes place over time, in which accounts of what is, what has occurred, and what is true of this past and present are negotiated and imposed through symbolic interaction. It may be correct, as Louis Mink (1987:60) argued, that "stories are not lived but told." But it is also the case that most of living is itself a telling of stories, including both the retrospective construction of for-the-moment completed stories and the conspective and prospective projection of candidate versions of the present and the future.

The metaphor of society as discourse also suggests that social structures can be understood as structures of language and that these structures are invented through acts of speech. This formulation invites us to analyze structural determinism from the viewpoint of a phenomenology of language or, conversely, to examine the intentionality of speech as engendered through language-like social structures. A number of theorists have taken up this challenge. By conceptualizing both *langue* and *parole* as emerging from discursive practices, they have sought to overcome the reification of language, on the one hand, and the subjectification of speech, on the other.[3] Basil Bernstein, for example, argued that speech performances express and embody different worlds of meaning that are ordered hierarchically in society. Such symbol systems are realizations and regulators not only of speech performances but also of the structure of social relationships. One might further say that social relations are themselves symbolic systems, in that society itself is a system of communicative action (see Bernstein 1971; Brown 1987; Harré 1979).

This perspective has been enlarged by Mary Douglas, who has sought to link structure to meaning in a model of society as language. In her work with Aaron Wildavsky, for example, Douglas interpreted contemporary political behavior in terms of structuralist concepts of purity and pollution (Douglas and Wildavsky 1982). Elsewhere (Douglas 1972) she elaborated empirically the assumption that symbols can symbolize only within a structured framework. Meaning depends on distinction, and distinction is an essential dimension of structure. The concept of a meal as a semantic unit, for example, requires a grammatical distinction between meals and other kinds of eatings. This binary structure of meal/non-meal is created by distinctions *within* eatings that are meals—distinctions that are absent or structured differently in non-meals. In the English-speaking world, the core of a proper meal consists of meat and two vegetables, preceded by soup and followed by dessert. Douglas also observed that the structural element "meat" in relation to "two vegetables" is homologous to the structure of a "proper meal" as a whole, with its main course and subsidiary soup and dessert. Meals also come in threes—breakfast, lunch, and dinner. This triadic structure makes it possible to distinguish meals from other eatings and so enables us to invest meals with semantic meanings. For example, a "meal" may mean "this is for family only," or "eating thusly with us, you are now a friend." As Douglas (1972) said, "Drinks are for strangers, acquaintances, workmen, and family. Meals are for family, close friends, honored guests. The grand operator of the system is the line between intimacy and distance." Those we know at meals we also know at drinks, but not the reverse. The semantics *of* the meal (closeness) is made possible by its syntactics (triadic structure) *as* a meal.

Perhaps the most successful attempt to integrate agency and structure in largely discursive terms is the work of Pierre Bourdieu. Bourdieu recognized the cognitive power of structuralist theories of objective economic and political relations that provide a framework for practice (1977:3). Instead of protesting against scientific objectification in the name of lived experience and withdrawing into a naive humanism, however, Bourdieu sought to put structuralism "back on its feet" (Bourdieu 1977:3–4). Structuralism is off its feet because it fails to recognize the dependence of its operations on the practical mastery of members. These members evoke the structure and deploy it for their own needs, which usually involve the imposition or evasion of domination. Concerning kinship structures, for example, Bourdieu (1977:39–40) qualified the formulation of Lévi-Strauss: "The genealogical relationship is never strong enough on its own to provide a complete determination of the relationship between the individuals which it united, and it has such predictive value only when it goes with the shared interests, produced by the common possession of a material and symbolic patrimony."

The genealogical relations charted by anthropologists as having law-like regularities are in practice invoked strategically either to establish greater inclusion by finding a common ancestor further back in time or to demark greater exclusion by shortening the lineage to include only more recent descendants and kin. Similarly, legal codes are "enacted" not only in parliaments but also through their performance—that is, through their strategic invocation or selective enforcement. As Garfinkel (1967) or Bourdieu (1977) might have said with Franz Kafka, "The verdict doesn't come all at once. The proceedings gradually merge into the verdict" (Kafka 1956). Those with sufficient authority and wit can solemnize an incident into a precedent. What would have been a private occurrence, say the affront of a woman named Helen, thus can become an official insult and a cause for war. Conversely, clever underlings may manipulate the formal structure for their own ends; for example, when employees "work-to-rule" they may subvert the intent of regulations. In this sense, determinism and agency, or social structure and individual consciousness, both emerge from the same discursive practices.

Another example of this relation of semiotic structures and hermeneutic contents can be generated by comparing structuralist and phenomenological analyses of the exchange of gifts. Marcel Mauss, and later Claude Lévi-Strauss, insisted on a complete break with natives' experience and their theories of that experience, and urged instead that the exchange, and not the actions or intentions of the individual engaged in it, constitutes the primary object of study. But, as Bourdieu noted, counter-gifts must be *deferred* and *different* if they are not to be taken as insults. Too hasty a discharge of one's obligations is a sign of mistrust and ingratitude, for it retrospectively redefines the initial gift as intended to put one under obligation. Similarly, a counter-gift that is identical to the initial gift redefines the relationship as one of swapping or lending. Contrary to the view of structuralists, then, the constitution of gift exchanges requires strategy and style, timing and tact. Gift exchanges are never simply a blind grammar that operates independently of the will or consciousness of members. At the same time, and contrary to a naive hermeneutics, this "subjective" dimension is not identical to the self-perceptions of members nor to their own vocabularies of motive. "If the system is to work," said Bourdieu (1977:6 [n.7], 4 [n.5]), "the agents must not be entirely unaware of the truth of their exchanges, which is made explicit in the anthropologist's model, while at the same time they must refuse to know and above all to recognize it."

LINGUISTICS AND ECONOMICS

One also can cast the textual net over the big fish of economics. One way to do this would be to expand Saussure's theory of linguistic value to include value in general. Stated slightly differently, one would create a Marxian semiotics that subsumed the political economy of commodities under a political economy of signs. To see how this might be done, we should first distinguish theories that see language as a system of signification from theories that view it as a system of representation. The discursive approach presupposes a conception of language as a system of signification rather than a system of representation. If language is viewed as a system of representation, objects, ideas, relationships, selves, or institutions exist independently from the language that is used to describe them. In this theory a message is formulated to convey (or disguise) the meaning of extralinguistic objects, intentions, or conditions. The speaker encodes this extralinguistic reality into words and sentences and transmits it to an audience in the form of a message, which the audience then decodes (Thompson 1989:7).

By contrast, in the view of language as a system of signification, the crucial category is the sign. The sign is made up of two aspects—the signifier (the sound image) and the signified (the concept). In this Saussurean view of language, "linguistic values do not involve any pre-existing ideas but emanate from the very system itself. The concepts (the signified) are purely differential and defined not by their positive content but negatively by their relations with other terms of the system. This means that in the case of the sign, the concept (the signified) only symbolizes a value determined by its relations with other similar values" (Ahonen 1989b:36). Likewise, on the material side of signification (the signifier, the sound image) only the difference between sounds is crucial, and the means by which signs are produced are therefore unimportant.

This "economy of signs" is not so different from a monetary economy. As Saussure noted, in linguistics "as in political economy we are confronted with the notion of *value;* both sciences are concerned with a *system for equating things of different orders*—labor and wages in one and signified and signifier in the other" (1982:11). And it is unimportant whether the signifier of value (the money image) is coins, paper, cowrie shells, or computer bits.

If we push this conception further, we could say that the sign constructs its own adequate signified. In this formulation, the signifier dominates the signified, and our attention is thereby directed to the conditions of discourse in order to understand the origin of meaning and sense. Meaning is not something already formed prior to its articulation, for which language serves only as a mechanism of transmission. Instead, the "play" of meaning and sense is a consequence of the play of signification itself, as exemplified by the system of signs that make up those very means of signification (Thompson 1989:8).

When this way of thinking is applied to the case of money, we see that both neo-classical and Marxist economics assume the representational theory of language and thus treat money as a sign of something else. Both consider money a means of representing value, although they differ as to what the value is. For neo-classical theorists, "value" is given by the utility obtained from the use of the commodity. "The amount of money consumers are prepared to pay for a commodity depends upon the utility they derive from it. Of course, that utility cannot be observed directly. It must be represented by money because it remains hidden. In Marxist theories, money is a phenomenal form of value, where value is determined by the abstract labor power embodied in that commodity" (Thompson 1989:8). Here again, labor value can never be seen directly but only as it is "transformed" into money and prices. In both neo-classical and Marxian conceptions, then, it is the representation of value that we observe— the realm of money and prices—and not the deeper reality of utility or labor that determines it.

This representational theory distinguishes appearance (representation) from reality (the deeper meaning, structure, and so on) and then decodes the reality as it is displayed through the appearance. The absent reality becomes present through its re-presentation. It is both absent and present at the same time. If we strictly applied positivist canons to such thinking, it would appear to be a logical contradiction, even an example of mystical thought, as in the absent presence of Christ's blood and flesh in the wine and the wafer. In Marxist literature this is called the "transformation problem."

By contrast, if we take seriously the view of language as signification, we understand the signifier to "construct" the signified. Analogously, money does not represent anything in terms of an extralinguistic domain of utility or value. Instead, money "constructs" value, but value on the same semiotic "surface" as money itself. Thus "value" and "money" are synonymous.

This view of money and value as "appearance" or "surface" would become more plausible if it were understood in the context of a general theory of economic action as a significatory system. Such a theory is hinted at in some of the writings of Saussure and Marx. Saussure (1982:33) held that "*a science that studies the life of signs within society* is conceivable," and he understood economics to be part of society. In a somewhat parallel notion, Marx (1971:17) compared the fetishism of language to the fetishism of money: "It is no less false to compare money with language. It is not the case that ideas are transmuted in language in such a way that their particular nature disappears and their social character exists alongside them in language, as prices exist alongside goods. Ideas do not exist apart from language."

We could extend this point and say that the world does not form speech but that speech forms the world or, more precisely, gives form *to* the world (Roche 1973:79–80; Mehan and Wood 1975:218–24). Class, economic exchange, and value take their existence and form in their linguistic enactment. In *Capital* Marx followed the logico-empiricism of Feuerbach, and so he conceived of the value of goods as an expression of the labor of those who produced them. But he also argued in the more Hegelian *Grundrisse* that under capitalism language becomes reified. Language becomes the "agent of divorce" (Marx 1971:71). Like virtue, love, or conviction, which men had once considered inalienable, language too becomes "an object of exchange, or traffic. . . . [What] till then had been communicated, but never sold; acquired, but never bought . . . passed into commerce."

Perhaps the most ambitious attempt to develop this homology between the thought of Saussure and that of Marx is Ferruccio Rossi-Landi's *Linguistics and Economics* (1975), a Marxist semiotics of economic life.[4] For Marxism, the problem was whether language in the social totality is determined or determining, whether it is part of the base or the superstructure. In admitting that language is neither of these, Rossi-Landi recognized that any rigid theoretical separation between base and superstructure was inadequate and that the analysis of language was not possible within this framework (Bodner 1987). Thus Rossi-Landi tried to provide a new theory of the relations between structure and superstructure. His working hypothesis is that what mediates between the two is the totality of sign systems that define any particular social formation.

Rossi-Landi (1975:6) described the categories of social reproduction and language as a homology between material production and linguistic production: "One of the most important aspects of this theory is that everything that has value (and therefore, as we shall see, everything that has meaning) is always a product of human work; value is something that man has introduced and continues to introduce into the world."

The central feature of all signs is that they have meaning that is produced by human work. Rossi-Landi assumed that there are two fundamental modes of social development: the production and circulation of goods (in the form of commodities) and the production and circulation of sentences (in the form of messages). These two modes are essentially homologous. To describe their coinciding properties, Rossi-Landi transcoded into semiotic terms such basic concepts of Marxist economics as work, material production, exchange, and consumption. These economic phenomena are akin to linguistic activities. Goods and words are both artifacts. The material production of goods and the linguistic production of sounds, words, or sentences are forms of human work. "We sustain, then, the Vichian and Marxian thesis that the notion of artifact is in principle applicable to language" (Rossi-Landi 1975:33).[5]

Following Marx's political-economic theory, Rossi-Landi (1975:155) distinguished production, exchange, and consumption, and then applied these concepts to linguistic production: "The operation of total linguistic capital, i.e., of a language as constant linguistic capital together with its speakers as variable linguistic capital, is communication: [communication is the] production, circulation and accumulation of messages within a linguistic community, in a communicative market."

Rossi-Landi (1975:183) also attempted to discover private ownership and exploitation of signs as a logical extension of his homology: "The major misunderstanding as regards linguistic private property is that the supra-individual, public, social character of the language is considered sufficient to exclude the possibility of the language itself being subject to private ownership." In advanced capitalist societies, for example, the game of economic semiosis is stacked in favor of oligopolistic owners. Through their domination of mass communication, the capitalists' discourse, with the help of Madison Avenue, may overwhelm the consumers' ability to respond effectively. Indeed, even if they do protest, in their protest *as consumers* they are reinforcing the dominant capitalist discourse. In more primal societies there also may be an elite ownership of customary or historical discourse. Thus A. M. Hocart's informant in Fiji (quoted in Sahlins 1985:49) "was said to know little because he had been brought up among the common people and not the nobles"; likewise, Gillian Feeley-Harnick (1978:402) in Madagascar found that "history is not evenly distributed because to have it is a sign of politico-religious power and authority."

Rossi-Landi's Marxist semiotics does not have a strong hermeneutic moment. There is much more structure of language than enactment of speech. His communicative agents do not have much freedom; instead, their behavior is preprogrammed by the deep grammar of the semiotic system. "Semiotics finds its proper place, its significance, and its foundation alongside the study of modes of production and of ideologies, within the sphere of the social programming of all behavior" (Rossi-Landi 1975:203).[6]

Seen linguistically, economics becomes a subject of semiotics. As objects have become commodities and relationships have become ones of commodity exchange, the use value of things or people is subordinated to their exchange value. This exchange value is stated in terms of money, the purest of signs as it now stands for virtually anything (Marx 1946; Simmel 1978; Lukács 1971b; Kelemen 1982). As Baudrillard (1981:63) said, "The object is *nothing*. . . but the different types of relations and significations that converge, contradict themselves, and twist around it." This semiotic critique of the political economy of the sign parallels the earlier Marxist critique of the political economy of the commodity. Indeed, in a Marxian semiotics, they become the same critique, because commodities are now seen as signs par excellence. The commodity combines use and exchange value, whereas "the sign . . . combines the signifier and the signified. A Marxian semiotics merges these two structures into a single structure that may be called the *signified commodity*" (Baudrillard 1975, 1981; Denzin 1987).

In this view, such economic concepts as "poverty" or "wealth" are themselves the outcome of human communicative actions that alter the horizons of experience and knowledge (Green 1984). "Goods acquire apparently necessary significances, much as language *seems* to lose its arbitrariness, because of a social context in which those goods are read as defining one's social availability" (Herzfeld 1985:170). Once the semiotic properties of economic exchanges are recognized, they cease to be an isolated facet of human experience. Instead, "the meanings of goods are viewed as construed within a fluid social environment that is itself negotiated. Production and consumption are active process[es] in which all the social categories are being continually redefined" (Douglas and Isherwood 1978:68). This is true of local firms and markets as well as of national and international economic processes, because ultimately producers and consumers alike remain actors in the creation of significance.

SOCIAL THEORY AND CIVIC DISCOURSE

In sum, the metaphor of society as discourse has certain logical and moral-political advantages over organistic and mechanistic ways of thinking. First, logically, social theory on this model can encompass such micro social phenomena as meals, such mid-level phenomena as gift exchanges, and such macro social phenomena as economic structures. The dichotomies of base and superstructure or structure and agency are also mediated by discourse. The structure, envisioned as language, is both a constraint and a resource for enactments, envisioned as speech. The semiotic moment of the linguistic metaphor deals well with structure; its hermeneutic moment deals well with meaning and action. Both these dimensions—syntactics and grammatics, on the one hand, and semantics and pragmatics, on the other—are contained and logically consistent within the metaphor of society as discourse. In effect, this metaphor combines in linguistic terms Durkheim's conception of constraining structures with Marx's idea that the system of exchanges is the source of values (Lemert 1992). But it also incorporates Mead's and Garfinkel's conceptions of social reality as constructed through symbolic interaction.

Second, on a moral-political level, the discursive approach is reflexive. It sees the social sciences as providing *logoi* by which members generate their own social texts. Thus general theory cast in the metaphor of discourse explicitly recognizes its moral and political functions. That is, it acknowledges that its discourse *about* society reflects and engenders discourse *within* society. It thus sees social science as value-soaked civic talk about our common life.

The discursive approach also challenges the notion of disciplines as well as positivist and humanistic dichotomies within them. Instead, it enables us to slice up modes of argumentation differently and understand "theory construction" in terms of various linguistic and textual strategies. Such an approach highlights the presuppositions and metalogics of all the social sciences and thus brings values back to the fore. The devices of discovery and judgment, or invention and legitimation, are of course rhetorical terms; under the aegis of the language metaphor of society they can now be used to develop social theories as discourses for reasoned civic judgment.

In abandoning the anti-rhetorical rhetoric of positivism, the discursive approach recovers the ancient function of social thought as a moral and political practice. In this critical rhetorical view, in constructing general theory we attend not only to logical propositions and empirical contents but also to linguistic methods and existential functions. From this perspective, the linguistic dimension of social theory is an integral part of its truth or falsity to social life. This is for two reasons. First, truth and validity are themselves rhetorically constructed (Brown 1990, 1989a, 1989b, 1987). Second, as rhetorical interventions, social scientific theories convey an existential as well as a propositional truth. Scientific truth about society is a truth of facts or meanings, an appeal to the telos of elegance and precision, predictability or comprehension. But seen discursively or rhetorically, such truth is also an implicit call to action. Its existential telos is understanding, critique, and emancipation. Positivists have sought to silence this existential dimension by treating general theory as an external object that makes no personal moral claim upon us. But social theories do convey an existential truth. And, unlike propositional truth, existential truth is not merely to be cross-examined. Instead, when it speaks we ourselves become its "object," and we must examine ourselves, for it is we who are addressed.

Thus, different approaches to theory are not merely competing or complementary language games without ethical consequence. Instead, each game implies a different moral affirmation. For a purely language-analytic philosophy, all interpretations are equally valid within the limits of the theory that provides their given rules of reading. But each such set of rules also has its own existential function (Ricoeur 1980:107). The telos of psychoanalysis, for example, is an archaeology of the subject, and the telos of positive social science is technical direction of society. The telos of a discursive analysis of society and of science is the human authorship of the social world.

To the extent that various theoretical approaches articulate the visions and interests of different social groups, a single general theory of society is not desirable. Indeed, the hegemony of general theory from a mechanistic, organistic, or cybernetic perspective is suspicious because it tends to legitimate technicians, managers, and experts and to depower ordinary citizens in their efforts to govern their lives rationally. Conversely, social theories based on metaphors of human intentionality are weak at identifying causal interdependencies or rule-governed regularities in complex social orders; hence such theories are inadequate as discourses for the guidance of late modern social-technical systems.

While the discursive approach goes far in overcoming such dualisms, we should not claim for it an absolute privileged status. As long as we remain committed to some form of democratic pluralism and open public discourse, as long as we require efficient systems management for survival, and as long as we seek self-understanding and dignity in our lifeworlds, we will need alternative social theories to articulate fully these different practical interests. Such competition, moreover, is crucial to the development of social theory itself.[7] The key question, then, is not how to create a single integrated theory but how various integrated theoretical discourses can be brought into ironic, dialectical play, each resonating with others, each contributing to a civic culture of citizens shaping their collective fate.

SCIENCE, NARRATIVE, AND CIVIC LIFE

These observations suggest that our canons for assessing the scientific truth of theories, or the moral adequacy of policies, are not transcendent but immanent within scientific, moral, and political discourses themselves. This implies that we should neither dismiss ethical language as beyond the realm of reason nor reduce science to ideologies or interests. Positive science seeks law-like explanations that accord with concepts of causes and effects. Moral discourse employs the vocabulary of purposes and ends. Like all intentional discourse and action, it is performed in the future-perfect tense. That is, it is oriented toward, or at least made intelligible in terms of, some in-order-to or because-of motive (Rouse 1987; Schutz 1970). Indeed, the very conception of "action," as opposed to mere behavior, presupposes such a temporal structure of intentionality (Carr 1986; Heidegger 1962; Okrent 1988:51; Rouse 1988). As a kind of discussion about the unfolding of intentions through action in time, moral-political discourse therefore has a narrative structure.

A central problem of contemporary public life is not merely the encroachment of scientific or technical discourse into areas of properly moral and political concern. It is also the deterioration of reasoned narratives in moral discourse itself. With the capture of rationality by positive science and its technical extensions, reason and narration have been separated in civic culture. Thus, today's crisis is not merely that one collective narrative is replacing another. It is more severe: the polity in general has lost a reasoned narrative form (Lyotard 1988). Reason in narrative discourse is being replaced in civic culture by scientific-technical calculation, on the one hand, and by irrational stories, on the other. And with this we have lost much possibility for unity in our moral traditions. As public moral meanings become fragmented or fraudulent, society becomes unsusceptible to emplotment in terms of some rational political ethos.

A good example of the reduction of the democratic language of participation to the elitist language of technicism is the work of Stafford Beer (1974:41–43). Beer affirms the value of workers' participation in industrial systems even while deploying a cybernetic conception of "system" that silences people or human judgment and renders participation irrelevant.

> The work people themselves . . . know what the flows are really like. . . . And if their interest can be captured in putting together the total model of how the firm really works, we shall have some genuine worker participation. . . . The vision I am trying to create for you is of an economy that works like our own bodies. There are nerves extending from the governmental brain throughout the country, accepting information continuously. So this is what is called a real-time control system. This is what I mean by using computers as variety handlers on the right side of the equation. They have to accept all manner of input, and attenuate its variety automatically. What they will pass on to the control room is whatever *matters.*

There is an animus in such writing against human natural languages, values, memory, and literacy. Such rhetoric excludes conflicts of politics, class, or other interests. "It shows no insight into the political nature of 'information,' no respect for 'information's' ambiguities of meaning deriving from moral paradoxes and situational diversities" (Stanley 1981:159, 182; for examples and discussion see Burke 1969; Gittell 1980; Helevy 1955; Piven and Cloward 1977). Partly because it can do certain things so well, however, the discourse of positive science and systems efficiency easily expands to include more and more social life and experience. It thereby leads us to ignore history and tradition, to turn political and moral questions into technical or instrumental ones, and to treat every "problem" as though it had a "solution" (Delli Priscoli 1979:10; Rappoport 1964:30). Scientized politics constitutes an official discourse of meaning and legitimacy that imposes a preemptive, cognitive closure on the present even as it suppresses the lived experience of society's members. Applied science thus is a discourse of power for experts and of alienation for citizens. It construes the actions that it recommends as neither whimsical nor arbitrary but as legitimate because they are the product of rational, objective deduction. Certain control replaces prudent counsel as the goal of reason.

By contrast, Giambattista Vico ([1744] 1972) viewed truth and experience as enacted through language that is available to all members of the community. Thus, he opposed philosophies that construed the knower as a passive spectator and the world as an object independent of our rhetorical construction of it. Vico specifically challenged Descartes' view that the truth of ideas is to be judged by their clarity and distinctness. In opposition to Descartes' conception of knowledge as consciousness of universal laws, Vico showed etymologically that certainty does not have universal validity: the Latin term *certum* means the particular or individual, not the universal (Vico 1965:par. 321). Instead, for Vico, doing and knowing, or the constructed and the true, are both rhetorically made, and each is "convertible" to the other.

Extending Vico's thought in the direction of Foucault's, we would include relations of power and domination in our understanding of the "doing" or "making" of knowledge. From this viewpoint, the *what* of any practical-cognitive system is convertible into the *how* of its writing, imagery, or speaking. Knowledge and power are built into our representational practices. Their convertibility becomes available to us through rhetorical self-consciousness. Such self-consciousness allows us to see how the ideological scripting of our messages masks exclusions, silences, and control and, thus, how knowledge and power, or knowing and doing, are ways of enscribing the social text.

Such a linguistically self-reflective posture is largely absent from scientific and civic practice today. And, indeed, it is explicitly eschewed by the dominant positivist epistemology. To that extent, even though modern science avoids explicit value commitments, it reproduces dominant discursive practices and thereby helps affirm existing categories and relations of things, persons, and classes (Shapiro 1988:5–9). By contrast, a textualist understanding of science and society stresses the constitutive rather than the causal or even the representational dimensions of knowledge/power practices. It thereby alerts us to the processes by which discourse becomes reified as a mirror of the very things, categories, and relations that it creates.

A rhetorically reflective civic narration would help citizens to see how technical discourse masks political issues *and* how political discourse can be informed by technical knowledge. The point therefore is not to eliminate either technical discourse or public storytelling but to make technical talk accessible to citizens and storytelling amenable to reason. We cannot know *how* to eliminate acid rain, for example, unless we understand that "sulphur" is a cause of it. Nor can we know *why* we should eliminate acid rain unless we have a conception of the character and value of human life. A rhetorically self-conscious, technically informed civic narrative discourse would fuse the "how" and the "why." It would help humanize technicians and, much more important, it would enlighten and empower citizens. In hopes of contributing to that project, the ensuing chapters argue that science is itself narration and, as such, is subsumable within rational ethical narratives of society.

Chapter 3 Social Science and
the Poetics of Public Truth

What I want is to represent reality on the one hand, and on the other that effort to stylize it into art. . . . I invent the character of the novelist whom I make my central figure; and the subject of the book, if you must have one, is just that very struggle between what reality offers him and what he himself desires to make of it.
André Gide (1955:207)

To exceed the limits of a formula without destroying it is the dream of every magazine writer who is not a hopeless hack.
Raymond Chandler (1980:9)

Social science and poetics would seem to have little in common. Scientists study language as a datum and use it, so they say, only as a medium for reporting facts or truths that are discovered and conveyed through nonpoetic means. Indeed, much of the research methodology of the sciences can be seen as an attempt to bypass, or at least to narrow, the symbolic resonances of language and to establish a one-to-one "pointer-reader" relationship between words and things. Francis Bacon attacked rhetorical devices because they led men to "study words and not matter," and Thomas Sprat in his *History of the Royal Society* attacked fine language as being "in open defiance of Reason."

Members of the Royal Society were resolved "to reject all the amplifications, digressions, and swellings of style: to return back to the primitive purity, and shortness, when men deliver'd so many things, in an equal number of words." In the same spirit, John Locke urged parents to stifle poetic tendencies in their children lest these block the direct relationship between thought and things. David Hume called poets professional liars, Jeremy Bentham imagined an ideal language altogether without words, and Samuel Johnson wished to establish univocal meanings in perpetuity in his dictionary (Richardson 1991:4; Levine 1985:4).

A contemporary expression of this anti-poetic tradition is the philosopher Moritz Schlick's (1959) concept of "protocol sentences" as the foundation of knowledge. These are sentences that "express facts with absolute simplicity, without any molding, alteration or addition, in whose elaboration every science consists, and which precede all knowledge [and] every judgment regarding the world" (Ward 1986:324; see Wolff 1986). Such a method, it is held, protects us from error and delusion.

By contrast, poetics is concerned with how poetry renews and refreshes language. Poetry does this by projecting meanings that are inherent in any poem's particular linguistic properties. That is, the *what* of any poetic text is radically entangled in the *how* of its expression. From a poetic viewpoint, therefore, even those texts that explicitly eschew rhetorical and ideational commitments end up reinscribing them in the linguistic mechanisms of their writing (DeMan 1984:210). In this view poetry, in its self-consciousness of its own rhetorical devices, is an exemplar of nondelusional writing.

There is one place, however, at which the interests of science and poetics converge: the text. "The social sciences are talking sciences, and achieve in texts, not elsewhere, the observability and practical objectivity of their phenomena. This is done in literary enterprises through the arts of reading and writing texts, and by 'shoving words around'" (Garfinkel, Lynch, and Livingston 1981:132). Both social scientists and poets are writers; both must inscribe their discoveries in language. And although economics and sociology and psychology may be sciences, writing, even scientific writing, is an art. As such, it is, like poetry itself, amenable to analysis through poetics, which is the theory, or science if you will, of linguistic arts.

If this idea is accepted for the moment, what might we gain from its elaboration? What metatheoretical benefits derive from analyzing social science as poetic practice? I think there are at least four. First, textual analysis of social theory can give us greater understanding and skill concerning the translation of human experience, including that of social scientists, into objective reports and analyses. As Aaron Cicourel (1986:247–248) put it, "Everyday thinking and talk are not self-evident objective processes and products that can be easily subjected to algorithmic, formal modeling. Yet both the researcher and the respondents or subjects make necessary but often tacit use of their everyday knowledge and language. Our efforts at social measurement invariably ignore this issue." I believe that this translation of everyday experience into social scientific reports involves a "textwork" that can be understood through such poetic concepts as genre and irony.

A second advantage of poetic analysis of scientific texts is that it invites a systematic pluralism. In seeing the poetic processes of different theoretical genres, for example, we may have greater critical appreciation of other people's approaches and greater understanding of our own. Thus, to reveal the poetic properties of social science is not to negate its scientificity but to make it more critical and self-reflective. If we more clearly understand how social science is constructed through language, we can better assess our own textual practices and their relative adequacy in light of other possible linguistic strategies. Such poetic deconstruction of social theory does not reveal an ultimate social stuff beneath or behind language, some extralinguistic foundation of empirical facts or hermeneutical meanings. Instead, it reveals yet another (mode of) representation. This may breed despair for finding absolute truth about society, but it also should encourage hope for more critical and judicious understanding.

Third, poetic analysis shows us how the translation of experience into objective formal language transforms what is experienced and thereby changes (our understanding of) the world. Objectification is thus not only central to the workings of science, but it also is a form of power or, more precisely, objectification gives one power to form or transform nature into technology and political desires into social programs. Success in shaping scientific insights into discoveries, and in translating discoveries into physical or social technologies, depends on the enrollment of allies, the weaving of networks, and the building of constituencies. Much of this is done through textwork. Persons, things, and processes are written into new roles and relations. Scientific writing recruits nature, other scientists, and other texts as allies for new ways of looking at things, or for reinforcing and deepening their already established ways (Schrum 1988:401). Words link actors to social agencies, or events to natural causes, in ways that reinforce old behaviors or encourage new ones.

Science facilitates technical or social change mainly by "problematization"—the familiarizing of the strange or the estranging of the familiar—by imposing linguistically what Burke (1964) called "perspective by incongruity," which first suggests and then establishes an equivalence between two fields or problems and which requires those who are interested to translate each into the terms of the other—a metaphoric transfer that may become a literal observation. "Is the *eradication of poverty* of concern? If so, then one clearly needs to understand *stratification in industrial societies*. *Occupational status* and *educational attainment* play important roles here; their causes and consequences vary for different *ethnic groups*. *Childhood socialization* can create barriers to attainment, particularly in *segregated communities*, a phenomenon that could well be studied in *North Baton Rouge preschools*. Successful scientists are extremely good at constructing these equivalences," (Schrum 1988:401) and most of this constructing is done through textwork.

Problematization thus involves the postulation of equivalence between otherwise unrelated people, processes, political problems, techniques, locations, or things. It involves the translation of each into the other through metaphoric associations. The more these elements are similar to each other and to the already accepted linkages, the more such work will appear as thickly encoded literal descriptions—conventional, normal science within the dominant paradigm. Conversely, the more the elements associated are unlike each other, or unlike the dominant conception of their linkages, the more the problematization will be ironic—that is, the more it will be a metaphoric equivalence of opposites and, thereby, more innovative, more a stretching of received ways of viewing things. In scientific writing, this kind of textwork can be partly done simply by linking words to each other (Callon, Law, and Rip 1986:107; Bijker, Hughes, and Pinch 1987). The higher the rate of co-occurrence of key words in the same article, the more dense and redundant the article is in such verbal linkages and, hence, the more forcefully their association is projected. The success of efforts at problematization or innovation, however, depends more on redundancy between texts than on redundancy within any one of them. One article does not a genre or paradigm make. Instead, other writings must incorporate the same or similar textual practices. Intertextual thickness, redundancy, and elaboration over time can turn an initial metaphoric association—"The heart is a pump"—into a literal description through a now-taken-for-granted genre or paradigm that realistically describes what is.

This leads to a fourth advantage of a poetic conception of science—its contribution to the debate over objectivity and ideology. In this debate three positions seem tenable: "We may see objective knowledge . . . as the only bulwark against ideology, as do the uncomfortable bedfellows of Louis Althusser and Karl Popper. Or we may see knowledge as saturatedly ideological and in effect an unwarranted defense of entrenched organizational power," as do followers of Feyerabend or the early Foucault. "Or thirdly, between these two, we may see knowledge as redeeming itself by first recognizing itself as ideological" (Ward 1986:328; see Lorrain 1979).

A poetic understanding of social science can contribute to this third position. By revealing the methods by which truth is encoded linguistically, poetics also reveals the constructed, rhetorical, persuasive, and, hence, ideological nature of any discourse. Through such an awareness social scientists can free themselves of the choice between either amoral objectivity or irrational ideology. Instead, the choice becomes that of a self-conscious and responsible use of language against naive and unreflective writing. To write is to shape linguistically a (representation of the) world. Understanding this helps us choose between metaphors, narratives, and genres that are more or less fruitful, that assert or subvert cognitive authority, that thicken or stretch our disciplinary canons, and that are politically and ethically responsible.

ON THE POETIC CONSTRUCTION OF TRUTH WITHIN PARADIGMS AND GENRES

All writers, whether of biology or biography, physics or phenomenology, confront certain choices inherent in the act of writing. These choices include the degree of consistency in the use of emplotment or narrative structure, in the deployment of authorial distance and point of view, in the allocation of textual space to the voice of the subject or the narrator, and in the use of such tropes as metonymy or irony. One such stylistic choice, under which those above may be largely subsumed, is that of genre.[1] In which genre should one write, and how closely should one adhere to or depart from its canons? I shall show that objectivity, realism, and credibility are yielded by consistency or thickness of representation according to the rules of a paradigm or genre. In contrast, subjectivity, relativism, and autonomy are yielded by stretching, making ironic, or mixing genres and their rules.

"Genre thickening" involves tightly coded descriptions, a semiotic denseness. The genre's rules of representation are applied literally, strictly, and redundantly in order to display a reality that is taken as pregiven. The "thick" text is traditional, readily analyzed, reinforcing assumptions that the reader already holds. It is a serious, closed structure that constrains and imposes meaning through repetition of the code or method. Thus, genre-consistent discourse elaborates a paradigm that is well established and taken for granted (Riffaterre 1984:159).

By contrast, "genre stretching" puts the polysemous properties of language in the foreground, and new meanings or relationships are suggested by shifts in point of view, ironic reframing, or metaphoric transfers. Genre stretching or mixing fosters scientific or artistic innovations, the shaping of new paradigms, the creation through articulation of a reality-in-formation. Thus the "stretched" text is elusive, escaping easy analysis because it "is playful, fluid, open, triumphantly plural and hence impervious" to the rule of fixed generic structure (Sulliman 1980:119). In terms of audience reception, genre stretching makes the reader a producer, and not a mere consumer, of the text (Barthes 1970:10–12).[2] In terms of disciplinary boundaries, thickness and "redundancy will increase efficacy and will thereby help a profession control its jurisdictions. [By contrast, stretching or] inconsistency between different ways of constraining problems will lead to specialization and possible differentiation in the profession" (Abbott 1988:56).

The relation between genre stretching and genre thickening is dialectical and temporal. Each form of truth telling, or of truth making, presupposes the other, and each may *become* the other over time. "Normal science" is by definition literal science; scientists who invest their energies in elaborating the dominant paradigm take it to be a true description of reality (Kuhn 1972). Such realism is achieved textually through thick encoding according to that paradigm's rules and, indeed, through elaborating, formalizing, and codifying these rules themselves. In practicing normal science, we tend to see the scientific reality that we project linguistically as being self-subsistent and exterior to our linguistic practice. Thus we come to take our literary devices literally. By thickening representations within our accepted paradigm, we thereby define as errors those activities that stretch the paradigm or mix it with others.

Stretched or thick genres respectively induce relativist or realist epistemologies. Theoretical inventions in science start out as relativistic ways of looking at things, but, if successful, they become discoveries of real objects or relations. Similarly, academic paradigms and disciplines start out as stretched discourses that, when successfully institutionalized, become generically thick and epistemologically realist. Indeed, the very stability, even rigidity, of their discursive practices guarantees both that their objects are constituted as already available for inspection and that "the truly clever practitioner will succeed" (Kuhn 1970:179).

Such realism is a rhetorical achievement. "Only when a community decides there is one right way can it achieve the confidence and narrowness of detailed prescriptions [for representations]. In rhetoric, 'one right way' implies not only a stability of text, but a stability of rhetorical situation and rhetorical actors, so that there is little room or motive for improvisionary argument. Within a stabilized rhetorical universe, people will want to say things to each other under similar conditions for similar purposes. In this context, prescribed forms allow easy and efficient communication without unduly constraining needed flexibility" (Bazerman 1987:137).

When sufficient anomalies arise, however, or competing perspectives challenge the dominant one, or shifts occur in the reigning habitus, then both old and new paradigms appear as metaphors for, rather than copies of, a reality that can be known differently through different poetic evocations. At such moments the conflicts between old and emergent paradigms can be more easily seen as political struggles between representatives of opposing definitions of the correct tradition, a tradition that is articulated in narrative form (Brown 1987:164–69; MacIntyre 1980; Fisher 1987). The dominant paradigm may ignore the new perspectives or data and thereby limit its relevance and range. It thus may remain internally consistent but will be able to truly represent an ever-diminishing portion of the relevant reality. Conversely, the dominant paradigm may be stretched to accommodate new information or viewpoints. But practitioners thereby run the risk of rendering their paradigm internally inconsistent, thinly encoded, and thus bereft of the thick consistency of representation that was the source of its realism and objectivity and, hence, of its authority and truth. Finally, the old image of the world will be reaffirmed or a new one will replace it. After such sea changes, when the waters again are calm, the revived or newly dominant paradigm will once more become the taken-for-granted code for truthful descriptions or realistic representations. And, in poetic terms, scholars will start thickening the new genres that they have created through stretching and mixing.

This dialectical interplay can also be understood as a process of structuration (and destructuring) of genres. Even thickly encoded, traditional genres need a measure of difference to justify the repeated use of the genre as a framework of meaning. When films or fictions or scientific texts are merely elaborations of verified rules of representation, for example, they do not arouse the interest of a thoughtful audience. Thus genre operates in a double-edged fashion, providing both regulation and innovation. It is a process "in which a rule-bound element and an element of transgression are both equally important. This accounts, on the one hand, for the fact that genres appear to constitute clearly defined systems and, on the other, for the fact that they are rarely, if ever, susceptible to detailed analysis as such" (Neale 1980:50).

The dialectic of genre thickening and genre stretching operates over time. Established truths begin as created fictions, a stretching from the known to the unknown, from the literal to the metaphoric. Conversely, what was taken as literally true today may be seen, tomorrow, as having been a metaphoric invention, a stretching of meaning from one domain to another. For example, through thickening, through elaboration, and through his Protestant tendency toward foundationalism, Sir Isaac Newton turned Descartes' heuristic metaphor—"the world *as* a machine"—into a literal assertion—"the world *is* a machine" (Newton 1966). Newton and others thickened Descartes' image to make mechanism into a scientific genre on its own. Elaborating his metaphor that the world is a machine, for example, Newton imagined that the eye is a camera, and he elaborated this submetaphor into a new subgenre—the science of optics. Mechanism became the new orthodoxy, the new way of representing the real and true. Westerners for centuries agreed with Newton that the world is a machine. Finally, however, genre stretching in physics recommenced, and a new genre or paradigm emerged—quantum mechanics and relativity theory. From this new perspective, people again could see the literal mechanistic mode of representation as a poetic metaphor and genre, a thing created, not a thing discovered.

Such processes of genre formation and transformation are always with us. Harrell and Linkugel (1978:263–264) suggest that "genres stem from *organizing principles* found in *recurring situations* that generate discourse characterized by a family of *common factors*. Such principles involve a *root term,* representing an idea, which serves a canopy-like function—enveloping through implied association all which falls within its authority." Much as the machine metaphor came to dominate in early modern physics, so a new root term—language—increasingly functions in molecular biology (which is itself a genre stretched from the study of forms of life to the study of molecules). Articles on DNA in such professional journals as *Science, Nature,* and the *New England Journal of Medicine* during the 1950s and into the 1960s are pervaded with such terms as code, expression, translation, messenger, and the like (Halloran and Buford (1984:186). Watson (1968) and Crick (1994) constituted their findings as a genetic code, and Crick sought to identify what he called a "comma-free code."

What began as a metaphor for an undescribed (under-scribed) and as yet undescribable domain was elaborated into a model, and as this model led researchers to develop evidence that could conform it, the metaphor and model of "code" and its "information" were thickened into what were then taken as literal descriptions of the newly constituted domain (Olby 1974; Judson 1979;

Prelli 1989:236–55). Thus an essay in a 1972 issue of *Scientific American* could assert as a literal claim that DNA communicates meaningful information: "The capacity to communicate is a fundamental feature of living cells. . . . The genetic information of an organism is embodied . . . in the DNA molecules of the nuclei of its cellular constituency. The meaning of that information is the specification of the precise sequence of the 20 amino acids in a myriad of different kinds of protein molecule." By such means a scientific half-truth invented through genre stretching may be thickened into an institutionalized discourse as a whole reality and doctrine, not only accepted but indispensable to further experiments done under its aegis.

All referential language carries a surplus of possible meanings. Normal science tries to narrow such potential meanings to a single monological one. But too much of this narrowing and thickening is counterproductive to scientific innovation itself. In conveying new ideas, or even in elaborating old ones, some imprecision is indispensable. This is because an image of the field of study has to be posited before it can be specified. Thus even the discourse constituted by sedimented metaphors and thick genres has to be stretched to extend to new inferences or applications. Fresh metaphors or stretched genres even more strongly imply dimensions yet to be spelled out or whole fields yet to be known. The only way to avoid this stretching of meaning is an impossible one: that we should know everything about a domain before we have conceived and explored it. By stretching genres, however, we can apprehend a new domain before we fully comprehend it. We use borrowed or stretched language to talk about the emergent domain until the new language, or the new usage of the old language, becomes elaborated and thick, a genre on its own.

THE RHETORICAL CONSTRUCTION OF ANTHROPOLOGICAL TRUTH

A good example of realistic representation through genre thickening is old-fashioned ethnographic texts. Ethnographers attempt to truthfully represent the principal features of one culture in terms understandable to members of another, different culture. From this essential purpose flow several rules of the genre: ethnographic texts must create a distance or otherness between the audience culture and the topic culture, they must present the author as a credible link between these two cultures, they must characterize and explain the core features of the alien culture, and they must do this within a tight narrative structure. All the classic ethnographers are effective in performing these generic tasks and thereby rendering their texts believable as true and adequate representations.

Ethnographies are not merely stories about other peoples (Chambers 1988:5). They must also enable the reader to imagine what it is like to be among, or even to be one of, such other peoples. To do this, however, ethnographies must establish otherness early in the account, often by opening with exotic travel instructions or descriptions of the danger of access to the topic culture. The report of such difficulties prepares readers for challenges to their conceptions of their world and themselves. For example: "The road leading east for Tawzar goes downhill across the desert-like steppe and through El Hamma, a paltry oasis spread out at the foot of a sandy cliff, eroded by wind and rain, whose crumbling mass threatens to fall upon it. Then it turns towards the *shatt* of El Bahri. . . . The bed of the *wadi* has been dry for years. . . . Only in April, or during autumn, does a mass of yellow, greasy liquid pass like a clot, through the unused passage, on whose clay banks, shaped by the winds, there accumulate tufts of the *euphorbia gruyoniana* in which camels occasionally seem to delight" (Duvignaud 1977:1). Jean Duvignaud describes a foreboding, desolate place, far away, with alien names like Tawzar or El Hamma. It is threatening, windy, and dry, where nothing grows that is either pronounceable or edible—a place fit only for camels.

Otherness also can be created by describing *social* distance or danger, as in the opening sentence of Whyte's (1969:xv) study of the denizens of Cornerville, who, though geographically close, are threateningly different from their neighbors: "In the heart of 'Eastern City' there is a slum district. . . . To the rest of the city it is a mysterious, dangerous, and depressing area. Cornerville is only a few minutes' walk from the fashionable High Street, but the High Street inhabitant who takes that walk passes from the familiar to the unknown."[3] Whyte provides details which show that those who journey with him into this unknown land will return with knowledge. With the narrator as guide, the danger and mystery will become safe and familiar. This is to be a magical journey that will transform both reader and object; it is a literal and literary (w)rite of passage.

A second task of the classic ethnographic text is to establish its author as a credible interpreter of the topic culture. Unlike some contemporary ethnographies, which are told by members of the alien culture (e.g., Bulmer and Majnep 1977; Bahr et al. 1974; Cisneros 1983; Chin 1972, 1981), classic ethnographies are books about other peoples that are written by someone more like "us" than like "them" (Chambers 1988:8). The reader thus must be kept mindful of the ethnographer's presence, her authorship and authority, even while she is describing the actions or reporting the speech of members of the topic culture.

This authorial presence shifts, however, as the narrative develops. At first, the ethnographer encounters the topic culture as a naive, unaccepted outsider; to show this, the ethnographer takes a position textually close to the reader. Because the job of the text (and perhaps of all science) is to render the strange familiar, in the "middle" of the story the ethnographer moves textually from outside to inside the topic culture, and the audience is invited on this journey.

Often this shift is marked by dialectical turning points, as when the ethnographer is accorded quasi-member status through some rite of passage that then permits a more intimate sharing of information. Conversely, a more intimate sharing of information may itself become a rite of passage. For example, when Clifford Geertz and his wife first entered his topic village, they were "nonpersons, spectres, invisible men." The Balinese "acted as if we simply did not exist, which, in fact, as this behavior was designed to inform us, we did not, or anyway not yet" (Geertz 1973:412–13). Geertz then describes the police raid from which he escaped with other fleeing Balinese, thereby achieving a local personhood. This partial acceptance by locals is marked textually by a shift in pronouns. Henceforth in the text, "I" or "we," or "my wife and I," becomes "you." This not only asserts Geertz's authority over the readers and his role as their guide, it also decenters the narrator in the space of intersubjective dialogue with his subjects—he can now speak of "the Balinese" with a certain authorial omniscience (Crapanzano 1986:171).

Geertz and other anthropologists begin in the first person and end in the third. Through first-person narration, the ethnographer is stating, in effect, "I was there." Once this authority-by-personal-narration has been established, however, the writer typically shifts to the third person and hence to an authority-by-objective-description. Now the ethnographer displays dispassion, distance, and scientific objectivity (Clifford 1983). In effect, the field diary is omitted from the middle of the narrative of the account, which now consists of statements about the people studied rather than about what and how the ethnographer saw and heard about the people studied (Van Maanen 1988, 1995).

Such turning points from outsider to insider can also be marked by a report of the author's becoming part of a "joking relationship" (see Bakhtin 1965, 1981; Fisher 1987; Karp 1985). Such relationships denote familiarity and mutual understanding across strict social boundaries such as, for example, those between a white anthropologist and a black family with which she was living: "One incident eased my communication with Viola's husband and his brother. Late one evening I was at the Jackson's home, still pregnant, my cumbersome silhouette similar to Verna's. I was wearing dark tights and the rooms were poorly lighted. . . . Leo, slumped down in his chair, called out to me, 'Hey, Verna, get your baby his bottle so he'll stop crying. . . . ' Leo had confused me with Verna. He laughed so hard it was difficult to stop. From then on, when any relative or friend dropped by, Leo recounted this story. All their kin in the Flats—more than seventy people—heard it sooner or later" (Stack 1974). By telling of herself as having been the object of her informants' humor, the ethnographer thereby transforms herself into someone who also gets the joke. The humor of her having been mistaken for a member signals that she now has been accepted as one, and is now a certified agent and guide to cross-cultural understanding.

By relating such experiences, the investigator shows herself as sufficiently immersed in the topic culture not only to describe it from the inside but also, perhaps, to use that new insider's perspective dialectically to assess the audience culture critically as well. Renato Rosaldo (1987:90–91) provides an example of such a dialectical movement: "When I was residing . . . among the Ilongots of northern Luzon, Philippines, I was struggling against a diffusely overwhelming reaction to one of their central cultural practices: headhunting. . . . I was shocked and disoriented . . . How could such caring hosts also be brutal killers? Some months later I was classified 1-A for the draft. My companions immediately told me not to fight in Viet Nam and offered to conceal me in their homes. . . . They told me that soldiers are men who sell their bodies. . . . 'How can a man do as soldiers do and command his brothers to move into the line of fire?' . . . My own cultural world suddenly appeared grotesque."

The ethnographer also must persuade the reader that the text is a significant representative of the social scientific genre "ethnographic text." This requires that every reported item of conduct of individuals of, say, Andaman Island, be displayed as a significant representative of "Andaman culture." Cultures in this sense are lived texts that the ethnographer re-presents by describing their details as icons of generic categories that make up the core code of that culture. This can be done stylistically through flat characterizations of "typical natives" or "common denominator people" that serve to describe a type rather than an individual (Chambers 1988; see Marcus and Cushman 1982). Roles, behaviors, and scenes can also be characterized flatly as though there were no significant variation within their representative members, thereby conveying a sense of unitary and elemental facticity through the linguistic category. Radcliffe-Brown, for example, does not speak merely of the nuptials of a particular boy; he also notes a general cultural rule operating in that specific instance: "When *the parents* of *a youth* who is of *suitable age* to be married. . . . " (Radcliffe-Brown 1958). Or, "When *a man* is undressing and his true *sister* is at his side. . . . " (Firth 1957). Or "*Nuer* generally marry within their tribe," and "When *a man* feels that he has suffered an injury. . . . " (Evans-Prichard 1940:151). The otherwise unorthodox Clifford Geertz (1973:412, 446, 425) also uses such phrases as "in a way only *a Balinese* can do"; "*the Balinese* are shy"; and "*the Balinese* never do." Even in an ethnobiography such as Marjorie Shostak's *Nisa: The Life and Words of a !Kung Woman* (1981), the author's voice regularly intrudes to contextualize and typify the particularistic words of her "informant": "Once *a marriage* has survived a few years beyond *the young wife's* first menstruation, the relationship between *the spouses* becomes more equal" (Shostak 1981:169; italics added in each quotation in this paragraph).

All these narrators follow a norm of the ethnographic genre: they textually represent people with a group noun or pronoun (the Nuer, the Balinese, a man, the young wife) instead of an individuating personal name. This distanced, decontextualized mode of discourse represents individual actors as media or carriers of social norms and forms, with little or no scope for their exercise of personal judgment in particular situations. In this manner the reflexive ad hoc character of lived experience is textually rendered as objective and general.

All such reports display facts and observations in order to reveal some more general cultural norm or attribute, which in turn reflects a dominant cultural norm of ethnographic writing itself: to be scientific is to account for particular observables in terms of general rules or laws. This norm may require the silencing of dissident voices in order to achieve monovocal authority and a seamlessly generalized account. It may involve the suppression of purportedly irrelevant details such as the fact that the field worker paid informants or gained access through the good offices of the bad colonial officer. And it always involves choosing a mode of representation that marginalizes the intersubjective "field" that is "worked" (Clifford 1986:6, 10).

These are only four features of the narrative structure of traditional ethnographic texts: establishment of distance, transformation and new understanding, description of particular practices as representative of general cultural norms, and the ordering of these textual moves into a unified narrative flow. Moreover, I have sketched these features so briefly as to present almost a caricature. Nonetheless, these observations illustrate my point: ethnographies have paradigmatic rules of representation that define them as a kind of literary genre, and their realism, credibility, and adequacy depend upon close textual adherence to these rules for ethnographic representation. Realism in ethnographic texts is created through thick representation according to that genre's rules.

THE OBJECTIFYING RHETORIC OF POSITIVIST SOCIOLOGY

Positivistic accounts use nonhuman root metaphors—the world as a machine or as an organism rather than as a language, drama, or game. They employ a metonymic form of emplotment in which the whole is known through its parts, or even reduced to its parts. Positivist accounts in sociology also assume the highly distanced and hierarchically superior point of view of an omniscient author who sits above the fray. Hence, such accounts allow little or no space in their texts for the speech of the subjects or natives.

Positivist sociology aspires to produce statements of the kind and authority associated with the natural sciences—statements that purportedly rise above rhetoric. Following this anti-rhetorical rhetoric, selected works will be canonized into classics or exemplars, and an emergent profession will be institutionalized to enforce boundaries of membership and correct usage. An emergent genre of scientific writing may be codified into explicit formalized rules of representation. Such rules project the belief that social science has a universal objective validity. They seek to persuade readers that they do *not* persuade but are instead compelled by reasoning and evidence that are self-evident, independent of local or historical contingencies, and convincing in and of themselves (Perelman and Olbrechts-Tyteca 1969:32).

Positivist language is deployed in a way that lifts actions from specific contexts of persuasion by *agents* and attributes them instead to various decontextualized causal *agencies*. Andrew Abbott (1988), for example, found that all the research articles he examined in major sociology journals attributed agency to such variables as "high socio-economic status," "educational attainment," or "access to resources." By contrast, persons as agents were invoked only when data failed to support predicted outcomes. Unlike the anthropologists who transpose co-temporal shared experiences into a timeless representation, positivist sociologists seek to eliminate lived experience altogether.

The appearance of universal objective validity is achieved through the use of nominalizations, transformatives, and passivizations (of which this sentence is an example). Thompson (1984:120–21) described this process: "Nominalizations occur when . . . descriptions of action[s] and the participants involved in them are turned into nouns. The effect is to . . . eliminate agency . . . to transform processes into objects. . . . Transformation involves the suppression and distortion of material contained in the underlying linguistic structures. Passivization—the rendering of verbs in the passive form—also involves the delegitimation of actors."

In addition, positivist sociologists project the objectivity of their reports by representing the author as superior to the persons under study. The ethnographer, ethnomethodologist, and positivist act and are acted upon by their subjects, but they engage in and report on this interaction in different ways. Each thereby establishes a different authorial voice, distance, and authority. The experimenter or analyst of social systems does most of the acting and severely restricts the ways he (or she) may be acted upon. He defines his subjects as a "subject matter" in advance, specifies the conditions under which their limited actions are to be considered relevant (to be taken as evidence), applies the appropriate stimuli, and controls the subjects and their contexts, logically and sometimes practically, so that they may finally (1) react, or (2) not react, in the predicted manner. This reaction is the sole contribution of the subjects to the process of observation or deduction.

Such authorial distance and omniscience are displayed in the writings of Talcott Parsons (1951:250–51): "It is not possible to make a judgment of deviance . . . without specific reference to the system . . . to which it applies. The structure of normative patterns in any but the simplest sub-system is always intricate and usually far from fully integrated; hence singling out one such pattern without reference to its interconnections in a system of patterns can be very misleading." The "structure of normative patterns" and the "interconnections within a system" are defined by the sociologist, not the actors. The actors, operating as they do within discrete situations, are almost always bound to be "misled." The level of discourse of the reporter is "superior" to the speech of any possible subjects, except other positivist social scientists. The "specific reference" is to "the system," not to meanings that the actors themselves may give to their situations. As a reduction of language to denotative meanings, the words are not placed in any context that could suggest nearness to phenomena actually observed.

Another rhetorical strategy of objectification in positivist sociology, also used by ethnographers, is to refer to individuals in terms of general social categories rather than particular personal biographies (Maynard and Wilson 1980). Because of this manner of naming, people's identities are shifted from that of individual agent to that of objective agency—people become the instrument or expression of some social category or role, the results rather than the creators of social structure.

Such negations of agency can take place "on line," as it were, by denying reflexivity in conversation itself. Conversation presupposes tacit understandings, such as the et-cetera clause or the let-it-be clause (Garfinkel 1967), that not only make the process of interpretation possible but also promote a multiplicity of interpretations. Recognition of reflexivity in conversation is thus an acknowledgement that speakers are agents who interpret and create meaning. By contrast, this agency can be suppressed by excluding the voices of ordinary social actors from the text. Thus, the subjects of positivists' research are rarely allowed to speak for themselves. Unlike ethnobiographies (e.g., Thomas and Znaniecki 1958; Walker 1982a, 1982b, 1983; Crapanzano 1980) or even most ethnographic or symbolic interactionist writings, which report their subjects' speech for them in the text, positivist sociologists keep their subjects entirely silent or reduce their "speech" to aggregated responses to preformed survey questionnaires.

All these are typical features of the textwork of positivist sociologists. There is a focus on facticity, numerical tabulations, forced-choice responses. The author presumes an omniscience far beyond that of any possible member. The author does the talking and has the knowledge because he is located above or outside the context of discourse of members and controls the tacit rules of communication and representation through the devices of denying that such tacit rules exist and of insisting, instead, that the communication exchange between sociologists and natives is exhaustively, or at least adequately, described by the rules of *his* paradigm for representation. This type of writing protects generic *and* professional boundaries. Stephan Fuchs argues, correctly I believe, that the admission of lay agents into social science texts "deprofessionalizes" these disciplines by lowering the boundaries between lay and professional discourse. Positivists tend to erect firm professional boundaries, whereas symbolic interactionists significantly lower them. In deciding to "accept lay interpretations as the premises of [their] own accounts, ethnographers vote for an organization with comparatively weak control" (Fuchs 1992:208).

The rhetoric of positivist sociology projects a certain role for the author, for science, and for the reader. Such scientific articles start with a review of the literature, an announcement of a hypothesis that fills a gap or advances prior work, a statement of methods, and a report and discussion of results. An image of the author is projected by this unfolding sequence of topics—an author who is cast not so much as a thinker about mind or society than as a designer of experiments, a manager of research projects, and a presenter of findings.

Science, too, is rhetorically constructed by positivists as a project of "incremental architecturalism," with each study or article being another building block for an ever-extending disciplinary structure. Even short articles that report research findings without any inherent theoretical interest are acceptable, indeed, useful, because they add a brick to the structure, and we should not expect each brick to contain the blueprint of the entire edifice. This incrementalism is also suggested by footnotes and citations to prior writings, indicating that a particular essay builds upon previous work. This method of citation discourages a critical overview of prior research, which, in any case, usually is not necessary because the researcher, like the reader, is inspired to be more a mason than an architect (Bazerman 1987:140–41). Indeed, the reader is also cast in the role of a person seeking additional bits of knowledge to fit with previous bits. More emphasis is placed on evaluating the author's competence at method than on examining the truth or significance of her ideas.

THE IRONIC GENRE INVERSIONS OF ETHNOMETHODOLOGY

Irony is a preferred trope of genre stretchers. Indeed, despite its dangers, irony seems indispensable to discourse that generates contrarian ways of thinking (Brown 1989a: ch. 5, 1987: ch. 8). As a way of knowledge, irony helps us understand things by framing them from the perspective of their antitheses. To render something ironic is to stretch it from its conventional context and place it in an opposite one. Through such a negation, we become more aware of what that thing is. Irony involves what Kenneth Burke (1964:94) called "perspective by incongruity . . . a method for gauging situations" by stretching their representation from a usual genre to a logically contrary one. By working out the negative implications of a concept or situation, one can see whether the sign system it implies is really consistent. Because of its power to reveal inconsistencies between paradigm and experience, or within our paradigms, irony is a privileged means of paradigm innovation.[4]

Situations may become new sociological problems when represented through irony. Ethnomethodology, for example, makes use of irony to reveal that social reality is constructed through minute practices that themselves have no ultimate ontological status (Garfinkel 1952:51). The methods of ethnomethodologists also make empiricism ironic in their obsessive recording of ever greater details, their showing that what social scientists and members take to be facts are empirically manufactured.

In these ways ethnomethodologists not only unmask the givenness of everyday realities as social constructions; they also show that in this regard the organized rationality of science is no different from common sense. By reversing the usual views of psychotherapy, for example, Harold Garfinkel (1967) showed that the "meaning" of the "doctor's" remarks is not inherent in these remarks or in their relation to the patient's "symptoms"; instead, they may as well be (and in this experiment were) randomly generated by a computer. Thus the meaning, and the doctor herself, are revealed as discursive (re)constructions of the patient. Similarly, by reversing the conventional assumptions concerning what is a real pulse and what is only apparent, Garfinkel showed the independent Galilean pulsar to be a cultural artifact and not merely a physical fact or natural object (Garfinkel, Lynch, and Livingston 1981).

Garfinkel (1967:116) also made use of ironic distancing by describing his own growing understanding of the management of sexual identity from the viewpoint of a sociologist who is being successfully conned by the person he is studying—an ambiguously sexed person who pretended to have always been a female in order to secure Garfinkel's approval of a sex-change operation. Thus, Garfinkel unmasked his own rationality as a social construction with no inherently superior status.

A central feature of Western societies and science since the Enlightenment has been the privileged status of Reason, not only as an abstract ideal or process but also as the practical, applied rationality or "rationalization" of social conduct and organizations. In this context, conventional social science has assumed that rationality is both a naturally occurring *topic* of research and an unproblematically available *resource* for explanation. Rationality is a topic to be studied, for example, as it occurs in bureaucracies or in the reasons that people give for acting as they do. And rationality is a resource, for example, as it is used in the scientific method. By contrast, Garfinkel reversed these assumptions and made all "rationalities" into artifacts produced in micro-interactions. Moreover, in looking closely at the microprocesses of their construction, he finds that specifically scientific rationalities, if practiced apart from ordinary everyday reasoning, "can be employed only as ineffective ideals in the actions governed by the pre-suppositions of everyday life. The scientific rationalities are neither stable features nor sanctionable ideals of daily routines, and any attempt to stabilize these properties or to enforce conformity to them in the conduct of everyday affairs will magnify the senseless character of a person's behavioral environment and multiply the disorganized features of the system of interaction" (Garfinkel 1967:283). Excessive (scientific) rationality yields senselessness and disorganization. Similarly, scientific rationality is a reflexive construction of the microprocesses of research, not a pregiven method that guides these processes. In this, Garfinkel construed rationality as precisely the opposite of what Hobbes, Bacon, Descartes, Bentham, Weber, Popper, and almost everyone else had taken it to be.

To become "real" for Garfinkel is to be rendered accountable, to be articulable within the background expectancies of some given historically situated community of speech, no matter whether this community is made up of master astronomers or Shi'ite mullahs. Thus, Garfinkel ironically deflated the absolutist claims of positive science and the various forms of expertise that are practiced in its name. For Garfinkel, rationality does not instruct us as to what the world is like or what actions we should take. Instead, rationality is seen as itself emerging along with the events it is supposed to discover or the actions it is expected to guide. Rationality is always processual and retrospective, providing public and official legitimations for the night's work of astronomers, coroners, or jurists only after, or while, this work is accomplished in its practical, vulgar, local, ad hoc ways.

To reveal this point textually and practically, Garfinkel (1967:35–37, my italics) uses the stylistic devices of distance and point of view: "The members of a society use background expectancies as a scheme of interpretation . . . [but they are] at a loss to tell us of what these expectancies consist. . . . For these background expectancies to come into view one must either *be a stranger* to the 'life as usual' character of everyday scenes, or *become estranged* from them."

Thus Garfinkel's experiments create a distance in members from such background assumptions. Then members, and sometimes experimenters too, perform, and thereby render observable, the conduct necessary to maintain these very background assumptions that make intelligibility possible. That is, they question, repair, or actively reconstruct normalcy—what everyone knows, what is taken for granted. For example (Garfinkel 1967:42–43),

SUBJECT: Hi Ray. How is your girlfriend feeling?
EXPERIMENTER: What do you mean, "How is she feeling?" Do you mean physical or mental?
SUBJECT: I mean how is she feeling? What's the matter with you? (He looked peeved.)
EXPERIMENTER: Nothing. Just explain a little clearer what do you mean?
SUBJECT: Skip it. How are your school applications coming?
EXPERIMENTER: What do you mean, "How are they?"
SUBJECT: You know what I mean.
EXPERIMENTER: I really don't.
SUBJECT: What's the matter with you? Are you sick?

And then the interaction either breaks down or repair work is done to restore it. Thus Garfinkel's field experiments—a kind of scientific theater of the absurd—make manifest the reflexivity of meaning construction in everyday life.

Garfinkel reveals a similar reflexivity in sociological reasoning by ironically inverting the background assumptions of positivist sociologists. For example, although he begins the first paragraph of "What Is Ethnomethodology?" in the third person, before its end he has switched to the first ("I speak," "I mean"). No distancing here; Garfinkel speaks directly to us. But this directness, and a certain tentativeness of voice (his studies "seek to treat" and "seek to learn"), are soon inverted by verbal pyrotechnics that create density and distance: "The practices are done by parties to those settings whose skill with, knowledge of, and entitlement to the detailed work of that accomplishment—whose competence—they obstinately depend upon, recognize, use and take for granted."

Garfinkel's prose seems to express the perennial flux and redundancy of the everyday activities that he describes. His style evokes "the endless, ongoing, contingent" character of the most commonplace activities of daily life (Jacobs 1989:5–7). For example: "We were encouraged. So? Encouraged by what? Why? and why that? . . . Their [the astronomers'] tasks can be collected by speaking of them as the exhibitable-analyzability-of-the-optical-pulsar-again. They consist *of* Cocke and Disney's competent practices in that *in* each other's witnessed practices the exhibitable analyzability exists *as* their competent-practices-evidently. This object, their competent-practices-evidently, was achieved *in,* it consisted *of,* and it was extracted *from* the night's work, *and in situ* it was rendered as the properties of the pulsar's Galilean independence of their practices, the IGP" (Garfinkel, Lynch, and Livingston 1981).

Garfinkel's prose—folksy openers, followed by hyperbolically reflexive iteration—parodies social scientific jargon but is itself pellucid, once one has entered the cult . . . uh, the code. Through his seemingly modest and garbled descriptions, Garfinkel stretches sociology toward a phenomenology of language. But for readers unfamiliar with Husserl, Heidegger, and Schutz, he appears to be something of a clown, a would-be magician who cannot get his tricks to work but who, in all this hesitancy and fumbling, manages to perform amazing feats of magic, all the while subverting any rational method that might guide him. In turning both professional and lay assumptions upside down, Garfinkel used the trope of irony to stretch the paradigms of both common sense and positive science until they almost break.

CODA

In sum, I have illustrated the concepts of genre thickening and genre stretching with examples from three representative genres of social science: classical ethnographies within cultural anthropology and symbolic interactionism, positivist writings within sociology, and ethnomethodology, a relatively new school and genre of social science. With my first example, ethnography, I emphasized narrative structure and the particular narrative development that defines certain texts as truthful or adequate representatives of the ethnographic genre. In the second example, positivist sociology, I stressed authorial univocality and distance as ways of textually creating scientific authority and objectivity. In the third example, ethnomethodology, I focused on the structuring of written discourse through a literary trope, irony. The first and second examples show genre thickness, the second more than the first. The third example is one of genre stretching, mainly through inversion, because irony juxtaposes opposites and invites the reader to determine which is to have the greater valence.

I also argued that genre stretching and thickening are temporal processes, which are convertible and reversible. Classical ethnographies, for example, once expressed the descriptive literalness and authorial confidence expected of visitors to the outer reaches of their empires. Since then, with the collapse of empire, decolonization, mass literacy, and the assertiveness of "native" peoples in general, readers are more aware of the historically local character of the old-fashioned ethnographic genre. Correspondingly, new, open, stretched, ironic, or mixed genre writing has become more characteristic of ethnographic texts (Clifford and Marcus 1986).

A reverse movement, from genre stretching to genre thickening, is visible if one compares early and later ethnomethodological writings. One must use a known language, with its inherent vantage point and presuppositions, to say anything intelligible. But it is difficult to convey a new vision in an established discourse. If the new perspective is too closely wedded to a new mode of representation, it will appear incomprehensible to users of the old. But if the new vision is encoded in the old language, this very language, although easily comprehended, may contradict the new message that the author is struggling to express. Hence, as Gellner (1964:54) noted, "those who succeed in communicating this [newness], tend to do so by means of self-directed irony, by saying something and then also indicating why that something is also unacceptable, by getting involved in regressive arguments until we catch on to the principle which generates them and the way in which they are inescapable."

As ethnomethodologists found their own voice and created their own audience, however, their textwork became less ironic and open, and more thickly encoded. For example, ethnomethodologists' earlier style of ironic unmasking has given way to the obsessively detailed description of interactions and the discovery of invariant properties of sense making. With stylistic devices more akin to those of positivists, ethnomethodologists now push the local speech and meanings of members to the margins of their texts and, instead, put observable data and universal processes in the center. It follows from all this that genre thickening or genre stretching is not necessarily a virtue or a vice. We need thick, stable, shared genres to make our discourse real and intelligible; we need mixed or stretched genres to create anything new. Greater self-awareness of such poetic processes should make us more effective and reflective in our own modes of telling truth.

That stylistic choices are inevitable, and inevitably shape the messages of texts, is suggested by reflection on my own rhetorical devices in this chapter. Generally, I have stretched the genre "social science" in the direction of "literary criticism," using the trope of irony. Moreover, in order to present the chapter as objective and scholarly, I have used many of the same stylistic devices that I note in the authors I discuss. For example, my statement "All these narrators represent people with a group noun or pronoun" precisely makes me a narrator who represents people (social scientists rather than Balinese) with a group noun or pronoun. Likewise, whereas I state in literary terms that truth is judged with reference to its generic context, Parsons says something similar in the language of systems. Both of us assume a rhetorical stance superior to those whom we analyze—actors or social scientists whom we hold to be "unreflective" or "misled." Moreover, with my redundancy of arguments, assertions, and examples, and with my canonizing into classics or exemplars the texts I discuss, I am thickly encoding a new genre, poetics of knowledge, as though readers already took it to exist.

Finally, my language and my silence tend to undermine ethnographers and positivists and to applaud ethnomethodologists, without explicitly stating this. For example, I characterize the discourse of positivist sociology as "highly distanced and hierarchically superior," invoking "authorial distance and omniscience," "excluding the voice of the 'natives,'" and making "absolutist claims." These are presumably bad characteristics from a humanistic perspective. Similarly, I undercut the authority of ethnographers by suggesting that they silence "dissident voices in order to achieve monovocal authority." Likewise, I speak more of textual processes of ethnography and positivist sociology, and more of

the essence of ethnomethodology, and I remain silent about both the achievements of the first and the failures of the second (for example, the failure of
ethnomethodology to provide a macro-theory of social action or structure).
Also, by choosing to discuss ethnography and positivism in their most institutionalized moments, and ethnomethodology in its more ascendant phase, I
imply that the former are inherently more stodgy and the latter more creative.

All this could be otherwise. Rather than speaking of Parsons, for example, I
might have focused on Comte's and Durkheim's proposal to use procedures of
natural science to describe and analyze social facts—a revolutionary stretching
of the boundaries of accepted discourse in their time. Similarly, I could have
discussed ethnography since its postmodern, postcolonial turn and could have
examined more relativizing reflective, polyvocal studies (e.g., Shostak 1981;
Lacoste-Dujardin 1977; Rosaldo 1987; Bulmer and Majnep 1977; Nash 1979).
From a positivist perspective, all these "errors" or "biases" in my text could be
seen as in principle correctable, if only I would use language more logically or
correctly. But any such usage itself merely constitutes another literary–social
science genre, with its own presuppositions and silences. Of course, usually we
should adhere to the rules of representation of the genre of our choice. Indeed, a
central aim of this chapter is to heighten awareness of such choices and their
incumbent responsibilities. How we are to do this in specific instances is a
matter of aesthetic and political judgment.

In all these instances, both literal description and figurative invention depend on differential deployments of language. Objective truth or relativistic
representations—whether in ethnography, positive sociology, or ethnomethodology—can be judged by the standards of that paradigm or genre.
Indeed, the very intelligibility of scientific statements depends on at least some
conformance to the relevant rules of representation. Yet, because such paradigms are themselves historically shifting, and because rules always lack exhaus-
tive further rules for their application, no judgments of truths emanating from
paradigms or their rules can be absolute. This relativity appears even more
ineliminable insofar as every discourse implies a higher-order discourse by
which to justify its axioms, and such an accession of epistemological fields is in
principle boundless. We cannot push the bus that we are riding in, even though
(while on the bus) we may ride in comfortable conformity with its rules. But
there are no ultimate rules for bus riding or for truth telling. Hence, all
epistemological positions must be penultimate and at least partly self-endorsing. By revealing the poetic processes of different theoretical genres, I have tried
to encourage greater critical appreciation of all approaches and greater self-

understanding of practitioners of each of them. Writers of different kinds of science deploy different root metaphors, different genres, different tropes and other stylistic devices to construct their representations of the real or to realize their representations. Attempts to combine such approaches into a single all-inclusive one yields reduction, exclusion, and, ultimately, intellectual impoverishment. Such combinations become a kind of theoretical Esperanto with no literature and no fully native speakers.

But in the discursive perspective, science, reason, and public life do not require ultimate or universal rules of procedure for their legitimation. Instead, the relevance and proper use of rules of reason are matters of prudent judgment within scientific fields or communities of discourse. Judgment is necessary because a precise rule of application is impossible, as such applications are dependent on nonuniversal local contexts, and there are far too many contexts to allow for full specification of the possibly relevant rules and how they might be locally applied (Saunders 1987:4; Grim 1991).

If scientists were to recognize the literary textwork of their theories and descriptions, this awareness would not degrade their studies to the status of mere ideology, propaganda, or fiction. Instead, it could help to correct the tendency to become captive of ideological preconceptions that they do not recognize but nonetheless honor as *the* correct perception of reality (Gadamer 1975). Such ideological thinking is created by taking theories as literal when they are enscripted, perforce, by literary means. By contrast, in a rhetorical view, political and stylistic preconceptions are recognized and used to explore or invent a given field of inquiry and experience. By analyzing different scientific paradigms rhetorically, we can see theoretical change or revolution as processes by which original, poetic metaphors become literal and prosaic, and we also see how a stretched genre that is taken as a poetic projection becomes thickened little by little into what is then seen as an objective or literal mirror of reality.

Each new genre, each new set of theories, allows us to enrich our view of human or natural conditions—how they came about and how they are experienced. By seeing genres as modes of telling stories, and seeing theory making as a kind of poetic or narrative practice, we also view language as a primary resource and topic of our investigations (Spence 1990; White 1978:128–29). Language is no longer seen as a neutral carrier of meanings or a mere transparent instrument of representation. Instead, it becomes the constitutive method and material of the world that it projects. And the ways we talk about the world become as important as the objects of the worlds that, when we talk about them, become what we experience.

Chapter 4 Science and Storytelling: Creating Truths through Narratives of Conversion

And in fact we are under the influence of some narrative, things have always been told us already, we and ourselves have always already been told.
Jean-François Lyotard (1977:45)

The Victory above all will be
To see clearly at a distance
To see everything
Near at hand
And may all things bear a new name.
Guillaume Apollinaire (1980:341)

Woyzeck, it makes me shudder when I
think that the Earth turns itself
about in a single day! What a
waste of time! Where will it all
end? Woyzeck, I can't even look at
a mill wheel any more without
becoming melancholy.
Georg Buchner (1963:109)

We can now explore in greater detail another aspect of the poetics of knowledge suggested in chapter 3—how narratives of conversion are used to represent or constitute "discoveries" in texts that claim to proffer new kinds of knowledge. In this, I leave out entirely the practices and contexts of reception of such texts, as well as the modes of representation other than narratives of conversion.[1] It does seem, however, that some kinds of discoveries characteristically take this narrative form—those that convey the reader into worlds that at first seem wholly other than anything seen before. This by definition would include "revolutionary" changes or expansions in our knowledge, especially if these were achieved by an actual journey. Charles Darwin, for example, presented his theory of the origin of species as a narrative of personal conversion by an overwhelming mass of facts, and this format was made all the more natural—that is, its rhetorical character was made less evident—by the fact that Darwin did make a sea voyage on the *Beagle* from 1831 to 1836.[2]

Logics of discovery as narratives of conversion are characteristic of "classical" ethnographies—those written from about 1920 to 1950, a period when exploration and travelogue had given way to settlement and description, yet before the topic cultures of ethnography had become part of independent and more familiar nations. That is, in the days of classical anthropology, to describe a "primitive" culture was to articulate an alien world and, in the course of the text, to move the reader from fearful ignorance to comfortable closeness. In this, classical ethnographies are narratives that convert the reader and the topic from strangeness to familiarity.

Less obvious uses of narratives of conversion as logics of discovery are those of philosophy and science, where the journey, and the new world that is discovered, are not literal but metaphoric and intellectual. Thus, I turn from classical ethnographies to textual representations of philosophic conversions, focusing on the ways René Descartes constituted his thoughts as a major discovery in the *Discourse on the Method of Rightly Conducting the Reason and Seeking Truth in the Field of Science*. Finally, I discuss what has come to be called the Copernican revolution, using mainly the work of a student of Copernicus, *Narratio Prima* by Rheticus, as the eponymous, self-named text that established the findings of Copernicus' later *De Revolutionibus* as a scientific revolution. These narratives of conversion move the reader from outside to inside, from the other to the self, thereby transforming the inchoate into the ordered.

NARRATIVES OF CONVERSION IN FICTION, TRAVELOGUE, AND ETHNOGRAPHY

If one looks closely at ethnographic texts, one realizes that they have great affinities with certain nineteenth-century novels and with journalistic travel books. Indeed, all three types of writing may be considered varieties of a "meta-genre"—the journey of discovery—which has a hoaried history in Western letters and social thought from Homer's *Odyssey* to Melville's *Moby Dick*. One can see their family resemblances simply by comparing the opening lines of representative texts of fiction, ethnography, and travel journalism. Such beginnings may have a special rhetorical and philosophical significance, as they are intended and taken to indicate the author's direction and meaning for the work.

In each of these three genres, a distancing of place and person is immediately effected. Compare, for example, the strangeness and distance of place that is achieved respectively by the opening lines of Marlowe's story in Joseph Conrad's novel *Heart of Darkness* (1973), of Charles Wagley's ethnography *Welcome of Tears* (1977), and of William Shawcross' journalistic account "The Mekong" (1984). In each of these, that to which the reader will be converted is placed far from the narrator and the reader.

> Going up that river was like traveling back to the earliest beginnings of the world when vegetation rioted on the earth and the big trees were kings. An empty stream, a great silence, an impenetrable forest . . . you thought yourself bewitched and cut off forever from everything you had known once—somewhere—far away—in another existence perhaps. (Conrad 1973)

> The first trip down the Araquaic River was an extraordinary experience. I did not feel secure with my canoemen, nor did I trust my own ability to give orders. I slept each night under a net, with a revolver in my hand. But the river was beautiful. As we floated downstream the canoemen fished for *pacu,* a small tasty fish, and we traded tobacco with Canada Indians for *tucunare.* (Wagley 1977)

> My first day on the river, after we had been sailing for about half an hour . . . , I suddenly heard shots from the bank . . . warning shots cross the bow. . . . At once the captain put the helm hard over and steamed fast towards the shore where a police post was situated. On a falling tide, we ran onto the mud about 200 yards from the beach. Policemen came and told us we were under arrest. . . . It was midnight before the unfortunate Comrade Long was able to clear up the problem and have us released. (Shawcross 1984)

In each of these examples, geographic, temporal, and cultural distance is achieved stylistically by explicit reference to the journey, real or imagined dangers, nonmundane characterizations of otherwise ordinary items, or exotic details. In Conrad, streams are empty, silences great, forests impenetrable, and persons—suddenly cut off from what they once had known—are now bewitched. This image is all the more powerful because of its contrast to the place within the novel where the story is being told—the placid waters of the Thames. Wagley is even less secure than Conrad's speaker; he does not trust his ability and must protect his sleep with a revolver and a net. Yet the forest is beautiful and the river languid, with exotic fish in its waters and exotic people on its bank. This may be an enchanted garden, but it is filled with unnamed dangers or, more precisely, with things dangerous because not yet named. For Shawcross, the shore activities include being fired upon and arrested, but in the end, as though to emblemize the course of his journey of discovery, problems are cleared up and one is free to proceed. Moreover, in all three accounts the river itself symbolizes a journey, like birth or death, into another world. Thus, these opening lines serve as microcosms for the respective narratives as a whole. They tell of danger that is overcome, the danger of the Other that is "solved" through its being made familiar in the course of the narrative so that, at the end, one is released from bewitchment into mastery and understanding.

Another feature of these narratives of conversion is that their authors establish both distance and authority by revealing their naiveté. Because this revelation is told in a text, however, it perforce is retrospective—it is an account of a *former* naiveté that has since been overcome. This element serves two functions: it creates a rapport with the presumably naive reader, and it establishes the narrator's authority as a competent guide. We can compare, as examples, passages from Herman Melville's *Moby Dick* and journalist Germane Greer's "The Sao Francisco" (1984), and remarks by anthropologist Paul Stoller (1989) on the Songhay of Niger.

> The prospect was unlimited, but exceedingly monotonous and forbidding; not the slightest variety that I could see.
>
> "Well, what's the report?" Said Pegleg when I came back [from the weather bow]; "what did ye see?"
>
> "Not much," I replied—"nothing but water; considerable horizon though, and there's a squall coming up, I think."
>
> "Well, what dost thou think then of seeing the world? Do ye wish to go round Cape Horn to see any more of it, eh? Can't ye see the world where you stand?"
>
> I was a little staggered, but a-whaling I must, and I would. (Melville 1976:71–72).

An old man is selling honey in the market at Juazeiro. . . . Stupidly I ask if he can sell me just half a litre. He gazes wordlessly at me and over his face steals a look I have come to know, a look which I was to see often in the valley of the Rio Sao Francisco. . . . The old man's look told me that I was not aware of his dilemma, that I was not within hailing distance of the reality of life for poor farmers in the Nordeste, and he had no hope that I or any other person of my age, class, and background would ever be, and that he did not resent it. There was no way that he, a poor farmer eking out a meager subsistence on a *roça*, a small farm which would grow a little corn, beans, and manioc if the rains were adequate, and nothing at all if they were not, could lay his hands on two half-litre bottles.

God knows he had scavenged to find the litre bottles he already had. He said nothing but turned his head slightly and stared into the distance. (Greer 1984:115)

It took me thirty days to complete 180 interviews. As I collected the data I began to analyze them, and I discovered that multi-lingualism was greater than I had anticipated. Toward the end of the Mehanna survey, I interviewed a shop-keeper named Abdou Kano. Abdou told me that he spoke four languages (Songhay, Hausa, Fulani, and Tamasheq). My work with Abdou completed, I walked next door to interview Mahamane Boulla, who, like Abdou, was a shopkeeper. I asked him how many languages he spoke.

"How many languages does Abdou say he speaks?" he asked me.

"Abdou," I said, "says he speaks four languages."

"Hah! I know for a fact that Abdou speaks only two languages."

"What?" I exclaimed. "How could he lie to me?" I stood up abruptly and strutted over to Abdou's shop.

Abdou smiled and greeted me. "Ah, Monsieur Paul, what would you like to buy today?"

"Abdou," I began firmly, "Mahamane has just told me that you speak only two languages. Is that true?"

Abdou shrugged his shoulders. "Yes, it is true. I speak only two languages: Hausa and Songhay."

"Why did you tell me you spoke four languages?"

Abdou patted me on the shoulder. "What difference does it make?" He glanced skyward. "Tell me, how many languages did Mahamane say he speaks?"

"Mahamane," I answered, "told me that he spoke three languages."

"He can speak Songhay and that is all," Abdou said.

"What?" I exclaimed. Turning red with anger, I strutted back to Mahamane's shop. "Abdou tells me that you speak only one language. But you just told me that you spoke three languages. What is the truth?"

Mahamane smiled at me. "Abdou is telling the truth."

"But how could you lie to me?"

Like Abdou, Mahamane shrugged his shoulders. "What is the difference?"

I spent the next week frantically consulting the other 178 people whom I had interviewed during the previous month. To my disgust, I discovered that everyone had lied to me, and that the data I had so painstakingly collected were worthless. (Stoller 1989:52)

In the passage from *Moby Dick,* Ishmael's view reveals the conventional attitude with which he began his voyage. He sees the ocean as monotonous and forbidding, as showing no variety. His motive for going whaling—in order to see the world—is equally conventional. Pegleg's question, "Can't ye see the world where you stand?" reveals the triteness of Ishmael's assumptions. Ishmael staggers as his conventional ontology is shaken. Unlike terra firma, the world as figured in the prospect of the ocean is both infinite and indefinite (Wood 1988:4). But Ishmael also is the narrator of this tale. Thus, in showing himself retrospectively as a naif, he positions himself prospectively as one who now is wise. By the end of the story, this implies, the reader will have joined the narrator in having shed his naiveté to see a new world full of nuance and dimension.

Germane Greer also establishes at once familiarity with the reader, estrangement from her surroundings, and retrospective understanding of the peasant's dilemma and his view of her as not even within hailing distance of his alien world. In the telling of this scene, she describes a look she has since come to know and conveys a closeness to the reality of poor farmers of the Nordeste, despite her (and the reader's) different age, class, background, language ("*roça*"), and gender. This early passage, like that of novelist Melville or the anthropologist Stoller, is thus a metaphor for the passage of the text as a whole, from ignorant outsider to enlightened insider, with the formerly naive but now wise narrator serving as guide.

Paul Stoller's tale achieves several purposes. He shows the reader how culturally distant is the world of the Songhay. They find it normal to "lie"; for them, perhaps, there is no difference between falsity and truth. Or is it that they do not know the visitor, or do not trust him because he is different? The tale, because it describes a foolish, narrated character in the past tense, also projects the narrator as presently wise. Finally, the tale reveals that the conventional scientific method—ask questions and quantify answers—is wrongheaded. Such a method, as the Songhay say, "kills something thin only to discover it is fat." In contrast, by implication, the road to knowledge of the Other is to sit and listen, to hear stories and, later, to tell them.

Stoller's anecdote, as it continues beyond the passage quoted previously, might also be called a little discovery story, in which the ethnographer interrupts the description to tell how she or he came to know what is described. Such interruptions become emblematic of the movement of the text as a whole. For example, Malinowski interrupts the continuity of his text to convey the process of discovery in his study of the Kula. Similarly "Mayberry-Lewis leads us through a series of errors and misinterpretations as he tells us how he finally understood one aspect of factionalism among the Akwe-Shavante" (Chambers 1984:9). Often the obstacles to doing fieldwork—the hostility toward outsiders, the natives' insistence on telling irrelevant stories—are suddenly understood as the content and topic of the fieldwork itself (e.g., Berryman 1962; Rosaldo 1987). In Stoller's case, his narrative and his own journey of transformation both end with the discovery of the lore and practices of a secret religious cult that for him represents the core values of the topic culture and, perhaps, the wisdom of humanity in general. More broadly, such textual representations of the author's experience of error, discovery, and rapport establish an authoritative narrative presence precisely because fieldwork, like direct observation in science, constitutes "the basic rhetoric of authority which legitimates whatever is said and claimed about 'the other'" (Marcus and Cushman 1982:39).

Sometimes "thick descriptions" themselves can mark a transformation of awareness, an opening to new ways of perception. Thick descriptions are fabricated—adding this, taking away that—in order to provide a coherent account of an exotic culture through a transformed understanding of one of its artifacts (Geertz 1973). For the ethnographer and the reader, however, the thick description is itself a rite of passage into understanding. After the thick description, at last one grasps the allusion or gets the joke.

Literature, travelogue, and anthropology, like invention and description generally, borrow each other's techniques of representation. Yet only travelogue and anthropology are considered factual, and only anthropology has claimed the status of scientific or formal empirical knowledge. This claim is supported through a number of textual practices that together are importantly different from those of either fiction of travelogue. As noted in chapter 3, this is most evident in the "middle" of ethnographic texts, which are occupied with the linguistic construction of scientific rationality. The classical ethnographies were converting *to* science, but they also were converting *from* accounts by travelers, missionaries, and novelists. Thus, unlike travelers, ethnographers showed that they had stayed in one place long enough to learn the language and really know the local culture,[3] and unlike fictional or missionary accounts, their texts reported close observations from an objective, value-neutral perspective that respected the natives' meanings and point of view and at the same time theorized them into accounts of systems, functions, and structures.

Thus the middle parts of classical ethnographies consist of observations and generalizations about the cultural Other that have been stated in theoretical terms and validated by evidence. Unlike the more personalized reportage of the opening sections, in the middle parts of ethnographies natives are described as members of categories rather than as individual persons. They become "common denominator people" (Marcus and Cushman 1982:32). Similarly, local happenings are displayed as instances of generalized processes or events, rather than as discrete occurrences (Tyler 1985:84). All this is described in a segmented, monadized place and frozen in an ahistorical, universalizing time. Such categories and events—like "maternal uncle," "clan," "religious rite," or "hunter-gather"—then serve as foci for arguments about functions, structures, and processes, the description of which form the "theories" for which the typified categories and events become the "evidence." The point of view and voice of the native, marked in the opening sections, is now silenced, and the narrator moves from naive listener to omniscient speaker. This also is a shift from subjectivity to objectivity and from communication with a human subject to analysis of a scientific object—a move from personal perception to public description. Presence and the authority of experience are replaced by representation and the authority of explanation.

In addition to all that is present in the classical ethnographies, they also seem to be driven by a powerful *absence*—by what they suppress or leave out. The classical ethnographies are so close to travel stories and missionary tales that they are forever in danger of losing their scientific status. Who, after all, is the father of anthropology if not the traveler storyteller Herodotus, the first to take the "barbarians" seriously on their own terms? Or perhaps the heroic founder of ethnography is Bernadino de Sahagún, or perhaps Bartolomé de las Casas, both missionaries who were converted to the Indian's perspective even while seeking to convert them and who partly preserved indigenous culture in texts even as their Christianity fostered its extermination. Is not the ethnographer—the defender of the indigenous, the voice of "his" or "her" people—also, like de las Casas, the mourning bird of their doom, whose appearance among them is the surest sign of their demise?

Classical ethnographies also contain the silence of knowledge that denies its dependence on power. From Herodotus' descriptions of people soon to be conquered, to de las Casas and Sahagún, whose work was suppressed by King Philip II, to the twentieth-century anthropologists who described everything about colonized peoples except that they were colonized, anthropology has always been ambivalent, and often silent, about its relation to power. Why else would Edward Evans-Prichard explain as "Neurosis" the fearful reserve of his subjects who saw him as a representative of colonial terror? This silence becomes even louder when we learn that anthropologists depended on colonial power for their access to their peoples, even as they insisted on their freedom from ideology and their objectivity as scientists. How discomforting, too, that many colonial administrators, as in the elite Indian Civil Service, were often at least as well educated as the ethnographers, or more adept at local languages.

These texts also suppress the voice of the very natives to whom, they say, they are giving voice. Instead, the natives' speech becomes an originating voice, like that of God, which appears in texts only as garbled syllables or silence (Lyotard 1954:45). And, homologously, the writers' experience becomes akin to revelation. The primary experience of the ethnographer becomes equivalent to the original past of the natives. "Fieldwork" establishes the former as a mimesis of the latter. But fieldwork is *not* a mimesis. Only textwork can make it so. Yet this textualization of experience in order to have *scientific* authority must suppress the very experience that it textualizes and that gives it *existential* authority. Thus the authority of "I was there, I lived their life" always is negated by and negates the authority of "I know, I have theory." All this leads to epistemological worrying, lapses, and aporia.

PHILOSOPHIC INVENTION AND NARRATIVE DISCOURSE

René Descartes' first book was written over a ten-year period and published in 1637, when the author was forty-one years old. The most striking aspect of the *Discourse on the Method of Rightly Conducting the Reason and Seeking the Truth in the Sciences* is that it is a travel story, an autobiographical journey of discovery. In this, the *Discourse* is presented in a manner precisely the opposite of that proposed by the *Method* itself. The *Discourse* advocates what today we would call a scientific, logico-deductive approach to knowledge, but the knowledge of that approach which Descartes provides is told as an autobiographical travelogue, a story in the first person and the past tense, of how he came to discover his method and, in so doing, to realize his nature and his mission.

The *Discourse* has six parts that together form a classical narrative beginning, middle, and end. Parts 1 and 2 ("Some Thoughts on the Sciences" and "The Principal Rules of Method") introduce the author and his subject. The next three parts ("Some Moral Rules Derived from the Method," "Proofs of the Existence of God and of the Human Soul," and "Some Questions of Physics") describe how the author came to apply his method and to demonstrate to himself its usefulness for gaining new knowledge. The final part ("Some Prerequisites for Further Advances in the Study of Nature") is a denouement, where the author reveals the "moral" of his story and invites his readers to participate through their own activities in the epic search for truth that his method enables. As such, the ending is also a new beginning, for it retrospectively frames the *Discourse* as an introduction to more literally scientific volumes that will follow.

Descartes was eminently successful in presaging and encouraging changes that were to come. Among these were the belief in the adequacy of each individual's reason for the discovery of truth, an optimistic and progressive view of science, a view of the self as a mental essence, the segregation of mind from body and ideas from world, and the conception of a science in which all natural phenomena must have material and not mental or supernatural causes.

These assumptions largely define what we might call the Cartesian paradigm, but none of them are deduced from Descartes' method. Instead, their acceptance is a precondition for our understanding of and belief in the method itself. Thus, Descartes was faced with a rhetorical dilemma similar to that of the ethnographers whom we discussed previously: how to describe a cultural artifact (the method) to readers who are not familiar with the world (the paradigmatic assumptions) which gives that artifact its sense and meaning. And, like the anthropologists, Descartes overcomes this dilemma with a narrative of his own conversion to the new worldview.

Descartes begins modestly. Like classical ethnographers, and like the Copernicans, Descartes admits "his fallibility in order to establish the overall credibility of his specific claims" (Marcus and Cushman 1982:33). In the first sentence he suggests that perhaps his discourse is too long to be read in one sitting and allows that the reader has a right to know "the author's reasons for writing this book" (1960:3). "As for myself," he says, "I have never supposed that my mind was above the ordinary. On the contrary, I have often wished to have as quick a wit or as clear and distinct an imagination, or as ready and retentive a memory, as another person" (1960:4). This places the narrator closer to, and perhaps slightly below, the reader, and far from the new world of ideas that his *Discourse* is to create: "I . . . stumbled in my youth upon certain paths which led me [to form] . . . a method of gradually increasing my knowledge as much as the mediocrity of my talents . . . will permit. . . . I should be glad to show in this *Discourse* what are the paths I have taken to search for truth, and to sketch of my whole life, so that each one can form his own judgment of it. . . . I only propose this writing as an autobiography, or, if you prefer, as a story" (1960:4–5).

Descartes presents himself as a conventional person who began with the greatest commitment to received ideas and opinions. He then stumbles upon certain methods that can serve anyone who uses them as a touchstone for knowledge. "From my childhood I lived in a world of books . . . I esteemed eloquence highly and loved poetry . . . I was especially pleased with mathematics . . . I revered our theology" (1960:7). Nonetheless, "when I noticed how many different opinions learned men may hold on the same subject . . . I resolved to consider as false any opinion which was merely plausible" (1960:8).

This resolve led to travel, as the author went to see "courts and armies, living with people of diverse types and stations, of life, acquiring varied experience, testing myself in the episodes which fortune sent me and, above all, thinking about the things around me so that I could derive some profit from them" (1960:8–9). What our traveler discovers, however, is an even greater variety of customs and opinions than he had found in his books, and an even greater contradiction between them. Thus, he determines to accept only clearly demonstrable truths and see "how they fitted into a rational scheme" (1960:12); "in this matter I patterned my behavior on that of travelers" (1960:9). "In the nine years that followed I wandered here and there throughout the world, trying everywhere to be spectator rather than actor in all the comedies that go on" (1960:22).

Descartes states his preference for clear ideas, correct order, and precise statement. This clarity and correctness is achieved in his *Discourse* through metaphors, among other literary devices. Some of these metaphors are merely illustrative, as when he says that it is as difficult to separate good from harmful precepts as it is "to bring forth a Diana or a Minerva from a block of virgin marble" (1960:14). Elsewhere, metaphors take the form of models, chiefly mechanical ones. Thus Descartes uses metaphors not only to illustrate but also to provide the basic shape of the topics and explanations that he reports in the middle parts of the book. For example, "I explained [how] . . . our bodies can move without the guidance of volition. This will hardly seem strange to those who know how many motions can be produced in automata made by human industry. . . . Such persons will therefore think of this body as a machine created by the hand of God, and in consequence incomparably better designed and with more admirable movements than any machine that can be invented by man" (1960:41).

Descartes' text also contains what we could call root metaphors of the self—fundamental images that project and define an essence to the person (Pepper 1965; Brown 1989a; Edelman 1974). In the *Discourse* Descartes employs three such metaphors: the traveler, the cogito, and the builder. I have already spoken of Descartes' characterization of himself as a traveler; his image of the self as a thinking essence also runs throughout the text and is elaborated into a central metaphysical position. This image of the solitary cogito is prefigured in the first sentences of part 2, "The Principal Rules of the Method." When traveling in Germany, the author "was caught by the onset of winter. There was no conversation to occupy me, and being untroubled by cares or passions, I remained all day in a warm room. There I had plenty of leisure to examine my ideas" (1960:10). The thinker in a warm room, without cares or passions, becomes an image of the disembodied mind, the idea without the world, the mental essence that reflects on material existence.

A similar image of the self as solitary thinker appears in the last lines of part 3, "Some Moral Rules Derived from the Method," only this time the self is able to maintain its seclusion even "in the midst of a great and busy people. . . . [In Holland] I was able to enjoy all the comforts of life to be found in the most populous cities while living in as solitary and retired a fashion as though in the most remote of deserts" (1960:23).

The third root metaphor of the self for Descartes is that of the architect or builder, which recurs throughout the text. This image refers to the philosopher and his activity, to the necessity of establishing a firm foundation for knowledge, to the need for the conservation of old customs before new ones are constructed, and to the possibility of using materials from an older, now crumbling structure to build a more solid one on a new design. The first such image appears in part 2:

> Thus we notice that buildings conceived and completed by a single architect are usually more beautiful and better planned than those remodeled by several persons. . . . It is true that we never tear down all the houses in a city just to rebuild them in a different way . . . ; but we do see that individual owners often have theirs torn down and rebuilt. . . . By this example I was convinced that a private individual should not seek to reform a nation by changing all its customs and destroying it to construct it anew. Nevertheless, as far as the opinions which I had been receiving since my birth were concerned, . . . never has my intention been more than to try to reform my own ideas, and rebuild them on foundations that would be wholly mine. . . . And just as in tearing down a building we usually retain the desire to help build a new one, so in destroying all of my opinions which seemed to me ill-founded, I made many observations and acquired much experience which has aided me in establishing more certain knowledge. (1960:10, 13, 22)

These three images—the traveler, the isolated cogito, and the builder—are not so far apart as they may seem, for each of them presupposes a mind independent of the cares and passions of the world. The traveler is a bit like the *flâneur,* a disengaged observer, more spectator than actor, who is distant enough to see human efforts as comedic. The solitary thinker is by himself in his winter room or alone amid the tumult of the city, his creature comforts forgotten because provided, or dismissed because he has learned "to conquer myself rather than fortune, to change my desires rather than the established order, and generally to believe that nothing except our thoughts is wholly under our control" (1960:20). The builder, too, is an architect, not a mason, a self that conceives and designs but does not get its hands dirty, does not mix the mortar, does not breathe the dust. Thus, all these images convey a mind detached from the cares of the world and the appetites of the body—a mind that designs but does not engage, a mind in pursuit of certain truth. This is a mind akin to God's.

A logical development of these three images of the self parallels the narrative development of the text as a whole. In this, the Cartesian self is akin to God's chosen people, and Descartes' narrative of conversion is like that of the conversion of the Jews from slavish idolatry to God-given knowledge. In the beginning of the narrative, and of the self's own transformation, Descartes represents himself as a passive conformist who leaves the world of polythematic opinion on a journey in search of certain knowledge. In the longer middle part of his conversion, the self is an isolated cogito, akin to both Moses on the mountain and his people in the desert. The self, the cogito, can now intuit God's laws of nature even as it is, amid people, solitary in the desert. Finally, once revelation has been granted, it is time to construct the new kingdom of knowledge. The self becomes a builder.

In this transformation, the self comes into its own. Descartes begins by representing the *Discourse* "as a story in which you may possibly find some examples of conduct which you might see fit to imitate" (1960:4–5). By the end of the tale he has shifted from a modest "I" to an implicit "we." The tentative "may" and "might" are abandoned as Descartes invites readers to join in the construction of a new world of scientific knowledge. "I have now reached the point . . . where I see clearly enough the direction in which we should go" (1960:47). "As far as the related experiments are concerned, one man is not enough to do them all" (1960:52). Descartes' conversion is now complete, and he conveys with the pronoun "we" that his world is now also that of the reader.

As with the classical ethnographies, visible and invisible tensions exist in the works of Descartes. Although I have re-textualized Descartes' dominant metaphors as a logical development, they remain resistant to such assimilation. How can the cogito at once explore and build, go further while also going higher? Such words as *recherche, voir, chemin, progrès, voyager, chercher, rencontrer, découvrir, trouver, suivre, conduire, fuir, s'éloigner, s'écarter, avancer, approcher, parvenir,* never quite accord with such terms as *fondements, ferme, solide, renverser, ébranler, bâtir, fonder, affermir, appuyer,* and *élever.*

Descartes' images—a straight road for the traveler, a solid foundation for the architect, a method true and *assurée*—seem to assure Descartes of his self-sufficient certitude. And yet it somehow is not quite convincing, either logically or psychologically. Descartes' "I think, therefore I am" only proves that there is thinking, not being. It is a tautology. His certitude is circular. And his metaphors are indecisive, not only contradicting each other but also often expressing ambivalence themselves—*fuir* (to flee), *s'éloigner* (to walk away), *renverser* (to spill), *ébranler* (to loosen or shake). Why, as Edelman (1974:117) asks, are images of mud, sand, loose foundations, tottering structures, or of straying, groping, falling and drowning voyagers, so familiar to his mind? Why, all along, does he also need to evoke so often the *firm* foundation and the *straight* road? By the very pressure of its persistence and repetitiousness, his figurative language, like a form of subconscious resistance, betrays—although it would deny—the pressure of an uncertainty that remains to be dealt with. Rationally, he may in good faith have thrust back all possible mental qualms, but a sense of insecurity obstinately abides, in regions where argument does not reach it. Beyond middle age, the philosopher is still rehearsing the two selfsame metaphors, as if by an old private ritual conjuring and warding off incertitude. And young or old, reciting those formulas as by rote, Descartes does it almost always on identical occasions: when questions of method arise—irrepressible questions, which spring up anywhere but especially at the beginning of each of his philosophical works, and at the head of various chapters—at those points, that is, where Descartes launches new enterprises in which his method will be at stake.

Perhaps this ambivalence is not so surprising if we remember that Descartes, though later considered a scientist and precursor of modernity, was an actor, dancer, and author of at least three plays and a ballet, which have not survived. His motto was *larvatus pro deo,* "Masked I go forward": "In order that the blush on their faces does not show, actors on the stage put on a mask. Like them, when I go out into this theatre of a world, where wither I have been but a spectator, masked I go forward." In this passage from *Les Preambles,* Descartes himself is a player, hiding his "blush," taking one role and then another. Where can certitude be found in this theater of the world? What constancy of identity can there be for the players? What surety for the spectator who sees masks but not faces?

And how is it that, despite his insistent rationalism, the primary source of Descartes' own certitude was not his logic or method but a dream on the memorable night of November 10, 1619, recorded in his lost book *Olympia?* This was a nightmare of tortured travel: "He was obliged to turn toward the left side in order to be able to advance to the place where he wanted to go, because he felt a great weakness in his right side, which he could not stand. He was ashamed to walk that way, and he made an effort to straighten himself up" (*Olympia,* as reported by Baillet 1946, my translation; see Cole 1993).

These images presaged Descartes' life mission—to walk upright on the straight path. The righteousness of reason, the unreason of righteousness— how do they fit? Did God the Father strike down Descartes for his ambition, showing him the fruits of wisdom even as he forbade his son to eat of them? Is not Descartes' traveler a wanderer in a wilderness of "*terre mouvante et le sable, pour trouver le roc ou l'argile"* (*Discours* 6:29), walking over moving earth and sand, seeking the rock, like Saint Peter, on which to found his church of method, the edifice on which he can climb to God, to return to the rejected and punishing Father, to return to the womb-like heated chambers to receive "*une lumière pure, constante, claire, certaine, sans peigne, et tousiers présente, . . . la lumière de Dieu"* (*Oeuvres* 5:136–37)? The repressed does not stay fully repressed; the hubris of dismissing God, of leaving Calgary Hill for Mount Olympus, returns as anxiety, the unnamed fear of the wrath of the Father.

CONVERSION NARRATIVES AND THE COPERNICAN REVOLUTION

The triumph of Copernicus' heliocentric view over Ptolemaic geocentrism did not occur with the publication of Copernicus' *De Revolutionibus* in 1543. Instead, it was projected in Rheticus' *Narratio Prima* three years earlier and was elaborated through more than a century of study and argumentation. In its own time, the heliocentric theory solved some problems but introduced new ones, was not clearly superior to its competitor either logically or empirically, and was clearly inferior to it psychologically and ideologically. Nor was it practically more useful (Gingerich 1983:140). Even today the U.S. Coast Guard navigates by Ptolemaic, not Copernican, astronomy.

How, then, did this great shift of paradigms come to occur? Two opposing answers invite our attention—those respectively of Paul Feyerabend in *Against Method* (1978) and of Stephen Toulmin in *Human Understanding* (1972). For Feyerabend, adherence to Copernicus' views in Galileo's day required "blind faith . . . [supported] by *irrational means* such as propaganda, emotion, *ad hoc* hypotheses, and appeal to prejudices of all kinds" (Feyerabend 1978:153–54). By contrast, Toulmin holds that the move from Ptolemaic to Copernican paradigms was made for rational reasons: "If the men of the sixteenth and seventeenth centuries changed their minds about the structure of the planetary system, they were not forced, motivated, or cajoled into doing so; they were given reasons. In a word, they did not have to be converted to Copernican astronomy; the arguments were there to convince them" (1972:105; see Finocchiaro 1980:4–5).

The curious aspect of these seemingly opposed views is that they both assume a strict bifurcation of language and truth, rhetoric and reason. For both, belief is either irrational because based on propaganda or cajoling, *or* it is based on arguments and reasons that are independent of persuasion. Along with Alan Gross (1989:97–110), whose research I draw on amply in this section, I believe that both these views are incomplete because they overlook the rational functions of rhetoric and the rhetorical functions of reason. Indeed, if we were to caricature Feyerabend only slightly, we would urge would-be paradigm innovators to develop theories in opposition to known facts, to lie about their purported observations, to maintain their positions despite sensible objections, and to defend their views through trickery and bluster. Conversely, if we were to follow Toulmin strictly, we would imagine that science operates almost without the mediation of speech, that reason is not itself a form of verbal persuasion, and that arguments are "just there" and not made through communicative interaction.

In contrast to both these views, is it not possible that people were made open to the Copernican view through a rhetoric of reason, a narrative of conversion that functioned as a logic of disclosure of the Copernican system for the reader? Such a conversion narrative, the *Narratio Prima* by Copernicus' disciple Rheticus, appeared in 1540, three years before the publication of Copernicus' own opus, *De Revolutionibus*. The *Narratio Prima* announced and advocated the heliocentric theory. Of course, Rheticus gives reasons for its superiority over the Ptolemaic system—reasons that training tells him are scientific. "But since, as a result of this very training, he cannot regard these reasons as sufficient for full conviction, he sets them within the frame of a conversion narrative: he unites argument and narrative into a single structure, a model for radical intellectual change" (Gross 1989:98).

"Copernicans shared with their master an austere and intransigent realism: the new astronomy must be a mathematically parsimonious system in exact agreement with accurate observations and in precise conformity with a correct physics. But the realization of this explanatory ideal was not possible until the advent of classical dynamics over a century after Copernicus' death" (Gross 1989:98). Thus, the conversion to the new model could not be fully justified in terms of facts and deductive logic because these would be invented only if the theories that they would support could be made sufficiently persuasive without them. In reductive terms, one could say that the narrative justified the theory that justified the search for the facts that justified the theory that justified the narrative.

This movement was not so much circular as reflexive and dialectical. That is, the very inconsistency between the narrative structure of the conversion and the governing mechanist epistemology created a fruitful tension. It became an irritant that stimulated Tycho Brahe, Michael Maestlin, and Johannes Kepler to generate the data and logic that would make that narrative unnecessary as the

Copernican paradigm thickened. This movement would not have been possible, however, except for the power of the initial narrative to persuade. "It was not until Newton that the task was completed to the satisfaction of a sizeable segment of the then scientific world; only then did astronomy rest, in their view, on a fully scientific base. On this reading, *Narratio Prima* becomes the opening move in an eventually successful campaign to create the first modern exact science" (Gross 1989:98). Let us turn to Rheticus' text and see how this movement was initiated.

Rheticus describes Copernicanism as the natural outgrowth of Ptolemaic astronomy. But in the midst of this portrayal the crucial Ptolemaic assumption of geocentricity is suddenly and completely discarded. Near the end of a section on lunar theory, Rheticus says: "These phenomena, besides being ascribed to the planets, can be explained as my teacher shows [*demonstrate*], by a regular motion of the spherical earth; that is, by having the sun occupy the center of the universe, while the earth revolves instead of the sun on the eccentric" (1982:54). This sentence, which comes without warning in a text that up to then is orthodox, certainly must have shocked its sixteenth-century readers—much more so than we can readily imagine today. "Demonstration" [*demonstrate*] in the sixteenth century was not a "showing" (as in the English translation) but had to be a strict logical proof. Thus, in its own context, Rheticus' claim must have been even more radical than it appears, first because it is stronger and second because it is false, or rather because it can be true only on the assumption that the observation can be shown to follow, logically deductively, from Copernicus' assumptions. Thus, to believe Rheticus' assertion "was to turn one's back on the central tenet of years of training, to discard completely the unquestioned assumption of respected colleagues and admired teachers, to desert forever the cosmos of fourteen centuries of astronomy. Little wonder that, for over a century, Copernicanism had relatively few significant adherents" (Gross 1989:102).

Rheticus does prepare the reader for this sudden shift by describing the conflict between Copernican and Ptolemaic astronomy as a conflict within the scientific tradition, a conflict that Copernicus struggled with himself. Rheticus presents the heliocentric view, despite its radicalness, as one that Aristotle himself would certainly have accepted. He thus seeks to normalize his deviant claims by placing them in the tradition of science of which Aristotle and Ptolemy are exemplars: "I am convinced that Aristotle, who wrote careful discussions of the heavy and the light, circular motion, and the motion and rest of the earth, if he could hear the reasons for the new hypotheses, would doubtless honestly acknowledge what he proved in these discussions, and what he assumed as unproved principle" (Rheticus 1982:58).

Copernicus' conversion and the reader's identification are made more powerful by the astronomer's initial unwillingness to give up conventional beliefs. While "walking in the footsteps of Ptolemy," Rheticus says, Copernicus nevertheless "became aware that the phenomena, which control the astronomer, combined with mathematics to compel him to make certain assumptions even against his wishes." Copernicus "had to assume his hypotheses . . . in obedience to the command given by the observations" (Rheticus 1982:81, 57, 63). Thus the phenomena control him and mathematics compels him even against his will, and, in any case, Aristotle would have approved. The reference to Aristotle also places the work of Copernicus in the same classical tradition as that of Ptolemy. By this rhetorical device, Rheticus has created legitimacy for Copernicus' work, for to deny the right to question geocentricity is now to reject the intellectual tradition within which Ptolemy worked.

In telling Copernicus' story of rational conversion, Rheticus is sensitive to the uses of contrast as well as of continuity. He shows how Copernicus began with the same observations as Ptolemy only to arrive, by force of evidence and logic and almost unwillingly, at a diametrically opposed central conclusion. Copernicus is especially reluctant to espouse heliocentrism because "he is far from thinking that he should rashly depart, in a lust for novelty, from the sound opinions of the ancient philosophers, except for good reasons and when the facts themselves coerce him." Moreover, even after Copernicus himself was entirely convinced of heliocentricity, says Rheticus, he published his results only after the repeated urging of the Bishop of Kulm. Rheticus thus dramatizes the power of the heliocentric theory by stressing Copernicus' initial resistance to it and his general respect for traditional belief and authority.

Rheticus' account of Copernicus' conversion to heliocentrism is also an account of his own: "In my teacher's revival of astronomy I see . . . with both eyes and as though a fog had lifted and sky were now clear" (1982:168; Westman 1975). He himself becomes slowly but increasingly convinced of the truth of Copernicus' theory in the course of his own text, which moves, like Descartes', from tentativeness to surety. Early in *Narratio Prima* heliocentricity is merely a hypothesis by which celestial phenomena "can be explained." But soon thereafter he asks, "Should we not attribute to God, the creator of nature, that skill which we observe in the common makers of clocks?" Some hesitation is conveyed by such terms as "should we not," "can," "suppose," and "as it would if" (1982:135, 137). But this tentativeness is abandoned near the end of the work, where Rheticus becomes openly assertive: "That this covenant of earth and planet might be everlasting, God ordained that the first small circle of liberation . . . should revolve once in the time in which one return of Venus to either of the movable nodes occurs" (1982:184). Copernicus has achieved a "restoration of astronomic truth" (1982:52). Indeed, by the end of *Narratio Prima,* the meaning of "hypotheses" has been converted from tentative heuristic for the scientist to physical truth about the universe.

As Rheticus' conviction grows, so does the status of Copernicus. From heir to Ptolemy he becomes king, general, philosopher, and mythical hero. Like Atlas, Copernicus now shoulders the world; like Orpheus, he rescues the muse of astronomy from the underworld (1982:131, 132, 150, 162–64). Such mythical status is in accord with Copernicus' own language, for rational conversion has led to the discovery of the neo-Platonic truth that the self-caused Sun, the source of all motion and light, rests in the center of the universe "as if on a kingly throne, governing the family of stars that wheel around" (1978:22).

Copernicus himself, along with other Copernicans, also used the strategies of the conversion narrative that Rheticus had deployed so ingeniously. Chief among these strategies is the affirmation of tradition as a means of establishing credibility for the author and his subversion of that tradition. Thus, Copernicus insisted that his theory was based on hypotheses concerning the nature of the universe that had been formulated by the ancients:

> We must follow in their footsteps and hold fast to their observations, bequeathed to us like an inheritance. And if anyone on the contrary thinks that the ancients are unworthy in this regard, surely the gates of this art are closed to him. (1971:99)

> I undertook the task of rereading the works of all the philosophers which I could obtain to learn whether anyone had ever proposed other motions of the universe's spheres than those expounded by the teachers of astronomy in the schools. And in fact first I found in Cicero that Nicetas supposed the earth to move. Later I also discovered in Plutarch that certain others were of this opinion. . . . Therefore, having obtained the opportunity from these sources, I too began to consider the mobility of the earth. And even though the idea seemed absurd, nevertheless I knew that others before me had been granted the freedom to imagine any circles whatever for the purpose of explaining the heavenly phenomena. Hence I thought that I too would be readily permitted to ascertain whether explanations sounder than those of my predecessors could be found for the revolution of the celestial spheres on the assumption of some motion of the earth. (1978:4–5)

Copernicus the tentative searcher becomes more certain and assertive by the end of his text. As in Rheticus' *Narratio Prima,* Copernicus' "hypothesis" or "opinion" of heliocentrism becomes, little by little, an empirical finding demonstrated with mathematical proofs, a near "certainty" that explains "the movements of the world machine" (Copernicus 1978:43). Indeed, Copernicus comes to assert, "I have no doubt that acute and learned astronomers will agree with me if, as this discipline especially requires, they are willing to examine and study, not superficially but thoroughly, what I adduce in this volume in proof of these matters" (1978:45).

With similar rhetorical moves, Copernicus' contemporary defenders also begin by insisting that he was astronomy's great *restorer*. "Even those, like Brahe and Clavius, who did not accept his system . . . called him a 'new Ptolemy'" (Hallyn 1990:59). Kepler stressed that Copernicus was interpreting the ancients and not nature (1971, vol. 3, p. 141) and that the author of *De Revolutionibus* took care "not to disorient the diligent reader by straying too far from Ptolemy" (1971, vol. 1, p. 50). And, indeed, *On the Revolutions* does duplicate not only the mathematics of Ptolemy's *Almagest* (Neugebauer 1967) but also its method, structure, and language, making only those slight changes that were required by, but also served to disguise and elide, the massive shift to heliocentricity (Prince 1969:215).

Such opening modesty also is imputed to Copernicus by Galileo in his "Considerations on the Copernican Opinion" (1989). The very title of Galileo's work signals that he is not engaging in a defense or an argument but only a "consideration," that Copernicus had put forth only an "opinion," that it was grounded in the writings of the ancients, that it was only a hypothesis, and that it also depended on the older computations: "We should therefore understand clearly that Copernicus takes the earth's motion and sun's stability for no other reason and in no other way than to establish it, in the manner of the natural philosopher, as a hypothesis of the primary sort; on the contrary, when he comes to astronomical computations, he goes back to the old hypothesis." (Galileo 1989:79).

Finally, however, Galileo comes to write that man is able to understand some propositions "perfectly" so as to have "absolute certainty," as in pure mathematics. God's knowledge is infinite, but within the finite range of the human mind, "I believe that [the mind's] knowledge equals the Divine in objective certainty, for it is able to comprehend necessity, above which it is not possible to have greater surety" (*Opere* 12:128.21–129.6 cited in Moss 1986:201). This for Galileo was probably a *modest* statement of his belief, as in the flypage of his own copy of the *Dialogue* he wrote that "in time . . . sensately and necessarily it will be demonstrated that the earth moves and the sun stands still" (in Moss 1986:203). Not only must the theologians take care not to defy "sense experiences, accurate observations, and necessary demonstrations," but even "one thousand Demosthenes and Aristotles would be cast down at the feet of every mediocre mind who had the good fortune to find the truth" through such methods (Galileo 1989:81, 1953:7:78.20–29). Galileo even excuses the Holy Spirit for speaking "differently from the truth" concerning "the motion of the earth and the stability of the sun; these propositions are very far removed from the understanding of the masses, for on these matters not relevant to their eternal life the Holy Spirit chose to conform its pronouncements with their abilities, even when facts are otherwise from the point of view of the thing in itself" (Galileo 1989:84).

In sum, for the Copernicans the renovation of the ancient learning is a way to clear space for the invention of the new. The ancients are cited not only for their theories and observations but also for their insistence and exemplification of the freedom to think. This freedom becomes all the more crucial because more information is available to contemporary astronomers than was to ancient ones: "For the number of aids we have to assist our enterprise grows with the interval of time extending from the organization of this art to us" (Copernicus 1978:8). Ptolemy himself affirmed this idea. Rheticus draws on this "tradition" of liberty of thought by quoting the *Didaskalikos* in the epigraph of *Narratio Prima:* "Free in his mind must be he who desires to have understanding." The ancients, in their respect for liberty, thus give authority to the liberty of Copernicus, in his respect for the ancients, to overturn them.

Renovatio, then, is closely related to *inovatio.* It not only establishes the modesty, credibility, and legitimacy of the innovators. Renovation of the tradition is also a logical prerequisite of innovation, because such renovation reconstitutes past thinkers in a way that reveals their systematic inadequacy. In this sense there never was a Ptolemaic *system* of astronomy before Copernicus (Hanson 1961:175; see Hallyn 1990:60, 312). Instead, the "renovation" by Copernicus was the *invention* of systematic astronomy. He constituted Ptolemy's views and data in systematic terms in order to show their *lack* of system and thus reveal their character as a "monstrosity" (Copernicus 1978:4). After criticizing the model of homocentric spheres and, indirectly, Ptolemy's equant, Copernicus says, "Nor have they been able thereby to discern or deduce the principal thing—namely the design of the universe and the fixed symmetry of its parts. With them it is as though one were to gather various hands, feet, head and other members, each part excellently drawn, but not related to a single body, and since they in no way match each other, the result would be monster rather than man" (1978:f.iii[v]).[4] This also was Galileo's observation: "But he [Copernicus] . . . in going about putting together all the structures of the particular orbits [of Ptolemy], there resulted thence a monster and a chimera, composed of members most disproportionate to [one] another, and altogether incompatible" (Hallyn 1990:80; see Gingerich 1975:89). In this way, systematicity was established (through "restoration") as the chief criterion for judging adequacy in the celestial science. And by this criterion the world system of Copernicus could be contrasted to the "system" of Ptolemy and found to be superior.

Tensions and silences, as though expressing a suppressed and unnamed fear of retribution, also are present and absent in the texts of the Copernicans. Perhaps, they seem to say and not say, God will be vengeful at having been displaced. And perhaps indeed the Copernicans have given offense. Rheticus writes the *Narratio Prima,* a genesis tale in its very name, the *logos* of a new science. Copernicus no longer is in the service of God but makes God to serve man. God made the world *for us* and for our use (*mundus propter nos*), he declared. "In place of a universe whose beauty and rationality escape us, and which therefore calls us to humility, Copernicus substitutes a cosmos for which man is the final purpose and whose plan he can reconstruct" (Hallyn 1990:55).

Copernicus casts his work in the tradition of astronomy, but he is silent about his radical stretching of that genre into what became a new discipline. Astronomy for centuries had restricted itself to predicting celestial phenomena with no effort or pretension to explain their mechanisms. This modesty of purpose, which continued decades after the appearance of *De Revolutionibus,* was expressed in the status of astronomy in the universities of the day as "art" to be learned prior to and only as a preparation for philosophy, including natural philosophy and physics. Thus Copernicus was simultaneously forcing philosophy to justify itself in terms of empirical calculations and pushing astronomy in the direction of philosophy and theology.

This move, although unspoken in the text, was radical ontologically, epistemologically, and politically, because, since Aristotle, a strict distinction was made between what could be known of the earth (physics), what could only be hypothesized about the inassessable sphere of the heavens (astronomy), and what could be known absolutely by and about God (theology). By fusing these deeply separated spheres of knowledge and reality into what eventually became theoretical astronomy, Copernicus asserts the powers of man to know the entire homogeneous world—a cognitive access that, according to the Scholastic and especially Nominalist theologians, was uniquely the preserve of the Almighty (Blumenberg 1987:part 2, ch. 3).

Some seventy years later, Galileo is much more explicit in this regard. He subordinates theology to astronomy on questions regarding nature, he insists that theologians must disprove his assertions before criticizing them, he presumes that his status as a lay astronomer authorizes him to lecture theologians on Scripture and its proper interpretations, and in his *Consideration* he puts into the mouth of a simpleton the advice given to him by Cardinal Barbarini, who was to become Pope Urban VIII (Galileo [1615] in Finocchiaro 1989:chs. 2, 3; see Moss 1983, 1986).[5] Heliocentrism had replaced theocentricism with homocentrism.

Moreover, the new knowledge that announces the scientific method and system is not told through scientific method and system. It exists in an aporia, a u-topia, a no-place space between a received literature and a science whose dispensation has yet to be fully granted. Thus Kepler writes an explicit proto-science *fiction*, putting a man on the moon so as to better imagine the earth in a different perspective, or *in a perspective* rather than as simply being there. This is Kepler's *Somnium seu Astronomia Lunari* ("Dream or Astronomy of the Moon"), which began to circulate in 1611. And in other writings Kepler also closely reports his own conversion to a heliocentric and mechanistic perspective.

In the same spirit, Galileo writes a dialogue occurring over a four-day period with four principal voices. Although the author insists in his title that he is merely discussing the relative merits of the "two chief World Systems, proposing indeterminately the Philosophic and Natural reasons for one as well as for the other side," the Copernican side is presented more forcefully. Summing up the exchanges of the first day of Galileo's *Dialogue,* Sagredo says that heliocentrism was found to be "more probable and reasonable . . . [to have] more verisimilitude than the other." Thus the indeterminate discussion is really about determinate decision, as expressed even in the Copernican Salviati's insistence that this is not his intention: "I am not deciding upon any other controversial proposition . . . [but will] leave the decision to the judgment of others" (*Dialogue* 157). Again at the end of the fourth day, after having argued persuasively for heliocentrism, Salviati says: "I do not claim and have not claimed from others that assent which I myself do not give to this invitation, which may very easily turn out to be a most foolish hallucination and a majestic paradox" (*Dialogue* 463). This "rhetoric of indecision" (Finocchiaro 1980:12) seems to have been sincere, not cynical. Far from being the hero founder of modern science, as later claimants construed him, Galileo, seen in his own time and context, was more a rebellious adolescent, between the childhood of faith and the manhood of reason, struggling against, because still beholden to, the

Father. Named later as the father of modern science, he also was, even more perhaps, the rebellious son of the Church.

TOWARD A CONCLUSION

Certain parallel features are evident in the three examples that we have considered—classical ethnographies, Descartes' *Discourse,* and Rheticus' *Narratio Prima.* Together these features might help define narratives of conversion as a literary or scientific genre. One such feature is the narrative construction of the self; in each of our cases this self converts from a textually "lower" to a textually "higher" level of authority. In the classical ethnographies, the narrator begins as a naive outsider and ends as a knowledgeable insider. In the *Discourse,* Descartes begins as a traveler filled with conflicting conventional opinions and ends as an architect whose method can build the edifice of certain truth. For the Copernicans, the astronomer begins as a follower and finishes as a leader; he starts at the feet of Ptolemy and arrives at the throne of Heaven.

The texts also share an implicit ontological development, not only from appearance to reality, or from doubt to certitude, but also from the material to the spiritual. This is an ancient pattern, seen in the movement in Plato's *Republic* from the shadows on the wall of the cave to material things in the world to the ineffable forms themselves; and again in the movement in Augustine's book, and of Augustine himself, from the "city of man" to *The City of God.*

This conversion from material to spiritual, or the transformation of the material *into* the spiritual, is seen in the progression of topics in ethnographic texts from early chapters on physical ecology and material culture, to economic organization, social structure, and kinship, to religion, ritual, values, and beliefs (Tyler 1985:87). Such an ordering of themes is typical of ethnographic studies and recapitulates the central topic of anthropology itself: the evolution of humanity from nature to culture.

A similar movement is seen in Descartes' text—a movement from variegated experience to indubitable truth. This truth was "a pure light, constant, clean, certain, effortless, and always present," "an illustration of the spirit . . . in the light of God . . . by a direct impression of divine clarity upon our understanding" (Descartes 1898 5:136, 137; my translation). The *Discourse* of 1637 was planned in 1636 to be "The Project of a universal science that could *elevate* our nature to its *highest* degree of perfection" (in Edelman 1974:120; my italics and translation). How much closer to God can one get?

Copernicus' work is full of astronomical observations and calculations, and these are often presented as part of his hypotheses and speculations. But soon we understand that our movement toward heliocentricism is also a movement toward God. The divine maker of everything could not create anything un-beautiful, and "What is indeed more beautiful than heaven, which of course contains all things of beauty?" (Copernicus 1978:4). Thus astronomy is "a divine rather than human" science, for "it is highly unlikely that anyone lacking the requisite knowledge of the sun, moon, and other heavenly bodies can become and be called godlike" (Copernicus 1978:7).

Like narratives in general, all these accounts have beginnings, middles, and ends. As all three are stories that aspire to scientific truth, the middle parts of each are filled with objectified and objectifying discussions that constitute the "contents" of the account that can be manipulated and understood through abstract categories and concepts. The ethnographers, for example, shift to the impersonal pronoun, use flat and highly typified characterizations, and de-scribe what natives do rather than what the ethnographer saw someone doing. Similarly, the middle section of Descartes' *Discourse* is made up of discussions of how he applied his method to specific problems. He thereby converts the problem of the existence of God or of the nature of human physiology into instances of his more general approach. In the middle of *Narratio Prima*, Rheticus provides a detailed summary of Copernicus' theories. In each case, the middle is not a journey in itself so much as a description of the promised land. That is, these middles describe what one can see after one has entered the alien tribe or adopted the alien method or perspective. And, in dwelling in these *contents* of the new world or vision, the strangeness of that world as a whole is lessened or forgotten.

The three accounts also make strategic use of similarities and contrasts or, stated topographically, of nearness and distance. In classical ethnographies the narrator begins at a location close to the reader and far from the natives. By the end of the text, however, the narrator is far removed from the earlier position and so, one hopes, is the reader. Similarly, Descartes stresses his conformity, his lack of wit or personal ambition, and this convinces the reader that the method or data have been strong enough to overcome the author's (and the reader's) initial resistance. Rheticus characterizes Copernicus in the same way, saying, for example, that he published his work only after the Bishop of Kulm pushed him to do so. Moreover, in Copernicus' text, the power of his *invention* depends on his contrastive *renovation* of Ptolemy.

Another feature of conversion narratives is their epistemological obsessiveness, a constant self-reflection on their own status and authority. Because the author wishes to describe a new kind of truth or reality, he or she not only must use old language to communicate intelligibly with the reader but also must stretch and bend this language to properly shape the new world to be described. Conversion is thus akin to translation as described by Willard Quine (1960:58): "Wanton translation can make natives sound as queer as one pleases. Better translation imposes our logic upon them." Thus the narrator who aspires to convey or create new forms must articulate them according to two contrasting codes of meaning—the old code of his readers, and the new code of the new readers that his old readers will become as they enter the new code that is created by their entering into it. This conversion is accomplished through stretched or double-layered language.

These rational narrative conversions give cause for epistemological worrying (Marcus and Cushman 1982:47). Such worrying can itself become a device of persuasion if it is made public within the text. It is a way to acknowledge the readers' initial skepticism, to join in it, and then to shift it toward a skepticism about the journey rather than the place of arrival. In such a shift, the question becomes "Am I able to convey to you (or, for the reader, will I be able to understand) this new culture, philosophy, or science?" rather than "Does such a new culture, philosophy, or science really exist?" Moreover, the narrator's authority is strengthened by the admission that what follows really is quite strange (ethnographers), that perhaps it is not for popular consumption at all (Descartes), or that at first the narrator had trouble believing it himself (Copernicus). Such modesty inspires credence. Further, self-reflexiveness heightens the contrast between the old and the new and therefore strengthens the value and power of the conversion that is to be achieved, thereby encouraging the reader to proceed (Marcus and Cushman 1982:47). By meditating on his own pre-understandings and assumptions, the author encourages readers to suspend their preconceptions and to be open to descriptions or analyses whose strangeness would otherwise seem abhorrent. Of course, the language used at the beginning of the text comes to have a very different meaning by the end. In the process of making the strange familiar, the reader must be estranged from the familiarity of the language through which this is initially done.

But epistemological worrying goes deeper than this; it seems to express an anxiety of the unstated, a fear of the abyss, perhaps, even, an incipient oedipal terror, as though the Father of tradition, however placated, might strike back as the intrepid thinker conquers the forbidden intellectual territory. Each of our texts claims scientific realism as the true voice of the world, yet each is written in a traditional literary form, before the scientific article or monograph had been invented for that discipline. Perhaps textual anxiety *is* modernity, at least insofar as epistemological worrying has become the central preoccupation of philosophers since Descartes (de Certeau 1980:25). Does this reflect an unease with the arrogance of the new objectivity, a suspicion that all is not really as represented in the kingdom of science, a fear of being pulled down Alice's hole into the world of prescientific wonder? Or does anxiety simply come with the liminal no-place between the fading old paradigm and the new one not yet formed, as when you step off a cliff in a dream without knowing whether you will fall or fly?

In all the narratives of conversion that we have considered, contradictions exist between the "scientific" claims and the "literary" modes of presentation, and also between the "private" prose and its "public" presentation: the field notes of the ethnographer and the published report; Descartes' lost dream book *Olympia* and his well-known *Discourse;* the rebellious notes Galileo wrote in the margin of his own copy of the *Dialogue* and the ambivalent, assertive humility of the *Dialogue* itself. In each of these texts, as scientific realism is being invented, these contradictions, this speech against itself, are kept before the reader. The force of these texts comes in large part from the maintenance of this tension between what is made up, a majestic hallucination, and what is really out there, an empirical reality codable as scientific truth (Seltzer 1984; Clough 1992). The maintenance of this undecidability, this keeping the problem problematic, is the condition of the narrative of conversion itself. For this is not only a *con*version from one world *to* another; it is also a *trans*version of fiction into truth.

If narratives like these are successful in converting their readers, a new form of representation is likely to take over, and the invented will become entrenched as the discovered. Indeed, it might be more precise to speak of a logic of invention rather than a logic of discovery, because discovery implies a world already existing and needing only to be uncovered. But this makes sense only *after* the process of invention has been successful. Once the new viewpoint has become regnant, the old language is seen as a sheet that covered the furniture of the world—a world that can be seen correctly, or seen at all, only when the sheet is lifted and the reality or truth is dis-covered. In a symbolic realist perspective, however, the sheets and the furniture, the words and the things, create each other. Indeed, rather than saying that words stand for things, it might be more correct, in this perspective, to speak of things standing for words. Things are words that get objectified through interactions; they are concretized micro-theories, or "entifications," to use Quine's term (1960; see Brown 1987:83–87).

In the conversion narratives that presaged a new paradigm, this process of entification is going on within the texts. This is done through self-reflexive stories that report on the discovery of methods or reflection even as they describe the results yielded by such research. In *Argonauts of the Western Pacific*, for example, Malinowski (1961:3–4) remarks, "In Ethnography, the distance is often enormous between the brute material of information—as it is presented to the student in his own observations, in native statements, in the kaleidoscope of tribal life—and the final authoritative presentation of the results." Such reflection on the narrator's construction of his or her own story is also built into Margaret Mead's work on Samoa, Raymond Firth's *We the Tikopia* (1957), and many others. Once the new ethnographic (or philosophic or astronomical) form has become a convention, however, and its early exemplars have become "classical," subsequent ethnographies do not need to include such epistemological worrying (that is, the extensive accounts of personal work in the field), because now these can be expressed metonymically, with a simple statement of method. For writers and readers already converted to the new ethnographic genre, a mere phrase is sufficient, such as that which opens Godfrey Leinhardt's *Divinity and Experience* (1961:vii): "This book is based upon two years' work among the Dinka, spread over the period 1947–1950."

Something similar occurred in the narratives that helped convert Westerners to modern science, and thereby to distinguish themselves and their science as "modern" and as "Western." After about one century, Descartes' heuristic and tentative "I will take the world *as* a machine" became Newton's literalistic "The world *is* a machine." The need for conversion to the Cartesian worldview eventually vanished in the West. Earlier, scientists from Brahe to Newton had been inspired by the conversion narratives and had sought to complete the initial vision by creating a (theory of the) universe that was adequate, structurally and dynamically, to the unfulfilled realism of Copernicus and Descartes. As this became achieved, the literalistic, anti-narrativist prose of modern science became the norm of philosophic and scientific writing.

Perhaps this is true more generally. As new perspectives become sedimented in discourse, their symbolic, constructed character fades from awareness, and they become more literal and objective. The new stretched genre becomes a thickened old one. A relativistic epistemological stance gives way to a more realist posture. Rhetorics of conversion, personal testimony, and individual commitment are replaced by their institutional surrogates, the rhetorics of authority and indoctrination (Gross 1989:109). Stretching toward new para-digms or genres, and thickly encoding those already created, are both needed. Without authority and indoctrination we would have no shared language and no intelligible world. Without narratives of conversion we would not be able to invent anything new.

Chapter 5 Narrative and
Truth in Scientific Practice

In the Book of Nature, as in a well contriv'd Romance, the parts have such
a connection and relation to one another, and the things we would
discover are so darkly or incompleatly knowable by those that precede
them, that the mind is never satisfied till it comes to the end of the Book;
till when all that is discover'd in the progress, is unable to keep the mind
from being molested with Impatience to find that yet conceal'd, which
will not be known till one does at least make a further progress.
Robert Boyle (1674:97)

An adequate paradigm for civic communication must join efficiency
in systems with significance in the lifeworld. That is, it must enable us
to govern our polities in a rational manner to ensure collective survival, while providing us meaning and dignity in our existential experience of ourselves. Hence, such a discourse must be adequate not only
on the level of science and technique but also on the level of ethics and
politics. I believe that a reasoned narrative discourse, a truthful kind of
storytelling, offers such a mode of civic communication. To develop
this contention I argue here for two subsidiary assertions: that the

logic of science can be subsumed under narrative discourse and that narration can be a mode of truth.[1]

Even if we were to accept that science is a form of truth telling and that human experiences are shaped through narrative form, we still would have to ask how representations or realities created through narrative discourse might properly elicit our reasoned credence. In the realist tradition since Plato, language was thought to play an insignificant or even harmful role in the discovery or constitution of truth. Plato denied that storytelling could have a central role in the uncovering of truth, and so he banished poets from his ideal kingdom. Early positivists envisioned a material reality that language could truly represent only when it served as a "pointer reader" to the empirical thing that it indicated, like a litmus that indicates acid or base. For positivists, properly used language was a mirror, and anything truthful that appeared in it was reflected from a reality external to language itself (Rorty 1979). Even some hermeneuticists posit brute meanings or intentions instead of the positivists' brute facts, and then they suppose that true statements are ones that correspond to these hermeneutic foundations.

Until recently, however, philosophers of science had done little to reveal how scientific discoveries are accomplished. Instead, they tended to separate the "context of discovery" from the "context of justification" in order to dismiss the first and defend the second. In this view, discoveries come from chance or intuition; what counts as science, however, is their logic and validity—not their discovery but their justification. Thus the title of Karl Popper's book, *The Logic of Scientific Discovery*, is unintentionally ironic. In its opening pages Popper banished discovery from the kingdom of philosophy to the netherworld of "empirical psychology"; he then devoted his entire work to the logic of verification (1959:31).

Norwood Hanson, in *Patterns of Discovery* (1958a) and later articles (1958b, 1967), created some space within philosophy for the logic of discovery. Hanson conceived of discovery in terms of certain types of hypotheses that eventually lead to what subsequently is recognized as a breakthrough or discovery in science. Yet he still conceived of discovery as something that occurs within the research setting, that is, as something interior to science itself.

Things began to change in the history, sociology, and rhetoric of scientific inquiry with the acceptance of the work of Thomas Kuhn and others, who conceived of science as a historically contingent, communal practice. This view opened up space for challenges to the positivist philosophy of science. One such challenge was launched by sociological ethnographers who showed how the objects and explanations of science are constructed through discourse in local settings (Knorr-Cetina and Mulkay 1983; Latour and Woolgar 1986; Pickering 1992). They found that facts—from the Latin *facta,* as in factory, manufacture, or artifact—are made through rhetorical practices. This finding undermined scientists' absolutist claims to truth by showing scientific findings to be locally contextualized, linguistic constructions.

Another challenge to positivist philosophy of science focuses on scientists as a community that constitutes itself through narrative (Brown 1990; Rouse 1987). That is, the validity, significance, or utility of any finding is constituted as such in terms of the shared and contested narratives that define the scientific school, paradigm, or discipline. A third group of post-Kuhnian researchers examines paradigm shifts and asserts that, because these take place *between* different sets of scientific assumptions, a preference of one paradigm over another must be due to extra-scientific forms of persuasion (Feyerabend 1978).

In these more sociological and rhetorical views, an understanding of discovery is an understanding not merely of a fact or idea discovered but also of the processes of documentation, presentation, and reception that create such facts and ideas as symbolic public realities. Sociologists of science, for example, have noted the absence of the idea of discovery in actual research settings. The scientists who inhabit laboratories every day would find it bizarre to hear their quotidian work described as the "context of discovery." Scientists do comment on their success or failure in "getting things to work" or "making it come out right," but they do not construe such activities, even when successful, as "discovery." Instead, discovery seems to hinge on the production of a document and the engagement of a public that lends it credence. Discovery is not merely an uncovering of what already exists but a social symbolic construction that persuasively defines some research practice as having yielded a finding that is to be taken as original and significant.

There are, of course, occasional moments of "Eureka!" in science, but these seem always to be the self-awareness of an original *conceptualization,* or of a significant experimental *confirmation,* which can be recognized as such only within the context of ongoing discourse and definition within a community of inquirers as to what might constitute original theoretical conceptualizations and what could be their empirical confirmations. In 1900, for example, Max Planck said to his son Erwin during a walk in the Grünewald of Berlin, "Today I have made a discovery as important as that of Newton" (Born 1966:473). But Planck never spoke that way publicly. Instead, he spent the next dozen years persuading his colleagues that what he "imagined" (*wir denken uns*) should be accepted at least provisionally as worthy of further elaboration. Planck spoke not of discovery but of what he "presumed," "considered," or "envisaged," "on a trial basis" concerning "certain arbitrary energies" (*versuchweise bestimmte willkurliche Energien*), and he left it to "the future" to "teach whether such an influence will ever be directly provable." How much further from "Eureka" could he get? Planck may have been convinced during his walk in 1900, but he must also have understood that what he then personally took as a discovery would not be so defined by other scientists without a great deal of persuasive public argumentation.

Eventually Planck's work came to be called "the first valid and authentic derivation of the relationship between mass and energy" (Ives, in Goldberg 1976:140). But this hardly settled the matter, and hardly settles it today. Instead, the narration of the "discovery"—its narrative constitution as a discovery during the course of research programs in progress—continues to occur in the historical accounts of the constitution of quantum mechanics as a discovery during the course of research programs in progress close to a century later. Thus Thomas Kuhn cites evidence of Planck's pattern of publications in order to move the "revolution" from 1900 to 1906 and to place it not in Planck's work but in Albert Einstein's interpretation and elaboration of it. In Kuhn's (1987) account of Einstein's contribution, an "important deduction" is investigated by "celebrated astronomers" who, "undaunted" by the requirement of "great accuracy," produce "thoroughly satisfactory" results. But such an epic narrative construction must omit certain candidate elements in the interest of cogency and concinnity. In this instance, the "thoroughly satisfactory" results were so unsatisfactory "that there were, between 1919 and 1952, *twelve additional attempts* to measure the bending of stellar light in the solar field, attempts that consistently failed to resolve the equivocation inherent in the original results. This repeated failure did not seriously impede the acceptance of general relativity. Nor should it" (Gross 1992:22).

In advocating Einstein's primacy, Kuhn (1987:170) writes of a passage in Einstein's 1906 paper "On the Theory of the Emission and Absorption of Light": "That passage is the first public statement that Planck's derivation demands a restriction on the classical continuum of resonator states. In a sense, it announces the birth of the quantum theory." Kuhn's metaphor of discovery as "birth" is significant because it allows him to favor Einstein's singular achievement over Planck's mere "conception." Moreover, in addition to his arguments from the historical events that he is emplotting, Kuhn provides a final argument not from the events but from the plot into which he is allocating them. "Told in this way," he says (1987:354), "the story makes better historical sense than the long-standard version." Kuhn argues that "the new narrative is more nearly continuous than its predecessor" and that his "reinterpretation eliminates a number of the apparent textual anomalies and inconsistencies" that appear in other versions. "Thus Kuhn's own agenda is one that accords well with classical physics—the criteria for validity in experiments and results include consistency and continuity, and elimination of anomalies and inconsistencies. It is the agenda with which he associates Planck up to a later date than that accepted by other historians. Implicit in Kuhn's historical narrative is a denial of the possibility of history as a discontinuous and disorderly, even chaotic, narrative" (Greenberg 1990:142–43). Thus both Planck and, later, Kuhn constitute narratively what they respectively hope will be taken as a scientific discovery. Planck tells his research as a discovery and his discovery as researched. More explicitly, Kuhn uses the same techniques of emplotment and eventment to achieve a different outcome.

The reflexive, narrative procedures that I identify here differ from those advanced by conventional philosophy (or even Kuhnian history) of science. These earlier approaches take as their central theme the logical "steps" that led up to the discovery. Instead, I foreground the narrative processes of representation and recognition that made a "discovery" out of the happenings that Kuhn and others describe. Moreover, I assume that these processes may be discontinuous and disorderly, even chaotic, and that retrospective re-narrations of them may also be so and that such (re)narrations are convertible and recursive, both iterative and reversible. Put slightly differently, philosophers and historians of science have assumed "that once a thing is discovered or made evident, then it is seen retrospectively to have been all along present, though covered" (Brannigan 1976:5–6). This view underplays the reflexivity of the identification of discoveries insofar as the retrospective identification of occurrences as "discoveries" is also an enactment of the very thing under study. By contrast, from a rhetorical and sociological viewpoint, the context of discovery *is* the practices of representation in the speech, texts, and contexts of presentation.

This is the view that predominates in much current philosophy of science. Popper's earlier dichotomy of contexts of discovery and of justification is put in the background or simply abandoned, and the focus is now on the character of scientific rationality as a process of invention and legitimation, and on whether such a process can still be called scientific rationality. Said another way, the process that was debunked by ethnographers of science is not dismissed but investigated more thoroughly as the place where rationality itself is constructed discursively (Newton-Smith 1989; Gralison 1987; Franklin 1986; Kuhn 1977). Similarly, such thinkers have criticized Feyerabend's opposition of the sociality and the rationality of science as a category error because there is no reason or evidence for believing that science is not both social *and* rational. The task then becomes that of articulating the sociality of rationality and the rationality of sociality. One way to do this is through the metaphor of science as narration.[2]

In sum, orthodox accounts describe scientists as seeking to choose from among plausible accounts of nature those that are true. This search is said to be done through logic and testing, a process of matching theory or mathematics to observable facts or, more broadly, of making language fit the world. The world is seen as obdurate, already just there, and it is language, theory, or numbers that need to be adjusted accordingly. Other thinkers argue that the world is always and only contained within language and that no special methods or realities could be properly demarcated as scientific. Both of these accounts are not so much wrong as limited: neither tells us how this fitting of word and world is done.

Instead, I argue in this chapter that scientific discourse is a kind of storytelling that articulates facts, theories, research programs or disciplines, and science in general, not only as these are already there but also as they *must* be there. That is, the just-thereness of data, of evidence, or of facts is constructed through narrato-logical must-be-thereness. Facts, theories, programs, and science generally, are not discrete ideas or entities that must be fitted together. Instead, they are co-generated through narration.

ON THE REFLEXIVITY AND PERVASIVENESS OF NARRATION

We may say that a narrative is an accounting of events or actions temporally that explains them causally or motivationally. Thus, "the king died, the queen died, the prince died, the cousin ruled alone" is not a narrative so much as a list of happenings. "The king died, then the queen died, then the prince died, then the cousin ruled alone" is still not a narrative because, although it establishes temporality, it does not explain the actions in necessary relation to each other. Perhaps it would qualify as a chronicle. By contrast: "The king died of natural causes, then the queen died of grief, then the prince was murdered by his cousin, who then ruled alone." This is a narrative because it temporalizes and explains the actions and events. In narrative terms, the actions and events are thereby "emplotted."

But what exactly does this emplotment involve? The way I told it, actions or events occurred, they occurred in a time sequence, and they were linked causally. This is how we usually think about life, nature, and narratives. But what if we were to reverse the flow: actions and events were linked causally, they occurred in a time sequence, and they occurred. On the surface this seems a bizarre way to order these clauses, but this version also makes sense and, indeed, has an implicit logic at least as strong as the first version. Let's make that logic explicit: actions or events are linked causally (through rules of motives or through laws of nature); therefore, they must have occurred in a temporal series; therefore, they must have occurred.

Notice that both these versions are narratives. That is, they can start with temporalized events or actions and then explain them, or they can start with explanations or meanings and then apply these to events that are thereby temporalized. From this we can infer that narratives are convertible. Further, each version ended almost where it started. That is, these versions both start and end with actions or events. But whereas the first version starts by positing actions or events, the second version ends by demonstrating them to have occurred. This suggests that narratives are not only convertible but also circular. They begin by positing what in the end they prove.

Notice, finally, that I have presented the preceding discussion in a narrative form. I said that there are "events or actions," in a "temporal series," with an "explanation" of them, in that order. But not quite. Why this order (version one and then version two) and not the reverse? Why did I start with the "data" and then get to the "theory" later, when, at the end, I asserted that this order is convertible with equal logic? I did it that way because I presume that the reader is more comfortable in a "realist" rather than an "idealist" ontology—that he or she gives priority to experience over interpretations, to facts over theories. I thought that the story would have been less plausible had its order of presentation been reversed. I even used the word "bizarre" at the turning point of the story, to validate the reader's skepticism and hence allow an easier entry into the less familiar, inverted way of viewing things. This suggests something else about narratives: narratives intend an audience. They are social communications or, in Bourdieu's term, a mode of "communicative interaction" that takes the audience's possible reception into account, that is, that incorporates it into the construction of the account. Notice, too, that I have just invoked an ally (Bourdieu), who, you are expected to presume, would approve of what I am saying. This suggests something else about narration. It is "intertextual." That is, narratives not only explain and tell actions or events to intended audiences but also refer to other narratives. Indeed, narratives may refer as much to other narratives as they refer to audiences or to actions and events. Oops, I became a realist. It would be improper, wouldn't it, to say that narratives "refer" to events, as though the events were exterior to the narrative, if my point is that the "reference" can go from explanation to events or from events to explanation? In the narrative view, actions or events come to exist as such through emplotment (accountings of their temporality, cause, and meaning), and plots or theories exist only in their eventment (their instantiation in particular actions or events).

Have I described the way we understand experience, or even *have* experience? Some, like G. W. F. Hegel (1977) or Wilhelm Dilthey (1957) or Walter Fisher (1987) might say so. But most would insist that narrative is at best one way of knowing among others, and that it has little to do with the facts of science and mostly to do with the fictions of literature. The first type of thinker gives primacy to language, the second to experience. The first says that experience is mediated by, or realizable in, or constructed through, discourse. The second gives primacy to experience as independent of language, but to which, when used correctly, language corresponds or refers. Sometimes these opposing positions occur within the same thinker, as with Ludwig Wittgenstein of the *Tractatus* and Ludwig Wittgenstein of the *Investigations.*

Whether literary or scientific, however, whether indispensable or unnecessary, narrating seems difficult to avoid. This is suggested by experiments done by such researchers as A. E. Michotte (1963), F. Heider and E. Simmel (1944), and Harold Garfinkel (1967). In each case, the experimenters constructed a device that generated a random series of events and then asked their subjects what they experienced. And in each case, the subjects generally constructed a narrative that "explained" or "gave meaning to" the randomly generated events. Subjects of Michotte's experiments, who were shown two or more rectangles in motion, made comments like this: "'It is as if A's approach frightened B and B ran away.' 'It is as if A, in touching B, induced an electric current which set B going.' 'The arrival of A by the side of B acts as a sort of signal to B . . . ' 'It is as if A touched off a mechanism inside B and thus set it going' and so on. Also this experiment often produces a comical effect and makes the observers laugh" (quoted in Sarbin 1986:12).

Similarly, in an experiment by Heider and Simmel, observers reported the physical movements of the nonhuman objects as if intended by humans. Three colored geometrical figures, which subjects saw moving at various speeds and directions on a film, became "characters" in a narrative drama with plots, subplots, characters, and action.[3]

Notice that I have used "realist" experimental evidence to support the "idealist" narrativist point—a point that, if correct, would undermine the very evidence that supports it. Or, conversely, if the above evidence is valid, the conclusion that it supports must be untrue. Perhaps this paradox is only apparent, and the problem here is that the samples used by the respective experimenters were of lay people, not scientists who, as scientists, observe objectively and speak with care and rigor. Could scientists, as scientists, regularly make the same mistakes, if mistakes indeed they are, and narratize their observations? Let's take as a datum a fairly typical snippet of writing of one exemplar scientist, Sir Issac Newton. In the thirty-first query of the *Opticks,* Newton asks: "And when *Aqua fortis,* or Spirit of Vitriol poured upon Filings of Iron dissolves the Filings with a great Heat and Ebullition, is not this Heat and Ebullition effected by a violent Motion of the Parts, and does not that Motion argue that the acid Parts of the Liquor rush towards the Parts of the Metal with violence, and run forcibly into its Pores till they get between its outmost Particles, and the main Mass of Metal, and surrounding those Particles loosen them from the main Mass, and set them at liberty to float off into the Water?" (Newton 1952:377). As Robert Markley (1990) noted, "This description of a chemical process is dominated by political metaphors of violence and liberty as though the acid and filings were enacting a microdrama of Newton's Whiggish political convictions. The language of observation, in this regard, becomes objective and dispassionate only if the reader accepts as natural the aesthetic and ideological presuppositions which anthropomorphize and politicize the realm of chemical processes."

It could be argued that Newton's Restoration style of writing imposes repressed or displaced political conflicts onto essentialized forces of nature (see Vickers 1985; Arakelian 1979; Markley 1990) and that contemporary scientists have outgrown such biases as their disciplines have matured. Such an argument, however, also implies a narrative of passage of science from a subjective youth to an objective maturity. Moreover, as we have seen in our discussion of the writings of Max Planck and Thomas Kuhn, even contemporary physicists seem to be unable to avoid narrating that which they wish to describe objectively. For both absolute realists and relativists this is a flaw, either to be overcome in the advancement of science or to be used in its devaluation. But from the narratological perspective, such practices are the ones through which scientific facts, theories, and programs are created.

THE NARRATION OF SCIENTIFIC FIELDS AS A MODE OF TRUTH

Contemporary discussions of narrative can be understood in the context of debates between scientism and historicism of the past century. Law-like explanations of general facts (the positivist or scientistic tradition) were opposed to story-like interpretations of particular meanings (the romantic or historicist tradition). Correspondingly, language was seen to have a logical and descriptive function appropriate to science, and an expressive or emotive one necessary for history, storytelling, or art.

These divisions were assumed by detractors and defenders of narrative alike. Both positivists and romantics strictly distinguished science from history, and so they respectively defined each as what the other was not. Narrative was taken to concern history or the human studies but not science or rational inquiry as a whole. Even today many anti-positivist thinkers, including Jürgen Habermas and Hans-Georg Gadamer, hold this outdated conception of positivism and of the romantic tradition. Yet few philosophers still adhere to the traditional positivism that Habermas attacks. Similarly, Gadamer builds his notion of interpretive procedures against the conception of natural science as based on inductive methods and the claims of absolute objectivity. But interesting analogies for Gadamer's distrust of method can be found, for example, in the mathematical theory of Bertrand Russell and Kurt Gödel and in the semantics of Alfred Tarski (Weinsheimer 1985).

The same opposition and interdependency can be seen in the views of the positivist Karl Popper and the historicist Hayden White. Both assume that facts or meanings are available for explanation or interpretation independently of the theories or forms into which they are cast. For example, Karl Popper's (1977) conception of independent evidence presumes a fact-world autonomous of the ways we apprehend it, but so does Hayden White's (1973) idea that a historical record is accessible apart from the various ways that we emplot it.

Given such shared assumptions, students of narrative located stories within texts and used hermeneutics as a kind of equivalent to theory. Correspondingly, the narrative properties of scientific discourse were forgotten, and stories were viewed as completed writings, not as ongoing practices of making sense of a contested past and a projected future (Rouse 1988:1–3). In this view, narrative was seen as a form imposed on unformed contents, rather than as a process that formed and essentialized these very contents by emplotting them.

Drawing amply on the work of John Rouse, I want to move beyond these assumptions and argue that all rational inquiry has a narrative structure, not just the humane disciplines such as literature or history. To do this, I must make several subsidiary points. First, I need to argue further that the most significant unit of analysis for the natural sciences is the ongoing, open-ended discourse of scientific communities, not a specific and completed scientific theory. I also need to remind the reader not only that scientific inquiry is a communal, social, and historical *activity* but also that this activity is central to the construction of what is to be taken as valid scientific truth.

Many critics of positivism have argued that science should be reconceptualized as something that scientists *do,* rather than as the body of representations that result from this activity. In this view, the distinction between creation and validation—or what positivists have called the context of discovery and the context of truth—is logically arbitrary and, for our purposes, misleading. Usually, however, ethnographers and historians who have studied the practices of scientists have aimed at debunking the claim that what scientists create is truth. This debunking project shares many assumptions with the positivism it attacks. Chief among these assumptions is that the warrant for truth claims must be universal laws (or at least general rules) of logic and method that are independent of scientific practices and results. Having shown that these cannot be securely established, such critics then conclude, gratuitously, that anything goes.

In contrast to both defenders and debunkers of scientific rationality, it is arguable that the epistemological warrant for scientific findings is contained in the rhetorical practices of scientists. That is, the truthfulness of scientific representations emerges from the discursive context of discovery that positivist philosophers reject and that anti-positivists use to debunk positive science. But what precisely is this discursive activity? What is its nature or form?

The beginnings of an answer to this question might be gained from a phenomenological analysis of "action" itself. All action is intentional. That is, it can be understood as action—and not mere behavior or motion—only in terms of "because of" or "in order to" motives or intentions. This intentionality also means that action has a social and temporal structure. Because action is oriented in terms of pre-understandings of the actions and reactions of others, and because it is intelligible as action only in terms of reasons, goals, or purposes, it can take place only in an ongoing social community—that is, a group with the same vocabularies of motive, rules of intelligibility, and contestable history.[4] In this sense, action presupposes a social teleology. As such, action takes a narrative form.

This is no less true of scientific forms than of other forms of human action. The rationality of scientific action is manifest in this temporal structure of action itself. Such action is always open and ongoing, always understood in the future-perfect tense. "It is being enacted toward the fulfillment of a projected retrospection, but one that is constantly open to revision, as befits a story not yet completed" (Rouse 1988). Like other social texts, the communal narratives of scientists are unfinished, contestable, and revisable projects. Indeed, it would be more accurate to speak of scientific activity as fields of competing narratives, rival versions of common traditions that alternately give priority to one or another research program or line of theoretical development. Each scientist strives to occupy the position of the storyteller with respect to the common narrative in her area of work, and thereby to heighten the significance of her own research (Carr 1986:61). Indeed, occupying a central role in an unfolding narrative of a scientific field is precisely what "significance" or "usefulness" of research is all about. Insofar as other contemporary practitioners accept one's own version of the narrative, one's own research becomes critical to the next developments of the collective plot. Likewise, insofar as later practitioners develop one's earlier initiatives, they retrospectively define these initiatives as important, even path-breaking. As Porter (1989:2) put it,

> What counts as knowledge is not quite the same as what can be defended with sound arguments and reliable evidence. I mean by this more than that humans are imperfect reasoning machines, or even than the standards by which arguments and evidence are judged are themselves culturally conditioned. My point is rather that ideas and methods are judged by what one can do with them. . . . Scholars and scientists . . . value most highly work that can be used to support their research, or occasionally to suggest new directions for it . . . a paper offering little promise of guiding new research may not even be read. However clever, however reasonable, such work earns the harshest condemnation that researchers can give. It is not even of academic interest.

Most voices that propose alternative lines of narrative development will be silenced in order to defend turf, avoid cacophony, conserve resources, maintain intelligibility, enforce consensus, establish closure, and direct further research into areas that are deemed more fruitful. Or such voices may simply be ignored because no scientific public can use their ideas or data. As Diesing (1992:195) noted, "Such a work exists in an empty space; it neither comes out of a current research tradition nor leads into an enrichment of some tradition. Who now has heard of Scudder Klyce's *Universe?* This was a large, scholarly systematization of existing knowledge, as of the 1930s, but it did not relate to the research interests of any active group of scientists, so no one paid any attention to it. Similarly Ludwik Fleck's 1935 book, *Genesis and Development of a Scientific Fact,* remained unread and unknown until the late 1970s, when the constructivists suddenly developed similar ideas and started citing Fleck as supporting evidence."

Self-promotion by individual scientists or teams plays a role in officializing their version of the proper development of the field, but they cannot determine the outcomes. This is because most of the life of what comes to be known as a scientific innovation lies ahead of it (see Latour 1987:29; Rouse 1988:21). New words, tools, or procedures that we invent do not exist by themselves or merely through the will of their authors. Their truth or falsity, efficiency or waste, fit or ineptness, depend as much on their contexts as on their contents, more on their reception than on their "internal" properties alone. And these contexts of reception are made up of other words, tools, and procedures that have been and will be invented and used by other people—people who are joined in a tradition and thereby share a history of customs, usages, and meanings. It is by incorporation into the narrative of this tradition that a scientific innovation acquires not only significance but even intelligibility.

"Insofar as improvement can be discerned in a sequence of theories, that is usually because they are all taken to be solving roughly the same set of problems. However, as Kuhn and his successors have emphasized, that set is subject to change, often because the problems simply lose their urgency, which makes any overarching sense of progress elusive" (Fuller 1993:218). By similar long-term processes, some theories are eventually reclassified as disconfirmed. Other frameworks are repeatedly deployed, and this generates "problems" that are eventually "solved," even though the original theory may continue to "suffer from bad data, flawed interferences, wrong techniques, and successes that cannot be replicated. No one test disconfirms a theory, except in retrospect" through a narrative logic (Diesing 1992:310).

The negotiation of different narrative versions of a scientific field—and hence of the significance of any item of research within it—is a political process oriented toward the future. On one hand, such negotiation includes explicit competition for resources such as grant monies, academic positions, journal space, and the like. But it is also, and more deeply, a competition over what will become the taken-for-granted definition of the scientific field itself. Thus the tacit function of alternative narratives of scientific fields is not to show their pasts in accurate dimensions but to shape their futures in specific directions.

For the winners, their narrative of the field, and hence their assessment of the significance of (their own) discoveries within it, becomes "what everyone knows" (Macomber 1968:201). Thus scientists share the same aspiration as the poet Baudelaire: "to invent a cliché."

Narratives make up the taken-for-granted background reality, the ongoing domain assumptions, that help define a field and provide for the possibility of agreement and conflict within it. The narrative character of science lies not in a story completed but in a story being told, a story constantly struggled over and adjusted. The narratives of science may be found in specific texts, such as review articles in physics or general essays in paleology (Landau 1984). But the main location of scientific narration is the sociotemporal discourse that constitute the origins, nature, and destiny of scientific fields.

In this narrativist perspective, the focus is on scientific fields or communities of discourse, not on individual scientific findings or on "science" as a whole. Scientists rarely talk about "science," and when they do they talk about it naively, as philosophers *manqué,* and not as working practitioners of their particular specialties. When they talk as practitioners, they discuss specific theories, methods, or findings, how correct these may be, who made them and how well, how they relate to other local works and workers, and how they might be useful for (one's own) further research. In other words, when scientists talk as scientists they do not talk as philosophers of the logical properties of "science" (Rouse 1988). Instead, they talk, as practitioners, of the works and their uses. And in so speaking they make up the ongoing narratives of their fields.

By this reasoning, the justifications-in-use for scientific truths are inherent within scientific discourse and not exterior to it. Seagulls don't need a theory of aerodynamics in order to fly, nor of the chemistry of guano in order to make it. And scientists can be successful as scientists with neither philosophic justifications of the correctness of their logical procedures nor social justifications of the utility of their empirical findings. Instead, warrants for the truth of scientific representations are largely emergent from the narrative discourse of scientific communities.

Such an institutionalist and rhetorical view of science encourages us to seek the narrative character of scientific rationality in the discourse of scientists, and not necessarily in particular theories or in the minds of particular scientists. In this view, science itself is envisioned as an open-ended story told collectively by members of a scientific community.[5] In this community of inquiry, the criteria of proof are public, not private, and the allegiance of scientists is toward the creation of consensus. "The rationale of the scientific attitude is not that there is a set of angelic qualities of mind possessed by individual scientists that guarantees the validity of their every thought, but that scientists learn . . . to further the consensible end" (Ziman 1968:78).

This formulation also suggests a modification of Thomas Kuhn's conception of paradigms, of scientific change, and of disciplinary cohesion. In the rhetorical view, paradigms are not merely shared cognitive orientations but also, and as such, shared communal practices. That is, through such practical activities as decisions on tenure, promotion, publication, or grants and fellowships, paradigms define what permissible discourse is within that disciplinary and disciplined community. Thus paradigms function politically as well as cognitively. In fact, expanding Kuhn's thought in the direction of Foucault's, we could say that the cognitive function of paradigms is political, in that the ability to define responsible inquiry or opinion is a principal source of power.

Kuhn (along with Feyerabend, Hanson, Polanyi, and others) also discusses paradigm crises and shifts as moments of abrupt discontinuity with traditions. In doing this, however, Kuhn fails to account for the continuity of intellectual traditions that is the precondition for the intelligibility of his own historical narrative. That is, the conception of scientific revolutions as complete cognitive ruptures denies to its object the very rationality that it claims for itself. Instead, rather than projecting a radical incommensurability that Kuhn saw in science onto the history of Western conscious as a whole, we can broaden our understanding of rationality to include what scientific rationalists, since Bacon and Descartes, have condemned as irrational—the various *traditions* of rationality themselves (Wallace 1987:xxxi; Blumenberg 1983).

Traditions, of course, are not unitary monoliths that press against the present. Instead, as anthropologists and historians have shown, they may be as diverse as the present, because every group in the present may seek to legitimate its contemporary claims by advancing its particular version of the past. And because scientific paradigms constitute and are constituted in traditions, struggles between paradigms become debates over which tradition is the more legitimate or adequate one. Such discourse of traditions is a form of historical—that is *narrative*—reason (MacIntyre 1980:69). In times of dominance of a particular scientific paradigm, narrative discourse may be overlooked by positive reason. But when paradigms clash, the intelligibility of each to the other, and the victory of the emergent one, depend on narrative form. The shift from one paradigm to another, therefore, is not merely a switch of psychological gestalts or an unreasoned leap in the dark. Instead, it is a leap into the logic of narrative, a construction (or reconstruction) of a cognitive tradition to make sense anew.

Given such a discursive, conflictual notion of the narration of scientific fields and of scientific truths, we need to revise Kuhn's representation of paradigms as tending toward unity. On the contrary, scientific fields tend toward fragmentation. Indeed, members of disciplines need constantly to be disciplined if that discipline is to remain cohesive or, simply, to remain. Thus, the hegemony of any given paradigm is the product not merely of the success of its elaborations but also of the discursive representation of successes *as* its elaborations and of work done in its name *as* its successes. This discursive activity is as much retrospective as prospective, as much retrofitted into a dominant narrative of that discipline as inspired by it.

These ideas are hinted at in Lakatos' (1974) notion of a research program, of which "the appraisal is rather of a *series of theories* than of an isolated *theory*." What is often taken as a single theory is, on closer inspection, "a growing, developing entity, one which cannot be considered as a static structure" (Burian 1977). This growing, developing series of theories must be assessed over time. Hence, falsification of particular discrete and static theories gives way to narrative accounts of the temporal development of research programs.

Orthodox views of theory and method dismiss narrative and tradition, and thus obscure the sources of their own intelligibility. By contrast, a narrativist approach understands theory and method within both their larger and their local social and historical contexts. Customs—that is, traditions within scientific communities—govern canons of evidence and falsification, rules for linking observations with generalizations, and norms concerning the degree and even the definition of exactitude that may be required. And when these customs compete, in order to make each of them intelligible and to resolve their antagonisms, not only must scientists narrate their positions, but the latent narrative structure of the taken-for-granted, customary, traditional practices becomes more visible.

THE NARRATED CHARACTER OF SCIENTIFIC THEORIES AND FACTS

The operation of narrative logic in science can be investigated at various topoi or places of inquiry, including the constitution of data into facts and facts into evidence, the formulation and validation of models, theories, or disciplines, and the narrative projection of an entire worldview. Often analysts confuse these distinct topics of inquiry. For example, one would be stretching the concept of narrative excessively to call a scientific equation, say $E = mc^2$, a narrative. It could be more plausibly argued that articles in scientific journals have an implicit narrative structure. Joseph Gusfield (1976), for example, showed the dramatic narrative structure of medical studies of alcoholism. A narrative structure is even more visible in texts of the human sciences, such as ethnography, history, or psychoanalysis. Here, one might say, whenever there is a case study, there is a narrative. The narrative character of texts in sciences of origins or development—like paleontology, geology, or evolutionary biology—is also fairly evident. In such fields, "to convey the sense and atmosphere of an analytic experience, means that we must tell a coherent story about it . . . without which the material remains inchoate" (Stein 1988:114).

Exactly how such truthful storytelling is done is a question of rhetorical persuasion, largely through narrative form (Spence 1990; Mahoney 1987). In theories of the mind, for example, we project rhetorically the referents that are not empirically observable even with instrumentation. Empirically, we either have behavioral or linguistic "expressions" of mind or we have physiological dimensions of brain. But such points of reference can only be metaphors of the theories of mind they are thought to indicate. In this sense, theories of mind are imaginative constructions of various aspects of our inner experience, not descriptions of empirical things. They evoke ways of feeling and thinking but do not refer directly to findable objects or places in the head. But perhaps this could be said of all science, especially of such sciences as nuclear physics whose objects often are not accessible, even indirectly, to human perception. To put it another way, in sciences of the mind, objects and places are always metaphoric representations for the stuff of mentation, not empirical presentations of it. And all these are given coherence and consequence through such narrative features as plot, choice of detail, point of view, rhetorical trope, and other ingredients of a good story (Spence 1990).

This metaphoric character of indicators, and the projective, imaginative character of theories, are perhaps most obvious in scientific theories that posit an inherently invisible referent, such as theories of the nature of the mind or the origin of the universe. But the metaphoric character of indicators and theories also obtains in more conventional scientific fields, even though these usually are understood in reductive empiricist or nominalist terms. Indeed, what makes such theories seem more objective or empirical is not the greater reality of their objects but the greater realism of their language. Or, more precisely, much of the reality of the objects of a discipline is created by the discipline of the language used to describe them. This linguistic realism is achieved through the very conventionality of these fields—that is, through the sedimented, literal, "thick" quality of their discourse. Their once spritely metaphors have been conventionalized into facts; their once speculative notions have become, for a time, conceptual black boxes (Latour 1987). This does not mean that matter doesn't matter; it does mean that, whatever the matter is, it is shaped into fact, and fact into evidence, through rhetorical action. This conception of truth is not merely logical but also rhetorical in that it subsumes logic as itself a compelling rhetoric in many situations.

Thus consensus is achieved through rhetorical action not only in the case of paradigms but also in the case of experiments, those instruments considered most objective for recording reality. Ethnomethodologists have shown that no algorithm or decision procedure or set of rules for experiments can provide a complete recipe for their application. Indeed, they have shown that these very decision rules constitute in effect a set of problems to be overcome in the course of their implementation. The practice of an experiment, for example, then becomes the problem not of experimentation but of representation—of representing credently that what one is doing is a reliably repeatable experiment. As a participant observer in laser research, for example, Harry Collins (1985:159,55) found that no scientist succeeded in building a laser by using only information found in published or other written sources. The TEA laser is not an exceptionally complicated or innovative piece of machinery, but Collins learned that a successful copy of the first one could not be built except by those with direct or personally mediated experience in the laboratory where it was invented. Hence the locus of knowledge was not the written word but the community of expert practitioners. Moreover, because these copies were not independently achieved, the "tests" and their resultant "findings" logically could not be counted as "independent confirmation." But of course they were so counted. The anomaly exists only in a logico-deductive, Cartesian individualist conception of scientific reasoning. In a rhetorical perspective—the perspective *in use* by scientists—the reproduction of the laser, and hence of its confirmation, was achieved by conversations, collaborations, and conflicts within the relevant scientific community. Scientists do a lot more than they can say, and they say a lot more than they can write (McCloskey 1988). And between the silent practice and the written word are stories. In the tribe of the laboratory or the forest, narratives mediate between the raw and the cooked.

This also means that we cannot test a hypothesis about flatworms or phosphates unless we already know a great deal about them, and especially about their behavior in natural and experimental settings. Thus the ideal of an exact replication to confirm an experimental finding is misleading, for it can be regularly achieved only after a great deal of searching and getting lost, that is, only after we have accumulated a great deal of ad hoc practical knowledge from laboratory bricolage. Indeed, until we have created such plausible knowledge about many factors of context, materials, and instruments, we cannot even specify what an exact replication might be (Diesing 1992:338). "The very word 'observation' implies some kind of steadiness across time, space, or observers" (Collins 1991:130), and the rule of replicability makes this temporal structure explicit. Like any other rule, however, replicability does not contain rules for its own application. To replicate means to do the same as someone else has done. But what "the same" is varies according to differing contexts. Replication theory involves not only a two-valued judgment in which something must be either identical or not identical to itself. Replication also involves a three-valued logic that includes the *intentional action* of scientists trying to achieve replications and judging their successes or failures. The two-valued logic is effective for describing an external world, but a multi-valued, narrative logic better accounts for science as a system that intends to describe this external world. This difference is illustrated by the Narcissus motif in Ovid's *Metamorphoses*. As interpreted by Fischer (1987:344), "Narcissus recognizes himself in the reflection of a pool as an object; 'Iste ego sum,' 'I am that one,' he exclaims when seeing the moving lips of his mirror image but does not hear speech. In this very moment, Narcissus becomes an *observer*. Were he to hold up another mirror which reflects him as a *subject* that is looking into the pool which reflects him as an object, then he would evolve from an observer to a *narrator*. A self-referential or recursive network is formed between experienced objects and experiencing subject, a network that can reverberate its own history and enable Narcissus to narrate both [his] jubilation and alienation." Through narrative logic, science becomes aware of itself in its efforts to observe, to replicate, and to explain the world.

One could also say that this recursive process is at work not only in experiments and replications but also in theorization. Models and hypotheses cannot be tested by data alone because data are never merely given but always made or taken, produced through archival research, experimentation, or clinical trials that take place over time. Moreover, the making or taking of data is so thoroughly infused by a context of "theoretical perspectives that the stock of data that is thought to exist at any time and, hence, the validity status of existing hypotheses, will be affected by the very theories that the hypotheses and data are intended to test" (Diesing 1982:367). It is this very provisionability and reflexivity of science that gives it its narrative character. Narrative rhetoric not only shapes data into evidence and evidence into theoretical plots, but it also adduces the evidence and theories that we cannot have, or cannot yet have, or, at any rate, do not have now. This is expressed with rare and playful candor by Francis Crick (in Judson 1979:113–14):

> The point is that evidence can be unreliable, and therefore you should use as little of it as you can. And when we confront problems *today*, we're in exactly the same situation. We have three or four bits of data, we don't know which one is reliable, so we say, now, if we discard that one and assume it's wrong—even though we have no evidence that it's wrong—then we can look at the *rest* of the data and see if we can make sense of *that*. And that's what we do *all the time*. I mean, people don't realize that not only can data be wrong in science, it can be *misleading*. There isn't such a thing as a hard fact when you're trying to discover something. It's only afterwards that the facts become hard.

Thus the establishment of both scientific facts and their theoretical relevancies is a rhetorical construction over time, a narrative process like the establishment of other social or historical facts. For example, few Americans dispute the fact that World War II began with the Japanese attack on Pearl Harbor on December 7, 1941. But perhaps it only seems this way. Perhaps the War began on September 1, 1939, as Poles and their historians say, when the German army crossed their border. Or did it begin in March 1939 when Hitler seized Klaipeda (Memel), as Lithuanians believe? Or perhaps there wasn't a "World War II" at all, but rather a "Great Patriotic War, 1941–1945," as Soviet scholars proclaimed. Or perhaps there was only a period of civil strife and foreign invasion, difficult to name, that began in 1931 when the Japanese entered Manchuria and ended only with the capture of the cities in 1949 by the People's Liberation Army, as most Chinese believe. Moreover, neither Americans nor Poles nor Lithuanians nor any others knew what "World War II" was when it started or even as they lived it. Such understandings of what happened or what it meant or how to explain it are retrospective, the products of narrative emplotment.

   That historical facts are retrospective social constructions is not too difficult to accept. After all, history is one of the humanities, a soft discipline, without hard facts because it lacks the experimental method. But is there really so much difference between the historical and natural sciences, as many have argued? Perhaps the experimental method—which most of all is used to distinguish science from historical narration—is itself a narrative practice. Perhaps the objectivity of scientific facts, like the historical fact of World War II, is a product of negotiation and contestation, and achieves its factivity retrospectively through narration. Perhaps what Kierkegaard said of life, that we live it forward but understand it backward, is also true of scientific experiments.

To see experiments this way requires that we understand that they are extremely hard to perform.[6] When my high school chemistry class tried to produce a Brownian ring, not even the teacher, who had been an industrial chemist, could at first make it come out right. And of course, he and even we knew *in advance* what "coming out right" or "making it work" meant. We could know it because chemists had already agreed on that point and had officialized their agreement in our textbook. Thus, we were simply trying to reproduce an effect that had already been produced, characterized as significant, and made reliably reproducible. And even this reproduction was very hard to do.

Imagine, then, if we, now seasoned chemists or biologists or other experimental scientists, are trying to produce experimentally what has not yet been produced—what experimentally has never been known to exist. In that instance, how do we know that we have it right? To what do we compare it? Theory may be a guide. It tells us what to expect. But isn't the experiment supposed to be a test of the theory? And if we use the theory to confirm the experiment, do we not then obviate the whole point of experimentation as an independent confirmation of hypotheses? Or does "making it come out right" mean doing a number of experimental runs until we obtain one that confirms the theory, and then reporting *that* run as the crucial test and calling all the prior ones "testing the equipment" or "defining the protocol" or "errors of instrumentation"—simply warm-up exercises that need not be reported? And then do we write up our report as though we knew what we were doing all along? Do we reconstruct our activities into an ideal logical development that must have led to the result that we stumbled on through informed trial and error, the result that we now say we "achieved?" Do we, in effect, present our "empirical scientific statement . . . by describing experimental arrangements, etc. in such a way that anyone who has learned the relevant technique can test it" (Popper 1959:99)?

Yes. That, roughly, *is* what we do. And that is what we *must* do to have an experimental science. As Karl Popper said (1959:45), "Only when certain events recur in accordance with rules or regularities, as in the case of repeatable experiments, can our observations be tested—in principle—by anyone. We do not take even our own observations quite seriously, or accept them as scientific observations, until we have repeated them and tested them. Only by such repetitions can we convince ourselves that we are not dealing with a mere isolated 'coincidence,' but with events which, on account of their regularity and reproducibility, are in principle intersubjectively testable."

Popper thinks what he is describing here is a logic of verification. But, following Harry Collins (1989:83), my point is that it is better understood as an ideal rhetoric of presentation, a rhetoric that can be fully enacted only retrospectively—after agreement has been reached among experimenters both on the team and in the relevant community. By contrast, during most of the lived time of scientific disputes, scientists disagree precisely about the particulars of the material world and the value of various efforts to elicit different versions of them. By telling and defending contested stories about the objects, relations, methods, and purposes of experiments in that scientific field, scientists eventually establish, for a time, agreed-upon facts.

Experiments, in other words, may be understood not only as formal rules of methods but also as rhetoric and practices in use. Indeed, rather than guiding the experimental procedures, we can understand rules of method as emerging from them. That is, the methodological justification for the experiment crystallizes at about the same time as do the "final results," or in many cases even afterward when a "methodological statement" is being prepared for a larger public (publication). Thus, in innovative science rationality neither instructs us as to what actions to take nor inheres in the facts under study. Instead it emerges along with the facts and then is used retrospectively to legitimize what has already taken place or is being enacted.

On this account, Popper's criteria serve as rhetorical norms of presentation, not as descriptions of how science is conducted. This conduct is not a matter of reasoning about evidence toward a conclusion. Instead, the "rationality" and the "evidence" emerge, along with the "conclusion," from ad hoc, conflictual, discontinuous bricolage as this is emplotted into a logical and necessary development. The "experimental activities" themselves are not performed "in accordance with rules and regularities." Nor can the activities of experimenters be said to be logical steps leading up to observations that can be tested—in principle—by anyone. Instead, the rules, regularities, observations, and repeatability are generated together over time and through rhetorical interactions about what *are* the rules (among alternate relevant ones), what *are* the regularities (*the* regularities, among the various plausible ways of construing what appears), what *are* the observations (as opposed to errors), what *is* a repetition (and not the production of something else and something independent). In sum, " 'replicate results' is a valuable imperative, but its value lies in the way it makes scientists attend to contentious issues, not in the way it demarcates the true from the false" (H. Collins 1989:85).

What I have said here does not refute the principal criterion of falsification—that true statements resist experimental attempts to refute them. How, in any case, could one "refute" a norm or definition? Instead, it is the source of this resistance that I question. According to rationalists, resistance to refutation "comes from the presence either of consistent logical rules, or of exact representation of an object out there, or of an efficient action. The problem is that, when a study of science in the making is carried out, these three alternative sources of robustness appear along with many others. Moreover the 'coherence' of a logical demonstration, the 'exactness' of representation, or the 'efficiency' of an action are words used *after* the statement has resisted trials" (Latour 1989:110).

All these points are of greater moment when experiments are done in order to establish what the right result should be, that is, without prior theoretical determination. In such often crucial cases it is not possible to inspect the outcome to know whether the experiment has been properly performed, for the experiment is meant to establish what the outcome is. "For example, in the early 1970s, Professor Joseph Weber's claim to have detected high fluxes of gravitational radiation was disputed. A number of scientists set out to repeat Weber's experiment in order to test the claim. It was not clear at the outset whether a properly designed experiment should detect gravity waves or should not detect gravity waves because their detectability was the very subject of the dispute. To settle this question, experimenters needed to know whether or not gravity waves existed, and to find this out they needed to do some well-performed experiments. But to know whether their experiments were well performed they needed to see if their experiments produced the 'correct' results, and to determine this they needed to know whether gravity existed— and so on" (H. Collins 1989:88).

If we look more closely, however, we can see this paradox or indeterminacy at work even when an experiment is designed to test a specific theoretical prediction. This is because the solidity of any given theory is itself a product of a network of assumptions about theory and method that make up the paradigm within which that particular theory has meaning. And in times of paradigm shifts this context itself is brought into question. Moreover, even a firmly held theory is not necessarily firmly linked to any particular experiment. A new theory, for example, might be tested with an old experimental design that is inappropriate to it, but there is no conclusive way to know whether the lack of fit is due to the inappropriateness of the experimental design or the inadequacy of the theory.

Thus "the objectivity and certainty of science seem to dissolve before our eyes" (Ravetz 1971:186), and we are left with paradoxes that an abstract epistemological analysis cannot hope to resolve. Such paradoxes, however, can be eliminated by a narrative approach. For the same objectivity that disappears under deconstructive critique reappears when understood as a narrativized construction. As various findings compete for attention, relevance, and acceptance as facts, some will be marginalized or rejected, others will fade into disuse, and still others will call for their own modification or improvement. Moreover, given the importance of utility and the variance between different scientific schools, a finding may be ignored or rejected in the discipline where it was invented even as it is declared truthful, significant, and immediately useful in a cognate field. In these ways, the established fact is embedded in spacial and temporal contexts of problems, and it will survive only as long as one or another of these contexts continues to give it relevance. Eventually, if the contextual relevancies of a fact continue long enough, it will become, for awhile, knowledge. "Facts stay alive only as long as they are useful in new contexts, and if they cannot be put into a convenient form for their limited functions, they are soon discarded and forgotten. Although such standardized facts comprise the body of scientific knowledge, it is not simply a collection of atomic units of hard, long-lived facts. Indeed, its special character results from the complexity and interconnectedness of its materials, as they evolve through the complex and fallible social processes of their use and adaption" (Ravetz 1971:209).

This means not that experiments cannot be "decisive" but that they can be so only if both the governing paradigm, the neighboring theories, and the appropriateness of the test are all taken for granted. But if this already were the case, nothing would be contested for the experiment to be decisive about. Instead, the taken-for-granted, general agreements about the validity of theories or results are rhetorical achievements of scientific communities over time. Such consensus does not spring from theories or results or methods because these are precisely what are in dispute in important scientific innovations. And, in the meantime, which for creative scientists means all the time, scientists depend on such things as the reputations of the experimenters, the authority of sponsoring institutions, the refinement of the apparatus, the personal ethos of the participants, or the metaphysical possibilities of the existence of the physical phenomena (H. Collins 1989:89). Advocates will gather proxies, allies, and *amicae juris*. Reputations may be challenged. The nonscientific public might become involved. Finally, if a consensus is reached, the victors will claim that what has been constructed—truth, objective facts, reproducibility—is what had guided the whole process all along. The outcome of the story will be said to be its cause, and the tropological, rhetorical action, through which the real-time happenings were made into a timeless story, are silenced by the victors.

World War II did, in fact, begin on December 7, 1941.

SCIENTIFIC NARRATION AS AN ALLEGORY OF FREEDOM

Stories of origins, nature, and destiny are narrated explicitly to recall and celebrate the definition of those who tell them. But this mythic function also can be seen in the foundational assumptions of science. Truth claims, whether in modern or primal societies, are defensible only in the context of norms and practices that are socially and historically variable and that are themselves legitimated narratively in terms of some tradition. In this sense, the scientific worldview has a mythic quality—it is a story told of origins and essence, an ultimate story that contains the world and hence has no referent external to itself.

Thus, in choosing the scientific vision as our global and primary one, we are choosing "a kind of society which sustains it and which is sustained by it. This cannot be done from the outside, for there is no external vantage point, no inter-social empty space from which it and its rival could be judged" (Gellner 1985:64). To choose such a society is to see oneself and one's thought as part of its tradition, to narrate one's own biography in terms of that society's own historic or mythic narration. In this sense, science is an allegory, the story of Western society's quest for freedom through mastery of nature.

Narrative is the principal way we translate observations into prose and happenings into experience. It gives temporal form to the senses. If we take a strong position and assert that all discourse, science as well as myth, has a narrative dimension, then we must distinguish, with Hayden White (1987:2–3), between a "discourse that narrates and a discourse that narratizes, between a discourse that openly adopts a perspective that looks out on the world and reports it and a discourse that feigns to make the world speak itself and speak itself as a story." In the latter, narratizing discourse, the narrator disappears and no one speaks excepts the events, which seem to tell themselves (Genette 1978:8–9; Benveniste 1971:208). Narratizing discourse is a thick encoding that attempts and perhaps succeeds to invest its objects with a realism independent of the discourse that tells them.

And, indeed, in the naturalistic and especially mechanistic world of modern science, real events do not offer themselves as a story, and for Kantians not even as a chronological series. Instead, they have to be ordered that way. That is, the scientific narratization of nature presupposes an invented temporality that enables science to emplot its objects as real and itself as true. Newtonian temporality afforded this for modern science. Issac Newton's invention of the dual conceptions of absolute space and absolute time enabled the ordering of all events, both terrestrial and celestial, on a single universal time continuum within a single universal space.

Thus, in the narrative view, science does not simply register a passive nature that gives itself up, voiceless and unresisting, to be mirrored in theories. Instead, nature is given voice by scientists through experiments, and these "speech acts" elicited from nature in the form of empirical events are solicited and emplotted theoretically into the narratives of particular scientific fields that together are science. Scientists thus textualize the materiality of nature into perception and reflection, and they fashion this materiality into new symbolic orders.

Scientists narrativize such inventions as discoveries. Their emplotment of nature allows us to see the empirical end of the story in its theoretical beginning. Anton Chekhov's emplotment of the shotgun over the fireplace in the first act presaged its going off in the last, just as Einstein's theorization of relativity elicited Eddington's experimental proof. In this way, theory is like the plot in relation to the events or facts of the story of science. And like any narrativized event, facts cannot be inserted into the story wherever the writer wishes. Instead, they first have to become "evidence" that may contribute to the development of the plot or, conversely, the plot must be revised to accommodate the included event. "It is as if the plot were an entity in process of development prior to the occurrence of any given event, and any given event could be endowed with [scientificity] . . . only to the extent that it could be shown to contribute to this process" (White 1987:51).

Thus, science is more than a mode of conveying precise information, more even than a mode of explanation. It also is a strategy for structuring events without which their temporality remains inaccessible to our understanding. One can make true statements about events without narrativizing them, as in chronologies or correlation series. And one can even provide explanations of events without narration, as science pretends to do. But without narration one cannot show that there is "progress" in science, or "development" of a research program, or greater "significance" or "fruitfulness" of one theory over another, or that something is a "finding" and not an "error," or, ultimately, why science is worth doing at all. In the narrative discourse of science is revealed the meaning, coherence, and significance of the events and theories that experimental scientists create. Narration makes a truly mysterious nature into mysteriously true versions of it.

Nature is not a text, but it is accessible to our understanding only through textualization. And to understand how science gives nature the voice with which it speaks to us, we must work through its prior and current textualizations. This is not to say that the scientific "significations" of nature are without a referent, as some deconstructionists might have it, but only that the cognitive and ontological status of this referent remains indeterminate. No matter how thoroughly they may be deconstructed, those indeterminate necessities called Nature, History, the Other, or Death will continue to impose their scarcities upon us because this is the very precondition of our capacity to assert our autonomy within the otherwise mindless implacability of the scarcities that we realize as objects of narrative reflection.

Science makes us mindful of nature, but science can become critical and therefore potentially liberatory only to the extent that we become aware of the conditions and processes by which its methods and insights are textualized into the cognitive authority of certain knowledge. Theory is not accounted for by its data or logic, nor is science determined or explained by its correspondence to nature. But we *can* account for the intelligibility of scientific discourse meta-narratively, by systematically emplotting it to reveal the historical production of the cognitive integrity of facts, theories, programs, and disciplines, their layered and interpenetrating relations to one another, their cognitive or historical ruptures, confrontations, and transformations. This would restore science to its central task, to help humanity wrest a realm of freedom from the realm of necessity.

Conceived in this way, science not only appears as a mirror of the nature of which it speaks but also as an icon of the kind of actions that produce the kinds of events that we call historical or social. It is not God's beneficence, as Descartes and Newton thought, that elicits from nature a response to the supplication of language. It is theoretical emplotment of empirical events within a narrative discourse that provides this response. As historical actors, we all to some degree fashion forms of social life out of the materials that we have narrativized as necessity. This indexical character of science as an exemplar of cognitive social production in general gives it a significance beyond its mechanistic or relativistic metaphors of nature. It permits what no specific scientific theory or set of data could permit: the adequacy of science as human truth

about an extra-human world. The enfolding of natural and human tempo-
ralities in scientific narration is the link between the language within which we
live and understand, and a world exterior to us that we seek to explain. Through
its narrative form, science provides an allegory of human temporality. It not
only offers literal accounts of natural events in time and causality; it also represents allegorically the timeless drama of humanity's struggle to give meaning
to its own "experience of temporality," a struggle to liberate itself from the
determinations of history and nature (Ricoeur 1984).

What desire motivates our search for the "true story" of nature, the correct
theorization of its events? What wish is enacted, what desire gratified, by
finding the truth of real events when their inner coherence is displayed in
formal theory? What is "the cultural function of narrativizing discourse in
general, . . . the psychological impulse behind the apparently universal need
not only to narrate but to give to events an aspect of narrativity" (White
1987:4)? Perhaps it is the desire to become human, to transcend the brute
determination of events into a self-determination through knowledge. Perhaps
the coherence and fullness that we imagine we attain in our story is the
fulfillment of our desire because we imagine such coherence and fullness in a
mastered human life and in the human mastery of nature. Narrative subsumes
aesthetically the integral truth of nature and the integrity of a truthful human
existence. It is an allegory of realized human freedom.

Those "leaps of the imagination" that become known as scientific discoveries
appeal in part because they seem to reveal some universal truth, having defined
a point of view that becomes the taken-for-granted frame of vision for whole
generations of those who elaborate the initial insight. But "great discoveries"
also appeal to us because they display the human capacity to order incoherence,
to overcome contradiction, to endow lived necessity with the possibility of
transcendence, to give voice to mute nature, to lift us above its determination of
our own natures, if not in life at least in figuration.

Dialogical processes proliferate in any complex discursive space, and science
is no different from the novel in this regard. Both art and science also possess a
"legislative" capacity, as Heidegger called it, to amplify some voices and to
silence others, to form its objects by imposing upon them artful form, and
thereby to give becoming the character of Being. Scientists, like poets, name the
forces or the gods of the heavens and the earth, and name all the things in which
they reside and that reside in them. This naming does not consist merely in
supplying a name to something already known. Rather, when scientists or poets
speak the essentializing words, that which is named is nominated as what it is to

be. It thus becomes known as being. "Poetry is the establishment of being through the word (Heidegger, in Bruns 1989:38; see Scult 1991). Science also evokes the world through symbolization. It is, in Vico's phrase, the "serious poem" of nature. Just as poetry helps solicit experience from existence, just as the human studies partake in the "invention of culture" (Wagner 1980), so science is a part of the invention of nature, a collective poeting of the world.

Of course, this is "illusion," because any narrative representation is always partly illusory in that it imagines an integral consciousness that views the world from the outside, and apprehends its logical structure and necessary processes, without realizing that this coherency of representation to consciousness is that of narrativity itself (White 1987:173). The "meaning" of scientific narration—that which emerges from its forming of events through emplotment—is not only that this emplotment both theorizes events and makes them empirical but also that it expresses what would otherwise be unutterable in language, namely, the ineluctable aporia between consciousness and the world, an aporia that language can only pretend to fill.

Thus we can read the epigraph of this chapter—Boyle's association of science and romance—not as a condemnation. Instead, the emplotment of science provides its cogency, making nature accessible for reflection. It also helps to explain the persistence and vitality of the scientific enterprise, its open-ended quest for truth, the unity that, in the Romance of Nature, is the object of desire.

Chapter 6 Modern Science: Institutionalization of Knowledge and Rationalization of Power

The former are convinced that among the false books flooding the world they can track down the few that bear a truth perhaps extrahuman or extraterrestrial. The latter believe that only counterfeiting, mystification, intentional falsehood can represent absolute value in a book, a truth not contaminated by the dominant pseudo truths.
Italo Calvino (1982:104)

For *True* and *False* are attributes of Speech, not of Things. And where Speech is not, there is neither Truth nor Falsehood. Errour there may be, as when we expect that which shall not be; or suspect what has not been: but in neither case can a man be charged with Untruth.
Thomas Hobbes (1958:105)

We can now expand our discussion to include the political economics of science—how the creation and transmission of knowledge re-create and transmit forms of power, and how power shapes and deploys forms of knowledge. The relation of scientific knowledge and political power is not simply one of knowledge guiding power or of power shaping knowledge. It also involves institutional mediations and reciprocal transformations of the character of knowledge and power themselves. Broad historical and institutional conditions influence cognitive processes in the sciences and constrain the deployment of political and economic power. Local factors are also important. Although scientists have always participated in structuring politics and society—at the very least through the discourses on nature and culture that they offer—they do so under circumstances, sometimes very local circumstances, that they have not chosen, and with consequences that they have not foreseen.

Thus the relation between the political and the cognitive is best seen as interactive and often dialectical in the sense that each can be transformed into the other. The politics of professionalization, for example, require practitioners to represent their services as of great value to patrons and clients, and even to shape these services accordingly. That is, scientists may tailor their topics, concepts, methods, and applications of knowledge to the needs of those who fund them. To the degree that professionalization is achieved, however, it brings to its members the independence and privilege of a self-regulating monopoly guild—an independence that is vital to the creativity that makes scientists useful. Moreover, especially in a technologically sophisticated society, power cannot be fully exercised through coercion but depends on specialized knowledge and is deployed through relations of trust. Thus the patron who wishes to control science by supporting it must delegate some discretion over funding to those scientists who are better able to judge the quality of the work that is supported. "The patron's delegation of authority is an act of trust" (Turner n.d.a:5; see also Barber 1983). Such trust gives discretion to scientists but is secured by affinities of interests, shared ideology, financial interdependence, and a record of mutually useful performance.

In exploring such relations between knowledge and power, we can begin by imagining the production of (scientific) truth and reality as akin to economic production. Like means of economic production, the modes of reality production also tend to be concentrated in the hands of a few. Of course, language, the principal such mode, is available to all socialized members of any community. Reality, however, is produced not through just any speech but mainly through those discourses that have achieved hegemonic legitimacy (Foucault 1980). Schizophrenic paralogisms, children's talk, or racetrack gossip can create or define only local realities shared by politically marginalized persons. Thus, the question arises as to the preconditions for a given discourse to attain a position of hegemony, to become *the* language through which the real and true are manifest. In the modern world, science is that hegemonic discourse.

Elaborating our economic metaphor, we note the preconditions for the oligopolization of discourse or commodities. First, the item to be oligopolized must be a staple—something without which people feel they cannot do. This is because nonstaples are not worth controlling, as monopoly pricing would simply result in a collapse of demand and, hence, of monopoly profits. Second, production of the staple commodity must be accompanied by some barrier to entry. That is, some means must be available to keep out competing producers, especially potential producers who would be stimulated to enter that sector once the privileges of monopoly become visible.

Applying this model to the production of reality, we assume that a reality is something that everyone must have—that is, we all need stability, continuity, and intelligibility in an intersubjectively validated lifeworld. Hence, to control the discourse through which reality is produced is to control a vital resource, because reality is quintessentially a staple. We still need to know, however, how one discourse that produces reality becomes privileged over others—how it beats out, and keeps out, the competition. Drawing on the political economic theories of Marx, we might speculate that to become dominant, a discourse must serve the needs of dominant groups in the society. That is, there needs to be a "market" for that (version of) reality among those who can dispense money, status, and influence to the masters of that reality-generating discourse. In addition, however, a barrier is needed to restrict control of that reality-producing discourse to certain persons. This barrier can be provided by formal or technical properties of the discourse itself—properties by which persons may be demarcated as correct users and, therefore, bona fide practitioners of that mode of representation.

In sum, these appear to be conditions for a discourse to become hegemonic: it must be capable of articulating a reality consonant with the habitus and interests of dominant groups, and it must possess sufficiently occult or formal properties to bar unwanted persons from its legitimate deployment. These broad conditions may be elaborated into three "ingredients" that help us to understand the institutionalization of modern science and the rationalization of modern institutions. These ingredients might be called, respectively, cognitive, political economic, and institutional.

The first, cognitive ingredient of hegemony is that the discourse must be perceived as specialized. That is, the proper use of the discourse must require more than ordinary socialization of would-be practitioners. Certain topics, concepts, methods, rites, or modes of representation must be known to require special training and discipline. The discourse must also be specialized not only in contrast to lay discourse or doxa but also in contrast to other specialized forms of representation. Indeed, this is part of what we mean when we speak of a scientific discipline. Correspondingly, the products or works of that discourse must require expert judgment in order to be properly assessed. In economic terms, one could say that the discourse must fill (and defend) a niche in the cognitive market.

The second, political-economic ingredient is that the mode of representation must be useful to dominant groups. Since the seventeenth century, for example, the arts in France, served to glorify and hence legitimate monarchical rule (Brown 1995). Similarly, the sciences, including the sciences of society and human nature, enhance the efficiency, legitimacy, and, hence, the profitability and stability of the capitalist state.

Finally, to achieve hegemony the discourse in question must be institutionalized—as the arts were under the French Academy or as the sciences are in modern universities and research institutes. Institutionalization provides a formal and continuing social basis for the patrons and practitioners of that discourse to exercise their power and enjoy their privileges. Indeed, this process has been called a " 'second' scientific revolution . . . marked by the eclipse of the generalized learned society and the rise of more specialized institutions, and by the concurrent establishment of professional standards for individual scientific disciplines" (Hahn 1971:275; see Ben-David and Zloczower 1962; Schneider 1991). Because institutionalization involves significant social investment, those who control the necessary resources can influence practitioners by proffering or withholding funds. Such institutions serve several key functions: as settings for specialized discourse; as social mechanisms for training, licensing, and exclusion; and as defenders of professional prestige, property, and privilege. Thus, practitioners are usually inclined to promote institutionalization and are usually willing to adapt their discursive practices sufficiently to accord with the interests, and to maintain the support, of their sponsors.

In exploring such interactions between science and politics, I begin by discussing ethnographies of scientific discourse and practice. I noted earlier that such ethnographies reveal the rhetorically constructed character of scientific knowledge, and hence its openness to social and political influence. But these studies also show how scientists strive for standardization in rendering their somewhat ad hoc activities in the laboratory into replicable and reputable public accounts. The norms and techniques of this locally created standardization emerged historically, mainly in the form of objectivity and numeracy. These standards in turn served politically to define legitimate scientists, demarcate them from amateurs or quacks, and exclude whole categories of persons, such as women, who were thought to be insufficiently rational (Mendelsohn 1977; Schiebinger 1989).

Such cognitive boundaries thereby enabled social boundaries, which were indispensable to three further processes: the definition of disciplines and the establishment of distinctions between them; the organization of practitioners of these disciplines into professional guilds; and the institutionalization of these disciplines and their practitioners in research universities and specialized scientific-administrative centers. Along the way, the disciplines, in seeking to demonstrate their utility to potential patrons, became more oriented toward utility and were shaped to conform to the requirements of professionalization and institutionalization. The very language of science changed in accordance with its new emphases. The close institutionalized affinity of cognitive and political interests was largely established in the late nineteenth and early twentieth centuries, and it continues in changing form to this day.

SPECIALIZATION THROUGH STANDARDIZATION

The research of David Bloor (1976) and of Michael Mulkay and G. N. Gilbert (1982) lends credence to these assertions. In their studies of laboratory life, these and other researchers found that scientists try to have their claims to knowledge accepted by telling stories, little conversion narratives, as it were, of how these claims emerged. But as the claims become successful with larger publics, such social explanations are soon dropped, and what was earlier described as a knowledge claim is told technically as a taken-for-granted object in nature. The style becomes impersonal (like the middle parts of ethnographies), focusing on objective agencies rather than human agents, almost as though the physical world were acting and speaking for itself (Halliday 1978; Mulkay, Potter, and Yearley 1983:197). Thus scientists speak in two different linguistic registers. One is a personal narrative of the emergence of knowledge claims. The other is the public and technical language of scientific objects. These discourses are incompatible in terms of formal logic but complement each other rhetorically, and through them, scientists continually revise their conceptions of the natural world as well as the meaning of their own and their colleagues' present and former actions (Gilbert and Mulkay 1984). In effect, the discourse becomes more specialized (more removed from ordinary language) as it becomes more public within the scientific community. It is no longer a story of human agents trying to understand; instead it becomes an objective analysis or description of the laws or facts of nature. Ethnographies of laboratory life reveal that truth in science is a rhetorical movement from personal experience to professional knowledge. To learn precisely how this shift is accomplished, Bruno Latour and Steve Woolgar (1986:136–39) sought to discover how problems were conceived and addressed before answers were established and their logic appeared self-evident. And they discovered how facts and truth in science are socially made. Was TRF a peptide, or were the assays anomalous because the purification of the supposed hormone was incomplete? As soon as scientists felt they had a believable solution, they tended to reconstruct a history of the work that led plausibly to their current understanding. Thus, they simplified complex contextual actions into formal logical procedures. The "objective" (in this genre, technical) aspects were separated from the "subjective" social (unpersuasive) elements and then inverted in sequence. This split and inversion of the technical and social factors was not dictated by either the method or the data. Instead it was a rhetorical (re)construction of data and method themselves.

Ethnographies of science like these tend to subvert foundationalist assumptions of science. The cases that Harry Collins (1985) presents do this too. Scientists rarely try simply to repeat earlier studies, as one would expect if they chiefly were interested in verification or falsification. Even when scientists do repeat earlier studies, as in the laser case discussed in chapter 5, the process of repetition becomes exceedingly troublesome in view of practical contingencies in following technical instructions. Furthermore, in the controversies that Collins examines, scientists set out deliberately to confirm or destroy rival claims on the basis of a priori beliefs about the credibility of the claims and the reputations of claimants. Depending on the experimenter's initial interest in outcomes, experimental results can be taken as publishable evidence or counterevidence, or merely as indication that the equipment was not working properly. Given the absence of independent criteria, the meaning of positive or negative results in controversial science depends on the experimenter's initial expectations. And considering the unequal and contested distribution of incentives and opportunities for circulating persuasive arguments in scientific communities, it is not surprising that researchers design, conduct, and interpret their experiments for polemical purposes (Lynch 1986:620). Yet all this seems inconsistent with a philosophy and rhetoric that present science as an objective, value-neutral, dispassionate pursuit of truths. Instead, it would seem that truth, in science as elsewhere, is socially created.

Collins and others (e.g., Ashmore 1989; Gilbert and Mulkay 1984; or Pickering 1992) unmask the absolutist pretensions of science by revealing the local, embedded character of scientific practice. They achieve this irony by showing how scientific results are "made" through poetic and political processes, and how their "discovery" is a retrospective construction. But their finding has a counterirony as well, for it also reveals that scientists strive for standardization. They try to create decontextualized results so that other scientists can create them, too. Indeed, given the operational concept of truth held by modern scientists, a fact can be acknowledged as such only after the steps through which it can be regularly made evident have been specified (van den Daele and Krohn 1983:237). This is not a matter of induction versus deduction or theory versus research. Scientists reproducing a result are not simply finding other instances of a general law, because the production or reproduction of the result requires skills and knowledge that are independent of, and have been *made* independent of, their original context. The new contexts may be different from the original ones; indeed, they must be different in order for the results to count as "independent confirmation" or an extension of the original "finding." And the making of these new results, new theories, and new findings also aims at standardization. In this way science *is* objective. But it also is *projective*. Or rather, it projects its own objectivity through poetic and political practices of standardization that invite intersubjective confirmations. Such processes of invention and discovery change reality, for reality *is* what appears in our standardized practices (Turner n.d.b; Rouse 1987). Relativistic inventions thereby become discoveries that are realistically confirmed; or, more precisely, they become real because they have been made confirmable.

Such representational practices of science emerged historically through much rhetorical struggle. Objectivity in science, for example, depends on standardization of weights and measures, but this standardization was achieved only through lengthy collaborations of scientists, who wanted consistent measurements for laboratory work, and state officials, who wanted national and, later, international standards to facilitate manufacturing and market exchanges in the capitalist economy. The historical construction of standards for objectivity also enabled and was enabled by the establishment of science as a social institution. Objectivity means intersubjectivity so broad and deep, so taken for granted, that the resulting uniformity of perception is seen as inhering in the objects themselves. In semiotic terms, a unity is seen between the referent and the signifier, with no role for the sign. Through these processes, the principal artifacts of science—laws about facts—come to be thought of as things, and people forget that they are created through institutionalized actions and protocols of perception.

Theodore Porter (1989:3) provided an example of such a development. His historical narration reveals the narrative character of scientific objectivity: "Scientists were disciples of Henry Ford *avant la lettre*. Their interest in standardization has, at least since the early nineteenth century, been unflagging. It was expressed in the enormous effort by late nineteenth-century physicists to produce standard units of electricity, magnetism, heat, mechanical work, light and the like. . . . Similarly, astronomers worked tirelessly to establish objective criteria—that is, quantitative rules—for admitting and rejecting observations [and] for correcting the discrepancies due to the different 'personal equations' of observers." By 1889 Lord Kelvin could assert the success of this movement with his famous dictum, "When you cannot express it in numbers, your knowledge is of a meager and unsatisfactory kind" (in Kuhn 1977).

Standardized methods and measures came somewhat later to the social sciences. Between 1890 and 1940 the dominant issue in these fields was how practitioners might establish them as independent scientific disciplines, free of any taint of religion (Bannister 1987; Longino 1990). Because science was thought to be empirical, objective, and ethically neutral, such sociologists as W. F. Ogburn and H. Stuart Chapin were "nominalists" who believed in statistics and in means rather than ends. "Others, like Bernard, were 'realists' who wished to provide 'objective' standards of control and, hence, to establish absolute standards for social construction" (Vidich 1989:406). Indeed, with the support of the Rockefeller and Russell Sage foundations and the Social Science Research Council, Ogburn supervised the triumph of quantification—"the frightful symmetry of statistics" (see Vidich and Lyman 1985:ch. 4).

The development of statistical approaches based on probability carried quantification a long step forward because it provided a framework for regression analysis to social scientists. This was crucial because social scientists, unlike astronomers, tested their theories with data shaped by many factors that were of little concern in the theory. Regression analysis made it possible to locate numerically the possible causal role of the factors of theoretical interest. For example, "Curnot could interrelate demand and price in theory, all other things being held constant, but he could not hold other things constant in the real world. A new conceptual approach was needed that would measure uncertainty, and it was supplied by the regression framework" developed by Galton, Edgeworth, Pearson, and Yule (Namboodiri 1987:762; see Stigler 1986:359). Statistical objectivity thus provided a common language within social science disciplines even while helping to define them as scientific and disciplined on the model of astronomy or physics. And, like astronomers and physicists, social statisticians also interacted with nonscientists, helping governmental agencies to standardize their definitions for data gathering and, beyond this, creating new statistical facts that then could be considered by laypersons.

As uniformity of measure was established more generally in society, it became more possible to apply innovations made within scientific contexts to larger nonscientific settings, because they now had a common measure. Through calculation and numerical control, the laboratory and the factory or classroom or welfare program or production line were brought closer together. The symmetry of mathematical models was extended to the rest of the world. Nonscientists articulated more and more aspects of life in terms of mathematical symmetry—the roots of which, *syn* and *metria*, mean a measuring together or a common measure (Hallyn 1990:72–74). The very impersonality and seeming impartiality of such measurement appeared to fit the democratic ideology of American institutions (Hornstein 1988:24). Thus, what began in the Renaissance as a neo-Platonic aesthetic ideal—a mimesis that elucidates principles of Creation as a coherent system of mathematical relations—was realized in modern science as a practice that wills the technical re-creation of the world.

THE PROFESSIONALIZATION AND INSTITUTIONALIZATION OF SCIENCE

The establishment of codified methods, measurements, and practices by scientists was crucial for their professionalization, because the acquisition of their guild monopoly privileges depended on the advancement of their intellectual agendas. Standardization gave them a precise shared discourse—a discourse that announced its availability for public inspection even while excluding all members of the public who were not also members of the guild.

Social scientists soon sought to imitate two features of standardization—numeracy and objectivity—that had been achieved by some of the natural sciences. In the United States such imitation was also an effort to justify and institutionalize the study of society as akin to the study of nature. In Sorokin's (1976) phrase, the Sinatras of scientism sang the song of objectivity. Their longing for certain knowledge also represented a secularization of male Protestant absolutism. "The celebration of 'hard facts' and the 'rigors' of research brought the Protestant Ethic into the era of modern Professionalism" (Bannister 1987:233; see Stigler 1986; Keller 1985). Similar processes occurred in France and in Germany. In France, Emile Durkheim advanced a positivist statistical method for the social sciences that was in opposition to his own theoretical work (Alexander 1988; Brown 1989b). In Germany, "a leading group in the

German Society for Sociology . . . reduced the theoretical ambition of sociology to a concept of a pure or formal approach which should stand beside, not include, history, economics and law" (Wagner 1989).

With the establishment of more universal norms of scientific exactitude, it became easier to say which practices were proper and, hence, which practitioners were scientists. The establishment of scientific canons of objective representation provided demarcations for membership into, and enabled the formation of, professional guilds whose privileges included greater property rights and control over their cultural products.

The cognitive and professional authority gained by scientists also enabled them to claim the authority to manage society's cultural capital, which was now seen as both collective and indivisible (Bourdieu and Passeron 1970:25; Bourdieu 1991). As their formal knowledge and organizations grew, scientists became able to restrict admission into the scientific professions and to the privileges that this provided. They now defined what was science and who was a scientist, what were proper objects and methods of inquiry, and how results should enter the public domain.

These gains made by scientists also depended on the conceptual and practical distinctions between science and technology and between basic and applied research. Emerging industrial elites and established public authorities wished to differentiate technological inventions from inherently unpatentable basic research. What was secretive, geared toward the discovery of new products or processes, or protected by patent or copyright was called technology. In contrast, what was to be open, geared toward understanding rather than doing, was called basic research (Root-Bernstein 1984). Science was supposed to take place in universities and public research institutes, where property rights mainly concerned the protection of the prestige attached to priority of discoveries (Nelkin 1984). This conceptual and practical distinction between applied and basic research extended and reflected the commercial distinction between proprietary and nonproprietary findings. Applied research led to patentable and profitable results. Thus it was privatized and motivated by money. Basic research was by definition nonproprietary and nonspecific in its applications. Thus it remained in the public domain of universities (a collective utility) and was rewarded by status instead of by cash. Each kind of research helped to legitimize the other. Pure science extended an intellectual warrant to applied science and technology, whereas applied research and technology proclaimed that basic science often led to something useful.

With the growth of industrial science in the post–World War II period, knowledge came to be produced through a complex integration of financial, governmental, technical, and academic resources, thereby shattering in practice the continuing ideological distinction between science and technology or pure and applied research. Particle physics was basic research, but the hydrogen bomb was technology. Or, conversely, Louis Pasteur's discovery of vaccines in the laboratory and their use on people in hospitals could both be called science (see, e.g., Perutz 1995). Evelyn Fox Keller (1991) provides a nice example of such ontological gerrymandering. Keller discusses two books that sketch out the emerging field of molecular biology, one by Mueller, a biologist, and one by Schroedinger, a physicist. Schroedinger's book had far greater influence because it promoted molecular biology as a quest for "unified, all-embracing knowl-edge,"—that is, as pure or basic science—whereas Mueller's work spoke of molecular biology as holding the potential for "molding the evolutionary future of the human race," which for most readers was a scary prospect. Ironically, however, the greater authority of Schroedinger depended precisely on the success of practical interventions said to be derived from modern physics.

Scientists of nature were the first to achieve relative independence as a group and, with this, greater control of their products. This control in turn encour-aged more members of upper social strata to join their ranks, which further enhanced their status. High social background and economic security enabled scientists to assert that their undertakings were self-validating enterprises that were in society but not of it. Indeed, scientists claimed that their deeds contrib-uted to a cumulating cultural progress (Merton 1973:348–350). This claim perhaps had more basis by the later nineteenth century than before, because many of the modern disciplines of natural science, and their technical applica-tions, were invented at that time.

The social scientific disciplines also began to crystallize in the late nineteenth century, with their respective professional journals and associations. In the United States these included the American Historical Association (1884) and its *Papers* (1886); the American Economic Association (1892) and its *Publications* (1886) and the *Quarterly Journal of Economics* (1886); the American Psychologi-cal Association (1892) and the *American Journal of Psychology* (1887) and the *Psychological Review* (1894); the American Academy of Political and Social Science (1889) and the American Political Science Association (1903) with its *Proceedings* and with the *Political Science Quarterly* (1886); and the American Sociological Society (1905) (See Manicas 1987:208; Furner 1975; Haskell 1977).

The diversity of knowledge-producing activities embodied in such professional associations and journals suggests the importance of the linguistic forms by which such knowledge is shaped. Getting the words right is more than fine-tuning one's personal style. Instead, it is a collective endeavor that defines the entire disciplinary enterprise. The words shape and are shaped by the discipline's practices. These include "its communally developed linguistic resources and expectations; . . . its stylized identification and structuring of realities to be discussed; its literature; its active procedures of reading, evaluating, and using texts; its structured interactions between writer and reader. The words arise out of the activity, procedures, and relationships within the community" (Bazerman 1988:47; see Harris 1988).

Thus, in addition to their theoretical and public functions, the rhetorical devises of scientific style also help shape the practical routines of day-to-day conduct that maintain the discipline's structure and cohesion. For example, root metaphors that guide discourse in various disciplines highlight certain commonalities in objects or situations and incline those who know how to use the lingo to act in similar ways. Thus, "if some psychologists conceptualize the mind as a hard wired computer, whereas others think of the mind as an adaptive organism, they will adopt very different methodological practices in their psychological investigations. Similarly, if clinical or counseling psychologists consider members of the public to be their clients rather than their patients, they are likely to orient their professional interactions in distinctive ways" (Leary 1991a:3). In ways like these, the development of a common language, including common numerical measures, is central to creating the shared concepts and methods that define that knowledge practice as a distinct, scientific discipline. Knowledge of such rhetorical devices, and practical skill in deploying them, is a hallmark of the professional.

Practitioners of a would-be science must show that theirs is expert knowledge, different and superior to "what everyone knows" (Freidson 1986; Haskell 1984). In addition to establishing their own distinct rhetorical or cognitive voice, however, practitioners also must create and defend a niche within the existing market for scientific discourse. Essential to this process is distinguishing their particular topics and methods from those of some disciplines, and making alliances with others. Distinctions help to define the enterprise as a unique and independent knowledge practice; alliances help to defend and validate this independent status. In the late nineteenth century, for example, America's would-be scientific psychologists distinguished themselves from philosophers and psychical researchers and allied themselves with physiologists. Thus they sought to establish their scientific bona fides even though they seemed, at first, to be asking philosophical or psychical questions (Latour 1987). Conversely, in Germany, where philosophy was a dominant discipline, psychologists stressed their linkages with philosophy rather than their distance from it (Danziger 1979b). Such alliances, however fruitful politically, often alter, or even halt, the would-be scientists' initial intellectual agenda. Nascent professionals, highly responsive to external pressures and eager to represent their discipline as a mature science, may cease to ask how or even whether their adopted methods fit their theoretical questions. Indeed, they may reduce the initial theoretical questions to the adopted established methods (Ravetz 1971:368). This seems to have happened with behaviorist psychology, for example; it eschewed inquiry into the structure or processes of mind, which was psychology's original topic, and focused only on experimentally producible behaviors. Moreover, because these behaviors were to be explained without reference to mentalistic concepts, it seemed appropriate to substitute rats or pigeons for people, especially as rodents and birds were more controllable than humans for use in experimental designs.

In sum, the institutionalization of a new discipline is a rhetorical, cognitive, and

> *political* process in which alliances have to be formed, competitors have to be defeated, programs have to be formulated, recruits have to be won, power bases have to be captured, organizations have to be formed, and so on. These political exigencies necessarily leave their mark on the discipline itself, and not least on its investigative practices. The political environment largely determines what types of knowledge product can be successfully marketed at a particular time and place. The goal of producing an appropriate type of product plays a crucial role in the selection of investigative practices within the discipline. Ultimately, the limitation of investigative practices results in corresponding limitations on the knowledge products that the discipline has to offer. So in the end, those with sufficient social power to have an input into this process are likely to get the kinds of knowledge products that are compatible with their interests. (Danziger 1990a:182)

THE POLITICAL ECONOMY OF MODERN SCIENCE

Before the 1850s science was more a gentlemanly craft than a professional pursuit. Soon, however, leading scientists sought to establish collaborative relations with governments. In 1862, for example, the German chemist Hermann von Helmholtz proposed that science was both the disinterested pursuit of truth and the promoter of national wealth and weal:

> Whoever, in the pursuit of science, seeks after the immediate practical utility, may generally rest assured that he will seek in vain. All that science can achieve is perfect knowledge and a perfect understanding of the action of natural and moral forces.

Men of science form, as it were, an organized army labouring on behalf of the whole nation, and generally under its direction and expenses, to augment the stock of such knowledge as may serve to promote industrial enterprise, to adorn life, to improve political and social relations, and to further the moral development of individual citizens. (1893:24–28)

In other words, a perfectly disinterested army of scientists directed by the government will produce such knowledge that will promote economic, social, and human growth.[1]

The proposals that Helmholtz and others advanced were more than realized in the deployment of science for state and industrial purposes and the bureaucratization and industrialization of science. Legitimated by positivist philosophy, industrialized science is a symbiosis of science, finance, industry, and the new state. In the twentieth century, industrial science has become an essential part of economic production. "This change in the mode of production of science . . . developed over a long period, with some branches, such as chemistry, becoming industrialized in the nineteenth century, and some still to fully undergo the transformation, but from 1945 onwards industrialized science has been the dominant mode" (Rose and Rose 1979a:16).

The establishment of a knowledge practice in the new marketplace of disciplines required would-be practitioners to combine cognition and control— control of cognition by experts, and cognition for control of others. And they have been largely successful. The penetration of a scientific vocabulary into numerous social domains, and the refashioning of science itself to serve such hegemony, are expressed in scientific warfare, scientific management, the conquest of space, the exploitation or conservation of natural resources, and the regulation of people through demographic planning, urban design, criminology, organizational development, and psychotherapy. Bentham's Panopticon is an emblem for such controlled and thence self-controlling observation in both laboratory experiments and social institutions. Specialized academic disciplines became linked with specialized administrative spaces. "Psychiatry was joined with the asylum, and education with the school, economics with the government, and management science with the corporation" (Bledstein 1957:218–19). The maintenance of such specialized social spaces required the development of expert professionals with specialized training, uncommon knowledge, administrative ability, and a distinct culture and way of life.

Professionalization and institutionalization were part of the restructuring both of scientific fields and of the criteria for assessing scientific work within those fields. On the one hand, scientific work became increasingly politicized and bureaucratized, especially with the growth of specialized research institutes that operated largely outside the traditional normative constraints of the university (Elzinga 1985). On the other hand, the epistemological justifications for such works became increasingly "internalist," rationalistic, and idealistic. Scientists were assumed neither to have a material existence nor to require funds, social approval, and political support to conduct their research. All that counted in the official version of science were conjectures and refutations (Popper 1963). Even as positivist philosophy reified science as an ascetic, interest-free pursuit of ideal truth, however, research in the natural and social sciences was becoming more closely linked to politics through contract research. Often this link was established against the intentions and without the awareness of investigators themselves, who might continue to adhere to epistemologically and politically purist conceptions of their work. A physicist working on vortex turbulence in fluid dynamics, for example, might receive funding from the navy and the air force, as well as from the National Science Foundation, to build a wind tunnel to measure the microdynamics of air movements around a foil. Although the researcher might be inspired to solve theoretical problems that have occupied physicists since Newton, her governmental sponsors would be thinking of stealth submarines and supersonic missiles.

Thus, although "pure science" is divorced from "practical applications" at the ideological level, in the practice of university administrators, governmental leaders, and corporate elites, they are closely interwoven. Not only is most university research sponsored by external sources that justify their investments in terms of ultimate social and technical applications, but industry and government themselves invest in "pure science." For example, Arno Penzeas, a director of Bell Telephone Laboratories, won a Nobel Prize, and Bell Laboratories also supported the work of William Shockley, which led to a Nobel for Shockley and the commercial exploitation of microelectronics for Bell. In addition, the great majority of scientists work on directly utilitarian projects in corporate and governmental settings.

Because the technical applications of social scientific knowledge are far less obvious, investigators in these fields tried much harder than natural scientists to convince publics and patrons of the practical utility of their work. Only in this way could they justify the social investments necessary for their institutionalization in university chairs, university departments, and research centers. Such justifications of utility were couched in terms of broader political, economic, and cultural conditions—conditions that in turn help explain why the social sciences emerged when they did and how they came to have their particular ideological, cognitive, and stylistic orientations. Chief among these conditions was the emergence of the modern nation state, of industrial capitalism, and of psychological individualism. Roughly speaking, these conditions first occurred in Great Britain, then in France, and then in the United States, Germany, and Italy. In Italy, for example, the emergence and function of sociology can be understood in relation to the achievement of Italian national unity (Sola 1985:5; Wagner 1989). Much the same could be said for the activities of the Verein für Socialpolitik (Association for Social Policy) in early German social science and for many of the Durkheimians in France and their use of sociology as the "republican ideology" of the secular and democratic Third Republic against the resistance of older aristocratic and Catholic elites (Girson 1984; see Brown 1987:ch. 4; Clark 1973; Jarausch 1990; Weisz 1979).

In the United States, the meliorative and later statist bent of social science is not surprising given its origins in Protestant reformism and its emergence at a time when the country was undergoing enormous social upheavals (Vidich and Lyman 1985). The tremendous economic development and state centralization that began with the Civil War was accompanied by industrialization, urbaniza-tion, floods of immigration, and the emergence of what was called the social problem. The federal state that emerged after the Civil War had been captured by the new industrial capitalist class (Birnbaum 1969). Their efforts at repres-sion, combined with the racial and ethnic fragmentation of labor and the relative scope and success of capitalism and democracy, help explain why the United States never developed a large radical labor movement. Instead, the orientation of most people was toward piecemeal reform rather than institu-tional transformation, and the characteristic role of social scientists was to give voice to these elitist and middle-class yearnings (Manicas 1987:223).

Social reformers, funded directly by capitalist elites and only later through the state (Kolko 1967), adopted methodological individualism in their ap-proach to social research, especially in England and the United States. This development provided a bridge between political and epistemological individ-ualism, and inclined researchers to look for causes of social problems in individ-ual behavior or attitudes rather than in social structural forces and relations. In the view of the new social scientific professionals, the problem was not class conflict or oppression by dominant groups but the ignorance and weak morals of workers.

Examples of the convergence of political and intellectual interests abound today, with drug companies powerfully present in departments of molecular biology, chemistry, and medicine; the intelligence establishment, IBM, and a few major makers of computer chips dominating departments of computer science; and the Pentagon pervasive in physics (Soley 1995). Indeed, "anyone trained in physics who reads the Annual Report of the Secretary of Defense will recognize the essential ways in which progress in science has become linked to 'progress' in modern weapon systems" (Woollett 1980:109). As the costs of production are extremely high in these fields, influence both of "external" funders and of "internal" elites tends to be correspondingly high. Even in research universities where the core disciplines may be more or less intact, new departments and programs are almost always created in response to corporate and governmental needs and funding, with managers, politicians, and bureaucrats thereby shaping the intellectual agenda. For example, programs in chemistry, criminology, gerontology, or computer science engage in research and development consisting of little theoretically oriented research and much product- or service-oriented development.

Traditional disciplines also have been institutionalized by being instrumentalized. Sociology, for example, was unable to legitimate itself until, a half-century after its inception, a theoretical and methodological synthesis could be credibly claimed. The quantitative research techniques of Paul F. Lazarsfeld and the functionalist theorizing of Talcott Parsons were conjoined in Robert K. Merton's program of building middle-range theory. But this new cognitive capital had to be invested in research that patrons would pay for. Thus, while many sociologists heralded the intellectual maturation of their discipline, "it is hard to imagine that the institutional breakthrough would have been achieved without the political concomitant of placing sociology in the service of the modern welfare state" (Wagner and Wittrock 1990:13). In order to seem useful, sociologists had to examine "variables" that could be affected by politicians or bureaucrats. The discovery of a correlation between rates of urbanization and rates of capital investment, for example, is not very useful because political leaders in capitalist societies are not prepared to manipulate these variables. Instead, it would seem more fitting to study attitudes toward contraceptive devices, because attitudes are subject to influence by governmental programs of persuasion (Waitzkin 1968:410).

Through such adjustments toward "middle-range theory," many policy-oriented subfields developed within the social scientific disciplines. Thus, a typical sociology department in the United States might specialize in demographic studies, social deviance, and military sociology. Funding would likely be secured, respectively, from the Agency for International Development, the National Institute of Alcohol Abuse, and the Department of Defense. All the funded studies would perforce have an experimentalist design and an instrumental telos—that of increased efficiency of social policy and control. All also would be framed to contribute to the literature of the discipline, although by now that discipline would be so shaped by statist interests that it would be almost an extension of them.[2]

Economics provides another example of the institutionalization of knowledge and the rationalization of power. Economic research was institutionalized during the 1920s and 1930s in government agencies, universities, quasi-governmental commissions, and research institutes directly funded by the government. Among the research institutes are the Brookings Institute in the United States, the Institute für Wirtschaftsforschung in Austria, and the Institut de Conjoncture and Centre National de Recherche Scientifique in France (Wittrock, Wagner, and Wollmann 1991:48). The institutionalization of applied economics helped shape economics into a two-tiered field. On top is a relatively small, hierarchically centralized academic discourse with clear demarcations and high prestige. Beneath this is a large base of applied economic work with low academic prestige and little intellectual relevance (Whitley 1987). The top offers the bottom an aura of intellectual legitimacy; the bottom offers the top an image of utility. Only rarely do they meet in common discourse, but together they create expertise that is their joint source of social power.

In the United States and elsewhere, the social sciences provided an apparently rational means for advancing policy goals determined by others (Geiger 1986; Wagner et al. 1990). "Intentionally or not, all these fields have adapted their theoretical language and their research practices to bureaucratic-technological priorities. The hope appears to have been either that such restructured knowledge would lead to power, inside or outside the academy, or that there might at least be some space for free inquiry. The ironic result has been that even the most esoteric inquiry has been carried out in a research style already settled in advance by the apparatus" (Ash 1991).

In sum, in the twentieth century funding for science, at first by the government and later by corporations and foundations, has increased exponentially. This sponsorship was crucial in the growth and industrialization of contemporary disciplines and also in the shaping of their topics, their methods, and the very definition of science itself. The institutionalization of scientific disciplines has depended on their convincing nonscientific sponsors of their utility. In the process, these disciplines advanced their intellectual agendas and preserved their intellectual autonomy, but often only after little was left in the disciplines' agenda to be autonomous about. And through the same processes, state and corporate entities were rationalized, both ideologically and practically. Scientific experts in their institutionalized disciplines, and political economic elites in their nationalized institutions, mutually supported each other and largely removed themselves from accountability to broader democratic publics. Francis Bacon's aphorism "human knowledge and human power meet in one" has achieved an ironic fulfillment. Instead of liberating the potentials of men and women, knowledge has become the power of domination, the capacity to control and manipulate physical and human nature.

DEFENDING DISCIPLINARY DOMINATIONS

The early establishment and defense of science as a distinct cognitive and institutional domain required struggle with other knowledge practitioners, principally the practitioners and guardians of religion but also the keepers of magic (Tambiah 1989; Merton 1979; Greenfeld 1987). As new social classes and modes of production emerged in the nineteenth century, many new professions also were formed, often, as before, at the expense of the clergy (Geison 1983). As science came to be established as the hegemonic discourse in Western societies in the late nineteenth century, such competition between cognitive systems continued, but now within the system of academic disciplines itself. Disciplinary groups struggled over which were more scientific and which were to dominate particular intellectual and social territories.

This process of differentiation and competition has been called "boundary work" by students of academic organizations and professions. It involves not only maintaining the boundaries of one's own discipline through the social reproduction of practitioners but also defending or extending these boundaries in relation to other academic groups (Becher 1989; Gieryn 1983). This boundary work is seen in the use of such geographical metaphors for knowledge as field, realm, domain, territory, or frontier that knowledge workers map, annex, or explore. In Becher's (1989:36) interviews with practitioners, for example, "economics was said to have one common frontier with mathematics and another with political science; some trade relations with history and sociology; and a lesser measure of shared ground with psychology, philosophy and the law. Biology was portrayed as being bounded on the one side by mathematics and the physical sciences (especially physics, chemistry and physical geography) and on the other by the human sciences (in particular by psychology, anthropology and human geography)." Thus, as Gieryn (1983:783) noted, the landscape (or market) for academic knowledge "has with time been carved up into separate institutional and professional niches through continuing processes of boundary-work designed to achieve an apparent differentiation of goals, methods, capabilities and substantive expertise."

Such interdisciplinary competition for legitimate domination of territories is a central feature of modern professional organization. Hence, jurisdictional disputes between disciplines, and not only jurisprudential reasoning within them, is much of the ongoing organizing activity of academic life. The disciplines are based mainly within university departments and are also organized as national and international associations and networks. They change their shape, commitments, and relations with other disciplines over time, and they thus form an ecology or system of competition and alliances. Because "jurisdiction is a more-or-less exclusive claim . . . every move in one profession's jurisdiction affects those of others" (Abbott 1988:34). This process has varied from country to country depending on, among other factors, the strength and role of the state. In France, for example, a centralized state established or shaped most major educational institutions for the purpose of training government functionaries. Thus Emile Boutmy, the founder of the Ecole Libre des Sciences Politique, was forced to abandon his project for a scholarly political science and to turn the Ecole into a training center for administrators (Favre 1981; Wagner and Wittrock 1990:4). By contrast, relatively more autonomous professions proliferated in the more decentralized and market-oriented United Kingdom and, especially, United States.

Much of the competition between disciplines goes on within universities, for this is where the disciplines are mainly based, funded, and in direct proximity with each other. Thus chemistry and biology departments might compete for the inclusion of agronomy; the law and business schools might struggle for the teaching of accounting; biology and geography may fight for control of courses and programs in ecology. Dollars, students, programs, and budgeted positions are not only constituents of disciplines but also stakes in competition between them.

The strength of a discipline in relation to other disciplines partly depends on how well it disciplines its members. Indeed, this is much of what the term "discipline" means, both historically (as in monastic discipline or discipline in the classroom) and today through ceaseless professional socialization of more disciplined effort (exams; grades; tenure and promotion; peer reviews of journal submissions, grant proposals, and books; invitations to or exclusions from meetings and networks; and the like). On the one hand, self-discipline strengthens internal cohesion, boundaries, and development and thickening of that discipline's central paradigm; on the other hand, it also provides the political solidarity and intellectual resources for appropriating, translating, absorbing, and elaborating the accumulated intellectual capital of internal factions and external rivals (Collins 1996; Fuchs 1992). Such appropriation also depends on the relative external political support garnered by different disciplinary groups.

Physics and economics are examples of internally cogent fields with high consistency, even rigidity, in the socialization of their members to an overarching paradigm or general theory. Such strong disciplines typically tend toward an unreflective realist epistemology, a purely internal justification of their own practices (such as their jurisdiction over some "natural kind" or their unique theories and methods), and a generally "holier-than-thou" attitude toward disciplinary competitors (Fuller 1988:191). Even when their statements turn out to be false, they always remain within that discipline's definition of the realm of what *can* be true. By contrast, such weaker disciplines as anthropology, speech communication, geography, and literary studies are more internally divergent and open. They have more permeable boundaries, a looser knit, more divergent structure, and a less stable, more diverse theoretical apparatus (Becher 1989:37–38). Practitioners of these disciplines engage in much reflection on methods, epistemology, and the origin and direction of the field.

Shifts in the larger political economy can create shifts in disciplines by generating new markets, new intellectual capital, and new influences on the intellectual factions that have allied themselves with one or another non-academic source of support. Sociology, for example, although still a multi-paradigm science (Ritzer 1975), diminished its scope dramatically after 1950 in favor of market specialization, focused socialization, and greater disciplinary strength. "Classical" thinkers like Weber and Durkheim are still hailed as founding exemplars, but their projects for a comprehensive social scientific discipline that would include law, history, politics, and economics has been largely abandoned in favor of the middle-range theories and statistical positivism appropriate to interdisciplinary competition for market shares of research support in the new social welfare state.

I can now elaborate another aspect of my initial metaphor of knowledge production as akin to economic production, and of disciplinarity as cognitive monopolization. Economists distinguish natural and artificial monopolies.

Natural monopolies are those in which features inherent in the production process restrict admission to that market. High start-up costs, as in the automobile or mineral extraction industries, is an example of such a barrier to entry. Weber elaborated this Marxian idea of technological barriers to competition in his discussions of the relation of technology to bureaucratic concentration of control. For example, much as the invention of industrial machinery facilitated the move from decentralized artisan production to concentrated factory production, so the invention of expensive weaponry facilitated the move from decentralized feudal warfare to the concentration of lethality in bureaucratic national armies.

Perhaps similar processes influence intellectual production, so that "the particular kind of research technology used within a science will have an effect on the degree of concentration of power" (Collins 1975:22). Some disciplines have expensive means of intellectual production, such as the cyclotrons of particle physics and the radio telescopes of astronomy (Swatez 1970). In such fields the means of intellectual production are highly concentrated, and hence the fields tend to be hierarchic and bureaucratic in style, and more unified intellectually. They are industrialized science, where highly controlled access to the means of intellectual production yields a high degree of control of intellectual products exercised by those few persons who control the necessary technology. Organization tends to be bureaucratic and tasks predictable. Authority of position and persons becomes important in the maintenance of claims and assumptions, because an enormous accumulation of resources is required before one can ever begin to establish or challenge black boxes, let alone reopen them. "Two-dimensional polyacrylamide gel electrophoresis is not impossibly difficult, but it is very expensive" (Schrum 1988:399), and such high costs of research tend to concentrate cognitive power and authority. Moreover, because leaders of such disciplines also control the allocation of credit and blame (Chubin 1988), they tend to have reputations for scientific brilliance and impeccable integrity.

Physics is the exemplar of disciplines with conceptually integrated paradigms, high disciplinary autonomy, and extremely concentrated resources: "Workers in such organizations depend very closely on the elites who control reputations and resources. Task uncertainty is generally low because the elites are too powerful for alternative modes of work and deviant styles of interpretation to challenge the orthodoxy. As a result, work in physics is rather routinized, well-structured, and theoretically integrated. At the other extreme of the spectrum, there are 'fragmented adhocracies' [such as literary studies]. In such organizations, mutual dependence is low while task uncertainty is very high. This is so because reputations may be gained from a variety of audiences, and resources are widely dispersed. The style of work differs greatly from that in bureaucracies: it is less well-structured, more idiosyncratic, and rather localistic" (Fuchs 1992). Biochemistry stands between these two extremes. Biochemical labs are costly, but not so costly as cyclotrons, and so there are many more of them. Hence, there is less centralization of intellectual production and less theoretical closure than is the case in high-energy physics. Sociology is still less concentrated. But if nationally projectionable statistical survey research becomes more important and its costs (currently about $1 million per survey) increase, we can expect greater genre thickening, intellectual focusing, and hierarchic organization in that subfield. Mathematics usually requires little more than chalk and a blackboard as physical technology for intellectual production. Hence this discipline is characterized by a multiplicity of perspectives, a personalistic, anti-bureaucratic style, and virtually no interest in an overarching unified theory (Collins 1975, 1996; Hagstrom 1965).

In sum, high costs of intellectual production tend to yield more concentrated control of intellectual resources, more uniformity of products, greater elaboration of dominant paradigms, greater epistemological orthodoxy and realism, and more jurisdictional hegemony of that discipline. Like monopolies in general, however, strong disciplines can engender resentment, and for that reason they can be special targets of attack. Moreover, to the extent that cognitive concentration and hierarchy inhibit competition between both disciples and disciplines, they discourage intellectual innovation. An institutionally powerful discipline, for example, can more easily avoid innovation by suppressing cognitive dissonance, ignoring anomalies, or absorbing anomalies through minor modifications in peripheral parts of the central theory (Quine 1953:43; Hesse 1980:83–87). Such moves may also make that discipline intellectually sluggish and, hence, ripe for poaching or invasion.

Concentrated control of crucial means of production characterized the material technology of scientific research in the seventeenth century. Those who possessed a microscope, telescope, or air pump could engage in the Big Science of their time, which was limited to persons of means—that is, men of the upper class. This exclusiveness also had a literary counterpart insofar as the restricted access to instrumentation made public replications extremely rare and difficult. Hence the credibility of observers required the establishment of textual authority in relation to those who could read about but not directly observe what was described. The inexpensive literary technology that supported the expensive experimental technology included reporting unsuccessful experiments to show that one's observational neutrality was untainted by personal interests; a humbleness of authorial voice by letting the facts, or at least the mechanical artifacts, speak for themselves, as it were; and the avoidance of ornaments of style to show that Bacon's idols had not addled one's mind (see Shapin and Schaffer 1985; Pinnick 1994).

Another important aspect of disciplinary innovation or boundary breaking occurs through genre stretching. This is usually conducted by innovative persons at the center of a field who are in close contact with similarly well-placed and well-connected persons in their own field and other fields. Most creative scientists are at the core of a number of overlapping networks of communication, that is, where subfields of different disciplines intersect. Innovators who stretch across these genres seek to combine various resources into new hybrids, fragmenting older disciplines and creating mutant nondisciplines which, if successful, eventually become normal science (Dogan and Pahre 1990:83; Zuckerman 1977:86–88, 99ff; R. Collins 1989; Hagstrom 1965:48–51; Menard 1971:96; Fuchs 1993). Newton's work on universal gravitation, for example, created a new hybrid out of the astronomy of the Copernicans, the mechanics of the Gallileans, the magnetic theories of W. Gilbert, R. Hooke, and others, and the algebraic and geometric traditions synthesized by Descartes (Collins 1986). Similarly, for centuries biology consisted largely of cataloguing the animal and vegetable forms of life. Once biologists created links to the theory of evolution and the conceptions of protoplasm and the cell, however, the central topic shifted from "What are the forms of life?" to "How did the forms of life come into existence?" and biology was completely revitalized.

These examples suggest that creativity is not a matter of inventing ideas de novo so much as the combining of diverse intellectual materials, often from different disciplines, into new precisely cogent formulations that resolve important questions in one or another field and open up new lines of fruitful, fundable research. This kind of innovative science is what most of the ethnographies of science are about, and it is here, as well, that the constructivist processes of scientific practice are most evident. As Fuchs (1993) put it, "At the research frontiers, work is too uncertain and innovative for formal procedures to determine how work is actually to be carried out. These may, at a later date, be used to *rationalize* scientific practice for journal publications, public presentations, or Whiggish historical success stories. But such rules of methods are not available to prescribe the steps leading to scientific innovation."

Sheer numbers also play a role in defending divisions of scientific labor, career opportunities, and intellectual innovation. The division of scientific labor is not merely a specialization and exchange for greater efficiency of knowledge production. It also opens up greater possibilities for attaining professional honor and status (Haber 1991). Or, more precisely, the organizational changes that yield efficiencies and innovations in knowledge production are driven by the competitive desire for greater status mobility of scientists. In economic terms, private greed for honor yields the public good of knowledge.

When scholars were few in number, the amount of respected positions was relatively great in relation to the total number of participants. Moreover, such systems tended to be more personalistic and less bureaucratic. Universities, however, in their very success as homes for disciplines and dispensers of social status, have expanded into mass bureaucratic systems. In the United States in 1900, for example, "2 percent of each cohort of twenty-three-year-olds received a bachelor's or first professional degree, and 6 percent of *those* would have another degree in two years. . . . [By contrast], in 1970, one-quarter of each cohort of twenty-three-year-olds received a bachelor's or first professional degree; one-third of these would have a second professional degree in two years" (Abbott 1988:209–10). University education has expanded still further since then, and with this has come an expansion of academic disciplines. Academic associations now include hundreds of thousands of members, making top or even highly respected positions much scarcer in relation to the mass of professors whose status may be ranked in terms of them.

This relative decline in the possibilities for attaining professional honor has found two solutions: specialization within existing disciplines, and creation of new hybrids at their intersections. Both specialty areas and disciplinary hybrids soon become status-granting communities themselves. Whether specialization or hybridization occurs is influenced by the relative dynamism of a given field both intellectually and financially. In disciplines where internal intellectual innovation and external funding are relatively static, more top positions can be created through the proliferation of subspecialties that deal with particular topics or applications, that produce their own local elites, and that work within the discipline's core paradigm. Such specialization is a way to create new opportunities for status mobility and "to avoid or restrict competition by claiming a new area of research as intellectual property, without the high risks of challenging the paradigmatic integrity of the larger field" (Fuchs 1993; see Hagstrom 1965:79, 1974:44; Crane 1972:38, 70; Merton 1973:330). Sociology of gender, of health, of organization, of development, of the military, and so on, are examples of such subspecializations, all characterized by orthodox methods and middle-range theory.

Conversely, in frontier science, or when new external constituencies develop, the tendency is to create new academic genres. Microbiology, neurolinguistics, cognitive science, feminism, and social studies of science are examples. All these hybrids were initiated with new constituencies, new social issues, or new sources of funds, and newly framed questions, newly combined methods, or newly created paradigms. The creation of agricultural chemistry, fluid dynamics, and behavioral psychology also provide examples of innovation through hybridization. Agricultural chemistry emerged about 1840 from a confluence of the mature methodological capital of organic chemistry and the socioeconomic problem of feeding a growing urban population. "It was not a product of problems internal to the research programme of organic chemistry, but rather an upshot of . . . external necessity" (Bôhme et al. 1983:15). Similarly, fluid mechanics is an outgrowth of hydrodynamics and the need for a theory of their application to aircraft construction. Likewise, at the end of the first decade of the twentieth century, psychology was a "colonial outpost" of philosophy— that is, a minor specialization of a quiescent discipline. Early in the twentieth century, however, psychologists translated philosophic questions into behavioral ones, formed alliances with experimental physiology, and garnered new external clients who sought new means of social control. Through these moves, psychology, a specialization in philosophy, fragmented into a new, rival discipline (Wilson 1990).

Both of the adaptations discussed here—specialization into subareas or fragmentation into hybrids—can occur simultaneously within the same discipline. Generally, however, "democratic" or egalitarian fields with less concentration of intellectual capital tend to generate subspecialties, whereas more "elitist," hierarchic fields tend to create new hybrids.

My analysis in this chapter draws on sociological theory of organizations and professions, ethnomethodological and ethnographic studies of science, and historical political economy. In this it also shows how Kuhn's early pathbreaking work has been radically extended. Kuhn (1972) illuminated key aspects of scientific organization and innovation with his idea of paradigms in normal and revolutionary science. The discussions in this section, following the many thinkers I cited, shift these terms in several ways. First, I have extended the concept of paradigm from its excessively cognitive meaning to include the practices and politics of intellectual production in particular fields. Second, I have shifted Kuhn's excessively "internalist" theory of scientific change to focus on the interpenetrations of "internal" and "external," which often become a single network or process. Third, I have stretched the diachronic or sequential narrative implied by Kuhn's concepts to a more synchronic view that is sensitive to the variety of activities, both "normal" and "revolutionary," that go on simultaneously within and across disciplines and paradigms. Finally, I have suggested that significant, albeit nonrevolutionary, changes occur within normal sciences, such as specialization or fragmentation, that are not accounted for in Kuhn's formulation.

THE INSTITUTIONALIZATION OF KNOWLEDGE THROUGH THE RATIONALIZATION OF POWER

An apparent paradox has become evident in our discussion of the institutionalization of science: the ideology of modern science (its epistemological purity as expressed in positivist philosophy of science) contradicts the actual practice of science (its massive involvement in and dependence on corporate and statist interests). This contradiction can also be formulated as a practical problem: How can one simultaneously maintain both the cognitive legitimacy and autonomy of science *and* the instrumental utility of science to the elites upon whom the institutional practice of science and the privileges of scientists depend? I believe that this question has several useful answers. The first is that the tension between autonomy and utility cannot be (fully) resolved because it is inherent in the conflict between the instrumentalizing interest of patrons and theorizing practice of scientists. A second response is that this tension is unimportant because the real utility of science is ideological. In a society in which formal rationality is itself a form of legitimation, the articulation of policies in terms of scientific findings is a way to legitimate them, regardless of the precise fit, or lack of fit, between such findings and the policies that are announced in their name. In this view, science also helps to suppress challenges to the elites who control the hegemonic scientific discourse. "For example, the nuclear power industry assures us that nuclear power is safe and cheap; nuclear scientists have said so, and they know" (Diesing 1992:214; Dickson 1984:323). Moreover, if people living downwind from nuclear plants hire their own scientists to show that nuclear power is both dangerous and expensive (if the "externalities" are considered), this challenge can easily descend into a "duel of experts" from which citizens are excluded and which the power companies, being wealthier and more focused, will almost always win. Science in this sense is politics by other means, and as such its truth value depends on its utility, not the reverse. Many studies of the disutilities of science in practice, and of the nonscientific sources of technological innovation, support this conclusion (see Weiss 1977; Weiss and Bucuvalas 1980; Formaini 1990).

Another, quite different interpretation of the tension between the autonomy and utility of science, which will be taken up in more detail in chapter 9, is that the utility of science depends on its autonomy. This is because only with the autonomy to pursue a program of basic scientific research will a discipline be able to accumulate enough intellectual capital to be invested in any practical project. Further, the "external" influences on science today affect not only choice of topic or practical uses but also the methodological and theoretical character of basic research. That scientific research is externally funded is usually reconciled with the ideal of autonomy by asserting a distinction between the development of theories and the deployment of findings for practical results (applied research). I have argued (along with Bôhme et al. 1983:5), however, "that it is possible for *theoretical* developments themselves to be subject to social influences and even political planning." External influences can be seen not only in the selection and definition of research problems but also in the specification of explanatory ideals and limiting conditions—that is, in what constitutes an adequate analysis beyond which it is not fruitful to proceed. This does not mean that the sciences are reduced to mere extensions of ideologies or political interests. On the contrary, the possibility of shaping inquiry in these basic ways suggests the success of such efforts to develop theoretical knowledge. In other words, the very success of the sciences not only makes them more socially relevant but also makes them more susceptible to social guidance. Thus the more a discipline is cognitively developed, the easier it becomes to steer the further development of its theoretical knowledge. This in fact is precisely the project of the "social epistemology" proposed by Fuller (1988) and others.

Another solution to tensions between autonomy and utility is not to socially guide science but to scientifically guide society or, in effect, to bring the context of investigation and the context of application closer together. One easily recognized way to accomplish this is to design the context of investigation to simulate the context of application. Thus ecobiologists might design microsystems as their laboratories that are metonyms for the larger context of application. Similarly, the psychological laboratory might be designed, consciously or not, as the ideal prison, army, classroom, or factory to which its findings may later be applied.

Alternately, however, the domain of application can be redesigned to match the laboratory. This way is much less obvious, but it may in fact be more characteristic. In modern rationalized societies, actual changes in practices are routinely transferred from the artificial laboratory setting to an increasingly controlled and artificial outside world. "In other words, the application of knowledge is possible only insofar as an artificial construction, derived from the investigative situation, is imposed on the natural [or social] world. This is what happens in the construction of industrial plants or in the adoption of sterile conditions in medicine, for example" (Danziger 1990b:189).

Developing this thinking further, one might even suggest that the very difference between the "inside" and "outside" of scientific inquiry is exactly what successful laboratories destabilize or undo (Latour 1983:143; see Callon 1981a). Scientific investigative practices can become new social practices. As such they are a source of power, even though, and partly because, this is rarely made explicit. For example, "it is clear that in political terms the influence of Pasteurian laboratories reached further, deeper, and more irreversibly since they could intervene in the daily details of life—spitting, boiling milk, washing hands—and at the macroscale—rebuilding sewage systems, colonizing countries, rebuilding hospitals—without ever being clearly seen as a stated political power" (Latour 1983:158).

Thus the application of laboratory findings is made possible by turning the context of application itself into a kind of laboratory. A further example of this is the standardization of measures discussed earlier. Initially such standardization was fostered in order to facilitate common and consistent discourse within the scientific community. Standardization helped remove the "subjective" dimensions of observation and reporting and thus enabled an impersonal, numerical common language within that scientific community—a language more precise, if more narrow, than lay discourse, a language that helped create scientists as a community, and later as a guild, of experts. But such standardization, as it became more universal outside the contexts of investigation, enabled the application of investigative findings to the world beyond the laboratory. Indeed, the extension of standard scientific measurements into general public standards of measurement was a precondition for the extension of what was invented in the lab to what could be discovered in the world. As Latour (1983:167) put it, "Most of the work done in the laboratory would stay there if the principal physical constants could not be made constant everywhere else. Time, weight, length, wavelength, etc., are extended to ever more localities in ever greater degrees of precision. Then and only then, laboratory experiments can be brought to bear on problems occurring in factories, the tool industry, economics, or hospitals. But if you just try in a thought experiment to extend the simplest law of physics 'outside,' without first having extended and controlled all the main constants, you just could not verify it, just as it would have been impossible to know the existence of anthrax and to see the efficacy of the vaccine without the health statistics" (see Aronowitz 1988:299).

In sum, science was institutionalized in the modern West through a number of different but closely interrelated processes. First was the formation and professionalization of disciplines. This involved the creation of standardized methods, procedures, and language, and the codification of a field of knowledge and the certification of certain practitioners through communal rites as bona fide users of that disciplinary discourse.

Another concurrent form of institutionalization was the rise of research universities. Because this involved considerable resources from outside the disciplines, it required practitioners to assert (if not demonstrate) the utility of their knowledge to would-be patrons—usually corporate or statist elites. Universities at Oxford, Paris, and Bologna had existed since the Middle Ages with ecclesiastical or noble patronage. But *research* universities like the Ecole Polytechnique (founded in 1795), the University of Berlin (1810), and, in America, Johns Hopkins University (1876), Clark University (1887), and the University of Chicago (1892), were the creations of modernizing statesmen and industrialists (see Clark 1973; Geiger 1986; Geison 1983; Manicas 1987; Shinn 1980; Veysey 1965; and Olson and Voss 1979). As scientific investigation was industrialized and came to depend on large-scale patronage, these and other modern research universities became the major self-policing recipients of funds for scientific investigations. Even though the interests and pursuits of such universities were much broader than pure research, their reputations at least provided a crude indicator by which corporate and governmental investments in research could be assessed. Moreover, the diversity of types and functions of American universities led to greater competition between similar specialized areas of excellence within universities (Ben-David and Zloczower 1962).

A third form of institutionalization was the creation of scientific-administrative organizations such as specialized laboratories, institutes, policy research centers, and think tanks. The earliest major examples are the national statistical institutes and centers for economic survey research (Whitley 1987). Through such institutions, and through the research university itself, the new scientific and professional disciplines were linked to politics through contract research, emergent informal networks of political and academic personnel, and new institutions and mechanisms for coordination and monitoring of developments in science and in science policy (Wagner 1989).

All these forms of the institutionalization of science realized science as a form of power. Not only was the world modeled within scientific experiments, but soon the scientific experiment became a model for the world. More and more of modern life has come to depend on science. But in order to apply and exploit the inventions of the laboratory, social reality outside the laboratory has become more like a controlled experiment. The institutionalization of science and the rationalization of power were mutually authorizing, but only because institutional power had become rationalized and because science was already constituted by power.

Chapter 7 Poetics, Politics, and Professionalization in the Rise of American Psychology

The Sea of Faith
Was once, too, at the full. . . .
But now I only hear
Its melancholy, long, withdrawing roar . . .
Matthew Arnold, Dover Beach

We live surrounded by an enormous body of persons who are most definitely interested in the control of states of mind, and incessantly craving for a sort of psychological science which will teach them how to act. What every educator, every jail-warden, every doctor, every clergyman, every asylum-superintendent, asks of psychology is practical rules. Such men care little or nothing about the ultimate philosophic grounds of mental phenomena, but they do care immensely about improving the ideas, dispositions, and conduct of the particular individuals in their charge.
William James (1892:148)

Science is not only speculative activity supported by technical equipment and methods but also practices of controversy, persuasion, and institutional power. Logic and philosophy provide cognitive ethics for science, but they hardly describe or explain it. By contrast, an approach that simultaneously addresses poetics and politics, and that views logic as a method of persuasion, can reveal homologies between stylistic and social practices and thereby illuminate relations between knowledge, power, and legitimation. That is the goal of this chapter—to show how, in one discipline, the creation and transmission of knowledge re-created and transmitted forms of power, and how power shaped and deployed this form of knowledge.

Just as economics can be transcoded into linguistics (see chapter 2), so scientific discourse can be understood in terms of political economy. In the previous chapter I developed this metaphor of knowledge production as akin to economic production, noting that the production of scientific truth is characterized by specialization, institutionalization, defense of territory, and service to elites. This is also the case for psychology in its rise to professional and scientific status in the United States. Unlike early twentieth-century physicists or chemists, however, American psychologists first had to demonstrate their "scientificity"—their cognitive worthiness for the privilege and prestige that had already been achieved by natural scientists. To make their incipient discipline conceivable and believable, the new psychologists shaped it to appear consistent with the newly dominant scientific habitus. This effort was encouraged by another transformation that accompanied industrialization and the rise of a capitalist elite—the replacement of unquestioned religious authority by secular materialism and a philosophy, rather than a theology, of the subject (see Konig 1987; Ferrarotti 1981; Wagner 1989). The secular modern habitus, and especially the centrality of the secular individual, was a condition of the plausibility of modern psychology.

Exceptions could be readily found to the ideal typification sketched so far. Nonetheless, to the three "ingredients" noted in chapter 6—specialization, service to elites, and institutionalization—we can now add a fourth: consistency with the scientific habitus. I will discuss these dimensions as they interacted in the creation of the discipline and practice of psychology in the United States.

PROFESSIONALIZATION AND THE RISE OF THE NEW PSYCHOLOGY

Although the history of psychology can be traced back through centuries of speculations about the mental life of humans, it is commonly accepted that something significant occurred in the period from about 1875 to 1935. From the standpoints of both historians and contemporary participants in Europe and the United States, certain recurring questions about human nature shifted from the spheres of theology and philosophy "to a domain of positive knowledge: the formation of psychology as a coherent and individuated scientific discourse" (Rose 1985:3). To understand this event, we need not only a history of ideas but also an analysis of the practices, techniques, and institutions that made such ideas thinkable and which, in turn, were influenced by those very ideas (Rose 1985). Some of these practices of representation can be seen in the style and serviceability of American psychology during the twentieth century. American psychologists defined themselves and distinguished their discipline in a way that served the dominant classes. These moves were successful in making psychology into a hegemonic discourse and in securing the professionalization, prestige, and privilege of psychologists.

In the colleges of nineteenth-century America, philosophy and psychology were often taught by the college president, who was frequently an ordained Protestant minister. The courses emphasized moral philosophy; their aim was to use philosophy to form character and produce educated, useful members of society. "Such training was not necessarily opposed to scientific endeavor. Rather, many of these educators promulgated Scottish common-sense realism and a Baconian, inductivist ideal of science, and tried to combine the latest findings from the German laboratories with their moral teachings" (Ash 1983:146; see Bozeman 1977; Hoeveler 1980). Although many of the first American laboratory psychologists had gone to Germany to learn such experimental techniques, they did not forget the injunction to be useful. G. Stanley Hall, William James, and James Mark Baldwin, for example, all carried out extensive empirical research even while insisting that their results did not undermine either philosophy or religion. Instead, they asserted that psychology offered a way of reconciling the moral consciousness demanded by religion with the experimental science demanded by the theory of evolution (Ash 1983:6; Bjork 1983:6; Marsden and Longfield 1992; Rieber 1980:103–23).

William James was the first to argue successfully for the creation and institutionalization of a new psychology that would help him and many others resolve personal conflicts concerning religion and science, spiritualism and materialism, and the movement of society in general from a more theological to a more scientific orientation (Bjork 1983; Karier 1986; Leary 1980, 1992; Morawski 1982). Thus, "when Sanford (1892:141) wrote that training in experimentation is a means to infuse 'new vigor' and provide 'healthy and virile' exercise, he was referring to a correct scientific attitude *and* a desirable psychological character. In Victorian culture, the vision of science as a noble activity—as a way to discipline the mind to be rational and pure—was not only a professional ideology but also a means to reduce the tensions between science and religious traditions" (Morawski 1988:xi). In the same spirit, the many self-help manuals of the period stressed that asceticism was essential for becoming a professional (Bledstein 1957:156–57, 216–17).

University presidents were particularly active in the various campaigns for reform and control, and they consistently linked these campaigns with scientific expertise. Harvard's president, Charles William Eliot, sought to use the public health services to battle promiscuity and protect the white race. Similarly, William Rainey Harper, the first president of the University of Chicago, persuaded John D. Rockefeller, its founder, that a research university in Chicago would be a greater force for social improvement than could be the small-town Baptist schools that had previously been candidates for Rockefeller's largess (Goodspeed 1916; Storr 1966; Veblen 1965).

Institutionalization of the new psychology involved not only conflicts of religious and scientific ideas, however, but also the local politics of various universities that often reflected shifts and conflicts in the larger political economy. The growing commercial, industrial, and financial classes successively came to produce and control more and more of the new wealth that was being created in America after the Civil War. These newly rich groups sought to break the established aristocratic monopolies (for example, the law) and to secure means for their own advancement and security, and they seized on the university as their leading institution. Now led by men epitomizing middle-class origins, conduct, and values, the universities established new norms and practices such as disciplines, grading, the elective system to the academic ranks, and the idea of academic administration. During the forty-year presidency of Charles William Eliot, for example, Harvard grew from sixty to six hundred faculty members and introduced or adopted all the new practices just mentioned (Hariman 1989:214–17; Bensman and Vidich 1987; Veblen 1965:104, 106, 129, 214; Marsden and Longfield 1992).

William James's experience at Harvard reveals the emergence of psychology within this context. James was an excellent teacher in the "modern manner" favored by Charles Eliot, and he earned the endorsement of Harvard's overseers by showing that the new psychology could be used to discredit radical materialism while still claiming a scientific status for itself.[1] Later James was allowed to teach "physiological psychology" as an undergraduate course in natural history in the fall of 1876. In 1890 James published his soon-to-be-classic *Principles of Psychology*, which provided an exemplar work for the new psychology as a scientific discipline. Although James's writings were important in the struggle to legitimate and institutionalize American psychology, his lasting impact on official psychology was slight (Johnson and Henley 1990). Indeed, his open-spirited, philosophically reflective brand of psychology is in stark contrast to the view that ultimately prevailed (Myers 1986).

The next generation of practitioners had more interest in measuring and experimenting than in history or philosophy. Psychology became a science in the sense described by Ravetz—"a special sort of craft work which operates on intellectually constructed objects" (1971:116). Key to the construction of these new knowledge objects were experimentation and quantification. Practitioners of the new psychology "became decisively committed to specific practical methods of data production. The application of these methods became the special characteristics of the field and distinguished it from everyday psychology as well as from its own intellectual predecessors. By the use of these practical methods, modern psychology created a new world of psychological objects that increasingly defined the field and to which any purely theoretical developments were forced to accommodate" (Danziger 1990a:4).

The emerging discipline of psychology made two other shifts toward numeracy, and hence scientificity, during several decades before and after 1900. "First, a wide range of psychological phenomena (for example, perception, intelligence, personality, and learning) were fundamentally *redefined* to make their basic properties quantifiable. Second, psychological phenomena that resisted quantitative treatment (for example, forms of consciousness, spirituality, and will) were *jettisoned* from the domain of legitimate empirical psychology. As a consequence, psychology shifted in the American context from being a discipline which seemed inherently qualitative to one that relied almost exclusively on quantitative approaches" (Hornstein 1988:2). At the same time, these practices served, shaped, and reflected the needs of growing bureaucracies of economic production and social control.

The new psychologists also pushed aggressively for institutionalization of psychology as a distinct academic discipline. The new practices of experimentation and calculation served these efforts by demonstrating crucial differences between laboratory psychology and either "mental philosophy" or physics or physiology, or the mundane situations in which everyday psychological knowledge was acquired. Wilhelm Wundt, for example, insisted, "As an experimental science physiological psychology aims at a reformation of psychological research, which in importance does not rank lower than the change which the introduction of the experiment caused in the thinking of physical science. . . . For so-called self-observation may be presented as observation only with certain essential restrictions and cannot at all lay claim to exactness" (1908:4 in Strasser 1963:12). Through such rhetorical moves the experimental method became a boundary marker between psychology and philosophy. But lest experimentation push psychology into the field of physics or physiology, Wundt trained his subjects to distinguish sensations from the physical objects "inferred" from them—for example, they might say "round shiny presence" instead of "apple." The philosophically dubious separation between sensations and cognition, and the artifacticity of the facts generated by Wundt's method, were little noted. What counted was the establishment of the disciplinary autonomy of psychology.[2] Indeed, the very artificiality of laboratory situations helped to legitimate "knowledge claims emanating from this source, and the imposition of a numerical form on otherwise trivial knowledge gave it an apparent significance with which lay knowledge could not compete. Replacing ordinary language with jargon helped too" (Danziger 1990a:185; see Koch 1985; Fuller 1988).

This "professional generation," as the historian Dorothy Ross (1979) called them, still asserted the potential social value of their work, but they now did this in the context of secular education rather than religious formation. In this they gave formal expression to the progressive views of the emergent middle and upper classes, that science and technology could stem the tide of social disorder brought on by immigration, industrialization, and urbanization. Just as college and university presidents had stressed social utility in their appeals to rich patrons, so enterprising professors made the same appeals to them. This was a key selling point with senior administrators "who had the power to establish new professorships, departments and laboratories, and with the businessmen who sat on the boards of trustees that appointed the presidents" (Ash 1983:147; see Ross 1979).

Many new psychologists sought not only to establish their own discipline but also to discredit their competitors, who at that time were mainly psychical researchers and philosophers. If the new psychologists were to become the acknowledged authorities on mind and action, they had to make certain that theirs was the language that would be heard. Thus, they publicly discredited and privately appropriated psychical research. Moreover, although parapsychology is a specialized discourse, its nonmaterialist presuppositions excluded it from the dominant scientific habitus and thus contributed to its marginalization (McClenon 1981; Brown 1982). The new psychologists extended their purview to unconscious states of mind, and they advanced theories that were remarkably similar to those of the rejected psychical researchers. As

William James (1902:501) observed, "occult phenomena" were introduced and "legitimated" within psychology "under newly found scientific titles."

In 1870s psychology was still a "colonial outpost" of philosophy, respected only as "introduction to all specific philosophic questions" and as an aide in the coming reconstruction of society (Dewey 1886). Soon, however, innovations in psychology were inducing "a change in the method and *personnel* of philosophic study" to a point that "to criticize these new developments at all, one must have gone through physiological training" (James, cited in Wilson 1990:79). Toward the end of the nineteenth century the prestige of science increased, the success of experimental physiology provided a model, and elite patrons became ready to finance research that seemed useful in addressing the emerging social problems of industrial society.

The concepts of certain types of psychology were soon made amenable to "scientific," experimentalist laboratory techniques of inquiry. This scientization of psychology led to its fragmentation into a new discipline that competed with philosophy for university resources, public patronage, and disciplinary power. In 1892, G. Stanley Hall organized the American Psychological Association, which played a key role in the institutionalization of the new psychology. The purpose of the association was to assert the existence and jurisdiction of a special field, to organize and articulate common goals of members, and to promote the scientific and political strength of the discipline (Camfield, cited in Wilson 1990:108). From the beginning, the APA was presented not simply as an alternate professional association but as the only organization that could certify individuals as bona fide psychologists. Together with their journals and various graduate programs, membership in the APA gave the new psychologists a decided advantage over their competitors. An image of scientificity was also promoted through disassociation with psychical research, a distancing from philosophy, and official alliances with the American Society of Naturalists in 1895 and with the American Association for the Advancement of Science in 1902. Proof of experimental skills and dozens of hours of training in statistics were requirements for calling oneself a psychologist, or at least for gaining entry into most professional organizations (Morawski 1988:xi). Quantification not only helped distinguish the emerging discipline from philosophy, psychical research, and "amateur" psychology but also allied it with science.[3] The laboratory itself became a metaphor for scientificity and only later a source of literal science. The first psychological laboratories in America were started in the 1870s. There were eighteen laboratories by 1882 and forty-eight by 1904 (Garvey

1929). Yet these laboratories were emblems of modern science more than places of scientific research. Thus the fact that they were used mainly to conduct demonstrations or train graduate students did not diminish their importance in enhancing the status, autonomy, and patronage of a psychology that now seemed truly a part of experimental science (Wilson 1990:100–103; O'Donnell 1979). Through quantification, objectification, and experimentalism, questions that psychology shared with philosophy in the nineteenth century—such as the nature of mind, the structure of consciousness, and the relation of mind and body—became less important than numerical and experimental *methods*. Indeed, as these methods began to limit and guide the range of questions that psychology could properly address, psychologists increasingly argued that they were not in fact investigating the same phenomena as philosophers. As Kuo (1924:427) said, "Any controversy in psychology must be capable of promoting experimental researches so that the issue can be settled in the laboratory, or it must at least have some particular value for laboratory procedure. Otherwise there is no justification for the existence of any such controversies or problems in the science." Such demarcations helped to define psychology in America as a distinct science and, with this, to support a strong claim on university positions and resources for psychologists (Hornstein 1988:18).

THE POETICS OF PROFESSIONALISM IN THE NEW PSYCHOLOGY

To foster their professionalization within the broad habitus of mechanism and instrumental control, the new psychologists needed to tell likely stories about mind and action, and to bring these stories into systematic coherence with one another and with the practical activities of research and application (Leary 1992; Gergen 1990:282). Many of the analogies and metaphors that shaped these stories were firmly established even before 1920. Thus Alexander Bain (1872) described the learning process in terms of "tracks" and "turning off steam," and William McDougall (1908) spoke of the instincts of organisms as the fires of a steam engine. Psychological language in general moved from explicitly metaphorical to insistently literal conceptualizations of phenomena. The terms "stimulus" and "response," for example, soon were taken by virtually all psychologists as objective and neutral in the description and explanation of behavior. Thus Zajonc (1965, 1980) argued that the mere presence of another member of the same species (the stimulus) will arouse an organism (the response), whether these organisms be cockroaches or persons. What occurred, then, was the importation into the social realm of the argot of animal experimentation, chiefly from the reflexological work of Ivan Pavlov (1928). "Persons" became "organisms"; their activities became "responses"; their life situations were transformed into "stimulus conditions." As E. C. Tolman (1932) said, "Personally . . . I am suspicious of . . . verbal reports. I prefer to try to work out psychology with the aid of more gross forms of behavior. My motto for the present is: 'Rats, no men.'" The stimulus-response metaphor and the associated practices of laboratory manipulation and control became most pronounced at the Institute for Human Relations at Yale University. Clark Hull, around whom the Institute largely revolved, was primarily an animal experimentalist. Yet he and his colleagues extended the language of the learning laboratory to treatments of human aggression (Dollard et al. 1939), personality formation (Dollard et al. 1950), communication and persuasion (Hovland, Janis, and Kelley 1953), and other domains. Thus the psychological deus ex machina became the biological machina ex deo, a new metaphor for human interaction.

These images were not merely decorative metaphors. Instead they fit and shaped their psychological theories and also had a social or ideological function. That is, metaphors of the human psyche as a steam engine, telephone exchange, computer, or cockroach operate within social relations of power and domination. The stimulus-response metaphor, for example, encouraged the essentialization of persons as self-contained individuals (Sampson 1977). Similarly, the metaphor of rats and other nonhuman animals as human eliminates agency and reflective consciousness from consideration. To the extent that such metaphors become literal prototypes for the functioning of the human mind or behavior, people assume that the organization of social life in which the metaphor operates is a reflection of a nonmetaphoric human nature and not a rhetorical creation (Danziger 1990b:350; see Lakoff 1987:183–84). Metaphors that are absolutized and universalized in this way become myths that turn culture into nature.

Thus metaphors are not only cognitive and poetic constructions but also part of practical discourse and programs. Metaphors not only invite us to *think* about the world in a certain way; they also invite us to *act* in terms of certain implied assumptions (Danzinger 1990:351; see Schon 1979). This can be seen in psychologists' understanding of perception, central to any theory of mind, as a process that is ethically and politically neutral. Drawing on Cartesian and Baconian ideas of a cogito that is autonomous of the fact world that surrounds it, the new psychologists took perception to be a one-way process whereby value-free data from the surrounding environment are collected and organized by an atomized human organism. Just as biologists had until recently assumed, for simplicity's sake, that life adapts to an essentially passive environment, so psychologists assumed that the senses are passive mechanisms adapted to an environment of random events. The interior human "mind" or "subject" is kept apprised of these random happenings in the exterior "objective" world by the sense organs, which were seen as mechanical structures that register whatever discrete bits of sensory data with which they come into contact and then transfer these bits into the nervous system, where these separate sensations are built up, step by step, into a representation of the external world. It is this internal representation that is ultimately viewed and given meaning by the innermost "mind" of the perceiver.

This is the model of perception described by the founders of modern scientific psychology toward the end of the nineteenth century (e.g., Gibson 1979; Reed and Jones 1982), and despite many revision and qualifications, it still underlies most of the scientific discourse of our time. Within this account, meaning and value are assumed to be secondary, derivative phenomena that result from the internal association of external facts that have no meaning in themselves. Such a theory of perception accords with the positivist habitus in which truth is of the mind and of the world, but no longer in God's *word* nor, for that matter, in any linguistic or intersubjective practice.

Why was this model taken by modern Western peoples so literally and so loyally? One reason is that it describes perception as we must conceive it if we are to continue the positivist program of instrumental manipulation of people and nature without hindrance of reasoned ethical restraint (Abram 1985:5–6). Given these commitments, American psychology advanced a view that emphasized "control, prediction, and classification, rather than personal freedom, spontaneity, and individuality" (Hornstein 1988:24). Approaches to the study of mind and perception that differed from statistical positivism were cast out, the boundaries of the discipline were jealously guarded, and the possible impact of alternative models of psychological reality and scientific practice were thereby kept to a minimum (Danziger 1990a:194).

This social role and ideological orientation of the new psychologists had their counterpart in the anti-rhetorical rhetoric and the scientistic use of language. For example, the objectivistic language of experimental reports stripped the identities of participants ("subjects") to suit intellectually idealized ends. By presenting results in highly formulaic language and organization, experimental reports created the illusion that these results were "not really the products of social interaction among particular persons in historical time, but instead were the manifestation of abstract transpersonal and transhistorical processes"

(Danziger 1985:51; see Wexler 1983:109). Such depersonalization and abstraction were intended to render psychological phenomena compatible with science and, thence, to enable psychology to serve as an instrument of social betterment. With this justification, animals were substituted for humans in experiments, the results of which were then generalized to all human conduct; subjects' viewpoints in experiments and reports were denigrated, and quantification was substituted for judgment. This method did not explicitly advance a particular political ideology. Rather, it masked its central concern with control by silencing the moral and social, and presenting a dehistoricized, depoliticized "environment" as the context of people's thinking and action (Stam 1987:147; Venn 1984:119–52).

These tendencies are visible in such behaviorist metaphors as Tolman's mazes, Hull's machines, and Skinner's selection by consequences and his use of pigeons to stand for persons. Tolman (1926:369) stated that "the world for philosophers, as for rats, is, in the last analyses, nothing but a maze of discrimination-manipulation possibilities." Similarly, Hull (1927–1928:206) felt "quite sure that all kinds of action, including the highest forms of intelligent and reflective action and thought, can be handled from the purely materialistic and mechanistic standpoint." Such root metaphors not only helped shape psychological theory, methods, and experimental routines; they also influenced the reception and use of psychology among broader publics (see Smith 1986; Leary 1991a; Soyland 1994).

One illustration of this power of prose is the unreflective and mystifying rhetoric surrounding Cattell's concept of "mental testing." Cattell drew his original metaphor from the "anthropometry" of Francis Galton, which Cattell reframed as "psychometry mental testing" and described in terms of social doctoring and human engineering, two fields in which modern science has most clearly proven its worth. From these initial metaphors "an entire rhetoric of abnormal and clinical psychology was elaborated. As doctors tested for disease and engineers for stress, so psychologists came to think of themselves, and presented themselves, as being capable of testing for intelligence or treating insanity or any number of psychological properties. As portrayed in their own literalistic rhetoric, these psychometricians were not simply *like* doctors and engineers; they *were* doctors and engineers, testing 'patients' for 'mental disease' and designing 'solutions' for their 'mental stress.' More significantly, a whole set of practical routines were tied to this conceptual framework—routines that still direct the professional activities of many psychologists" (Leary 1991a:135–36).

This type of language and action was appropriate for a legal-rational bureau cratic order as described by Weber, in which people are conceived of either as functionaries following rules (like experimenters following methods) or as subordinate and passive things that are media or subjects of these functions. In military contexts, for example, the term "debriefing" eliminated active agents through the impersonal passive voice. "Instead of saying 'the pilot reported,' 'the pilot briefed the intelligence officer,' or even 'the pilot was interrogated by the colonel,' the military would say, 'the pilot was debriefed.' Thus the pilot is never allowed to become someone of special status (either high or low) because of something that he has done. Instead, the pilot is someone who proceeds through (that is, 'is processed by') the system" (Harris 1988:205).

Objectivity is achieved in texts through various stylistic devises (see chapter 3). Among these are authorial omniscience concerning the situation and the persons being discussed, and the aggregation and suppression of the voices of such persons. In psychological writing this was achieved by reporting the results in such a way that they were not attributed to individuals with particular personal and social identities; that is, scientific psychologists attributed causality not to specific agents but to abstract agencies "observed" in aggregated statistics elicited in experimental settings. This device distinguished reports on the outcome of experiments from everyday reports on most other social situations, and this difference helped to establish the experimenter's claim to be communicating something of general significance (Danzinger 1988:37). Thus it became a principle of psychological reporting that the experience of participants in experiments was to be discounted and that their social identities were to be reduced to their functions within the experimental setting—for example, as "subjects" or "observers." Indeed, "the names of persons participating in experiments appeared less and less frequently in articles in American journals of psychology during the early decades of this century" (Danzinger 1988:42; see Danzinger 1990a:183, 38; Adair and Spinner 1981). Such personal attributes were deemed irrelevant to or even obstructive of American psychology's mission to find universal laws concerning objective facts.

Given this orientation, the principal criteria for the acceptability of subjects was that they be available in numbers and capable of being subjugated in environments totally controlled by the experimenter. Infants in the families of psychologists were manipulable but statistically insignificant, although early psychologists did make use of them (as in Skinner's program of "hierconditioning"). Ordinary citizens were sufficiently numerous but insufficiently controllable. By contrast, undergraduate students were both numerous and malleable, as were inmates of prisons, asylums, and other institutions. Such persons became the preferred subjects of psychological experiments. The reports of the interactions that made up such experiments suppressed the personal and social identities of their members along with their hierarchic relations of power. Thus interaction, identity, temporality, and domination all were textually eschewed in order to present "results" as the manifestation of universal and timeless laws.

A further example of the rhetorical construction of objectivity is provided by the efforts of Freud's American disciples to render his work more scientific. Reading Freud in German, one finds his prose at turns didactic, hortatory, serious, playful, straightforward, full of military and managerial metaphors, and always adapted to the material he was seeking to evoke. In other words, it is a self-consciously persuasive narration. Not only does Freud invite the reader to participate in his efforts at linguistic construction, but the reflexive form of his message also expresses what the message is about (Mahony 1987:136; 1989). For instance, in his *Interpretation of Dreams* (1953:536), Freud openly admitted that his metaphors needed improvement, but he said that he saw "no necessity to apologize" because they were only provisional aids, intended to assist his initial descriptions and thoughts about previously unremarked psychical processes (Leary 1991b). As Freud wrote to Sandor Ferenczi on April 8, 1915, the critical "mechanism" of scientific creativity was the "succession of daringly playful fantasy and relentlessly realistic criticism" (quoted by Grubrich-Simitis 1987:83; Leary 1991b). In the same spirit, Freud acknowledged that "you will say that these ideas [about "resistance" and "repression"] are both crude and fantastic . . . more than that, I know that they are incorrect, and, if I am not very much mistaken, I already have something better to take their place" (Freud 1963:296).

This gift for rhetorical reflexivity was not appreciated by Freud's American translators. They were bent on placing his thought into the prevailing realistic mode by shifting from the accessible language of the original to an objectivistic language of technical terms and Latinate constructions. Thus, both Ernest Jones and James Strachey deployed technical language that was etymologically dependent on dead languages in order to create a sense of empirical objectivity and formal abstraction distant from experience. "The result, Jones thought, would be the securing of precise definitions and the avoidance of personal associations and emotional slippage and spills. Following in Jones' path, Strachey rejected an affect-laden vocabulary, with the result that Freud's fluid, resonant expression acquires a rigid and abstract cast" (Mahony 1987:173; for similar statements see Spence 1990; Bettelheim 1983; Ornstein 1985).

The rhetorical construction of scientific representation can also be seen in the formalization of rules for writing and reading psychological discourse. A good example is the editions of the *Publication Manual* of the American Psychological Association, which reflect the emergence of behaviorism in psychology and of a scientific realist style in the human sciences as a whole. The first "Instruction in Regard to Preparation of Manuscript" appeared in 1929 as a six-and-a-half-page style sheet. It grew to thirty-two pages by 1944 and sixty-one pages by 1952. By 1983 these rules of representation had become a tome of some two hundred oversized pages of detail on discipline that covered everything from apparatus to organization, grammar to grants.

As Charles Bazerman noted, the emergence of the *Manual* paralleled the historical emergence of the behaviorist movement, and as one might expect, the *Manual's* requirements of style project a reality that embodies behaviorist assumptions. In this rhetorical universe, people follow rules, check each other out, and gather information (Bazerman 1987:127). Articles are to be empirical in content and experimental in design. Method of logic is transformed into technique of research. First-person accounts of what the investigator did and what she perceived are replaced by impersonal renderings of what the instruments measured or the data revealed. Prior operational definitions become more important than emergent conceptual ones. Words take on a narrow technical usage far removed from ordinary language, intelligible only to an expert in a highly specialized field. Research is focused on narrow ranges of behavior, each experiment adding a further finding to an implied but never discussed intellectual architecture. Thus, articles become shorter, reduced to examinations of behaviors that are observable under certain conditions with little or no concern about how experimental findings might illuminate philosophic or theoretical questions or personal experience. Prior writings on the subject become an objectified foundational "literature" to which "further research" is to "contribute."

The author projected by these rules must display competence in the method rather than understand the truth of an idea. She is not a reasoner persuading reasoning readers about mind. Instead, mental processes of both the investigator and the subject are removed from the report. The individual author is replaced by her method, and the individual subject is replaced by the statistical patterns of behavior that are reported. The author becomes a "doer of experiments, a maker of calculations, a presenter of results . . . a follower of rules" who subordinates herself "to the group endeavor of gathering more facts toward an ultimately complete description of behavior" (Bazerman 1987:138–41).

Readers in this rhetorical universe are presumed to be seeking further bits of knowledge to add to their previous bits. They are not aiming to solve some intellectual problem, weigh alternatives, or be persuaded. Instead, the reader's role is to seek faults in the experimental apparatus that would disqualify the findings as an additional brick for the edifice to be constructed.

These practices of representation aligned psychology with the dominant habitus of instrumental scientism and created an occult vocabulary of expertise that excluded nonspecialists from the status and privileges of the emerging discipline. All this turned out to be an ironic inversion of John Locke's call for plain language that would be accessible to ordinary people (1974:bk. 3, ch. 10, secs. 33–34). Instead of addressing an educated lay public, the prose of the new psychologists bespoke an exclusive expertise and a knowledge that was "public" only to those already initiated into the monopoly guild of practitioners.

RENDERING PROFESSIONAL SERVICE TO THE NEW ELITES

In spite of these pedagogic, intellectual, and organizational developments within the emerging discipline, it is unlikely that the new psychology would have succeeded institutionally if it had not also responded to the needs of the elites of the emerging mass industrial society. In 1905 more than half the population of the United States consisted of either immigrants or children of newcomers—persons of mainly peasant and non-Protestant stock. In responding to this demographic and cultural onslaught, progressive reformers and enlightened capitalists had converging interests: the new masses were to be socialized to become Americans through schooling, and they were to be disciplined to become factory workers through scientific management. The new psychologists, progressives in the service of capitalism, became psychological engineers, specialists in getting children to learn in factory-like schools and in motivating workers to efficiently perform inherently uninteresting tasks.

In the competition among the social sciences to see which was to become the new theoretical infrastructure for legislation, politics, and social conduct, psychology had a major trump card: the use of its scientific credentials to depoliticize public issues. By treating social questions with a scientific discourse that focused on individuals, the new psychologists undermined the civic and moral contents of these questions by redefining political dissent as personal deviance (Apfelbaum 1986:9). They thereby stripped nonconformity of its political implications even while providing an instrument of social control—an instrument that was compassionate because therapeutic and unbiased because scientific. The nascent discipline and profession promised far more than it could deliver, but because the promise of psychologists was one that both they and their clients wanted to believe, few bothered to challenge it. Moreover, as psychological experiments and social institutions in America became more similar to each other as mechanisms of calculation and control, the advice of psychological experts became more plausible and, in its plausibility, more useful.

Distinguished academic psychologists also sought to sell services directly to corporate elites. In 1921, for example, "several of the nation's leading psychologists, including James McKeen Cattell, John B. Watson, Lewis M. Terman, Walter D. Scott, Walter V. Bingham, and Robert M. Yerkes, formed the Psychological Corporation, to provide psychological consultants to industry" (Gillespie 1988:131). In the same year the Personnel Research Federation was established under the aegis of the government's National Research Council in order to encourage and coordinate scientific research on industrial relations.

Although experimenting psychologists trumpeted the potential practical applications of their work, most of them operated within universities. In a 1929 survey of the field, James McKeen Cattell characterized psychologists "as the most academic of all scientific workers. Of the 307 members of the American Psychological Association in 1916—a ten-fold increase over the 31 of the founding year, 1892—84% held the Ph.D., and 88.6% (272) were employed as university or college teachers" (Ash 1983:147). "By 1917, the British publication *Who's Who in Science* could report that America had more psychologists than the combined numbers in England, France, and Germany" (Manicas 1987:208–9; see Cranfield 1973).

However much or little the new psychologists were actually able to offer to the new system of mass compulsory schooling and other expanding institutions, educators were certain that their association with psychologists would pay off. This belief seems to have been driven by the educators' own quest for professionalization, which depended on the development of scientific and technical bases for educational expertise. The mere promise of assistance to education carried the new psychology a good deal closer to its own institutionalization.

In comparison to the new psychologists who were based in universities, most industrial psychologists labored as technicians, not as scientists. This accorded with changes in the mode and relations of production. Around the turn of the century, control of the technical organization of production passed increasingly from the shop floor to production engineers. Then between 1910 and 1930 many firms began "to create special personnel departments. Foremen increasingly lost their power to hire, fire, or promote their workers, and personnel managers in many large manufacturing companies operated a system of paternalistic welfare policies designed to weaken and discourage unionization and win the loyalty of the work force" (Gillespie 1988:131). Training in psychology was a desired background for the new scientific management of people. Industrial psychologists and personnel experts, hired to solve specific problems, had to produce what appeared to be practical solutions and to concentrate exclusively on the narrow issues of productivity, personnel allocation, and industrial loyalty as defined by their bosses.

The subordination of industrial social science to the interests of management is illustrated by the work of Elton Mayo (1945) and his associates from Harvard University. In their studies of assembly workers at General Electric's Hawthorne plant in Cicero, Illinois, Mayo and his co-researchers found that their manipulations of the work environment to enhance productivity were almost always effective. But they failed to report that this was true only so long as the experimenters collaborated with the workers in developing the experiments. Thus, instead of respecting their experience in the field where they were equal to, or students of, the workers, Mayo and his associates reframed this experience "scientifically." Rather than interpreting their experience as "worker empowerment yields higher productivity," for example, they discovered that "management concern for workers yields higher productivity." When the experiments were finished, however, and the only thing left of collaborative decision making was management expressions of concern, productivity declined to previous levels or below, and the workers who had co-managed the workflow with the experimenters either quit or were fired. Such "anomalies" were then attributed to various "pathologies" of the workers. At the very least, Mayo's account of the Hawthorne studies as dramatic breakthroughs in scientific understanding suppresses the ambiguity of the actual proceedings (Gillespie 1988; Mariner 1971; Walter 1989).

By viewing labor-management conflict as workers' pathology, industrial psychologists served themselves through service to management. This was the norm, not the exception. Throughout their professional history, industrial psychologists have insisted that management should authorize studies of its workers in order to learn their wants, instincts, desires, aspirations, and motivations, and so to be able to enhance productivity and ward off costly strikes. From the pioneers of industrial psychology to the human relations experts of the current era, industrial psychologists have either avoided the political and ethical implications of their work or have faced them from the viewpoint of management. Hugo Munsterberg (1913) formulated this comfortable and ethically lobotomizing position in the dictum that industrial psychologists should concern themselves with means only, not with goals, aims, or ends, which could and should be determined only by the industrial managers.

As the role of the state became more important in regulating the capitalist economy and advancing American interests abroad, the state also became a consumer and then an arbiter of psychological knowledge. Perhaps the earliest breakthrough was "the use of intelligence tests to classify more than two million American soldiers during the First World War. With the army intelligence tests, psychology had achieved a previously unknown level of public notice and acceptance" (Samelson 1979). Seizing their moment, the "psychologists who had worked together on the development of group intelligence tests during World War I decided immediately after the war to adapt tests of this sort for use in schools. This effort was phenomenally successful: by 1922, three million children a year were being tested with one or another of the resulting tests" (Hornstein 1988; see Callahan 1962; Thorndike 1923:1–9; Apfelbaum 1986:9). By the mid-1920s, the use of tests was widespread in school systems that "tracked" students by ability. Such tests provided educational administrators with "an efficient way to divide students into homogeneous ability groups, and thereby to meet the problems of size in postwar schools" (Wigdor and Garner 1982:89–90).

Psychologists had created a product that met the needs of administrators of the emerging mass institutions. "Some of these products were the direct results of quantitative work itself (for example, statistical tests and scaling procedures); others were more indirect and resulted from the application of quantitative approaches to particular lines of research (for example, intelligence, personality, and vocational tests derived from testing research and signal-detection procedures, and hearing devices derived from psychological research)" (Hornstein 1988:19).

As knowledge products were created to meet the administrative market, so institutions were shaped along more "scientific" lines. "Since the end of the Second World War, psychological expertise has been increasingly deployed around a range of practical problems and within a large number of administrative and reformatory practices. Psychological agents and techniques are involved in assessment and diagnosis of problems of individual conduct in institutional sites such as hospitals, schools, prisons, factories and in the army. An analogous range of psychological specialisms has risen—clinical psychology, educational psychology, criminal psychology, industrial psychology, military psychology and so forth" (Rose 1985:1).

Psychologists seemed to have achieved the longed-for status of expert, with control over esoteric but apparently exact and recognizably useful knowledge. Accordingly, the discipline in the United States expanded from learning and industrial psychology to other areas of research and application. During World War II, the military's desire for knowledge of the psychology of enemy peoples fostered culture-and-personality studies. Likewise, the insufficiency of personnel to care for psychologically disturbed military men contributed to the establishment of clinical psychology (Ash 1983:156; Murphy 1949:12–22, 418–28; Simpson 1994).

The growing involvement of the state in shaping the character and direction of psychology has continued since World War II. The institutionalization of clinical training in universities, for example, occurred against academic resistance under pressure from governmental funding agencies, especially the Veterans' Administration and, later, the National Institutes of Mental Health (NIMH). In a similar fashion, social psychology and educational psychology were stimulated by governmental funding for the War on Poverty in the 1960s (Bakan 1980:133f). By focusing on individual pathology rather than institutional oppression, government-funded studies encouraged an inherently conservative ideology. In advancing a conception of the individual for whose encapsulated qualities all social relations were external, psychologists were conforming to a dominant assumption of those who financed them. Indeed, by taking for granted the ideology of individualism in a context that was supposed to be devoted to objective knowledge, the scientific psychologists gave this ideology a scientist justification (Danzinger 1990a:186; see Sampson 1977, 1983; Unger 1975; Venn 1984; Herman 1995).

More recently, two areas of growth in psychology have been cognitive behavioral studies of mental illness and artificial intelligence. Both serve the interests of dominant groups ideologically and practically. The first provides a scientific vocabulary for "medicalizing" social deviance and legitimizing new forms of social control of persons who cannot, or will not, adjust to the dominant system. Similarly, artificial intelligence aims at mapping the human mind on the model of the computer. This serves the technostructure ideologically because it projects a vision of citizens and politics as a cybernetic system that can be guided by techno-elites. This subcommunication both justifies the supposedly meritocratic expertise of the new class and masks the continuing power of older financial elites.

By secularizing, individualizing, and depoliticizing human suffering, psychologists also created a new jurisdiction, that of problems of everyday living or "adjustment." Whereas private therapy was the province of psychiatrists, psychology dominated part of the mental disorder market through the university and through federally funded research. By the 1960s, more than half of NIMH investigators were psychologists, whereas only fifteen percent were psychiatrists. Moreover, through their university base, psychologists could socialize students to their ownership of "abnormal psychology" and could thereby pre-sell the next generation of potential clients. Indeed, abnormality became a central focus of psychology even to the extent of defining normality as the absence of abnormal or socially ineffective conduct. Pragmatic behavioral theories and technologies of the person construed normality and pathology in terms of the regulation necessary to achieve conformity, whether through drugs, talk, or coercion. Psychiatrists retained their monopoly on pharmaceutical ministration, leaving psychotherapy largely to the psychologists (Abbott 1988:213, 311–13). By the late twentieth century, political issues had been turned into personal troubles through the new psychological science.

Artificial intelligence began as a subspecialty of psychology but has emerged as a new discipline—cognitive science—through fragmentation from psychology and alliances with subareas of neurology, computer science, and linguistics. Patronage for this discipline has been provided by the Pentagon since World War II. The control mechanisms needed to pursue and destroy an unpredictably moving target required an internal representation in which to register, update, and compute the relevant information (J. Miller 1995:65). The practical necessity of such a mechanism, along with Noam Chomsky's theories of a linguistic unconscious, undermined behaviorism and fostered the idea of unconscious information processing central to the ensuing "cognitive revolution," a revolution that supports and was supported by the military-industrial and corporate development of computer technologies.

In sum, the success of the new psychologists depended on their fitting the intellectual premises of their discipline with both the dominant habitus and the conditions and demands of their clients and patrons. Poetic and political practices of representation deeply commingled in the shaping of American psychology as a discipline, profession, and institutionalized discourse. The new psychology was established as a profession and an academic discipline in the late 1800s and was "applied" in schools, factories, and the military in the ensuing decades. The formalization of psychology served its professionalization, and as new professionals became servants of power, psychology became a hegemonic discourse within the larger culture.

TOWARD A POLITICAL ETHICS OF SCIENCE

Questions of the proper relations between science and power have been posed at least since Archimedes devised new weapons for his city-state and hoped that the requisite knowledge would remain a Greek monopoly (Nandy 1988; see Brown 1989b; Rouse 1987). In our own times, science has received patronage for its institutionalization, but this dependence threatens the very autonomy that is the source of utility of science to patrons. Like other modern disciplines, psychology has moved from the pastoral ideals of aristocratic play or professional communitas toward commercial greed, military secrecy, and scientistic nihilism.

A more humane and liberating relation of knowledge and power would seem to require, among other ingredients, a reflection not only on the ways knowledge is "applied" but also on how the knowledge system itself encodes categories of the culture that produces the knowledge system and is reproduced by it. But who will do the reflecting for whom, and will it be enough? Sociology, for example, has established a subspecialty called "theory," which does the "reflecting" that is almost entirely divorced from sociological "applications," which are the preoccupation of the rest of the discipline. And because the careers of most scientists depend on their uncritical acceptance of the institutional presuppositions of their discipline, it seems unlikely that reflexivity will have much currency or consequence. Thus, the tension between occasionally critical scholarship and usually uncritical practice is likely to continue. Any significant change would seem to require that reflexive modes of scholarship be institutionalized in new degree programs of their own (Ash 1991). And such alternate programs require alternate forms of patronage—as, for example, when the ruling Social Democrats in Germany sponsored the Starnbruck Institute directed by Jürgen Habermas. Most important, however, the democratization of science requires democratic social movements that can subsume its disembodied rationalism and instrumentalism within prudent civic discourse. After elaborating Pierre Bourdieu's critical theory of science, I shall discuss the prospects for a democratic science supported by a grassroots social movement.

Chapter 8 Toward a Field Theory of Knowledge/Power in Science and Civic Life

There is a real world independent of our senses; the laws of nature were not invented by man, but forced upon him by the natural world.
Max Planck (1959)

I cannot think of any Nobel Prize–winning discovery in physics, chemistry, or medicine that was based on anything other than empirical evidence or mathematical insight.
M. F. Perutz (1995:58)

If you want to understand what a science is, you should look in the first instance not at its theories or its findings, and certainly not at what its apologists say about it; you should look at what the practitioners of it do.
Clifford Geertz (1973)

For a long time, perhaps since Plato, Westerners have tended to assume strict separations between politics and reason, between power and knowledge, and between the external and internal criticism of science. In these bifurcations, the interest-driven, ideologically laden, external domain of politics was distinguished from, and made inferior to, the objectivism, value neutrality, and disinterestedness said to characterize science and scientists. In Marxian external analyses, for example, "bourgeois" science was viewed as a reflection of political economic forces. In positivist and functionalist internal analyses, scientific practice was seen as completely independent of political or economic influence.

Since about 1980 such demarcations between science and non-science have been challenged logically and assailed as efforts to disguise the politics *within* fields of knowledge. Perhaps this critique was inevitable given the new political context of science—the industrial scale of knowledge production, the now indispensable patronage of the corporate state, the consolidation by scientists of their guild privileges, the opening of the academy to persons from non-elite groups, and the extension of science and its technicist derivatives into almost all areas of contemporary life.

Scientists have traded utility for patronage. The intellectual, material, and social technologies that their work generates have bought them many institutional privileges. The chief of these is autonomy, not only to produce knowledge but to remain almost totally exempt when this knowledge has negative consequences or when their false or inappropriate hypotheses lead to bad policies. A central justification for this freedom was the presumed public character of science, which enabled it to be judged or used by all (Van den Daele and Krohn 1983:239). This liberal individualist and positivist distinction between the production and consumption of knowledge is less and less viable in an era of industrialized, hyperspecialized proprietary and often secret scientific research. Of course some consumers of knowledge, such as corporations, foundations, or governmental agencies, have a say in what kind of knowledge will be produced—even theory, it seems, can be planned "externally" in some disciplines (Böhme et al. 1983:5). But most citizens are only passive consumers of knowledge created to serve the interests of others, and they have no more say in its production than people who live downstream from petrochemical plants have in the disposal of waste products (Shumway and Messer-Davidow 1991).

For all these reasons, the sciences, though riding high, have fallen lower in repute. Even exalted French intellectuals have renounced their Enlightenment role as "masters of truth and justice" or as "spokesmen of the universal" (Foucault 1980:126). Scientists, like other professionals, are now seen as necessary but perhaps dangerous, and as vulnerable as any other professional group to the temptations of power and privilege.

Among sociologists and philosophers of science, a key move in this "normalization" of science has been their challenge to its distinctive epistemological stature. Thus Feyerabend (1978) equated knowledge of physics with knowledge of safecracking. Similarly, ethnographers have shown that both the demarcation between science and society and, indeed, the norms of rationality of science are construed differently in different contexts and, hence, that both science and its methods are "essentially contestable" (Pels 1995; Brown 1987:64–79; Gieryn 1983; Shapin 1990). As the boundary between knowledge and power becomes weaker and the overlaps greater, efforts at epistemological demarcation are now seen as ideological covers or political maneuvers to mask and advance professional power and privilege (Latour 1980, 1983; Woolgar 1988).

Once one has shown that everything both inside and outside science is a contested social construction, it is an easy step to view everything that is constructed as political and to see both acting and knowing as forms of power (Turner n.d.a:8). Epistemology and ontology are conflued in "knowledge practices" through which the world is made to appear, or made real, for us. Thus, for example, the Copernican revolution was not merely about changing views or paradigms; it was also about the legitimation of changing knowledge practices and, thence, about changing the world that structures the range of possible action (Rouse 1987:185). Moreover, rather than science being determined by extra-scientific forces, power is now seen not only to operate within the observatory but also to emanate outward from it.

These extensions of the concepts of rhetoric and politics to the domains of science and expertise also undermine such binary distinctions as science versus politics, and reason versus rhetoric. These distinctions have been useful for many purposes and perhaps are essential to the project of modernity. The creation of a separate sphere of politics and the depoliticization of religion that emerged from the European wars of religion and the French Revolution were a great political achievement. They provided a model for liberal political thought and led to the analogous creation of distinct spheres of the legal, artistic, and scientific, all of which were "thought to be antithetical to 'the political'" (Turner n.d.b:1–2). These demarcations continue to be central in liberal societies today and, indeed, are inseparable from the origins and self-definition of modern scientists.

In an important sense, then, the new rhetorical and sociological studies of science appear to challenge not only the status and privileges of scientists but also the legitimacy of the entire science-driven, rationalized liberal polity. This accounts in part for the attacks launched by members of the scientific establishment against the dreaded postmodernists, social relativists, and discourse constructionists. Targets have included ethnographers like Bruno Latour, who show how scientific "black boxes" of firm belief are constructed through networks of influence; sociologists of scientific knowledge like Harold Garfinkel and Malcolm Ashmore, who document the retrospective invention of scientific discoveries; Marxian theorists like Jerome Ravitz and Stanley Aronowitz, who expose the interests that drive scientific research; feminists like Donna Haraway and Evelyn Fox Keller, who argue that scientific methods are gendered; philosophers like Steve Fuller and Sandra Harding, who seek more democratic approaches to knowledge production; communication theorists like Alan Gross and Herbert Simons, who analyze the rhetorical making of scientific disciplines and discoveries; and critical theorists like Jürgen Habermas and Manfred Stanley, who reveal how scientific language corrodes the public culture (Ross 1995:348).

Defenders of positivist conceptions of science correctly note that such thinkers subvert demarcations between science and politics and between scientists and the slumbering masses. Positivists also fear that science will become more accountable to lay citizens. And they ignore the most evident demarcation—that between the idealized image of science as a pristine pursuit of truth and the actuality of science as mainly a creature of the corporate state. Indeed, scientists, rather than being embattled, disinterested seekers of truth, are largely proletarianized producers of processes and information that are useful to commercial or military interests. "By far the majority of professional scientists today are industrial workers, producing local, technical knowledge, not publishable research. Research and production science dominates the leading weapons, chemicals, biotechnology, energy and microelectronics industries" (Ross 1995:348). Scientific expertise has become a critical political resource, as scientific knowledge is used more and more to define or legitimate public policy and as "technicism" has spread as a model and ideology of rationality in public affairs (Nelkin 1979:106).

The critique of science as social, rhetorical, or political construction is not necessarily an attack on scientific rationality, however. Instead, an understanding of the politics of science or, more strongly, a view of science *as* politics, is not inherently an argument against science as a form of reason. But it does bring reason down from the imperium of Platonist or Cartesian philosophy to the level of observable practices. Scientific rationality is now seen as a hard-won social achievement, and not as something that magically appears from epistemological norms or pre-existing forms. In this view, reductions of science to either ideology or epistemology are misleading because both reproduce the dichotomy between power and knowledge; both see science as a mere reproduction or representation of something else (logic, a natural order, political interests), not as something made through scientific practices.

If a demarcation between science and non-science on epistemological grounds cannot be sustained, does this mean that no difference exists between scientific and other fields of practice? Not at all. It only means that warrants for such distinctions should be sought on the level of practical human activity. That is, following Pierre Bourdieu, the critique of epistemological demarcations is most valuable if it directs attention toward other *sociological* warrants for a distinction between science and non-science, an alternate *social* demarcation that resolves the old dilemmas of reason versus politics in a sociological and discursive conception of scientific fields.

The social, rhetorical, or political character of knowledge production does not compel us to equate science with politics nor to abandon every useful distinction between scientific and other practices. Nonetheless, social constructionists and philosophic deconstructionists often do equate the collapse of epistemological defenses of science with a social conflation of the scientific and political fields, as though politics and science were the same institution within the broader political economy. That is, having discovered science to be thoroughly driven by interests, they tend to assume that interests within the scientific field are identical to interests within any other field of social practice. On the contrary, however, the full significance of the insight that science is social or political appears only when these social and political contexts and practices are specified. Science is a field or discourse like any other; and, like other fields, it is also a distinct world that to greater or lesser degrees operates according to its own norms and conventions (Bourdieu 1990:300). Scientific practices are influenced by money, status, and power, but not just in the ways that money, status, and power operate in the worlds of finance, cinema, or politics, despite the frequent efforts of political and economic groups to make science a direct extension of their interests, and despite the efforts of some scientists to become celebrities. Science retains its special character in part because the highest political and economic utilities of science can be generated only if scientific communities remain autonomous. Basic science is still the driving force of corporate capitalism and the military industrial state. And because basic research is by definition not directed toward specific immediate technical or commercial applications, it remains nonproprietary and largely conducted in such nonmarket institutions as universities and research institutes. These institutions are crucial elements of scientific fields—fields in which the practice of science is partly protected from pressures external to the scientific community. Work within the scientific field is governed by canons of craft, rules of representation, protocols of professionalism, and norms of excellence that are intrinsic to the social field of science.

This functional or institutional separation between science and politics is different from the epistemological separation between knowledge and power. Indeed, whereas the epistemological distinction may be usefully suspended, the social distinction provides a now fully sociological demarcation between the institutional domain of politics and the institutional domain of science. This shift of focus does not dismiss epistemological or normative differences between different subsystems of the political economy. But even here, "epistemology" is translated into logics-in-use, that is, into the practical activities of knowledge production (Kaplan 1964; Pels 1995). In this sense, if there is a "foundation" of scientific thought, it can lie only in the collective belief in this foundation among scientists, whose very activities presuppose, produce, and ratify that foundation (Bourdieu 1991b:8; Durkheim 1965:21–36). In this sociological and rhetorical view, craft practices—such as writing, talking, arguing, publishing, criticizing—now replace a positivistic "logic of justification" as the bases for claims to cognitively or methodologically superior knowledge. Such a position against epistemological foundationalism does not dismiss epistemology. Instead, epistemology itself is relocated within the scientific field. This shift also restores agency and accountability to individual scientists, but only by locating that agency within the same field of social constraints that deploy an epistemological rhetoric of presentation.

Put slightly differently, earlier philosophy of science described the activities of scientists in terms of epistemological differences between science and nonscience. But if we focus on specialized social systems as practices of knowledge production, then the analytic flow is reversed. We no longer see epistemological differences creating social distinctions; instead, we see social distinctions as generating the conditions for epistemological ones.

A similar shift is made from methodological validity to social validity based on rhetorical practices within the scientific community. Here Bourdieu's concept of cultural capital extends to scientific capital as well, including material resources and professional authority acquired in previous struggles. This authority is strictly scientific insofar as it is gained only from recognition by peer competitors for finding solutions (that are accepted as legitimate) to problems (that are themselves held as legitimate) within that scientific field (Bourdieu 1991b:7).

The partial social segregation and privileged autonomy of producers of academic knowledge are the very social preconditions for their *internal* politics and their dependence on *external* support. That is, the social demarcation of science as a subsidized ivory tower, relatively free from the pressures of deadlines (as in journalism) or decisions of life and death (as in medicine or the military) or profits and payrolls (as in business), permits academic scientists not only to be disinterested in these goals or constraints but also, and more important, to become focally interested in the scientificity of their own professional pursuits. Thus the scientific field, like other discursive fields, generates its own specific interests. Scientific practices are as much oriented towards durability as journalistic practices are oriented toward deadlines; scientists are as disinterested in popularity with lay voters as politicians are disinterested in approval by specialized experts. But within the competitive game of science, practitioners are thereby freed to be intensely interested in acquiring technical resources, symbolic capital, and scientific status.

This logic-in-use exists in and through rivalry between scientists and the resultant criticisms and cross-checkings of their products. Thus rivalry, politics, and professional self-interest operate within the scientific field as stimuli to scientific progress. "The anarchic antagonism of private interests is transformed into a scientific dialectic, as every actor is forced, when challenging and resisting his opponents, to adopt an instrumentarium which lends his polemical purposes the universal scope of a methodical critique. This is how social mechanisms press with necessity for the realization of universal norms of rationality" (Pels 1995; see Bourdieu 1981:273–75, 277, 1990:300, 1992:91). The very autonomy of the scientific field encourages the full development of competition among its members and, indeed, such competition in asserting, criticizing, and defending knowledge claims is the successful performance of scientists' professional activity.

The distinction between science and non-science as different social spheres of practice also implies a new conception of the scientist as agent. Rather than being viewed as human clones of political and economic forces or as passive recorders of laws that nature forces upon them, scientists are now viewed as agents who create not only hypotheses but also discoveries and their validations. Of course, scientists do not create these any way they choose. Instead, creative scientists, being neither methodological drones nor isolated geniuses, actualize potentialities that are latent within and available through their scientific communities. "These potentialities in fact exist as such only for agents endowed with the socially constituted dispositions that predispose them to perceive those potentialities as such and to realize them. But this also means that these potentialities, which may appear as the product of the development of the immanent tendencies of science, do not contain within themselves the principle of their own actualization. Rather, they become historical reality only through the intervention of agents capable of going beyond the science already constituted (by other agents) in order to perceive in it (thanks to it and beyond it) possibilities to be realized" (Bourdieu 1991b:10–11).

Because of this self-constitutive aspect of scientific fields and innovations within them, what is at stake in important scientific disputes is not only the veracity of a particular finding or the validity of a particular theory but also, in and through these, the definition of what is scientific or what is "legitimate science," "appropriate methods," or "adequate data." These "meta-debates" become most evident in disputes between paradigms, where the intra-paradigmatic rules for adjudicating differences are by definition inadequate. Instead, in meta-debates the usually subterranean struggles over "correct" science, methods, and so on, come to the surface and are often explicitly contested. "It is indeed because the definition of the stake of the struggle is a stake *in* the struggle . . . that one endlessly runs into the antinomy of legitimacy: in the scientific field, as elsewhere, there exists no judiciary for legitimizing claims to legitimacy, and claims to legitimacy carry a weight proportional to the symbolic power of the groups whose specific interests they express" (Bourdieu 1991b:14).

The degree to which such struggles are "internal" or "external" to the scientific field is a measure of the autonomy of science, and of that particular discipline, in that time and place. Thus autonomy varies across different disciplines and fields and also within a given discipline over time according to the amount of scientific resources that that group has accumulated. Control of these resources constitutes, in effect, the social symbolic boundary between scientists and non-scientists. A high degree of resources possessed by a scientific community or field is thus equivalent to a high degree of autonomy, that is, freedom from constraints outside the scientific field *and* subordination to constraints within it. In highly autonomous fields, for example, only those with the legitimated symbolic capital are permitted to compete, but those who do compete have their rivals as their only relevant publics and their only source of authority (Bourdieu 1991b:15).

In contrast to highly autonomous disciplines, which can usually manage even dramatic changes while maintaining a social if not intellectual cohesion, paradigm revolutions in less autonomous disciplines (such as early behavioral psychology) are more vulnerable to influence by allies who are socially external to that scientific field. This assertion challenges Thomas Kuhn's (1972:153,162) view that the Copernican revolution is "typical of every other major scientific upheaval." In the case of the Copernican revolution, science was not yet established as a distinct and relatively autonomous social field. Thus the Copernican revolution was not merely a paradigm shift within science but a much more general revolution in establishing a new way of both knowing and doing, and in their legitimation. For science to disentangle itself and affirm an autonomy from religious, philosophical, and political fields meant that the battles fought over methods or numbers by Copernicus, Galileo, and others were also struggles to think and act in a new way, free of domination by either church or state, free indeed of any authority except that emanating from the nascent field of science itself.

Once a scientific field is strongly established, however (and again contra Kuhn), it by definition can contain within its own mechanisms of governance those now quiet revolutions that need not disestablish the scientific field itself (Bôhme et al. 1983:4; Lakatos 1974:105). This is because the intellectual and material resources for making a scientific revolution now exist largely within that scientific field and, hence, "permanent revolution" can occur alongside "legitimate dogmatism" (Bachelard 1953:41). As more scientific resources are accumulated within a given field and the barriers to entry rise, the means of relevant intellectual production become more concentrated within that community, and hence, the capital necessary to define or even to address scientific problems will be available only to certified practitioners. The "outsiders" who are most likely to make a revolution then will likely be outsiders to that particular discipline or subfield but insiders to the larger field of science.

One indicator of the degree of autonomy of a scientific field is the length of time it takes to achieve consensus on important innovations. Thus the Copernican revolution took a century to complete. Innovations in nineteenth-century biology also partly depended on religious belief, just as social theory today remains highly entangled with political and ideological interests. Thus it took decades of controversy before Darwin's theory or Weber's models became guides for disciplinary research. By contrast, it took only three weeks for Linus Pauling to acknowledge the importance and priority of Crick and Watson's model of the structure of DNA (Watson 1968:138–41; Collins 1992). Because autonomy also involves well-developed networks of internal communication, critical or supporting evidence can be more quickly mobilized to facilitate the formation of a new consensus.

The relative autonomy of scientific disciplines also will be linked to their costs of intellectual production. Big Science requires big money, which becomes available only if such science promises to be useful to those who possess the economic resources upon which Big Science depends. Thus high-energy physics is almost wholly dependent on government, and biology is highly dependent on the pharmaceutical industry. Yet paradoxically, these disciplines appear to be both highly dependent on external support *and* highly autonomous. These are interdependent phenomena, however: autonomy brings intellectual power that may generate useful findings that become a lever for gaining financial support that also supports the autonomy that is the source of intellectual innovation. If one punctuates this interaction as a one-way causal process—either political or intellectual—one obviates the dialectical character of power/knowledge discourses in which science/society or inside/outside are mutually transformed. The transformation of the worksite into a site of knowledge production, for example, was achieved jointly by academic departments of mathematics, computer science, and engineering, by corporate research laboratories, and by the telecommunications and information-processing industries. This transformation in turn created new prestige for science, new markets for industry, and new dollars for research, in addition to establishing a scientific cyberculture with its own international lingua franca. Similarly, as Latour (1993) shows, the application of Pasteur's germ theories to milk production or public sanitation required that farms and cities be reconceived and redesigned as enormous laboratories. In the many cases such as these, strict segregation of "inside" and "outside" loses its analytic power.

The issue of autonomy and of the relations between scientific and political revolutions is somewhat different in the sciences of society insofar as these are more crucial than the natural sciences for social and ideological control. It is intellectuals in the social sciences who are silenced first by despots, not the chemists and technicians. As Bourdieu (1991:10) put it, "all powers—and especially symbolic powers—cannot but feel threatened by the existence of a discourse claiming truth about the social world and especially about powers." Hence the temporal or spiritual powers-that-be tend always to reduce discourse about society to a range of representation that supports their own reproduction. Social sciences for elites are useful mainly as instruments of control or legitimation.

In sum, Bourdieu's theory of science as a special field of social practice accepts the deconstructive critique of the positivist version of science as well as the critical theorists' analysis of scientism. But it goes beyond these critiques by reinstating a sociological distinction between knowledge production and other specialized activities and by showing how political activities within science are thereby deployed in creating scientific knowledge.

SCIENTIFIC FIELDS AND THE SPACE FOR CIVIC DISCOURSE

Our efforts to elaborate a field theory of reason/politics lead us to reconsider the role of science in a democratic society. First, rather than applauding or rejecting science as an occult practice inaccessible to lay understanding, we have seen that scientific facts and theories begin as stories advanced and contested in communities of relatively free and open discourse, where each in principle has equal rights to speak, to criticize, to agree, or to dissent. This formulation also gives a sociological grounding to the speech ethic defined by Habermas. His apolitical ideal of discourse is realized in practice through the politics of scientificity within the otherwise ideally apolitical scientific field. Habermas' ideal speech situation is simulated, in effect, not through an absence of power relations but through the disciplining and focusing of such relations as a "politics of truth" within a scientific field.

This, of course, is a very rosy picture, perhaps a too easy reconciliation of particularistic power interests that pursue universal knowledge through the invisible hand of scientific fields (Pels 1995). That is, Bourdieu's model tends to ignore the real lack of autonomy of scientific fields and the self-serving oligopolistic practices that limit competition and knowledge production within them. Moreover, even in "ideal" conditions, the same structural features that make scientists so productive and useful also make them dangerous. The very autonomy necessary to the creation of new knowledge—the freedom for professional thinking, researching, speaking, and writing—also breed insularity and privilege and encourage scientists to take the role of experts, often in areas in which they have no special competence. And even where their competence is unparalleled, they may exclude others from access to public forums or from the acquisition of the now requisite credentials (Pels 1995). It does not take a Ph.D. in physics, after all, to know that hydrogen bombs are dangerous, nor expertise in epidemiology to notice that rates of childbirth defects are high near the waste dump known as Love Canal.

Thus the questions raised by such "anarchists" as Feyerabend or Foucault still need to be taken seriously: How can citizens defend themselves against the intellectual imperialism of many scientists and the policy experts who depend upon them? How can citizens influence the applications of scientific findings and even the research agendas of scientific disciplines? The external influence of corporate or state patronage provides no succor to citizens, for these forces are likely to be even less democratic than scientific elitists. Here Habermas' (1970a, 1984, 1987, 1992) critique of technicism is useful, for he shows how the rise of scientific expertise can drive a wedge between the efficient management of sociotechnical systems and the practices of everyday life from which democratic consensus can arise. But, contrary to Habermas, we can now see that rationality is preserved not by eschewing politics but by recognizing their very omnipresence and then channeling them, as in a scientific field, to support the advancement of agreements achieved through unfettered critique. It becomes clear, also, that the autonomy of scientific fields must be politically defended. Academic freedom and, more broadly, democratic rights, are not epistemic or ethical universals that always will exist. Instead, they are social achievements whose preservation requires ceaseless political struggle by scholars and citizens. Scientists need allies in the preservation of their autonomy, just as citizens need science to help articulate key issues and define strategies for defending and extending the autonomy of citizens and the "field" of civic discourse.

The scientific field is different from the field of public life, but each have their criteria for admission. Entrance into the scientific field requires certain specialized skills and institutional certification through credentials. Access to the public sphere usually requires only citizenship, which in principle includes all members who create and are created by that political community. Nonetheless, each vision of a viable public life is accompanied by some specification of access to it. John Dewey, for example, criticized the rising manufacturers of opinion for limiting access. For Dewey, the denial of access to the public sphere restricts the free marketplace of ideas, but his solution is to restore the marketplace, thereby reaffirming a market conception of politics. Similarly, Jürgen Habermas' justification of open access derives from his conception of the ideal polity as a rationalistic apolitical competition among ideas. Habermas thereby fails to interrogate his own Enlightenment assumptions concerning the segregation of knowledge and power (Klumpp 1991; Klumpp et al. 1995).

In contrast to such economistic, utilitarian, or rationalistic visions of public space, in the narrativist perspective, the representational theory of truth is replaced by a constitutive one in which the polity is made through discourse and the focus is not on essences of ideas or materiality but on how communicative action composes both scientific and civic communities.

The narrativist perspective also foregrounds the civic or scientific audience or community, rather than the individual rhetor. Scientific disciplines and whole societies develop paradigmatic strategies for defining situations and responding to them—strategies that guide and constrain the acts of individuals. A narrative theory of science is interested in these strategies and in how scientific communities generate and deploy them to shape and discipline their members and thereby reproduce themselves. Thus the narrativist perspective engages the linguistic forms through which a scientific or civic public "socializes its material and ideological situation into its daily activity. As a result it frames the powers of speech—generally considered—in terms of the community's exercise of power over its world" (Klumpp 1991; see Burke 1954:35–36). In this formulation, narrative and other rhetorical practices emerge not as modes of expressing ideas and materials that are apprehensible exterior to discourse. Instead, people re-present what already has been formed in prior discourse, and stretch and bend that discourse, and so they renew and reknow their worlds through communicative action. Hence, the quality of both scientific and civic fields depends on the development of strategies and practices of communication that enrich human responses to situations that such communities face.

The field theory of science also reallocates older Weberian notions of disinterestedness or value neutrality. The scientific community does have interests, but they are different from those of other institutions. And "better" knowledge is produced precisely because of the specialized, power-laden, interest-driven practices of the scientific community and its relative autonomy from external political forces that are not so directed at generating scientific truth. The autonomy of the scientific field thus becomes the collective interest of scientists and their allies, as this autonomy is the precondition for their internal competition through which rationality is advanced. This formulation also suggests a kind of autotelic consensus and sometimes advancement in science, though now driven socially, not epistemically.

Our analysis of science as a field of practical discourse also serves to integrate the more "internalist" chapters 3, 4, and 5 of this book with the more "externalist" chapters 6 and 7. Whereas the field theory preserves the validity of science by showing how its truths are socially generated, it also shows their limits. That is, because validity is always socially generated and constrained, the epistemological status of scientific claims are *in*valid, or meaningless, outside the scientific field. Of course, this field can expand to the extent that, say, the factory is turned into a laboratory for experimental psychology. Or the field can shrink to the degree that factory owners begin dictating scientific agendas and methods to serve only the interests of business. Thus scientific findings may be valid within their proper (and flexible) domains. But the sociological recovery of scientific validity after its philosophic downfall does nothing to justify the obsequious reliance on science in other realms of inquiry and other spheres of life. Such deference to science seems ubiquitous—in state funding for scientific research, in the teaching of humane disciplines in a "scientific" way, and in the legal and moral authority conferred to "scientific" experts in public institutions and civic culture. Such deference is buttressed by post-Enlightenment philosophies of history that link science to modernity—to rationality, technology, and economic growth (Rouse 1988:31). But this has no basis in the necessarily self-endorsing warrant for science that emerges from scientific discourse. And this is the only credible warrant for science that we possess. Hence, a rhetorical perspective, a critique of science and scientism, is needed. By rejecting any global legitimations of science as an inherently progressive and rational enterprise, this perspective opens space for political and moral awareness of the interactions between scientific and other social practices, and encourages a view of ourselves as the collaborative and conflicting narrators of our scientific and social worlds.

Finally, in the narrativist perspective, those who debunk science should redirect their critique—not toward the efforts of working scientists to keep their conversations going but toward the absolutist claims often made in the name of science, and toward the use of scientific discourse as a legitimation of modern politics and culture. This redirection implies a range of possible political objectives. At the least, scientists should be more self-critical about the political nature and social origins of their research. More ambitiously, scientists and their allies should seek to cleanse their fields of abuse by members and of exploitation by funders. More radically, we would hope to "create new scientific methods rooted in the social needs of communities and accountable to interests other than those of managerial elites in business, government and the military. The latter claim is driven by the principle that people whose lives are greatly affected by the effects of scientific superindustrialism ought to have a role in the decision-making that determines research. But it also involves taking seriously the proposition that Western technoscience is unlikely to have a world monopoly on good scientific ideas" (Ross 1995:348).

Such changes would not only help us toward a more just appreciation of scientific activities; they would also support a more profound critique and transformation of modern societies. Perhaps both these purposes can be served through coalitions of scientific groups and democratic social movements. At the least, such alliances might counterbalance the dependence of science on the corporate state and thereby reinforce the autonomy of scientific fields, even while curtailing anti-democratic scientism and the elitist exploitation of science.

RHETORICAL CRITICISM OF SCIENCE AND REASONED CIVIC NARRATIONS

A main thrust of rhetorical criticism has been to relativize absolutist claims in philosophy, science, and social engineering and, thereby, to open space for alternate discourses. Rhetoricians attack the central claim of positivists that language is a neutral vehicle that can transport the features of extralinguistic reality unadulterated into our conceptual apparatus—that scientific language constitutes a literal, nonfigurative transcription of the real. Rhetorical criticism implies that the constitutive functions of language have been obscured and that this obscurity can be replaced by reflexivity and insight.

The claim that rhetorical analysis can demystify literal or scientific language stems from two assumptions: that rhetoric can reveal the figurative workings of language and that the "literality" of scientific discourse is itself a linguistic construction. For example, Brown (1987:115, also 75, 113–17; see 1995, 1992, 1989a:219, 230) argues that "rhetorical analysis demystifies by showing that scientific theories are rhetorical constructions and that their key terms are ineliminably metaphorical." Similarly, Paolo Valesio (1980:96) asserts that "rhetoric . . . is the most . . . precise tool that can be used to show that every positive ontology is an ideological construction." In the same spirit, Chiam Perelman and Lucie Olbrechts-Tyteca (1969:512) argue that "the assertion that whatever is not objectively and indisputably valid belongs to the realm of the arbitrary and subjective *creates* an unbridgeable gulf between theoretical knowledge, which alone is rational, and action, for which motivations would be wholly irrational."

To fill this "unbridgeable gap" between knowledge and action, positivists have recommended a scientific politics of expertise and social engineering. By contrast, rhetoricians reject such amoral, technicist discourse and instead affirm the central role of civic intelligence in reasoned moral political action. Indeed, it is here that rhetoric comes into its own, for a good or noble rhetoric *is* civic intelligence at work and in the making.

Such civic intelligence is prudential. It is the making of political ethical decisions through reasoned judgment that adapts shared principles to changing circumstances and creates a politics of both. Of course, to the extent that situations are routinized and predictable, they are more susceptible to routinized methods of interpretation, even to scientific algorithms or decision techniques. Such devices such as building codes or actuarial tables, for example, can be routinely applied by structural engineers or insurance brokers to provide useful interpretations of bridges or populations. Situations of moral and political moment, however, rarely manifest the regularity and predictability that may be found in stress loads or mortality rates. Indeed, the more publicly significant the issue, the less likely it is to be predictable.

Thus, civic decision making is almost always conducted in a field of uncertainty. A prudent approach to such decision making cannot be either a purely expediential innovation or a rote adherence to rules, as either approach would thwart the capacity to adapt prudently to new conditions. Thus a reasoned civic practice faces two large dangers—opportunism and irrelevance.

Rhetoric, Aristotle tells us, has to do with "things about which we deliberate but for which we have no systematic rules." In more contemporary language, rhetoric concerns uncertainty. In the centuries since Aristotle wrote, our uncertainty has extended beyond the ethics and politics of Athenian civic life to include philosophy, science, and the academic disciplines in general. Indeed, our former resources for knowledge have now become topics of skepticism. This extension of uncertainty also extends the scope of rhetoric. Deliberation, which is made possible and useful by uncertainty, is central to both the old, Aristotelian, rhetoric and this new, extended rhetoric. Thus rhetoric offers not only a theory of choice in human affairs but also a way of understanding how consensual choices between alternative theories and data are achieved in scientific fields.

Contrary to the view of many rationalist philosophers, a narrative approach in science as in civic life insists that the abstract rationality of a given position is insufficient to convert most audiences to it. This is because "the audience will still be left wondering why the speaker would *want* to hold such a view and, more important, why anyone else *should*. After all, a defensible view is not necessarily worth defending" (Fuller 1993:306). Thus rhetorically adept speakers begin their stories where their audience is located in order to combine cognitive agreement with motivated action. A truly democratic rhetoric, one comprehensive enough to include scientific talk as well as lay and minority voices as parts of civic discourse, requires that changes of mind be products of sweet persuasion rather than dominating deduction. Steve Fuller (1993:306–7) notes this as a difference between the "facilitative syllogism" and the "belligerent syllogism." The belligerent syllogism says:

> One of us must move.
> I won't.
> Therefore, you must.

By contrast, the facilitative syllogism states:

> We're already trying to move in the same direction.
> There is an obstacle on your side of the road.
> Therefore, let me help you remove it.

For such a facilitative rhetoric, the polity is where realities are formed. Accordingly, democratically responsible institutions are those that provide the maximum space for public discourse and self-direction of citizens. Reciprocally, such discourse is precisely the means for engendering democratic institutions. This is rhetoric as affirmative, dialogical, and dialectical practice. Against positivist conceptions of science, against technicism and reified bureaucracies, rhetoric affirms the centrality of the human authorship of the world.

Critics of such a radically democratic conception of science and civic discourse claim that it relativizes and debases reason into ideology. Rhetoricians usually have responded *tu quoque*—the same to you. They defend a limited sort of relativism and insist that all that is human—including philosophy, science, and criticisms of rhetoric—is rhetorical constructions. But perhaps we now can more fruitfully understand this conflict between science and rhetoric as one between two different fields of practice—autonomous science and democratic politics—each of which has a different primary aim. The aim of a scientific field is the construction of knowledge. The aim of a democratic political field is the construction of citizenship. Defenders of scientific fields have encouraged practices with the highest levels of epistemic productivity, regardless of their ethical or democratic implications. That is, the philosophic or scientific "impulse is toward maximizing the *production* of knowledge-and-power, even if the means of production are concentrated in an elite cadre of [scientists, technicians, and their paymasters whose superior knowledge] enables them to mask their own interest in bringing the world into alignment with their normative model. The ultimate source here is Plato. Unlike the Aristotelian *phronesis* approach to politics, in which the rulers are no smarter than the ruled except in their ability to represent several constituencies at once, the Platonic *episteme* approach involves the ruler in strategic over-clarification and illusion in order to guide the populace toward a normatively acceptable end" (Fuller 1993:27; see Proctor 1991).

By contrast, radical democrats have focused on schemes for enhancing the construction of citizenship, without much considering the institutional and economic costs involved in implementing those schemes. Workplace democratization is an example of such a dialogical process, as are community justice and anti-psychiatric community-based mental health. Within the latter, for instance, "madness" is seen as generated by language practices, and "the usual 'monologue of Reason' about madness is no longer sufficient to sustain a diagnosis" (Murphy 1989:85–87). Instead, mental illness is seen as an inadequacy of communication, and treatment is aimed at re-integrating patients into their communities as effective citizens. The democratic impulse of such experiments is to maximize the distribution of power and knowledge, even if this undermines the autonomy or productivity of current scientific practices (Fuller 1993:27).

Just as the industrial revolution brought great concentrations of economic power, the industrialization of science has brought great concentrations of knowledge power. With such concentrations has come the belief that society should be run by experts. Thus the very success of science in extending the powers of humanity has yielded a condition of shrinking powers of ordinary men and women. As the alliance between capitalism and democracy becomes less feasible in mass industrial societies, so the link between knowledge and emancipation becomes less feasible with the advent of mass industrial science.

This change also has ironic consequences for the epistemic justification of science (Fuller 1993; Willard 1991). As the scale of science increases, traditional epistemology no longer offers guidance in evaluating knowledge claims. This is because the huge number of such claims that are produced today, and the even greater number of plausible contexts for assessing them, makes it impossible and irrational to assess each of them on its particular epistemological merits. In this circumstance, technicists claim that we must rely on experts. This is plausible for highly specialized or routinized problems in which expert knowledge is relevant and dependable, but it is not true of larger, more general and complex issues of public concern. Indeed, the epistemological limits of expertise in the public sphere provide a strong argument for democratic participation and rhetorical deliberation.

This democratic conception of knowledge/power also implies revised criteria for assessing knowledge and its value. Against epistemological or utilitarian views, democratic rhetors would assess the value of knowledge by the ability of its possessor to influence the subsequent course of knowledge production. For example, a chemist's knowledge of chemistry is worth more than, say, an undergraduate's knowledge of the subject because the knowledge of the trained chemist allows her with greater ease to effect the further production of such knowledge (Fuller 1993). Similarly, a lone individual complaining about pollution is likely to have zero effect on scientific practices, whereas a well-organized social movement might engender an entire new scientific discipline—ecology. Thus a democratic rhetoric shifts the question under discussion. No longer do we question *whether* knowledge is contaminated by, or shaped by, or independent of, power. Instead, we take for granted that the construction and propagation of knowledge are infused with power; then we ask how different kinds of power/knowledge differently empower citizens or knowers. This unifies the epistemic idea of demonstration and the political idea of empowerment into one conception: science and democracy are both forms of representation. Truth in each lies in the power to produce (and not merely passively consume) more knowledge/power. In the age of Big Science, a rhetoric of reason as empowerment subsumes epistemology, science, and techniques. Rhetoric becomes the creation of civic culture, the discourse through which we can make and guide our civic life.

Chapter 9 Democratic Science in Practice:
The Experience of the Environmental
Justice Movement

with Robert J. Brulle

The breakdown of narrativity in a culture, group, or social class is a symptom of its having entered into a state of crisis. For with any weakening of narrativizing capacity, the group loses its power to locate itself in history, to come to grips with the necessity that its past represents for it and to imagine a creative, if only provisional transcendence of its "fate." . . . In the dialectical movement by which a unity of plot is imposed upon the superficial chaos of story elements, narrative serves as a paradigm of the kind of social movement by which a unity of meaning can be imposed upon the chaos of history
Hayden White (1987:149, 157)

How can we restore and enhance moral agency and civic initiative in a society that depends on scientific knowledge and is infused with social engineering? How can we reclaim public policy from experts and subsume their scientific knowledge within larger narratives of our common life? One step would be to understand science as a kind of storytelling and to construe persons as authors of their worlds, including the world of science. This would help liberate science from its positivist ideologues and make it more accessible to persons who know how to narrate their lives and worlds, that is, all members of human communities, including citizens creating themselves and their democracies through reasoned, ethical public discourse.

Thus, to construe science as narration is to invite a morally enlightened alliance of science and politics or, more precisely, to render scientific narratives subsumable within more inclusive narratives of the political community. Such a move also helps to demystify those uses of expertise and specialized knowledge that mask the privileges of elites. A narrative conception of science also supports its democratization. Science as practiced—what scientists are doing when they are doing well as scientists—is also what citizens are doing when they are doing well as citizens, that is, when citizens are creating their polity through collaborative or argumentative discourse. Thus the democratization of science is not only a liberation of citizens from technicism in the service of the corporate state. It is also a liberation and relegitimization of scientists.

We have argued so far that science has a narrative structure, that it is a poetic and political practice. We have also shown that this rhetorical character of science does not negate its rationality but instead is its primary source. The industrialization of science, its enlistment in the service of elites, and its use as an ideology of expertise all have little to do with the discovery of truth, which is the telos of science when narrated as an intellectual pursuit. But these other features are indispensable to science as a major factor of production and control, and they have much to do with the use of science as an instrument and justification of statist and corporate domination.

Although many analysts have thoughtfully criticized the political economy of knowledge production along these lines, little has been written about what an alternative "democratic science" might look like. Moreover, most proposals for reform focus on humanizing individual scientists or altering funding priorities for science, without addressing the anti-democratic features of contemporary knowledge production as such. To move beyond technicist versions of science, antinomian rejections of them, or suggestions for limited reforms, we must imagine how a more radically democratized science could help us develop a civic community.

This involves a redefinition of the cultural idea of science—from a technicist practice, accessible only to a specialized priesthood, to a rhetorical practice in which all competent adults can engage. A democratic science seeks to replace the hegemony of scientism by subsuming science within a democratic civic discourse. When science is conceived this way, the autonomy and independence of the scientific communities must be preserved as a vital part of civic narrations. Moreover, an autonomous scientific discourse can also serve as a heuristic example of democratic argumentation. Thus the practice of science would be integrated into the development of larger communities of civic intelligence and would be part of such communities' rhetorical activity of creating knowledge, guidance, and themselves as a democratic polity. By viewing science as rhetorical practice, competent citizens are invited to join the scientific discourse as active partners in the development and implementation of research programs.

To realize such a democratic science requires changes in the patterns of interactions and self-definitions of both scientists and communities. One effort to develop scientific practice within a democratic civic discourse is the movement for environmental justice. Using this social movement as an instructive example, we will explore the development of a democratic science.

CIVIL SOCIETY AND THE PUBLIC SPHERE

It is taken for granted within the radical democratic wing of the environmental movement that the construction of a humane and ecologically sustainable social order will require major changes that involve all existing institutions in society. As Jaeger (1994:273) asserts, "Only if a huge process of cultural degeneration can be reversed into a fairly rapid process of cultural regeneration, is there a chance of overcoming the environmental crisis." For such changes to be accomplished, however, our society's capacity for social learning needs to increase greatly. This, in turn, entails the integration of science and narration, or system and lifeworld, that were discussed in chapters 1 and 2. That is, the problem for environmental planning or action is parallel to the problem for philosophy, the human sciences, and politics in modern democratic societies: how to reconcile systems efficiency with human agency. Theoretically, this requires the interconnection of two apparently opposite paradigms—positive science of nature and narration of the lifeworld. Practically, it requires that persons be prime agents in maintaining and changing their collective systems by mastering internal complexity and environmental inconstancy. Stated in more traditional terms, the practical requirement for reconciling systems efficiency and human agency is that citizens effectively govern their polities (Brown 1989b:148–49). Put slightly differently (Keane 1988:14), this involves "two interdependent and simultaneous processes: the expansion of social equality and liberty, and the restructuring and democratization of the state."

Civic communication is vital to the capacity of institutions to meet new circumstances. Because both the market and the state are infused with and propagate a technicist culture, they are unlikely to create effective alternatives either to this culture or to the ecological crisis that it engenders (Brulle 1998). By contrast, one space of activity outside the state and the market where such creative actions might originate is civil society (Habermas 1987, 1992; Cohen and Arato 1992). The modern notion of civil society was developed by Hegel (1967:122–55), who saw it as containing the social spaces and civic institutions in which deliberative discourse takes place. Civil society defines the site in the current social order where groups and organizations operate and interact outside both the market and the state, not merely as functionaries or consumers but as citizens.

Organizations based in civil society ideally provide an arena in which an ethical life can be developed and citizenship exercised. Because all members of such organizations are treated in principle as full participants and active agents in the co-creation of meaning and community, they ideally are seedbeds of moral and civic competence from which citizens can influence both the market and the state. Organizations in civil society are thus a prime source for actions that could lead to the reconstruction of the public sphere. Operating in and constituting civil society, these organizations are able to articulate and mobilize the concerns of citizens, thereby enhancing democratic control over political and economic institutions (Brulle 1994; Offe 1990:76; Habermas 1987:142, 1994), including the development of new alternative institutions that can foster an ecologically sustainable society.

Given the necessary orientation of capitalist economic entities toward profit, and given their concentration of economic and political control, a vibrant civil society appears to be necessary not only for the freedom and dignity of democratic citizens but also for the long-term survival of society and its natural environment. Indeed, public participation is necessary not only to ensure the accountability of large organizations but also to generate informed support for appropriate innovations of culture and policy that perforce elude the technocratically managed corporate state (Jaeger 1994:273–74). Within the environmental movement, for example, the direct involvement of citizens in decision making about hazardous wastes has been essential for defining and ensuring the general welfare. As Morgan (1994:29) concluded, "if public bodies are to make good decisions about regulating potential hazards, citizens must be well informed. The alternative of entrusting policy to panels of experts working behind closed doors has proved a failure, both because the resulting policy may ignore important social considerations and because it may prove impossible to implement in the face of grass-roots resistance."[1]

Opening the decision process to greater democratic participation enhances the testing of the validity of the information on which collectively binding decisions are made. Just as creative scientific communities generate alternative theories and findings and contest them through alliances in vigorous debate, so a more open social order allows for both the incorporation of more ecological knowledge into the decision-making process and the noncoercive achievement of assent to resultant decisions. This increases the use of ecological information and the overall rationality of the decisions. It also expands civil society and the democratic polity in general insofar as *civitas* is created through the very process of such open discourse. Thus the process of integrating more ecological information into the making of civic and institutional decisions is not merely a question of enhancing the technical rationality of such decisions, much less a question of engineering popular consent. Most important, it involves making our political and administrative institutions more open and democratic (Taylor 1984:3; Brulle 1994:115–17; Dietz 1987; Webler, Kastenholtz, and Renn 1994).

The development of a democratic science can contribute to such efforts. The practice of democratic science expands the notion of science as a narrative constructed in a human community and thereby provides an alternative to the technicist models of scientific inquiry. Social movements, like scientific movements, attempt to alter shared realities through the promotion of an alternative discourse. In this light, the political struggles of the radical democratic elements of the environmental movement are acting as scientific innovators, in stretching the existing narrative of scientific practice to more adequately address community concerns (Eder 1985:873–74). To understand how this has occurred, we need to explore the relation between a movement's discursive frame and the authorization of different scientific practices.

DISCOURSE AND SOCIAL MOVEMENTS

A rhetorical analysis of the discursive framework of a social movement can begin by examining key tropes, the terms that are regularly clustered around them, and the core common beliefs that are created from and maintained by such usages. One such belief is about the nature of the reality in which a social movement exists. Other core beliefs concern that movement's basic character and mission. The discursive practices through which such beliefs are engendered and enacted are, in effect, that movement or organization. That is, just as scientists constitute Galilean pulsars or peptides as objects of scientific inquiry in the very practices of talking about them (see chapter 3), and just as scientific communities constitute themselves through their practices of scientific discourse, so also social organizations and movements define their worlds and become what they are through communicative interactions.

From a rhetorical and phenomenological viewpoint, social order is constituted discursively through the development and maintenance of a dominant definition of reality. Along with this goes the suppression or marginalization of alternative coexisting definitions of reality. These subjugated discourses represent the lifeworlds of individuals who are not dominant within the social order. The use of these subjugated discourses is limited to particularistic, local, or noninstitutional interactions. The lack of existential fit between lifeworld experiences and the dominant discourse provides the impetus for symbolic challenges in the form of social movements. Such contestation of the dominant definition of reality may undermine its naturalness and taken-for-granted character. Then a symbolic space is created in which contending versions of the real can appear. The interest of dominated groups lies in reducing the reign of the dominant discourse and in broadening this space for creative transgressions. The interest of the dominant groups lies in increasing the reign of the reified and dominant reality.

In this perspective, social order is a practical, historic accomplishment, brought about through everyday struggles over the nature of reality. Similarly, social movements are creative activities of society remaking itself. This remaking often takes the form of moral dramas and quests for salvation (Burke 1945, 1955, 1989; Griffin 1969; Stewart, Smith, and Denton 1989:137–56). These dramas and quests are not inherently irrational. On the contrary, they deploy a narrative logic that implies criteria of consistency, verisimilitude, cogency, and form. Their rationality is a kind of reasonableness or prudence akin to what we have seen in effective scientific judgments-in-the-making.

The narrative of the environmental movement is one in which the drama of both humanity and nature are played out. This drama unfolds as the old social paradigm becomes overextended and thereby more subject to contradictions, challenges, and entropy. In sacral terms, as the old paradigm falls into corruption, it increasingly contaminates its users. From this emerges a new, redemptive definition of social and natural reality that eliminates the cause of corruption and restores the purity of believers (Stewart, Smith, and Denton 1989:152–55; Touraine 1985:59). Thus social movements, like scientific movements, alter stated realities by promoting an alternative discourse.

A first step in the development of the identity of a social movement is the delegitimation of the existing model of reality. This takes the form of a rhetoric of discontinuity that justifies dramatic change in society due to the invention and then discovery of unsolved problems (Jablonski 1980:289; Griffin 1969:460). For a social or scientific movement to gain an identity, a new narrative of its field must also be created (Stewart 1980:298–305; Kurtz 1983; Ash 1983). This voicing of a new representation of the social world is an act of identity formation of a movement that later may elaborate and instantiate itself as an organization. In addition to constituting the movement's identity, a discourse also provides a viewpoint or frame through which both the organization's reality and its appropriate collective action can be newly conceived. The discursive frame is a source of motivation for individuals to participate in the movement because it provides good reasons for seeking social change and positive identities for those who seek it (Fisher 1992). In brief, the movement's discourse defines the situation, identifies crucial interactions and places them within a specific historical and social context, and provides a positive personal identity from which collective action can be developed.[2] These alternate frameworks tend "to legitimate a particular set of participants and a particular set of resources in the conflict, and to delegitimate other actors and resources" (Dietz, Stern, and Rycroft 1989:53). The framework of discourse guides the thinking of those engaged in the conflict about what is really at stake, what the motives of participants must be, and what acceptable tactics can include. Such an analysis of discursive frames can also illuminate how science is used by environmental organizations. That is, insofar as a particular discourse legitimates certain actions and delegitimates others, one way to understand the different uses of science within the environmental movement is to examine the dominant discourse through which that organization's identity is shaped.

CONSERVATIONIST AND ECOCENTRIC DISCOURSE AND TECHNICIST SCIENTIFIC PRACTICE

The environmental movement in the United States is the product of more than one hundred years of collective action and is composed of various discourses and organizations that were formed in particular historical circumstances (Brulle 1994, 1998). Many different forms of organization, identity, action, and objectives are realized and legitimated through these discourses, which together form the discursive field of the current environmental movement. The two most politically dominant environmental discourses—conservationism and ecocentrism—both authorize a technicist scientific practice.

Conservationism was the first environmental discourse to emerge in the

United States. It articulates a utilitarian and technical or managerial view in which nature is a resource to be used by society to meet human needs (Oelschlaeger 1991:201–2, 286–89). In this view, collective action is aimed at ensuring that natural resources are used by applying the criteria of means-ends rationality or efficiency to achieve the maximum utility to society. Like other discourses, conservationism advances several key assumptions about the nature of reality:

- Physical and biological nature is nothing more than a collection of parts that function like those of a machine.
- Nature is a resource that humans need in order to maintain their societies.
- Nature can be managed by humans through application of technical knowledge by competent professionals.
- The proper management philosophy for natural resources is to realize the greatest good for the greatest number of people over the longest period of time.

This conservationist discourse began in the United States with the publication of *Man and Nature* by George Perkins Marsh in 1864. Marsh argued that humanity was "a destabilizing environmental force whose impacts portended an uncertain future" (in Oelschlaeger 1991:107) and, therefore, that humanity must develop a stewardship of natural resources. Marsh's ideas took root in the 1890s as people perceived a need for some sort of control over the reckless exploitation of nature. At the same time, technical, managerial, and professional elites became concerned about the continuing availability of natural resources.

These concerns were shared and even stimulated and extended by national corporate and political elites to develop a program to conserve natural resources and thus ensure continued capitalist development. Results of this effort include the establishment of national forests and the management of grazing on federal lands. More important, however, a program of resource management was to serve an economy that was technically managed by professionals. Conservation, above all, was a scientific movement, and its role in history arises from the implications of science and technology in modern society. Its essence was rational planning to promote efficient development and use of all natural resources. Conservationists envisaged a political system guided by the ideal of efficiency and dominated by the technicians who could best determine how to achieve it (Hays 1972). Under the leadership of the professional forest manager Giffort Pinchot, several political initiatives were taken to form governmental programs of action based on this viewpoint, among them the founding of the U.S. Forest Service.

Ecocentrism is the other environmental discourse that contributed to the development of a technicist practice of science within the environmental movement. Ecocentric discourse draws on the notion of the natural and especially biological sciences that humanity is part of natural ecosystems: it therefore links human survival to ecosystem survival (Oelschlaeger 1991:292–301). In this discourse, nature is a delicate web of interdependent relationships of which humans are a part. Because humanity is a dependent part of the global environment, its health is intimately connected with the state of the natural environment. Hence, this discourse animates action to identify and eliminate the physical and biological causes of environmental degradation. Key components of this perspective are:

- Natural systems are the basis of all organic existence, including human existence, and therefore possess incalculable value.
- Humankind is an element within natural ecosystems, hence human survival depends on ecosystem survival.
- Ethical human actions (actions that promote the good life for humankind) necessarily promote action toward all life on earth in an ecologically responsible manner.
- Proper use of natural sciences can guide the relationship between humanity and its natural environment.

One paradigmatic statement of this perspective is *Silent Spring,* by Rachel Carson, which appeared in 1962. This book combined concern for natural ecosystems with that for public health. The public awareness that it inspired was crucial for the founding in 1967 of the Environmental Defense Fund (EDF), which marked the beginning of the wave of new environmental organizations based on the ecocentric discourse. EDF describes itself as "a nationwide public interest organization of lawyers, scientists, and economists dedicated to protecting and improving environmental quality and public health" (Gale 1990). It was established after an informal team of lawyers and biologists working on behalf of the Audubon Society successfully halted the spraying of DDT on Long Island. This court action united scientific and legal competencies in the interests of public health and environmental protection. Following this initial success, the Audubon Society, the Rockefeller Fund, and the Rachel Carson Fund provided the seed money to start EDF. The fund's objective is "to encourage and support the wise use of natural resources, and the maintenance and enhancement of environmental quality" (EDF bylaws). The pattern established by the EDF has served as an exemplar for many other organizations, including the Natural Resources Defense Council, which also uses scientific research and legal action to protect the environment and human health.

In both conservationist and ecocentric organizations, the practice of science is based on a technicist image. First, the discursive frames of both conservationism and ecocentrism assume that environmental problems will be solved through top-down, expert intervention (Taylor 1992:27–50; Evernden 1992). Scientists, because of their expertise, must play a prominent role in the "scientific management of the environment" (Taylor 1992:50). Citizens and even elected officials play only bit parts; they are to heed the advice of scientists or lawyers. This is shown by the mechanistic metaphor of Paul Erlich's title— *The Machinery of Nature*—and by his discussions of how environmental problems will be solved: "To protect and (to the extent possible) repair the machinery (of nature) will require many more scientists delving into its complexities, as well as a much deeper appreciation by the general public and decision makers of both its importance and its basic design" (Erlich 1986:291). In this technicist discourse, there is no identified need to involve the public, except as objects to be instructed or from which to obtain financial support. Indeed, there is not even the existence of a public in the sense of an actively deciding, self-creating citizenry.

As groups become more organized, they, like scientists, need funds to sustain their institutional practices. In the environmental movement, the largest and richest organizations are mass-based ones with a multitude of "checkbook members." To obtain support from the public, conservationist and ecocentric organizations use mass mailings to members who have little loyalty to any particular organization. This practice results in episodic swings in levels of membership and funding. To stabilize this funding and to promote their own growth, the organizations turn to corporations and foundations and usually come to depend on them. The organizations thus become responsive to corporate discourses and interests, which further isolates the membership from participation in organizational policies and practices. Instead, the corporate and foundation funding pursued by such organizations involves them in a technocratic policy process. This is not only a matter of adopting positions acceptable to funders. To even apply for such funding requires specialized technical expertise to prepare grant proposals, administer them, and monitor and report on their progress. Thus, such organizations have developed professional staffs and bureaucratic structures, which further excludes members from participation. Moreover, given their technicist discursive framework, staffing pattern, sources of funds, and their passive membership, conservationist and ecocentric organizations tend to pursue insider political strategies and to keep their initiatives well within the framework and institutions of corporatist capitalism. They are well funded, oligarchic in structure, and generally headquartered in Washington, D.C.

The great limitation of this approach is that it leaves the basic social production of environmental problems untouched. Indeed, this technicist practice has failed to deal effectively with environmental problems. Twenty years after the first Earth Day, Barry Commoner (1991:63) reviewed the U.S. effort (which may be the world's most rigorous) and concluded that "the environmental effort has largely failed." Commoner's conclusion was confirmed and amplified by the updating of the volume *The Limits to Growth* (Meadows, Meadows, and Randers 1972) with the title *Beyond the Limits* in 1992, and by many independent and governmental studies. According to these analyses, the current use of natural resources by the human population is already exceeding the carrying capacity of the globe (Meadows, Meadows, and Randers 1992: xv–xvi). Thus, despite achievements in imposing regulations and responding to crises, the social production of environmental degradation is still greatly outpacing its repair. All this points to the difficulty of reorganizing our social order so we can function without destroying its biological basis. Although we have made incremental progress in reversing some of the worst forms of visible pollution, our efforts pale in comparison to the changes necessary to halt this destruction. "Indeed, many environmental regulations and interventions are little more than cosmetic" (Pointing 1991:400).

An examination of these environmental discourses shows their political limitations. By emphasizing technical knowledge, these discourses discourage mass political action. Moreover, the narrowly scientific analysis of environmental problems assesses current ecological problems but cannot provide a plan or theory for social change. Instead, the naive technicism that is adopted obscures new political visions that see beyond the current social order (Taylor 1992:173). In effect, this use of technicist language to assess the problems of a technicist culture reproduces the existing order. As Theodor Adorno and Max Horkheimer (1944:xiv) noted, "Even the best-intentioned reformer who uses an impoverished and debased language to recommend renewal, by his adoption of the insidious mode of categorization and the bad philosophy it conceals, strengthens the very power of the established order he is trying to break."

These failures of existing environmental discourses and organizations created a need for alternatives. Many members, cut off from active participation in these organizations and seeing only meager results, turned elsewhere to develop new ideas and strategies. Other persons, who have experienced environmental degradation in their own neighborhoods and who feel little affinity with national politics or Washington-based national organizations, have also been creating alternative discourses and interventions. Of particular interest among these is the movement for environmental justice and its discourse of political ecology.

POLITICAL ECOLOGY AND THE MOVEMENT FOR ENVIRONMENTAL JUSTICE

One major environmental discourse that promotes a democratic and participatory scientific practice is political ecology. In this discourse the organization of society itself is the source of ecological problems (Oelschlaeger 1991:307–8; Merchant 1992:132–54; Borecelli 1988:38; Sandbach 1980:26–27). Hence, in this view, the solution of environmental problems lies in changing the social order. Key tenets of this discourse are:

- Domination of humans by other humans also entails the domination of nature.
- The economic system and the nation-state are the core structures of society that create ecological problems.
- Commoditization and market imperatives force consumption to increase continually.
- Environmental destruction in racially distinct communities or in developing countries originates in the exploitation of these areas by economically dominant groups.
- Resolution of environmental problems requires fundamental change of these social arrangements—change that can come through empowerment of local communities.

The origins of political ecology can be traced to the works of Leo Tolstoy and of Peter Kropotkin (1993). Kropotkin argued that industrialism was unsustainable because of its destruction of communal economies and excessive exploitation of the natural environment. The Frankfurt school of social theory also contributed to political ecology, especially in the critiques of technicist discourse or instrumental reason by Theodor Adorno and Max Horkheimer (1944) and by Herbert Marcuse (1972). These authors argued that modern forms of domination of people and of nature express an alienated instrumental consciousness. Persons become atomized individuals for whom the external reality is made up of objects, natural or human, that are to be manipulated and controlled though the application of technical knowledge. In this instrumentalist or technicist view, say critical theorists, nature becomes merely a resource to be exploited, and the individual is merely a personality to be modified to fit the dominant social order (Adorno and Horkheimer 1944:57). The outcome is the reduction and depersonalization of our social relations to ones of calculated manipulation or exchange, and the severing of links to the living world of which we are a part. Technologies for regulating human nature and exploiting physical nature are gained in a Faustian bargain in which humanity exchanges its soul for wealth and power.

In such a perspective, the solution of the environmental crisis is linked to the resolution of our cultural crisis, because the ways we think about ourselves and nature shape our social actions toward both. Moreover, because the ecological and cultural crises are both outcomes of the use of instrumental reason to organize society, the resolution of these crises requires the creation and enactment of a new definition of social reason and reality that would enhance both human dignity and ecological sustainability.

From these initial sources, political ecology developed into a number of distinct environmentalist communities (Brulle 1998), one of which is the movement for environmental justice. Unlike mainstream environmental organizations, this movement is highly decentralized in several thousand local groups throughout the United States (Schwab 1994; Bullard 1993). The movement's central concept, "environmental justice," invites a view of environmental problems as the result of social organization. The environmental justice movement focuses on the disregard by government and corporations of community health and environmental needs. Indeed, this movement sees environmental problems as originating in the unprincipled quest for profits by corporations and in the power politics of the state. Similarly, the distribution of environmental problems is seen as a result of the distribution of wealth and power in society. Groups that are disadvantaged by class, race, and gender bear the brunt of ecological problems in the form of degraded living conditions, high levels of pollution, inadequate public services, and the dumping of toxic wastes in their communities. Environmental problems are thus concentrated in these communities, resulting in a significant degradation of the health of their residents.

Accordingly, the development of collective action based on the discourse of environmental justice originated in highly local struggles against pollution from toxic wastes that endangered people's health (Freudenberg and Steinsapir

1992). These citizens saw their communities and families threatened by degradation that resulted from pollution by companies and complicity or inaction by governmental agencies (Bullard 1993:8). In response, they created themselves as a movement through grassroots organizing. Many of the organizations formed by citizens in these communities were led by racial minorities or white working-class women and grew out of their direct personal experiences (Krauss 1993a, 1993b, 1994). They organized locally to respond to local threats. In the process of seeking amelioration of local problems, however, these citizens were regularly put off, lied to, or threatened by governmental and corporate officials. Hence, they came to challenge official channels, beliefs, and procedures, and to move beyond particular local problems to wider political issues. Thus the original focus on toxic wastes within the environmental justice movement has expanded to a broad agenda of issues of social justice, especially those concerning race, class, and gender (Krauss 1993b:259). In sum, rejection of environmental reform led to the development of broader and more radical approaches.

A key example of this development is the community situated on the dump site for abandoned waste known as Love Canal in New York State (Cable and Cable 1995:75–84). This community organized itself as the Love Canal Homeowner's Association. Originally focused on this specific instance of toxic pollution, this local association inspired the foundation of a national environmental organization, the Citizen's Clearinghouse for Hazardous Waste. Founded in 1981 by Lois Gibbs, a leader in the original Love Canal Homeowner's Association, this organization serves as a center for information and support for community organizing to more than seventy-five hundred local environmental groups nationwide. Its stated purpose is to facilitate the development of local environmental organizations by supporting, encouraging, and providing assistance to members and citizens generally who would seek to initiate, develop, and conduct programs within the fields of hazardous waste, toxic chemicals, and related environmental concerns, or those who would seek to increase public and professional awareness and understanding of the problems faced within these fields (bylaws of the Citizen's Clearinghouse for Hazardous Waste).

These kinds of organizations define their objective as changing the social order in some manner to solve environmental problems. The means to carry out this goal range from holding specific governmental agencies and corporations accountable through democratic processes, to ending race, ethnic, or economic exploitation. This is a democratic bottom-up approach, rather than scientistic and top-down. After years of skirmishes to achieve a local victory over powerful interests, groups that initially mobilized around a local issue become concerned and competent to define issues and take collective actions at the national level, only now with the broad power base of a social movement.

THE DEVELOPMENT OF "PEOPLE'S SCIENCE"

A major component of the movement for environmental justice has been the development of democratic scientific practices that empower local communities to conduct their own epidemiological studies of the impacts of toxic wastes (Bryant 1995:13). Such studies also encourage civic enlightenment and involvement because in the course of the investigation and through dissemination of its results there is an increase in both the community's knowledge of the presence and impacts of toxic wastes and its organized resistance to these conditions. Through these practices, the environmental justice movement suggests an image of what a democratic scientific practice might be.

Starting informally, community members usually begin by noticing the occurrence of possible links between health and toxic wastes. These links are the topic of local conversation, typically followed by inquiries and requests to governmental officials regarding potential health hazards. This is usually followed by governmental inaction or a series of governmental studies that find little direct proof to validate the community's concerns about pollution and health. Citizens, not convinced by official assurances that there is nothing to worry about, recommit themselves by forming their own community group and developing their own scientific knowledge, both by hiring their own experts and by enhancing the capacities of the local citizenry. Such actions lead to confrontation with the government and with corporate representatives over the impacts of toxic wastes in the community (Brown and Masterman-Allen 1994).

One key example of this process was the activities of the citizens who lived around Love Canal. In the summer of 1978 Lois Gibbs and several other residents of the houses built on or near an abandoned waste dump noticed extraordinary levels of illness in their area. Gathering information from local newspapers and court records, local citizens gradually recognized that their community had been built on an abandoned waste site. They set in motion a process of surveying the community for health problems. Informally, through door-to-door canvassing efforts, the true extent of the health problems in this area began to surface. In recollecting this process, Lois Gibbs reports, "The entire community seemed to be sick! Then I remembered my own neighbors.

One who lived on the left of my husband and me was suffering from severe migraines and had been hospitalized three or four times that year. Her daughter had kidney problems and bleeding. A woman on the other side of us had gastrointestinal problems. A man in the next house down was dying of lung cancer and he didn't even work in industry. . . . I continued to go door-to-door. I was becoming more worried because of the many families with children who had birth defects. Then I learned something even more frightening: there had been five crib deaths within a few short blocks" (Gibbs 1982:16–17).

Seeking answers, the community members contacted their local and state governmental officials. Initially, the officials denied that a problem existed. As community pressure for action expanded, however, officials began to make proposals to remedy the problem. Community activists entered discussions with the governmental experts who had been assigned to implement these "solutions." In this dialogue, the technicist discourse of science was encountered by the activists as a foreign language that obstructed the realization of community interests. This "scientization of politics," as Habermas (1970b:68) called it, was a technocratic reaction to community concerns. The community activists, unable to speak the specialized discourse of science, responded within their own narrative logic to challenge the adequacy of this technicist jargon. One such exchange is detailed by Lois Gibbs: " 'What about the underground streams?' He said they would be taken care of and gave me a technical explanation I didn't understand. 'Excuse me,' I replied. 'I'm just a dumb housewife. I'm not an expert. You're the expert. I'm just going to use a little common sense. You will have underground streams running through the canal beneath those pipelines. The chemicals will get out. There's no way they are going to go into your pipe. They will be under it. Now, how do you take care of that?' He answered with some more incomprehensible engineering terms" (Gibbs 1982:31).

On one side we see the technical language of the engineer who is attempting to convince the nonexpert of the utility of the proposed remedy. In the response, by contrast, we see the individual whose agency is validated as part of the larger logic of a community narrative. Although the statement made by the engineer might be technically correct, it lacks validity in the eyes of the community activist, who views the statement as the product of an unauthentic communication, based in a normative tradition outside her own community. At this point, however, the community lacked a technically adequate discourse of its own. A general failure by governmental officials to meaningfully address the problem of toxic wastes from Love Canal led to the founding of the Love Canal

Homeowner's Association. One of the earliest actions of this association was to build statistics about the incidence of health problems in the Love Canal area. With the assistance of a local university instructor, Dr. Beverly Paigen, local homemakers gathered data about hospitalizations and deaths in their community. Based on these data, a study was completed and presented to the state health officials. "Dr. Paigen finally went to Albany to meet with the health department. She had everything prepared, . . . all the statistical correlations and tables. . . . She thought something was going to come of it. Then we read in the newspaper that the state said there was no evidence to back up the claim [that Love Canal was causing major health problems] . . . all we had was what people told us. It didn't mean anything because it was put together by a bunch of housewives with an interest in the outcome of the study" (Gibbs 1982:81). Although later studies performed by government agencies verified the results of the Love Canal Homeowner's Association, the key in accepting the results was a social criterion. As often happens when embarrassing findings are presented within the scientific community, the attempt to disqualify this study focused on the lack of credentials of the individuals gathering the data, not on its methodology or empirical content.

Out of this and other similar experiences, the environmental justice movement has developed a community-based scientific method. This "people's science" seeks to empower citizens to use science as a tool in developing healthy and ecologically sustainable communities. This method is outlined in *Experts: A User's Guide* (CCHW 1985), published by Citizen's Clearinghouse for Hazardous Waste (CCHW). The cover of this book carries an image that ordinary people can understand. It illustrates the struggle of citizens to maintain their own definition of community needs in the face of the omnipotent technical experts.

People's science empowers local citizens by subsuming scientific rationality within a larger civic intelligence.[3] One of the first steps in developing a local scientific capacity is the pooling of common knowledge about the particular situation. Much as a scientific community learns by integrating diffuse data, citizens combine their knowledge to form a pool of local expertise. Expertise about the local community is not seen as the province of specialists in the university. Instead, each citizen is viewed as possessing a particular type of expert knowledge about the local community to which the academic world does not have access. "Community experts are people like you. You live in the neighborhood and know more about the community than anyone on the outside. . . . Isn't it common sense that people who've worked the land all their lives will have opinions about the ground that are at least as valid as some 'hired gun' expert from some far-away university?" (CCHW 1985:19).

In addition, this people's science appropriates scientific epistemology and enables local citizens without formal credentials to perform valid and reliable scientific research in accordance with the canons of positive science. The Citizen's Clearinghouse has developed a series of easily readable tutorials and short courses that enable ordinary citizens to conduct basic epidemiological studies of their own communities. It also provides advice on community resources that can be used to assist citizens in performing such studies. In addition, the CCHW's staff offers limited technical advice. One activist who engaged in such an experience reported: "I have learned so much. I learned a little basic chemistry. I have also learned a lot about engineering. . . . I learned about sewers and water and geology. . . . I have not learned anything that I could pass a test on to get a degree or anything, but I have learned a lot. A lot in a lot of different fields. It has been a real education" (Brown and Masterman-Allen 1994:277).

In environmental justice groups the expert's knowledge is subordinated to larger community concerns. The technical knowledge and credentials of the expert do not warrant a dominant position in the community's dialogue. The expert is seen simply as the holder of specialized and limited knowledge in a certain area. The CCHW provides citizens with guidance on how to use experts in this limited role: "Experts only understand their own narrow area of expertise and should not be used outside of it. For example, when you buy a house, you hire an inspector to check it out. You don't then ask the building inspector to be the one who takes those findings and negotiates with the seller over the final purchase price. That's your job and nobody can do it better! The same principle applies to public hearings and court cases. The expert should only speak after you do, to support your statements and needs—never to testify INSTEAD of you" (CCHW 1985:2). To ensure that the expert hired by the group operates within the limits established by the community, guidance is provided on how to hire an expert with whom citizen groups can work. Steps are included to help ensure that the expert understands his or her role in the community group, to examine potential conflicts of interest in hiring any particular expert, and to develop a research strategy and report that will be understandable in the cultural context of the community. Hence, the correct reason for hiring an expert is "to help us ask the right (technical) questions and to teach us how to be our own experts" (CCHW 1985:4).

Finally, the political characteristics inherent in scientific activity are recognized. In accord with both Foucault and Habermas, the CCHW understands that experts are usually used to scientize politics, deflect and limit citizen participation in government, and insulate political figures from public accountability. "Do you honestly think that you can win your issue JUST by presenting the truth? If we had a perfect world, this might be true, but this is far from a perfect world. . . . For every strong, well-documented statement your expert makes, your opponents will find other experts to say the opposite. Then you have a case of what we call 'Dueling Experts' rather than a clear-cut victory" (CCHW 1985:2). When the specter of dueling experts arises, the citizens' groups are advised to be aware of what their opponents are attempting to accomplish. "The basic idea of 'Dueling Experts' is to focus your attention on this expert whose job is to confuse and deflect you, distracting your attention away from the political policy makers. The idea is to either intimidate you into silence or seduce you into spending huge amounts of time and energy coming up with your own data. . . . [And] all while this is happening, you are losing your base of support in the community" (CCHW 1985:18). Instead of attempting to match the experts' credentials and engage in an endless debate over data, citizens' groups are advised to reveal the inherently political character of the supposedly value-neutral knowledge of the expert. In addition, the community needs to focus its efforts on influencing politicians and developing an organized community with enough political power and resources to sustain itself in a long public debate.

DEMOCRATIC SCIENCE AND CIVIC DISCOURSE

In sum, these ideas and actions suggest the development of a democratic scientific practice. First, such actions create a link between ordinary citizens and the practice of scientific research. Rather than seeing science as a remote and specialized discourse driven by epistemological rules, the environmental justice movement sees scientific inquiry as a collective, persuasive, and political activity in both its production and its use and , hence, as comprehensible within the narrative capacities of all citizens. Members of the community are recognized as possessing expert knowledge about local conditions and as being capable of performing scientific research. Consistent with these views, the use of science in the public arena, as within scientific fields, should be based on open communication and democratic access to the means of intellectual production. Such a people's science enables citizens to develop their own valid knowledge with their own resources. Finally, in this scientific practice, the local community in the form of citizens' groups provides the civic will and intelligence that animates scientific inquiry. The expert is hired not as a omnipotent seer but as a contributor to a larger body of community-based knowledge used for self-determination. The scientific knowledge of the expert is subordinated to a larger civic intelligence of the polity.

When science is conducted in this manner, it meets the requirements of an ethics of communication. "For it means that you put the responsibility for decisions on the shoulders of those who anyhow will suffer their consequences, and that at the same time you stimulate the participants who have to make up their minds in practical discourse to look around for information and ideas that can shed light on their situation—which can clarify their understanding of themselves" (Habermas 1986:207). In sum, the view of science as narration invites the development of a larger human community in which citizens guide experts in their pursuit of effective and morally sensitive actions.

A truly democratic rhetoric requires that changes of mind emerge from the kind of open critical discourse among peers that were described in the previous chapter. Central normative features of the narrative development of such a speech community are described in Habermas' ethics of communication. Instead of seeing rationality as the result of properly following epistemological rules, we can stretch Habermas toward Bourdieu and see rationality as emerging from the social organization of communication. Such a rationality is not the narrow or instrumental rationality of the technicist but the reasonable or prudent judgment of a community. Such substantive rationality, in Max Weber's terms, addresses the questions "What shall we do?" and "How shall we arrange our lives?" (Weber 1978b:152–53). These questions involve more than instrumental calculation. More important, they require prudent judgment in the self-creation of community.

Central to this position is the idea that substantively rational action requires an intersubjective consensus for which valid arguments can be made (Habermas 1984:22). These are the shared grounds that enable the kind of critical competition over data and theories in scientific communities that we described in chapter 8. Formulated this way, they are also a basis for democratic civic life. These grounds include a speaker's providing good reasons why his or her audience should accept that statements about the world are empirically true, and the speaker's engaging in authentic communication, that is, telling the truth. The requirement of empirical truth is similar to the notion provided for in the technicist frame of rationality. In addition to this requirement, however, the speaker must provide morally compelling motives for engaging in a particular action—motives drawn from the cultural tradition of that community.

That is, such moral reasoning must "resonate with cultural narrations, . . . with the stories, myths, and folk tales that are part and parcel of one's cultural heritage and that . . . inform events and experiences in the immediate present" (Snow and Benford 1988:210). In addition, the communication must be authentic insofar as the hearer of the statement believes that the speaker is being sincere in the communication process, and that the statement has existential validity with the individual's lived experience. Through providing these reasons, an intersubjectively accepted narrative is constructed that describes the relevant states or events in a situation, places the interaction within a specific historical and social context, and ties the individual's personal identity to the interaction (Habermas 1984:136; see 1990:65).

In this sense, a thriving citizenry and a thriving science have a common interest and a similar rhetorical practice: freedom from statist and corporatist domination and an open, nonmanipulative conversation leading to prudent judgments. Accordingly, democratically responsible institutions are those that provide the maximum space for open discourse and self-direction by members. Reciprocally, such discourse is precisely the means for engendering democratic institutions. This is rhetoric as affirmative, dialogical, and dialectical practice. Against positive science and philosophy, against technicism and reified bureaucracies, such a rhetoric affirms the centrality of the human authorship of the world.

Chapter 10 Science and Citizenship in a Technicist Culture

PASHA: The story of your life interests me.
KOKA: Story?
PASHA: The story of your life. *(pause)*
KOKA: *(almost in tears)* Thank you.
PASHA: For what?
ROKA: For calling my life a story [or history]. I wouldn't call it that . . . it's just fragments and tatters. It used to be fine lace . . . now only tatters . . . tatters, sir, and you see that history . . .
PASHA: You have suffered, and where there is suffering there is history.
Viktor Slavkin, Cerceau (1985)

Scientific knowledge and its technical extensions have become a central force in our political economy and our culture. Science and technology are so useful for so many purposes that they easily come to dominate in areas of ethics and politics where they are not appropriate guides.[1] Moreover, many people claim that the objectivity of scientific language qualifies it as the one universal discourse for pluralistic societies—a discourse that transcends the ethnic or cultural biases of particular groups. With the spread of technicism, however, the value-neutral manipulation of things easily becomes an amoral manipulation of persons. In this technicist discourse and practice, all things (including nature, machines, humans, traditions, ethics, and institutions) are conceived as a field for the application of scientific rationality, which is understood as instrumental calculation—that is, as theory supporting technique. In this view, science is focused on prediction and control, ends are reduced to means, values become utilities, and people become objects. This is the cultural and moral threat that technicism poses to citizenship and human dignity.

At the same time, however, such global dilemmas as nuclear proliferation, imbalances of food and population, and ecological breakdown threaten our physical survival. Moreover, even apparently simple problems like the reduction of crime or poverty are today complex. Shall we extend welfare support, or will that create a disincentive to work? Shall we raise the minimum wage, or will that encourage mechanization and the reduction of jobs? Such questions are ones of social engineering that require for their resolution scientific and technical knowledge of sociology, economics, mathematical statistics, and other specialized disciplines. Without some use of technical rationality, we will not be able to address such complex threats either globally or locally. Yet the very instrumentalism of such techniques undermines the autonomy and dignity of persons who are its objects. By making experts superior to and more competent than citizens, technicist discourse undermines the cultural bases of freedom and dignity.

Scientific knowledge helps create policy expertise by providing a theoretical legitimation for rational planning and management. This is because knowledge of the laws of nature, including those of social and human nature, are held to be applicable to the redesign of society and humans. As technical control comes to predominate, power shifts from citizens to experts. "Democratic consensus" may become just another problem of social engineering for the techno-administrators and the corporate and statist elites whom they serve. Stated phenomenologically, this means that politics as well as aspects of the lifeworld are redefined as technical or economic or scientific problems to be handled by experts, whereas formerly they were not so considered. By contrast, to be a citizen has meant to act as a moral agent in the public sphere. In Western culture, moral agency was institutionalized above all in civic and political life, where the person was seen to act with reason and freedom. Thus, the increasing privilege of experts in directing society displaces reasoned ethical judgment by citizens.

Technicism is difficult to avoid because science has become integral to the operation of modern political economies. Earlier liberal democracies had a market conception of politics that matched their market conception of economics. But in advanced capitalist societies, centralized direction is necessary to rationalize the market and guide the welfare state. With this, planning and administration come to be viewed as necessary to rationalize society in general. In such a society, "citizens" can act "rationally" only when they conform to scientific, economic, or technical "necessity." Life, history, and society have no meaning any more than nature does, and reason lies only in the methods used for the study and control of things. Given this view, there can be no rational basis for morally committed civic action. Public action by citizens, when it is not simply conformity to the requirements of the cybernetic state, is possible only as a nonrational, even a noncognitive, expression of wishes, desires, and interests.

In this model of societal guidance the public sphere is equated with mass behavior that can be aggregated into statistical facts that in turn are ideally manipulable by cost-efficient techniques of communication and control. At the same time, the private realm is seen as that area into which one can withdraw from the corporate state. And given the dominance of scientific techniques of organization and decision making, this private area is increasingly narrowed to contain only that which is irrelevant to administrative interests or market calculation. The result is that freedom to express one's moral volition comes to be defined negatively, as the right *not* to participate in the rationalized society. All morally and politically affirmative definitions of freedom become obsolete, and participation is restricted to those "public" roles deemed functionally necessary by social scientists and systems engineers. Politicians and other people do continue to assert ethical claims. But to the extent that technicism has replaced ethically rational public discourse, such claims become a kind of moralism or activism, with no genuine moral action emerging from reasoned public judgment. Thus, technical rationality as public discourse renders the public irrational. This is technicism rampant—an official ideology promoting civic incompetence.

CONTEMPORARY CIVITAS AS NARRATIVE TEXT

We need to preserve scientific and technical intelligence in order to address complex issues even while enhancing moral agency of citizens in public life. This dual objective requires us not only to imagine alternative social orders but also to invent alternative means for achieving them. We need visions of democratic practice that are, in Mannheim's terms, more utopian than ideological.

One utopian alternative contrasts substantive democracy and merely procedural democracy. In substantive democracy, legal procedures are defended, but the overriding goal is to enhance the political, economic, and cultural bases of citizenship—that is, to expand the public space available for the enactment of ethical-political choices. This expansion would include above all the involvement of people in controlling the decisions that most effect their daily lives. Citizens would not only vote on the ends of policy, they also would control the means of its formation and implementation, including scientific and technical expertise. Moreover, because economic power in market-oriented societies is easily translated into political power, such a utopian vision of democracy also includes dispersion among the citizenry of control of the means of economic production. This would be matched by a deconcentration of the means of intellectual production, thereby enhancing the competition of ideas, broadening the bases of consensus, and reducing at least some forms of mystification (Dallmayr 1981:245).[2]

It seems to me that this utopian image of substantive democracy of citizens is preferable to the ideology of procedural democracy guided by experts, not only because of possible pragmatic advantages but mainly because it strengthens human dignity and agency. In this vision, dignity and agency are ends in themselves, not merely the means for legitimating procedural democracy. In a substantive democracy, reason would again become a prudent guide to citizens' moral and political participation in the enterprise of human self-creation.

The contemporary scene, however, is characterized by the replacement of reasoned public narration by either a-rational moralism or amoral technicism. For this reason both Robert Bellah et al. (1991) and Alisdair MacIntyre (1981) bewail the vacuity of a public discourse that has been torn from its roots in collective historical experience. Their advice is to connect with tradition, extend our historical depth, and build a collective narrative that would help shape and regulate public action and make it ethically intelligible. Such a unifying meta-narrative, they imply, would embrace the various subsidiary narrations that negate or ignore each other and that encourage the reduction of democracy and freedom to interest-group pluralism and narcissistic individualism.

In a mass, post-industrial, postmodern society with more than 250 million people and a multiplicity of traditions, such recommendations do seem utopian. But the separation of reason and narration has always been a potential of pluralistic societies. Indeed, it might be that the more a society becomes large in scale, culturally diverse, and dependent on science, the more it will require an ethically neutral language of efficiency for "public" or at least intergroup communication, and the further its collective meta-narratives will be removed from particular experiences of specific individuals and groups.

Such a circumstance is not wholly new in Western history. The invention of rhetoric as a discipline in the ancient polis was itself partly a response to the multiplicity of discourses and the fragmentation of a single ethical ontology. In Aristotle's time it was still possible at least to imagine shared, taken-for-granted moral ends, even though their specification in practical cases required rhetorical interaction and prudent judgment. Thus, the function of civic discourse for Aristotle was not to persuade an ignorant public of the rightness of policies made by its leaders but instead to help citizens enact morally defensible decisions. Such a public was presumed to share a sense of how their own moral histories were involved with the moral life of the community and how their personal choices extended the impersonal teleology of the Greek tradition. Reciprocally, this tradition and community existed and was constantly re-created through such publicly reasoned moral argumentation. By critically assessing the original vision, "the classical rhetorical audience continually renewed that vision," thereby serving as "the ultimate guardian of moral action" (Frentz 1985:4, 16).

What would be a contemporary equivalent of such a rhetorical situation? Some thinkers, such as MacIntyre, have argued that there is none. The moral categories of today are so confused that it is fruitless to seek ethical guidance through formal argumentation because contesting groups do not share commensurate "intellectual traditions" (to use MacIntyre's term) or "argumentative fields" (to use Stephen Toulmin's). Without such fields or traditions, persuasive moral discourse cannot be framed because there is no ethical common knowledge, no *sensus communis,* to render its assumptions significant or even intelligible. Aristotle posited such shared knowledge as a natural corollary to his conceptions of human nature, reason, and public decision making. But even in Aristotle's day such common social knowledge was posited as an *ideal* consensus—that is, a consensus attributed to an audience that might not in fact share it. The assumption of consensual knowledge may even be counterfactual—some persons may disagree with what is attributed to them. Yet it is this assumed understanding of agreement, virtual rather than factual, that makes intelligible disagreement and civil argument possible (Farrell 1976:2; Pearce and Chen 1989).

How, then, might we create such a shared moral world, even one in which we are held together by a mutually understood set of differences and conflicts (Shotter 1997)? One way might be to speak as though an ethical community and tradition already existed and, in so speaking, to help create it. As a quotidian example, consider the political role of planners and demographers who make technical population projections concerning land use and zoning. A high demographic projection will satisfy groups that have a stake in higher growth: developers, investors, and merchants. A low number will please conservationists, traditionalists, and patricians. Because statistical projections involve much practical judgment, a large space remains for nontechnical political negotiation over numbers. To discuss the value of high or low growth by negotiating statistical projections, however, easily becomes a technicist mystification that excludes lay participation and fosters civic incompetence. The costs for whatever limited consensus that is thereby achieved are paid by the many citizens who are excluded from it. By contrast, an ideal meta-narrative for that community could well include the technical elements of demography and the particular interests of the competing groups, all within a common story. By appealing to such a not-yet-existing communal narrative, rhetors might be able to criticize the pretensions of technicists even while incorporating the knowledge and benefits of applied science within stories susceptible to prudent judgment and adherence by rational moral publics. In such ways, citizens can re-interpret science as part of the history of their own human community, subject to their own guidance, part of the narration of their own moral telos.

Thus, the public rhetor, in addition to needing technical competence in the issues at hand (for example, she must know that more housing requires more sewers), must also be able to interpret traditions. That is, she casts technical knowledge in a narrative of the ethical sensus communis of her public. To do this effectively requires what Hans-Georg Gadamer (1989) called "good will"— a specifically moral quality. For a conversation to succeed to produce understanding or agreement ("truth"), the interlocutors must desire to come together in understanding. "Both partners must have the good will to try to understand one another" (Gadamer 1989:33). "When good will is lacking, the conversation will fail, either in that it will not generate (real, effective) understanding at all, or in that the 'understanding' that it does generate will simply be a misunderstanding, the mere projection of one's own prejudices onto the other" (Madison 1989:270). In seeking to persuade the other, or in soliciting a response, civic narration is a kind of moral action (Schrag 1986).

Such rational ethical narration is the prudential discourse appropriate for the realm of ethics and politics. Prudence is different from expert knowledge in important ways (Sullivan 1977). Expert knowledge concerns fitting means to ends. It can help us to judge the effectiveness or utility of a means but has nothing to say about the moral appropriateness of ends or of the means to achieve them. Thus expert calculation is a necessary but not a sufficient condition for prudent choice. In addition, prudence involves a knowledge of ethical purposes and consequences. It is a substantive type of rationality that seeks the good for human beings and citizens in particular circumstances. Further, because prudence is a moral kind of knowledge, virtue in the knower bolsters prudence with ethical steadfastness and intuition of the good.

In the positivist image, science strives for universal and necessary laws and decontextualizes data into evidence to verify them. In contrast, prudence, like science as practiced, concerns particular and contingent states of affairs. Even when moral knowledge is formulated into general rules, prudence is always necessary to relate them to specific cases. Aristotle warned that "precision cannot be attained in the treatment of all subject matters alike. . . . A well-schooled man searches for the degree of precision in each kind of study as the subject matter permits." In claiming the authority of positive science or of her expertise, the expert thereby omits ethics, which are not amenable to either quantification or standardization. Thus the expert is open to corruption because of the value neutrality of skill itself. Both virtue and prudence are necessary to make an expert a good human and a good citizen.

Reason and ethics are not mere properties of individuals, nor are they merely abstract concepts. Instead, like language and science, both reason and ethics are discursive practices that are institutionalized within given communities over time. These institutions and communities compose their members and themselves as persons listen and speak in their efforts to reach public agreement (Klumpp and Hollihan 1989:93; Pearce and Chen 1989:129). Such rhetorical transactions gradually generate what initially they can only assume, and thence they provide both criteria for their own assessment and felicitous conditions for their achievement.

Giambattista Vico elaborated on these ideas when he suggested that all knowledge—both scientific and humane—is constructed through language. Thus Vico opposed philosophies that construed the knower as a passive spectator and the world as an object available to us independent of our rhetorical construction. Vico specifically challenged Descartes' view that mathematics is the exemplar of truth because of its universal self-evident clarity. By contrast, said Vico, we know the truth of things because we have made them. Mathematics seems fully true only because it is a system of signification that has been fully made by man. Thus, the only knowledge that the Cartesian cognito can have is knowledge of itself. For Vico, knowing and doing, or the true and the constructed, are both rhetorical enactments, and each is "convertible" into the other—*verum et factum convertuntur.* Knowledge of the world requires a reflective judgment in which the particular case is related to the general context, and the actions of individuals are seen as part of a shared making of history through language (Makkreel 1980:100).

The mistake of Cartesian rationalists, said Vico (1972:34), was to abandon this conception of reflective judgment or prudence in favor of technical decision making based on supposedly universal laws.

> But now to speak of prudence in civic life, as human affairs are governed by chance and choice . . . , those who solely have [law-like] truth in view only with difficulty understand the paths which these affairs take and, with still greater difficulty, their goals. The impudent scholars [such as Descartes or Hobbes] who go directly from the universally true to the singular, rupture the interconnection of life. The wise men, however, . . . make a detour, as it is not possible to attain [practical wisdom] by a direct road; and the thoughts which *these* conceive promise to remain useful for a long time, at least insofar as nature permits.

The impudent scholars remove reasoning and decision making from the practical contexts from which they are derived and to which they are applied. In contrast, for Vico knowledge and decision making must be located in specific situations that are assessed prudentially in terms of the paths that these affairs take and, with more difficulty, in terms of their goals.

Following Vico, I have suggested that even the most scientific and abstract rationality emerges from, and can be deployed in, specific situations only by reflective aesthetic and practical judgments that interpret the local situation and its particular requirements. Such judgments, whether in science or in public life, are inherently problematic because they refer to human situations characterized by chance and choice. Thus, contrary to the hopes and assumptions of technicists, a prudent civic narration would not attempt to prescribe definitive rules for applying any general theory to particular situations. Instead, it would construe public decision making as a practical activity that draws on accumulated cultural wisdom.

In the modern West, however, wisdom tends to be reduced to knowledge and knowledge to information; discourse as such no longer has magical, sacramental, or hierophantic associations; and "science" and "theory" have attained a unique significance. In Weberian terms, rational-legal authority has emerged to unparalleled prominence. To the degree that rationality in the West is a basic means of legitimating political authority, all formal language tacitly belongs to the political domain. As such, it may be exposed for its potential ideological relevance. Scientific language may mention little about specific political issues, but it nevertheless may be particularly ideological precisely because its rationalistic appeal directs attention away from the absence of explicit political content even while conveying it implicitly. The ideological significance of scientific discourse, then, is not merely that it abstracts the concrete significance of the material under study but also that its very abstractness is of concrete *political* significance to contemporary people. Rationality is one of the paramount symbols of modernity and authority in the world today. A deconstruction of scientific discourse and practice thus becomes a critique of contemporary ideology: it shows how the language of science, when used as a politically neutral public discourse, is actually politically charged.

Such a linguistically self-reflective posture is largely absent from both scientific and civic practice today. And, indeed, it is eschewed by the dominant realist epistemology, marginalized by orthodox science, and excluded by scientistic politics. By avoiding explicit value commitments and disavowing reflection, conventional applications of modern science reproduce orthodox discursive practices and thereby affirm existing categories and relations of things, persons, and classes (Shapiro 1988:5–9). In contrast, a narrative understanding of science and society stresses the constitutive rather than the causal or even the communicative dimensions of social practice. It thereby alerts us to the processes by which discourse becomes reified as a mirror of the very things, categories, and relations that it creates, and it highlights and supports the human authorship of both science and the social world.

NARRATION IN PUBLIC KNOWLEDGE AND CIVIC LIFE

Classical philosophers asked how people become members, and come to recognize themselves as members, of a community and heirs to its moral tradition. But in the contemporary world this question of politics and ethics should be asked with qualifications. Ours is a time of urbanization, social and geographic mobility, fragmentation of neighborhoods, the breakdown of families, the decline of legitimacy of institutions, the rise of ethnic nationalism, struggles among peoples and nations over scarce resources, and concentration of control of the economy, polity, media, and knowledge. Thus today the question might be better put more modestly: "How can dissociated, or unhappily associated, or unreflectively entangled people create a sense of interdependence and common fate and shared obligations that leads to joint actions and a sense of community, without individuals being homogenized into conformist or repressive collectives?" (Williams 1991:19–38, 111–19). The answer given by many today is simply to give up on the idea of community or tradition beyond the local and ephemeral, and to celebrate diversity, difference, and individual freedom without concern for a shared moral culture (Fisher 1987:75). If peace and justice are to be pursued and the rights of particular groups protected, however, these ethical commitments must be justified in terms of the larger narrative of democratic society (Stanley 1986).

If we cannot escape the need for a common discourse, community, and tradition, how should these be formed or enhanced? One answer is, through reasoned ethical narration. Communities are made when we communicate with each other about our shared concerns. In this process we co-author a story that has coherence and fidelity for the life that we wish to lead—a story that provides an honored perception of ourselves and a moral grounding for what we are and what we might become (Scult 1988).

Such stories, like every rhetorical act, not only communicate their content but also imply an audience—in this case, persons who can conceive of themselves in the specific ways of that narration (Fisher 1987:75, 187). By this reasoning, the moral value of each story may be judged by the sort of person it shapes (see Booth 1988). In this spirit Chaim Perelman held that an argument is as good as the audience that would adhere to it, suggesting that the best such audience would be a universal one (Perelman and Olbrechts-Tyteca 1969:31). The task, as Perelman (1984:192) saw it, "is not, as often assumed, to address either a particular audience or a universal audience, but in the process of persuasion to adjust to and then to transform the particularities of an audience into universal dimension." Similarly, the function of moral traditions and civic narrations is to articulate identities and meanings for particular persons and groups that retain their particularity while drawing them into our common humanity.

Central to reasoned moral political discourse is the cultivation of what might be called civic intelligence. The American tradition has always prized a strong sense of civic culture. We trace it to the Founders. Tocqueville lauded it. John Dewey captured its spirit when he wrote: "I am inclined to believe that the heart and final guarantee of democracy is in free gatherings of neighbors on the street corner and in living rooms to discuss what is read in the uncensored news of the days."

This tradition implies a certain consensus about individual freedoms and rights, about the common good and about the nature of government. It also assumes a strong conception of civic intelligence. Civic intelligence involves the special creativity of a "we" that is thinking together, a public in the making. Only in this context can we properly speak of public truth and public knowledge. The public is the active agent of its own creation, not just a passive entity to which information is publicized or made public, as in the manipulations of "public relations" or "public opinion." The public creates what only a public can: itself. Along with sound public philosophies and good public practices, the highest use of intelligence of which we are capable is the constitution of ourselves as citizens. We need other citizens "to make our judgments *with*—to help us uncover and deploy the tacit moral knowledge that we share, to help us make the sorts of decisions that are essential to living out our lives as moral beings" (Scult 1988).

What, then, would be an appropriate rational ethical way of guiding our civic life? Although he is advising princes, not citizens, Machiavelli provides a clue by redefining the operative terms of politics—virtú and fortuna. Rather than referring to such abstract virtues as truth or justice, virtú becomes the capacity to impose form onto matter and to stabilize innovation amid changing fortune. But lest the prince be seduced into merely parroting procedures or copying exemplars, Machiavelli invites the prince to attend his textual strategies as a model of both adaptation to and initiation of change. "Just as in teaching by case method (in law for example), the focus is not on the subject matter or result but on the method of *locating* these, [so] Machiavelli implicitly directs the attention of the prince to the deployment, exploration, and use of topics to innovate amidst change without sacrificing principles (including the traditional values of the people) or reifying or valorizing them" (Jost 1991:73–75).

In a similar way, citizens solve the problem of (re)creating a tradition that defines them as citizens by rhetorically deploying commonplace themes or values whose meanings are renewed in the practice of their new applications. Vico provides an example of this when he says that the Athenian plebes "invented" the historical figure, Solon the law-giver, in order to legitimate their claim to rights formerly reserved for nobles (Vico 1972, pars. 1086–87). People thus create themselves as a public by telling stories of their civic coming-to-be.

The Athenian polis—which was the model of democracy for humanists like Vico and Machiavelli—was a believable ideal of political community among citizens who knew each other and regularly engaged in face-to-face civic conversations. Indeed, rhetoric was invented as a discipline at this time precisely to understand and create links between reason, ethics, and traditions for decision-making publics. But how can these ancient conceptions make sense in an age in which rhetoric has lost much of its philosophical and moral significance in favor of technique? Indeed, one result of technicism in modern societies is that it is difficult to discuss questions involving moral or political values in an intellectually responsible way. Without a prudential rhetorical discourse, the kinds of value talk available become voluntarism (what I want), emotivism (what I feel), or utilitarianism (what is efficient). One consequence is that human knowing and doing incline toward the amoralities of will, emotion, or calculation, and political discourse and action become power politics legitimated by a-rational moralism.

Perhaps there is an alternative to scientistic discourse—the rhetoric of narration. I have tried to show that such a civic discourse is possible without abandoning science, because science itself is a form of narration that can be subsumed within meta-narratives of public life. I believe further that the intelligibility of our moral and political life depends on the restoration of reasoned narrative discourse. This is for two reasons. On the one hand, the sense and meaning of individual acts and identities are construed through attributions of motive and intention that depend on temporal contexts of rules and roles and on the larger moral traditions of which these contexts are a part. Thus, attributions of meaning, motive, and identity presuppose narratives that help us make sense of particular acts and give unity and continuity to particular lives. On the other hand, the moral life of the community or polity as a whole inheres greatly in the narrative of its origins, development, and destiny. Narrative thereby links personal conduct with the possible impersonal good of the community by showing that past actions have shaped the present and that the future is a potential extension of current conduct (Frentz 1985:5).

It would seem today that this is utopian, and that any reasoned public narration must be characterized by an awareness of its own impossibility. There is no ethical ontology or moral telos outside human experience around which human conduct in general might be organized in narrative form. Nor is there agreement about telos within the diversity of people's experience. But perhaps we may say that the *quest* for such a telos *is* the moral telos of contemporary humanity; just as the quest for truth, not truth itself, is the telos of modern science. Viewing this quest for a moral telos as itself a telos is properly ironic, because it recognizes the dialectical nature of the human condition—that our self-determination presupposes us to be determined beings. This may not make men and women happy, but it might elevate the melodrama of human existence to the level of tragedy. To be a morally enlightened person is to accept this tragedy and, so, to embrace the quest for what may not be fully realized—an emancipated political community. Narrative truth today evokes the tragedy of our efforts at self-transcendence. We are, as Heidegger said, a conversation. But this conversation, to be truthful to the contradictory conditions of contemporary life, must be cast in the ironic mode. This irony includes not only the profound hopelessness of the struggle but the even more profound hopelessness of its abandonment (Lukács 1971a:85–86; Gruman 1991:5). Between the utopian need to create our history and the actuality of our historical disillusion lies the openness of narrative desire. This openness is a wound that precedes desire. It provides not the fulfillment but the advent of our hope.

Notes

CHAPTER 2: TEXTUALITY, SOCIAL SCIENCE, SOCIETY

1. "In philosophy, sociology, and psychology much has been written about how people explain their actions to themselves and to others through stories (Mishler 1986; Sarbin 1986). MacIntyre (1981) argues that rather than offer categorical principles, rules or reasoned arguments, people tend to describe, account for, and perhaps relive their activities through narratives: sequences of statements connected by both a temporal and a moral ordering (cf. Ricoeur 1984). Todd (1988, 1989) and Reissman (1993) suggest that narratives bridge the gap between daily social interaction and large scale social structures: language organized temporally to report a moral reflects and sustains institutional and cultural arrangements at the same time as it accomplishes social action. So foundational to human interaction is narrative, that Polkinghorne (1991:135) proposes that the self, the fundamental concept of psychological theory, be conceptualized as an unfolding narrative" (Ewick and Sibley 1995:198–99).

2. This section, "The Rhetorical Constitution of the Social and Political Text," is co-authored with Robert Brulle, drawing from his 1988 unpublished paper. Several other paragraphs of this section are adapted from my previous work (1987:137–40, 1989b:40–41).

3. Many critics have argued that semiotics and other structural theories of discourse are a "new equivalent to Marx's 'fetishism of commodities,' one fitted to an Age of Abstraction" (Rochbert-Halton 1986:95). Certainly "it is possible,

if not particularly desirable, to establish a semiotics of signification independently of a semiotics of communication," as Umberto Eco (1976:9) pointed out. My point here, however, is that such a reification is unnecessary.

4. My comments on Rossi-Landi draw heavily from the work of Judith Bodner, whom I happily thank. For other interesting attempts at a linguistic analysis of economics see Ahonen 1989a, 1989b; Amariglio 1988; Goux 1973, 1984; Irvine 1987; and Thompson 1989. For relevant general works see Bilmes 1986; Lemert 1979; MacCannell and Flower MacCannell 1986; and Perinbanayagam 1985.

5. There are interesting parallelisms between Rossi-Landi's ideas and those of Pierre Bourdieu. As Axel Honneth (1986:56) noted, "Bourdieu offers a theory of action which analytically puts symbolic practices on the same level as economic practices, so that the former can be interpreted as strategies in the competition for prestige or standing in the social hierarchy. Both forms of activity, symbolic representations as well as economic accumulation, serve as means by which the social groups can improve their social position." In Bourdieu's idea of an "economy of practices . . . all actions, even those understood as disinterested or non-purposive, and thus freed from economic motives, are to be conceived economically as actions aimed at the maximization of material or symbolic gain" (Bourdieu 1977:235). Like Rossi-Landi, Bourdieu has been accused of reducing the symbolic order to a materialistic or utilitarian one. Mary Douglas (with Baron Isherwood) has also developed a symbolic economics. See, for example, their book *The World of Goods* (1978).

6. For example, Rossi-Landi's concept of homology implies that the similarity between work and language is so deeply rooted that these two phenomena no longer need to be distinguished. He also elaborates the homology in only one direction—language or communication is seen as work, but the idea of work as language or communication is less developed. Rossi-Landi's view of the exchange of commodities as a semiotic system could be enhanced by more discussion of the universal equivalent, money, as described in Marx's chapter in *Capital* on value, use value, and exchange value, or in Georg Simmel's *Philosophy of Money.* Yet Rossi-Landi seems to miss these points.

   Albert Bergesen (1993) notes the emergence of Semiotic Marxism, on the one hand, and Rational Choice Marxism, on the other, both of which disdain analysis of social structure. Rossi-Landi's project invites such an interpretation, perhaps because he fails to adequately distinguish language as communication and language as signification. Thus, his promising approach has the "infantile disorders" of an early Marxist semiology.

7. I develop this point in chapters 6 and 8. See Ben-David and Zloczower (1962:82, my italics): in the United States especially, "eagerness to recognize and develop innovations into new disciplines depended on the existence of a decentralized competitive market for academic achievements; . . . willingness to try and develop bits and pieces of practical insight and professional tradition into systematic theory depended on [the] . . . relationship [of the universities] to *the different classes of society.*"

CHAPTER 3: SOCIAL SCIENCE AND THE POETICS OF TRUTH

1. The term "genre" in literary criticism usually refers to a kind, category, or group of things, as in the biological term "genus." The classification of any set of texts or discourses as a

genre assumes that the entities so classified share important characteristics that differentiate them from all other entities. Genre criticism of literature has sought both to identify the central features that pervade a class of texts and to determine the best classification of particular texts. By clarifying the traditions and affinities of a textual class, genre criticism foregrounds "a large number of literary relationships that would not be noticed as long as there were no context established for them" (Frye 1957:247–48; see Schuppe 1991:1). "Prior to its recent revival, the notion of genre had fallen into disrepute because it seemed as though genres had to be treated either as sets of prescriptive norms (every tragedy, ode, and so forth must obey certain rules of the genre if it is to be a good tragedy, ode, and so forth) or as purely descriptive categories (any group of works which have common features could be treated as a genre). The first approach leads to incorrect normative judgments and the second makes the notion of genre trivial (for example, works in which the heroes ride horses could be treated as a genre). But once genres are treated as sets of norms or conventions which make possible the production of meaning, much as linguistic norms do, then the notion of genre is restored to a central place in literary theory. Generic conventions account for the meaning that is produced when a work violates or evades these conventions, and generic codes are postulated in order to explain the way we treat details in different sorts of works" (Culler 1977a).

Although analysis of genres is conducted in virtually all fields as a way of articulating and understanding similarities and differences, there are varying degrees of self-consciousness and different sorting criteria for such analyses in different disciplines. In anthropology, Bronislaw Malinowski (1961) came close to describing the genre of ethnography, although he did so through discussions of ideal standards and methods. In her assessment of Malinowski, Kaberry (1957) provides a brief but explicit sketch of ethnography as a genre. George Marcus' (1980) essay "Rhetoric and the Ethnographic Genre in Anthropological Research" heralded a decade of literary and rhetorical studies of ethnography as a genre, upon which the present chapter draws.

Within sociology and the sociology of knowledge there was little in the way of genre criticism until the 1980s. Classification systems abound, but they almost always focus on the topics or ideas advanced in texts and ignore the textual practices through which these are constructed. One early exception, though little developed by later thinkers, is Karl Mannheim's concept of "styles of thinking," by which he hoped to borrow methods of stylistic or generic identification and attribution used by art historians (Wessely 1991:271). For Mannheim the task of the sociology of knowledge was to reconstruct "integral styles of thought and perspectives" (Mannheim 1936:307; see Fleck 1979).

More recently, the study of generic aspects of social scientific texts has been booming. "Economist Donald McCloskey (1985), sociologist Richard Harvey Brown (1987), anthropologist James Clifford (1986b), and feminist theorist Sandra Harding (1991) are only a few of the scholars broadly studying the discursive constitution of science. Their work shows how objectivity is constructed narratively, how rhetoric affects the reception of scientific works, and how 'professional knowledge producers' seal narratively their ownership of that knowledge" (Cohen and Rogers 1994:304).

Within the fields of rhetoric and speech communication (which is my main resource for analysis in this chapter) there is a wide diversity of criteria and uses for genre criticism. For example, Edwin Black (1965) has "identified genres by the type and intensity of language chosen as a strategy by the rhetor. Zyskind (1950) and Mohrmann and Leff (1974) have maintained Aristotle's classical genres of forensic, deliberative, and epideictic speaking, which focused more on similarities in audiences. Osborn (1967) . . . investigated archetypal metaphors in order to develop genres. . . . Ware and Linkugel (1973), Halloran (1978), Theodore Windt, Jr. (1972), along with Harrell, Ware and Linkugel (1975), approached generic classification from similarities in situations. Campbell and Jamieson want to see indivisible wholes before they allow for a genre (1978:21). Bruce Gronbeck (1978) and Raymond S. Rogers (1982) base their classification on similarities in modes of thinking" (Schuppe 1991:1–2).

2. A similar distinction, advanced by Roland Barthes (1970, 1971, 1973), is that between the "readable" (*lisible*) and "writable" (*scriptible*), which define two opposite genres or spaces for discourse. Focusing on authorial voice, Cohen and Rogers (1994) mark a related distinction between the "credibility" of readable or generically thickened prose and the "antonomy" of writable, generically stretched texts. Genre stretching is also akin to Bakhtin's (1981) idea of "novelization," which does not permit the monologue of thick canonical generic texts. The "novel" always stretches to admit those styles and voices that are otherwise excluded from literature. Likewise, such new genres as neurolinguistics or film criticism emerge by stretching or novelizing older genres.

3. Whyte's beginning lines echo those of Sims (1984:3) in his study of the London poor: "I propose to record the result of a journey into a region which lies at our own door—into a dark continent that is within easy walking distance of the General Post Office." The reader, through the author, is made to feel estranged and vulnerable, as was Malinowski (1961:4): "Imagine yourself suddenly set down surrounded by your gear, alone on a tropical beach close to a native village while the launch or dinghy which has brought you sails away out of sight."

4. This is one reason why Goffman's early texts (e.g., 1961), in being open to subjects' voices and lay interpretations, are credible and popular but not very fruitful for further professional sociological inquiry. By contrast, Garfinkel ironizes *sociologists'* preconceptions, not merely lay ones. His more distanced voice is also more autonomous and has yielded more radical intellectual innovations (see Fine and Martin 1990; Cohen and Rogers 1994). I elaborate on this point in chapter 8.

CHAPTER 4: SCIENCE AND STORYTELLING

1. One could also develop accounts of the conversion to heliocentrism that focused on changes within the emerging scientific community or in the larger historical context. During Copernicus' lifetime, for example, the voyages of Columbus and Magellan had made Ptolemy's geography obsolete, the translation of Greek and Roman authors encouraged freer speculation and offered neo-Platonic ideals, the authority of Catholic dogma was being challenged by Luther and others, a need was felt for a new calendar, and the advent of printing accelerated and broadened the exchange of ideas.

2. For example: "When on board H.M.S. *Beagle,* naturalist, I was struck with certain facts in the distribution of the inhabitants of South America. . . . " (Darwin 1985:65).

3. Fluency in the native language usually remains merely a claim that is only rarely documented by the inclusion of dialogue in the text. See Tyler 1985:92.

4. The focus by Copernicans on Ptolemy's *Almagest* and their reference to it by its Arabic rather than original Greek name are also significant rhetorical moves. The commonly named *Almagest* (literally, "the greatest") was titled *Syntaxis* ("mathematical treatise") in the original Greek, which suggests a cogent geometrical and numerical account on the model of Euclid. Moreover, in a subsequent, more cosmologically oriented work, *Planetary Hypotheses,* Ptolemy "described how the individual mechanisms for the various planets could be assembled into a whole, truly a 'ptolemaic system'" (Gingerich 1983:157).

5. "Other dimensions of Galileo's rhetoric have been examined by Moss (1983, 1984, 1986). Aspects of Kepler's rhetoric in the sense of literary structure have been examined by Jardine (1984:72–79), who shows that Kepler's 'Defense of Tycho' has the structure of a judicial oration in the style of Cicero. Another author has spoken of a 'classical' rhetoric for modern science in general (Schollmeier 1984). A systemization of these and other types of rhetoric would be very valuable; I mean the sort of thing Croce (1965) does for rhetoric and poetry, though oriented towards science rather than towards poetry" (Finocchiaro 199x:189). See also Vickers (1983) on what he calls Galileo's epideictic rhetoric, and Finocchiaro's (1980) general treatment.

CHAPTER 5: NARRATIVE AND TRUTH

1. For perhaps the most systematic attempt to understand human communication as narration, and to establish criteria for narrative truth, see Fisher 1987. For poetic criteria of truth, at least in the social sciences, see Brown 1989a. For a nice summary of work in narratological theory as it extends outward from literary studies (as for example in special numbers of *Poetics Today* 1980a, 1980b, 1981) see Jackson Barry 1990. A fine sketch toward a sociology of narrative is Ewick and Sibley 1995; toward a narrative psychology, see Sarbin 1986.

2. In this I disagree with Bruno Latour (1989:104) when he says that "to the study of reason we prefer that of network, or, to say it in French, to *raison* we prefer *réseaux*." I find such a choice unnecessary and misleading. The workings of reason and its working through networks are both comprehended within a narrative perspective, or, to say it in French, I prefer to conjoin *raison* and *réseaux* in *récit*. This formulation brings the microprocessual analyses of Latour and others together with the macro-structural orientation of Thomas Kuhn. See Culler (1980) for a similar model of narration with applications to *Oedipus Rex,* George Eliot's *Daniel Deronda,* and some of Freud's case studies.

3. After viewing the film of geometric figures moving at various speeds and directions, one subject stated, "A man has planned to meet a girl and the girl comes along with another man. The first man tells the second to go; the second tells the first, and he shakes his head. Then the two men have a fight and the girl starts to go into the room. . . . She apparently does not want to be with the first man. The first man follows her into the room after having left the second in a rather weakened condition leaning on the wall outside the room. The girl gets worried and races from one corner to the other in the far part of the room. . . . The girl gets out of the room in a sudden dash just as man number two gets

the door open. The two chase around the outside of the room together, followed by man number one, but they finally elude him and get away. The first man goes back and tries to open his door, but he is so blinded by rage and frustration that he cannot open" (Heider and Simmel 1944).

4. As Mark Okrent (1988:51, 46) said, "My end, the for-the-sake-of my behavior, is impossible as an end unless I belong to a community and the end is a type of end within that community. . . . [It is] necessary that there be a certain standardization of ends and of ways of reaching those ends which we share or, at least, which the artificer takes into account in his work."

5. This view is adumbrated by certain latter-day positivists. Their effort to eradicate metaphysics and establish an objective standard of truth led them perilously close to a communitarian standard. For example, "in both Feigl's (1945:257) and Nagel's (1961:44) formulation of 'testability' as a criterion of meaningfulness, it is a *collective agreement* of scientists which establishes that a statement is testable or has been satisfactorily tested" (Overington 1977:143).

6. Hermann von Helmholtz (1893:320–21; see Ravetz 1971:81), the great nineteenth-century physiologist and physicist, provides an account of this research process: "At one time, we have to study the errors of our instruments, with a view to their diminution, or, where they cannot be removed, to compass their detrimental influence; while at other times we have to watch for the moment when an organism presents itself under circumstances most favorable for research. Again, in the course of our investigation we learn for the first time of possible errors which vitiate the results, or perhaps merely raise a suspicion that they may be vitiated, and we find ourselves compelled to begin the work anew, till every shadow of doubt is removed. And it is only when the observer takes such a grip of the subject, so fixes all his thoughts and all his interest upon it that he cannot separate himself from it for weeks, for months, even for years, cannot force himself away from it, in short, till he has mastered every detail. . . . In every good research, the preparation, of the results attainable in the time from those that cannot be attained, consume far more time than is really required to make actual observations or experiments. How much more ingenuity and thought are expended in bringing a refractory piece of brass or glass into subjection, than in sketching out the plan of the whole investigation! I believe I am correct in thus describing the work and mental condition that precedes all those great results which hastened so much the development of science after its long inaction."

CHAPTER 6: MODERN SCIENCE, KNOWLEDGE, AND POWER

1. These same tensions, and often the bad faith of denying them, continue today in the uneasy collaboration between science and its funders. For statements of the position that the relation between science and government is a fruitful collaboration or partnership, see Price 1967; Brooks 1968; Lyons 1969; Lyons and Morton 1965; Reagan 1969; and Gilpin and Wright 1964. For the critique, see Dickson 1984; Bôhme et al. 1983; Saloman 1992; Schuon 1972; Rose and Rose 1979a; Arnove 1980; Berman 1983; and Manicas 1987. For a summary and assessment of these positions, see Diesing 1992:207–41 and Wagner et al. 1990.

2. This is not always or necessarily so. Sometimes intellectual innovations within disciplines shape the very criteria by which they will be evaluated. We saw this in our discussion of the Copernicans. Something similar happened in response to Newton's work. He so thoroughly incorporated discourses of geometry, physics, and astronomy, besides inventing calculus, gravity, and absolute time and space, that there was little room for development of research programs exterior to his new, unifying perspective. Cartesians, for example, "were forced, almost against their will, to oppose the tyranny of self-evident, a priori first principles and thus to change standards of scientific proof and criticism and indeed, the very concept of knowledge" (Lakatos 1978:207; see Chalmers 1990:20–23; Hunter 1982; Hahn 1971).

CHAPTER 7: THE RISE OF AMERICAN PSYCHOLOGY

1. Similarly, G. Stanley Hall convinced the president of Johns Hopkins University, Daniel Coit Gilman, that psychology "could bridge the gap between the physical sciences on the one side, and philosophy and theology on the other" (Wilson 1990:79) and could thereby stave off criticisms of the alleged materialism of the new institution. Hall was rewarded with a lectureship and a new laboratory in 1881 and a professorship in psychology and pedagogics in 1884.
2. The project that could be said to begin with Wilhelm Wundt's *Grundzüge der Physiologischen Psychologie* (1908) was largely completed by Edwin G. Boring's *A History of Experimental Psychology* (1929), which sought to show that philosophy, though once important, had been superseded by experimental psychology. Boring (1929:494) summarized the situation in 1929 succinctly: "By 1890 the characteristics of American psychology were well defined. It inherited its physical body from German experimentalists, but it got its mind from Darwin. American psychology was to deal with mind in use. . . . Thorndike brought the animals into the formal laboratory, . . . then went over the study of school-children and the mental tests increased. Hall helped here too with his pioneering in educational psychology. . . . Then Watson touched a match to the mass, there was an explosion and behaviorism was left" (see O'Donnell 1979 and Manicas 1987:234–37).
3. Quantification also served the industrialization of psychology. Once quantification had become the criterion of acceptability of results, discussions about the appropriateness of research methods for theoretical questions or interpretations were put aside, and attention was more fully directed to the technical aspects of operationalization, instrumentation, and statistical analysis. Moreover, "researchers could take a complex phenomenon, decompose it into its constituent elements on the basis of quantitative transformation of its basic properties, and then divide up the work in a coherent and systematic way" (Hornstein 1988:20), thereby reducing artisanship and turning the laboratory into a more efficient research factory.

CHAPTER 9: DEMOCRATIC SCIENCE IN PRACTICE

1. For similar remarks see Graham and Sadowitz 1994; Dietz 1987, 1988; Dietz and Stern 1993; Fischer 1990; Forester 1985; Webler 1992; and Stanley 1983.

2. The use of framing analysis has expanded within the study of social movements. For examples of the development and use of this perspective see Gamson 1988, 1991, 1992; Klandermans 1992; Snow and Benford 1988, 1992; and Snow et al. 1986. Gamson 1992 is an excellent summary of this work. Also see Gerhards and Rucht 1992 for an application of this type of analysis to social movements in Germany.

3. In *Usable Knowledge,* Lindblom and Cohen (1979) argue that academic knowledge is only one of many valid forms of inquiry, and that it can only supplement ordinary knowledge that is widely dispersed among informed members of society. "Furthermore, professional social inquiry will usually not be accepted as a basis for political action unless it is supported by ordinary knowledge, nor is there any reason why it should be. There is a range of alternatives to it as a method of social problem solving" (Wagner and Wittrock 1990).

CHAPTER 10: SCIENCE AND CITIZENSHIP

1. Much of this discussion depends on the writings of Manfred Stanley and of James Klumpp, and on conversations with them over many years.

2. Steve Fuller, by contrast, advocates a social epistemology that could provide a basis for making investments in science that would have a higher than current chance for payoffs in actual knowledge produced. As for a scientifically enlightened public, he wonders whether this would be a drain on resources that might otherwise be invested in cutting-edge research or could "give the impression that . . . the public may act with confidence on matters where it would not have previously" (Fuller 1988:274–75). Others (e.g., Hirsch 1987) have extended the idea of "cultural literacy" to a popular literacy in science, which might lead to a "public science" akin to Walter Lippman's (1955:pt. 2) "public philosophy." Such a public science would allow members to identify themselves as a public in terms of the knowledge that they share. From a radical democratic perspective, Fuller's social epistemology seems elitist and technicist, whereas Hirsch's proposal seems technicist and mystifying, especially given his conception of cultural literacy as the possession of certain items of information. Indeed, Hirsch's conception of public science could polarize knowledges of science and legitimize elite societal guidance with little or no democratic participation. My discussion of ideal steps in developing a democratic science draws heavily on Dickson 1984 and Diesing 1992.

References

Aaron, R. I. 1952. *The Theory of Universals.* London: Oxford University Press.

Abbott, Andrew Delan. 1988. *The System of Professions: An Essay on the Division of Expert Labor.* Chicago: University of Chicago Press.

Abram, David. 1985. "The Perceptual Implications of Gaia." Manuscript.

Ackerman, James. 1969. "The Demise of the Avant Garde: Notes on the Sociology of Recent American Art." *Comparative Studies in Society and History* 11, no. 4, 371–84.

Adair, J. G., and B. Spinner. 1981. "Subjects' Access to Cognitive Processes: Demand Characteristics and Verbal Report." *Journal for the Theory of Social Behavior* 11, no. 1, 31–52.

Adorno, Theodor, and Max Horkheimer. 1944. *Dialectic of Enlightenment.* New York: Continuum.

Aeschliman, M. D. 1983. *The Restitution of Man: C. S. Lewis and the Case Against Scientism.* Grand Rapids, Mich.: Eerdmans.

Agger, Ben. 1989. *Fast Capitalism.* Urbana: University of Illinois Press.

Ahonen, Pertti. 1989a. "The Meaning of Money: Comparing a Peircean and de Saussurean Perspective." Manuscript. University of Tampere, Finland.

———. 1989b. "Tracing the Meaning of Money." Manuscript. University of Tampere, Finland.

Alexander, Jeffrey G. 1988. "Culture and Political Crisis: 'Watergate' and Durkheimian Sociology." Pp. 187–224 in Jeffrey G. Alexander, ed. *Durkheimian Sociology: Cultural Studies*. New York: Cambridge University Press.

Allport, Floyd. 1924. *Social Psychology*. Boston: Houghton Mifflin.

Althusser, Louis. 1970. *For Marx*. Ben Brewster, trans. New York: Random House.

Amariglio, J. L. 1988. "The Body, Economic Discourse, and Power: An Economist's Introduction to Foucault." *History of Political Economy* 20, no. 4, 583–614.

Apfelbaum, Erika. 1981. "Origines de la psychologie sociale en France: Developpements souterrains et discipline méconnue." *Revue française de psychologie* 22, no. 3, 397–408.

——. 1986. "Prolegomena for a History of Social Psychology: Some Hypotheses Concerning Its Emergence in the Twentieth Century and Its Raison D'Etre." Pp. 3–13 in Knud S. Larsen, ed. *Dialectics and Ideology in Psychology*. Norwood, N.J.: Ablex.

Apollinaire, Guillaume. 1980. *Calligrammes*. Anne Hyde Greet, trans. Berkeley: University of California Press.

Arakelian, Paul. 1979. "The Myth of a Restoration Style Shift." *The Eighteenth Century: Theory and Interpretation* 20, 227–45.

Arendt, Hannah. 1989. *The Human Condition*. Chicago: University of Chicago Press.

Aristotle. 1943. *On Man and the Universe*. Louise Loomis, ed. Roslyn, N.Y.: Walter J. Black.

——. 1983. *Nicomachean Ethics*. D. Ross, trans. Oxford: Oxford University Press.

——. 1991. *On Rhetoric*. George A. Kennedy, trans. New York: Oxford University Press.

Arnove, Robert F., ed. 1980. *Philanthropy and Cultural Imperialism*. Boston: G. K. Hall.

Aron, Raymond. 1968. "Evolution of Strategic Thought, 1945–1968: The Rise and Decline of Strategic Analysis." *Archives européennes de sociologie* 9, no. 2, 151–79.

Aronowitz, Stanley. 1988. *Science as Power*. Minneapolis: University of Minnesota Press.

Ash, Mitchell G. 1983. "The Self-Presentation of a Discipline: History of Psychology in the United States between Pedagogy and Scholarship." Pp. 143–89 in Loren Graham, Wolf Lapenies, and Peter Weingart, eds. *Functions and Uses of Disciplinary Histories* 7. Norwell, Mass.: D. Reidel.

——. 1990. "Psychology in Twentieth Century Germany: Science and Profession." In K. Jarausch and G. Cocks, eds. *German Professions, 1800–1950*. New York: Oxford University Press.

——. 1991. "Rhetoric, Society, and Historiography of Psychology, Comment on Danziger." *Annuals of Theoretical Psychology* 9.

Ashmore, Malcolm. 1989. *The Reflexive Thesis: Wrighting Sociology of Scientific Knowledge*. Chicago: University of Chicago Press.

Bacheland, Gaston. 1953. *Le matérialisme rationel*. Paris: Presses universitaires de France.

Bahr, Donald M., Juan Gregorio, David I. Lopez, and Albert Alvarez. 1974. *Piman Shamanism and Staying Sickness*. Tuscon: University of Arizona Press.

Baillet, Adrien. 1946. *La Vie de Monsieur Des-Cartes*. 1691. Reprint, Paris: Table ronde.

Bain, Alexander. 1872. *The Senses and the Intellect*. 1855. 3rd ed., New York: Appleton.

Bakan, David. 1980. "Politics and American Psychology." In Robert W. Rieber and Kurt Salzinger, eds. *Psychology: Theoretical and Historical Perspectives*. New York: Academic Press.

Bakhtin, Mikhail. 1965. *Rabelais and His World*. Cambridge: MIT Press.

————. 1981. "Discourse in the Novel." Pp. 259–442 in Michael Holquist, ed. *Discourse in the Novel.* Austin: University of Texas Press.

Bannister, Robert C. 1987. *Sociology and Scientism: The American Quest for Objectivity, 1880–1949.* Chapel Hill: University of North Carolina Press.

Barber, Bernard. 1983. *The Logic and Limits of Trust.* New Brunswick, N.J.: Rutgers University Press.

Barnes, Barry. 1988. *The Nature of Power.* Cambridge: Polity Press.

Barnes, S. B., and John Law. 1976. "Whatever Should Be Done with Indexical Expressions?" *Theory and Society* 3, 223–37.

Barrett, William. 1977. *The Illusion of Technique.* New York: Doubleday, Anchor.

Barry, Jackson G. 1990. "Narratology's Centrifugal Force: A Literary Perspective on the Extensions of Narrative Theory." *Poetics Today* 11, no. 2, 195–307.

Barthes, Roland. 1967. *Elements of Semiology.* New York: Hill and Wang.

————. 1970. *S/Z.* Paris: Seuil.

————. 1971. *Sade Fourier Loyola.* Paris: Seuil.

————. 1973. *Le Plaisir du texte.* Paris: Seuil.

————. 1983. *Barthes: Selected Writings.* Susan Sontag, ed. London: Fontana.

Baudrillard, Jean. 1975. *The Mirror of Production.* St. Louis: Telos Press.

————. 1981. *For a Critique of the Political Economy of the Sign.* St. Louis: Telos Press.

————. 1983. *Simulations.* New York: Semiotext(e), Foreign Agent Press.

Bazerman, Charles. 1987. "Codifying the Social Scientific Style: The APA *Publication Manual* as a Behavioralist Rhetoric." Pp. 125–44 in John S. Nelson, Allan Megill, and Donald N. McCloskey, eds. *The Rhetoric of the Human Sciences: Language and Argument in Scholarship and Public Affairs.* Madison: University of Wisconsin Press.

————. 1988. *Shaping Written Knowledge: The Genre and Activity of the Experimental Article in Science.* Madison: University of Wisconsin Press.

Becher, Tony. 1989. *Academic Tribes and Territories: Intellectual Enquiry and the Cultures of Disciplines.* Milton Keynes, England: Open University Press, Society for Research into Higher Education.

Beedstein, Burton. 1976. *The Culture of Professionalism.* New York: Norton.

Beer, Stafford. 1974. *Designing Freedom.* New York: Wiley.

Bell, Daniel. 1976. *The Cultural Contradictions of Capitalism.* New York: Basic Books.

Bellah, Robert N. 1970. "Civil Religion in America," in *Beyond Belief.* New York: Harper and Row.

————. 1985. *Habits of the Heart: Individualism and Commitment in American Life.* Berkeley: University of California Press.

Bellah, Robert N., Richard Madsen, William M. Sullivan, Ann Swidler, and Steven M. Tipton. 1991. *The Good Society.* New York: Knopf.

Ben-David, Joseph. 1984. *The Scientist's Role in Society: A Comparative Study.* Chicago: University of Chicago Press.

Ben-David, Joseph, and Awraham Zloczower. 1962. "Universities and Academic Systems in Modern Societies." *European Journal of Sociology* 3, 45–84.

Benjamin, Walter. 1968. "The Storyteller: Reflections on the Works of Nikolai Leskov." Pp. 83–109 in Walter Benjamin, *Illuminations.* New York: Harcourt Brace.

Bensman, Joseph, and Arthur J. Vidich. 1987. *American Society: The Welfare State and Beyond*. South Hadley, Mass.: Bergen and Garvey.

Benveniste, Emile. 1971. *Problems in General Linguistics*. Mary Meek, trans. Coral Gables, Fla.: University of Miami Press.

Bergesen, Albert. 1993. "The Rise of Semiotic Marxism." *Sociological Perspectives* 3, no. 1, 1–22.

Berman, Edward. 1983. "The Influence of the Carnegie, Ford, and Rockefeller Foundations on American Foreign Policy." In *The Ideology of Philanthropy*. Albany: SUNY Press.

Bernstein, Basil. 1971. *Class, Codes, and Control*. 3 vols. London: Routledge and Kegan Paul.

Berryman, Gerald. 1962. *Behind Many Masks*. Monograph 4. N.p.: Society for Applied Anthropology.

Bettelheim, Bruno. 1977. *The Uses of Enchantment*. New York: Vintage.

———. 1983. *Freud and Man's Soul*. New York: Knopf.

Betti, Emilio. 1980. "Hermeneutics as the General Methodology of the Geisteswissenschaften." Pp. 51–94 in Josef Bleicher, *Contemporary Hermeneutics: Hermeneutics as Method, Philosophy, and Critique*. London: Routledge and Kegan Paul.

Bhaskar, Roy. 1978. *A Realist Theory of Science*. Atlantic Highlands, N.J.: Humanities Press.

———. 1979. *The Possibility of Naturalism: A Critique of the Contemporary Human Sciences*. Brighton, England: Harvester.

Bijker, Wiebe E., Thomas P. Hughes, and Trevor J. Pinch, eds. 1987. *The Social Construction of Technological Systems: New Directions in the Sociology and History of Technology*. Cambridge: MIT Press.

Bilmes, Jack. 1986. *Discourse and Behavior*. New York: Plenum.

Birnbaum, Norman. 1969. *The Crisis of Industrial Society*. New York: Oxford University Press.

Bjork, Daniel W. 1983. *The Compromised Scientist: William James in the Development of American Psychology*. New York: Columbia University Press.

Black, Edwin. 1965. *Rhetorical Criticism: A Study in Method*. New York: Macmillan.

Bledstein, Burton J. 1957. *The Culture of Professionalism: The Middle Class and the Development of Higher Education in America*. New York: Norton.

Bleicher, Josef. 1980. *Contemporary Hermeneutics: Hermeneutics as Method, Philosophy, and Critique*. London: Routledge and Kegan Paul.

Bloor, David. 1976. *Knowledge and Social Imagery*. London: Routledge and Kegan Paul.

Blumenberg, Hans. 1983. *The Legitimacy of the Modern Age*. Cambridge: MIT Press.

———. 1987. *The Genesis of the Copernican World*. Robert M. Wallace, trans. Cambridge: MIT Press.

Bodner, Judith. 1987. "Another Approach to Semiotics." Manuscript. Department of Sociology, John Hopkins University.

Bôhme, Gernot, Wolfrang van den Daele, Rainer Hohfeld, Wolfgang Krohn, and Wolf Schäfer. 1983. "Introduction." In *Finalization in Science: The Social Orientation of Scientific Progress*. Boston: D. Reidel.

Booth, Wayne. 1988. *The Company We Keep: An Ethics of Fiction*. Berkeley: University of California Press.

Borecelli, Peter. 1988. *Crossroads: Environmental Priorities for the Future*. Washington, D.C.: Island Press.

Boring, Edwin G. 1929. *A History of Experimental Psychology*. New York: Appleton.

Born, Max. 1966. "Max Karl Ernst Lugwig Planck." Obituary Notices of Fellows of the Royal Society 6 (1948) 161–80. Reprinted in Henry A. Boorse and Lloyd Motz, eds. *The World of the Atom*. New York: Basic Books.

Bourdieu, Pierre. 1977. *Outline of a Theory of Practice*. Cambridge: Cambridge University Press.

———. 1980a. *Le Sens pratique*. Paris: Minuit.

———. 1980b. *Questions de sociologie*. Paris: Minuit.

———. 1980c. "The Production of Belief: Contribution to an Economy of Symbolic Goods." *Media, Culture, and Society* 2.

———. 1981. "The Specificity of the Scientific Field." In Charles C. Lemert, ed. *French Sociology: Rupture and Renewal since 1968*. New York: Columbia University Press.

———. 1984. *Distinction: A Social Critique of the Judgment of Taste*. Cambridge: Harvard University Press.

———. 1987a. "The Biographical Illusion." *Working Papers and Proceedings of the Center for Psychosocial Studies* 14. Chicago: Center for Psychosocial Studies.

———. 1987b. *Choses dites*. Paris: Minuit.

———. 1988. *Homo Academicus*. P. Collier, trans. Cambridge: Polity Press.

———. 1989. "The Corporatism of the Universal: The Role of Intellectuals in the Modern World." *Telos* 81.

———. 1990. "Animadversiones in Mertonem." In Jon Clark, Celia Modgil, and Shohan Modgil, eds. *Robert K. Merton: Consensus and Controversy*. London: Falmer Press.

———. 1991a. *Language and Symbolic Power*. Cambridge: Harvard University Press.

———. 1991b. "The Peculiar History of Scientific Reason." *Sociological Forum* 6, no. 1, 3–26.

———. 1992. *Réponses: Pour une anthropologie réflexive*. Paris: Seuil.

Bourdieu, Pierre, and Jean Claude Passeron. 1970. *La Reproduction*. Paris: Minuit.

Boyle, Robert. 1674. *The Excellency of Theology, Compar'd with Natural Philosophy*. London: T. N. for Henry Herringman.

Bozeman, Theodore Dwight. 1977. *Protestants in an Age of Science: The Baconian Ideal and Antebellum American Religious Thought*. Chapel Hill: University of North Carolina Press.

Brannigan, Augustus. 1976. "Discovery in the Social Organization of *The Origin of Species*." Manuscript.

———. 1981. *The Social Basis of Scientific Discoveries*. Cambridge: Cambridge University Press.

Brinton, A. 1985. "On Viewing Knowledge as Rhetorical." *Central States Speech Journal* 36, no. 4, 270–81.

Brooks, Harvey. 1968. *The Government of Science*. Cambridge: Harvard University Press.

Broughton, John M. 1986. "The Psychology, History, and Ideology of the Self." Pp. 128–64 in Knud S. Larson, ed. *Dialectics and Ideology in Psychology*. Norwood, N.J.: Ablex.

Brown, Joanne. 1986. "Professional Language: Words That Succeed." *Radical History Review* 34, 33–51.

Brown, Phil, and Masterson-Allen, Susan. 1994. "The Toxic Waste Movement: A New Type of Activism," *Society and Natural Resources* 7, 269–87.

Brown, Richard Harvey. 1978. "Bureaucracy as Praxis: Toward a Political Phenomenology of Formal Organizations," *Administrative Sciences Quarterly* 23, no. 3 (September), 365–82.

———. 1979. "Epistemological Scandal or Sociological Liberation? A Note on Overington's Doing the What Comes Rationally," *The American Sociologist* 14, no. 1, 14–17.

———. 1982. Review of *The Elusive Science: Origins of Experimental Psychological Research*, by Seymour H. Manskopf and Michael R. McVaugh. *American Historical Review* (October), 1045–46.

———. 1987. *Society as Text: Essays on Rhetoric, Reason, and Reality.* Chicago: University of Chicago Press.

———. 1989a. *A Poetic for Sociology: Toward a Logic of Discovery for the Human Sciences.* 1977. Reprint, Chicago: University of Chicago Press.

———. 1989b. *Social Science as Civic Discourse: Essays on the Invention, Legitimation, and Uses of Social Theory.* Chicago: University of Chicago Press.

———. 1990. "Narrative in Scientific Knowledge and Civic Discourse." *Current Perspectives in Social Theory* 11, 313–30.

———. 1993. "Cultural Representation as Ideological Legitimation." *Social Forces* 7, no. 3, 657–76.

———. 1995. "Realism and Power in Aesthetic Representation." Pp. 134–67 in Richard Harvey Brown, ed. *Postmodern Representations: Truth, Power, and Mimesis in the Human Sciences and Public Culture.* Urbana: University of Illinois Press.

Brown, Richard Harvey, ed. 1992. *Writing the Social Text: Poetics and Politics in Social Science Discourse.* New York: Aldine de Gruyter.

———. 1995. *Postmodern Representations: Truth, Power, and Mimesis in the Human Sciences and Public Culture.* Urbana: University of Illinois Press.

Brubaker, Roger. 1985. "Rethinking Classical Theory: The Sociological Vision of Pierre Bourdieu." *Theory and Society* 14, no. 6, 745–75.

Brulle, Robert J. 1988. "Power, Discourse, and Social Movements." Manuscript. Department of Sociology, George Washington University, Washington, D.C.

———. 1994. "Power, Discourse, and Social Problems: Social Problems from a Rhetorical Perspective." In James Holstein and Gale Miller, eds., *Current Perspectives in Social Problems* 5, 95–121. Greenwich, Conn.: JAI Press.

———. 1998. *Agency, Democracy, and the Environment: A Critical Theory of the U.S. Ecology Movement.* Cambridge: MIT Press.

Brummett, Barry. 1976. "Some Implications of 'Process' on 'Intersubjectivity': Postmodern Rhetoric." *Philosophy and Rhetoric* 9, no. 1, 21–51.

Bruner, Jerome. 1986. "Ethnography as Narrative." Pp. 139–55 in Victor W. Turner and Edward M. Brunner, eds. *Anthropology of Experience.* Urbana: University of Illinois Press.

———. 1987. "Life as Narrative." *Social Research* 54, no. 1, 11–32.

Bruns, Gerald. 1989. *Heidegger's Estrangements: Language, Truth, and Poetry in the Later Writings.* New Haven: Yale University Press.

Bryant, Bunyan. 1995. *Environmental Justice: Issues, Policies, and Solutions.* Washington, D.C.: Island Press.

Buchner, Georg. 1963. *Woyzcek.* Berlin: Wedding-Verlag.

Bullard, Robert D. 1993. "Anatomy of Environmental Racism and the Environmental

Justice Movement." In Robert D. Bullard, ed. *Confronting Environmental Racism: Voices from the Grassroots.* Boston: South End Press.

Bulmer, Ralph, and Ian Majnep. 1977. *Birds of My Kalam Country.* Auckland: Auckland University Press.

Burian, Richard M. 1977. "More Than a Marriage of Convenience: On the Inextricability of History and Philosophy of Science." *Philosophy of Science* 44, no. 1, 1–42.

Burke, Kenneth. 1945. *A Grammar of Motives.* Berkeley: University of California Press.

——. 1954. *Permanence and Change.* Berkeley: University of California Press.

——. 1964. *Perspectives by Incongruity.* Bloomington: Indiana University Press.

——. 1968. "Dramatism." In *International Encyclopedia of the Social Sciences* 7. New York: Free Press.

——. 1969. "'Administrative' Rhetoric in Machiavelli." Pp. 158–66 in Kenneth Burke, *A Rhetoric of Motives.* Berkeley: University of California Press.

——. 1989. *On Symbols and Society.* Chicago: University of Chicago Press.

Burtt, E. A. 1954. *The Metaphysical Foundations of Modern Science.* Garden City, N.Y.: Doubleday.

Cable, Sherry, and Charles Cable. 1995. *Environmental Problems: Grassroots Solutions.* New York: St. Martin's.

Callahan, R. E. 1962. *Education and the Cult of Efficiency.* Chicago: University of Chicago Press.

Callon, Michel. 1981a. "Les Operations de traductions." In P. Roqueplo, ed. *Incidence des rapports sociaux sur le developpement scientifique.* Paris: Centre National de Recherche Scientifique.

——. 1981b. "Struggles and Negotiations to Define What Is Problematic and What Is Not." In Karin Knorr-Cetina and Richard Whitley, eds. *The Social Process of Scientific Investigation. Sociology of Science Yearbook* 4. Dordrecht: D. Reidel.

Callon, Michel, John Law, and Arie Rip, eds. 1986. *Mapping the Dynamics of Science and Technology.* London: Macmillan.

Calvino, Italo. 1982. *If on a Winter's Night a Traveller.* William Weaver, trans. London: Picador.

Campbell, Karlyn Kohrs, and Kathleen Jamieson. 1978. "Introduction to *Form and Genre.*" Pp. 9–32 in Karlyn Kohrs Campbell and Kathleen Jamieson, eds. *Form and Genre: Shaping Rhetorical Action.* Annandale, Va.: Speech Communication Association.

Capel, Leo M. 1965. "Historical Introduction." Pp. 7–41 in Søren Kierkegaard, *The Concept of Irony.* Leo M. Capel, trans. Bloomington: Indiana University Press.

Capon, Eric. 1965. "Theatre and Reality." *British Journal of Aesthetics* 5, no. 3, 261–69.

Carr, David. 1986. *Time, Narrative, and History.* Bloomington: Indiana University Press.

Carson, Rachel. 1962. *Silent Spring.* Cambridge, Mass.: Riverside Press.

Carson, Robert, James N. Butcher, and James C. Coleman. 1988. *Abnormal Psychology and Modern Life,* 8th ed. Glenview, Ill.: Scott Foresman.

CCHW (Citizen's Clearinghouse for Hazardous Waste). 1985. *Experts: A User's Guide: Where To Find Them, How To Get Them, How To Pay for Them.* Alexandria, Va.: CCHW.

Chabot, Dana. 1993. "In Defense of 'Moderate' Relativism and 'Skeptical' Citizenship." Manuscript. Department of Political Science, Indiana University, Bloomington.

Chalmers, Alan. 1990. *Science and Its Fabrication.* Minneapolis: University of Minnesota Press.

Chambers, Erve. 1988. "Rebellion in Fact: The Narratives of Ethnographic Representation." Manuscript. Department of Anthropology, University of Maryland, College Park.

Chambers, Ross. 1984. *Story and Situation: Narrative Seduction and the Power of Fiction.* Minneapolis: University of Minnesota Press.

Chandler, Raymond. 1980. "Introduction." In *Pearls Are a Nuisance.* London: Pan.

Chin, Frank. 1972. "Confessions of a Chinatown Cowboy." *Bulletin of Concerned Asian Scholars* 58–70.

———. 1981. *The Chickencoop Chinaman and the Year of the Dragon.* Seattle: University of Washington Press.

Chubin, Daryl E. 1988. "Allocating Credit and Blame in Science." *Science, Technology, and Human Values* 13, nos. 1 & 2, 53–63.

Chubin, Daryl E., and Sal Restivo. 1983. "The Mooting of Science Studies: Research Programmes and Science Policy." Pp. 53–84 in Karin D. Knorr-Cetina and Michael Mulkay, eds. *Science Observed: Perspectives on the Social Study of Science.* London: Sage.

Cicourel, Aaron V. 1986. "Social Measurement as the Creation of Expert Systems." Pp. 246–70 in Donald W. Fiske and Richard A. Shivider, eds. *Metatheory in Social Science.* Chicago: University of Chicago Press.

Cisneros, Sandra. 1983. *The House on Mango Street.* Houston: Arte Publico Press.

Clark, Terry Nichols. 1973. *Prophets and Patrons: The French University and the Emergence of the Social Sciences.* Cambridge: Harvard University Press.

Claval, Paul. 1980. *Les mythes fondateurs des sciences sociales.* Paris: Presses universitaires de France.

Clifford, James. 1981. "On Ethnographic Surrealism." *Comparative Studies in Society and History* 23, no. 4, 539–64.

———. 1983. "On Ethnographic Authority." *Representations* 1, no. 2, 118–46.

———. 1986a. "Introduction to Partial Truths." Pp. 1–16 in James Clifford and George E. Marcus, eds. *Writing Culture: The Poetics and Politics of Ethnography.* Berkeley: University of California Press.

———. 1986b. "On Ethnographic Allegory." Pp. 89–121 in James Clifford and George E. Marcus, eds. *Writing Culture: The Poetics and Politics of Ethnography.* Berkeley: University of California Press.

Clifford, James, and George E. Marcus, eds. 1986. *Writing Culture: The Poetics and Politics of Ethnography.* Berkeley: University of California Press.

Clignet, Remi. 1985. *The Structure of Artistic Revolutions.* Philadelphia: University of Pennsylvania Press.

Clough, Patricia. 1992. *The End(s) of Ethnography: Narrativity and the Rhetoric of Sexual Difference.* Newbury Park, Calif.: Sage.

Cohen, I. Bernard. 1980. *The Newtonian Revolution.* New York: Cambridge University Press.

Cohen, Ira J., and Mary F. Rogers. 1994. "Autonomy and Credibility: Voice as Method." *Sociological Theory* 12, no. 3, 304–18.

Cohen, Jean L., and A. Arato. 1992. "Politics and the Reconstruction of the Concept of Civil Society." In Alex Honneth, Thomas McCarthy, Claus Offe, and Albrecht Wellmer, eds.

Cultural-Political Interventions in the Unfinished Project of Enlightenment. Cambridge: MIT Press.

Cohen, Ralph. 1986. "Reply to Dominick La Capra and Richard Harvey Brown." *New Literary History* 17, no. 2, 229–32.

Cole, John. 1993. *The Olympian Dreams and the Youthful Rebellion of René Descartes.* Urbana: University of Illinois Press.

Coleman, James S. 1980. "The Structure of Society and the Nature of Social Research." *Knowledge* 1, 333–50.

———. 1986. "Social Theory, Social Research and a Theory of Action." *American Journal of Sociology* 91, no. 6 (May), 1309–35.

Collins, Harry M. 1983. "An Empirical Relativist Programme in the Sociology of Scientific Knowledge." Pp. 85–113 in Karin D. Knorr-Cetina and Michael Mulkay, eds. *Science Observed: Perspectives on the Social Study of Science.* London: Sage.

———. 1985. *Changing Order: Replication and Induction in Scientific Practice.* Los Angeles: Sage.

———. 1989. "The Meaning of Experiment: Replication and Reasonableness." Pp. 82–91 in Hilary Lawson and Lisa Appignanesi, eds. *Dismantling Truth: Reality in the Post-Modern World.* New York: St. Martin's.

———. 1990. *Artificial Experts: Social Knowledge and Intelligent Machines.* Cambridge: MIT Press.

———. 1991. "The Meaning of Replication and the Science of Economics." *History of Political Economy* 23, no. 1, 12–142.

Collins, Randall. 1975. "The Organization of the Intellectual World." Pp. 470–523 in *Conflict Sociology.* New York: Academic Press.

———. 1986. "Is 1980s Sociology in the Doldrums?" *American Journal of Sociology* 91, no. 6, 1336–49.

———. 1989. "Toward a Theory of Intellectual Change: The Social Causes of Philosophies." *Science, Technology and Human Values* 14, 107–40.

———. 1992. "On the Sociology of Intellectual Stagnation: The Late Twentieth Century in Perspective." *Theory, Culture, and Society* 9, 73–96.

———. 1996. *The Social Causes of Philosophies.* Cambridge: Harvard University Press.

Commoner, Barry. 1991. "The Failure of the Environmental Effort." In *Environment in Peril.* Washington, D.C.: Smithsonian.

Conrad, Joseph. 1973. *Heart of Darkness.* New York: Penguin.

Cooper, John M. 1980. "Aristotle on Friendship." Pp. 301–40 in Amelia Rorty, ed. *Essays on Aristotle's Ethics.* Berkeley: University of California Press.

Cooter, Roger. 1984. *The Cultural Meaning of Popular Science: Phrenology and the Organization of Consent in Nineteenth-Century Britain.* New York: Cambridge University Press.

Copernicus, Nicolas. 1971. *Letter against Werner.* New York: Octagon.

———. 1978. *On the Revolutions.* J. Dobrzycki, ed. E. Rosen, trans. London: Macmillan.

Corvoisier, André. 1978. *Arts et sociétés dans l'Europe du XVIIIe siècle.* Paris: Presses universitaires de France.

Coward, Rosalynd, and John Ellis. 1977. *Language and Materialism.* London: Routledge and Kegan Paul.

Crane, Diana. 1972. *Invisible Colleges: Diffusion of Knowledge in Scientific Communities.* Chicago: University of Chicago Press.

Cranfield, Thomas M. 1973. "The Professionalization of American Psychology, 1870–1917." *Journal of the History of the Behavioral Sciences* 9, 66–75.

Crapanzano, Vincent. 1980. *Tuhami: Portrait of a Moroccan.* Chicago: University of Chicago Press.

———. 1986. "Hermes' Dilemma: The Making of Subversion in the Ethnographic Description." Pp. 51–76 in James Clifford and George E. Marcus, eds. *Writing Culture: The Poetics and Politics of Ethnography.* Berkeley: University of California Press.

Cress, D. A. 1985. *Discourse on Method.* Indianapolis, Ind.: Hackett.

Crick, Francis. 1981. *Life Itself.* New York: Simon and Schuster.

———. 1994. *The Astonishing Hypothesis: The Scientific Search for the Soul.* New York: Scribner.

Croce, Benedetto. 1965. *Aesthetic as Science of Expression and General Linguistic.* New York: Noonday.

Culler, Jonathan. 1973. "Phenomenology and Structuralism." *Human Context* 5, no. 1, 35–48.

———. 1977a. "Foreword." In Tzvetan Todorov, *The Poetics of Prose.* Ithaca, N.Y.: Cornell University Press.

———. 1977b. *Structuralist Poetics: Structuralism, Linguistics, and the Study of Literature.* Ithaca, N.Y.: Cornell University Press.

———. 1980. "Fabula and Sjuzhet in the Analysis of Narrative." *Poetics Today* 1, no. 3, 27–37.

———. 1981. *The Pursuit of Signs: Semiotics, Literature, Deconstruction.* Ithaca, N.Y.: Cornell University Press.

Dahl, Robert. 1961. *Controlling Nuclear Weapons: Democracy versus Guardianship.* Syracuse, N.Y.: Syracuse University Press.

Dallmayr, Fred. 1981. *Beyond Dogma and Despair: Toward a Crtical Phenomenology of Politics.* Notre Dame, Ind.: University of Notre Dame Press.

———. 1984. *Polis and Praxis: Exercises in Contemporary Political Theory.* Cambridge: MIT Press.

Danziger, Kurt. 1979a. "The Positivist Repudiation of Wundt." *Journal of the History of the Behavioral Sciences* 15, 205–30.

———. 1979b. "The Social Origins of Modern Psychology." Pp. 27–45 in A. R. Buss, ed. *Psychology in Social Context.* New York: Irvington.

———. 1985. "The Origins of the Psychological Experiment as Social Institution." *American Psychologist* 40, no. 2, 133–40.

———. 1988. "A Question of Identity: Who Participated in Psychological Experiments?" Pp. 35–52 in Jill G. Morawski, ed. *The Rise of Experimentation in American Psychology.* New Haven: Yale University Press.

———. 1990a. *Constructing the Subject: Historical Origins of Psychological Research.* New York: Cambridge University Press.

———. 1990b. "Generative Metaphor and the History of Psychological Discourse." Pp. 331–56 in David E. Leary, ed. *Metaphors in the History of Psychology.* New York: Cambridge University Press.

Darwin, Charles. 1985. *The Origin of Species by Means of Natural Selection.* 1859. Reprint, London: Penguin.

Directory of Experts, Authorities and Spokespersons. 1988. 5th ed. Washington, D.C.: Broadcast Interview Source.

Dear, Peter. 1985. "Totius in verba: Rhetoric and Authority in the Early Royal Society." *Isis* 76, 145–61.

de Certeau, Michel. 1980. "On the Oppositional Practices of Everyday Life." *Social Text* 3, no. 1, 3–43.

Deleuze, Gilles, and Félix Guattari. 1983. *Anti-Oedipus: Capitalism and Schizophrenia.* Minneapolis: University of Minnesota Press.

Delli Priscoli, Jerome. 1979. "Future Thinking: Fad or Necessity?" *Water Spectrum* 7, 7–32.

DeMan, Paul. 1984. *The Rhetoric of Romanticism.* New York: Columbia University Press.

Denzin, Norman K. 1986. "The Death of Sociology in the 1980s: Comment on Collins." *American Journal of Sociology* 91, 175–80.

———. 1987. "On Semiotics and Symbolic Interactionism." *Symbolic Interaction* 10, no. 1, 1–19.

Derrida, Jacques. 1974. *Of Grammatology.* Baltimore: John Hopkins University Press.

———. 1978. "Structure, Sign, and Play in the Discourse of the Human Sciences," in *Writing and Difference.* Alan Bass, trans. Chicago: University of Chicago Press.

Descartes, René. 1898. *Oeuvres de Descartes.* Charles Adams and Paul Tannery, eds. Paris: Leopold Cerf.

———. 1960. *Discourse on Method, and Meditations.* Lawrence Lafleur, trans. Indianapolis, Ind.: Bobbs-Merrill.

Dewey, John. 1886. *Psychology.* New York: Harper Bros.

———. 1954. *The Public and Its Problems.* Chicago: Swallow Press.

Dickson, David. 1984. *The New Politics of Science.* New York: Pantheon.

Diesing, Paul. 1982. *Science and Ideology in the Policy Sciences.* New York: Aldine.

———. 1992. *How Does Social Science Work? Reflections on Practice.* Pittsburgh: University of Pittsburgh Press.

Dietz, Thomas. 1987. "Theory and Method in Social Impact Assessment." *Sociological Inquiry* 57, no. 1, 54–69.

———. 1988. "Social Impact Assessment as Applied Human Ecology: Integrating Theory and Method." In Richard J. Borden, Jamien Jacobs, and Gerald I. Young, eds. *Human Ecology.* College Park, Md.: Society for Human Ecology.

Dietz, Thomas, and Paul C. Stern. 1993. "The Value Basis of Environmental Concern." Manuscript. Department of Sociology, George Mason University, Fairfax, Va.

Dietz, Thomas, Paul C. Stern, and Robert W. Rycroft. 1989. "Definitions of Conflict and the Legitimation of Resources: The Case of Environmental Risk." *Sociological Forum* 4, no. 1, 47–70.

Diggins, J. P. 1988. "Can-Do Cant." *The New Republic* 199, nos. 3843–44 (September), 14–15.

Dilthey, Wilhelm. 1957. *Gesammelte Schriften.* Stuttgart: B. G. Teubner.

DiMaggio, Paul. 1987. "Classification in Art." *American Sociological Review* 52, no. 4 (August), 440–55.

Dogan, Mattei, and Robert Pahre. 1990. *Creative Marginality: Innovation at the Intersections of Social Sciences.* Boulder: Westview Press.

Dollard, J. 1939. *Frustrations and Aggression.* New Haven: Yale University Press.

Dollard, J., L. W. Doob, N. W. Miller, O. H. Mowrer, and R. R. Sears. 1950. *Personality and Psychotherapy.* New York: McGraw-Hill.

Douglas, Jack. 1988. *The Myth of the Welfare State.* New Brunswick, N.J.: Transaction.

Douglas, Mary. 1972. "Deciphering a Meal." Pp. 249–75 in *Implicit Meanings: Essays in Anthropology.* London: Routledge and Kegan Paul.

———. 1985. "Pascal's Great Wager." *L'Homme* 25, 13–30.

Douglas, Mary, and Baron Isherwood. 1978. *The World of Goods.* New York: Basic Books.

Douglas, Mary, and Aaron Wildavsky. 1982. *Risk and Culture: An Essay on the Selection of Technological and Environmental Dangers.* Berkeley: University of California Press.

Drake, Stillman. 1986. "Reexamining Galileo's *Dialogue.*" Pp. 155–78 in William A. Wallace, ed. *Reinterpreting Galileo.* Washington, D.C.: Catholic University of America Press.

Durkheim, Emile. 1965. *The Elementary Forms of Religious Life.* 1915. Reprint, New York: Free Press.

Duvignaud, Jean. 1977. *Change at Shebika: Report from a North African Village.* Austin: University of Texas Press.

Eco, Umberto. 1976. *A Theory of Semiotics.* Bloomington: Indiana University Press.

Edelman, Nathan. 1974. "The Mixed Metaphors in Descartes." Pp. 107–20 in *The Eye of the Beholder: Essays in French Literature.* Baltimore: Johns Hopkins University Press.

Eder, Klaus. 1985. "The New Social Movements: Moral Crusades, Political Pressure Groups, Social Movements?" *Social Research* 52, no. 4, 869-900.

Edwards, Derek, Malcolm Ashmore, and Jonathan Potter. 1992. "Death and Furniture: The Rhetoric, Politics, and Theology of Bottom Line Arguments against Relativism." Discourse and Rhetoric Group, Loughborough University, England.

Ehrenhaus, Peter. 1993. "Cultural Narratives and the Therapeutic Motif: The Political Containment of Vietnam Veterans." In Dennis Mumby, ed. *Narrative and Social Control.* Newbury Park, Calif.: Sage.

Eliade, Mircea. 1959. *The Sacred and the Profane: The Nature of Religion.* New York: Harcourt Brace.

Elkana, Y. 1977. "The Historical Roots of Modern Physics." In C. Weiner, ed. *Proceedings of the International School of Physics "Enrico Fermi": History of Twentieth Century Physics.* New York: Academic Press.

Eisenberg, John A. 1992. *The Limits of Reason: Indeterminacy in Law, Education and Morality.* New Brunswick, N.J.: Transaction.

Elzinga, Aant. 1985. "Research, Bureaucracy, and the Drift of Epistemic Criteria." Pp. 191–220 in Bjorn Wittrock and Aant Elzinga, eds. *The University Research System: The Public Policies of the Home of Scientists.* Stockholm: Almquist and Wiksell.

Erlich, Paul R. 1986. *The Machinery of Nature.* New York: Simon and Schuster.

Evans-Prichard, Edward J. 1940. *The Nuer.* Oxford: Oxford University Press.

Evernden, Neil. 1992. "Ecology in Conservation and Conversation." In M. Oelschlaeger, ed. *After Earth Day: Continuing the Conservation Effort.* Denton, Tex.: University of North Texas Press.

Ewick, Patricia, and Susan S. Sibley. 1995. "Subversive Stories and Hegemonic Tales: Toward a Sociology of Narrative." *Law and Society Review* 29, no. 2, 197–226.

Farberman, Harvey A. 1980. "Fantasy in Everyday Life: Some Aspects of the Interaction between Social Psychology and Political Economy." *Symbolic Interaction* 3, no. 1, 9–22.

Farrell, Thomas B. 1976. "Knowledge, Consensus, and Rhetorical Theory." *Quarterly Journal of Speech* 62, no. 1, 1–14.

Farrell, Thomas B., and T. Thomas Goodnight. 1981. "Accidental Rhetoric: The Root Metaphor of Three Mile Island." *Communication Monographs* 48, 271–300.

Fashing, Joseph, and Ted Goertzel. 1981. "The Myth of the Normal Curve." *Humanity and Society* 5, 14–31.

Faust, D., and J. Ziski. 1988. "The Expert Witness in Psychology and Psychiatry." *Science* 241, no. 4861, 31–35.

Favre, Pierre. 1981. "Les Sciences de l'état entre déterminisme et libéralisme." *Revue française de sociologie* 22, no. 3, 429–65.

Feely-Harnik, Gillian. 1978. "Divine Kingship and the Meaning of History among the Sakalava of Madagascar." *Man* 13, 402–17.

Feigl, Herbert. 1945. "Operationalism and the Scientific Method." *Psychological Review* 52, 250–59.

Ferguson, Thomas. 1973. "The Political Economy of Knowledge and the Changing Politics of Philosophy of Science." *Telos* 15 (Spring), 124–37.

Ferrarotti, Franco. 1981. *Introduzione alla soziologia.* Rome: Riuniti.

Feyerabend, Paul. 1977. "The Expert in a Free Society." *Amsterdams Sociologisch Tijdschrift* 3, 4.
———. 1978. *Against Method: Outline of an Anarchistic Theory of Knowledge.* London: Verso.

Fine, Arthur. 1986. *The Shaky Game: Einstein, Realism, and the Quantum Theory.* Chicago: University of Chicago Press.

Fine, Gary Alan, and Daniel D. Martin. 1990. "A Partisan View: Sarcasm, Satire, and Irony as Voices in Erving Goffman's Asylums." *Journal of Contemporary Ethnography* 19, no. 1 (April), 89–115.

Finocchiaro, Maurice. 1980. *Galileo and the Art of Reasoning: Rhetorical Foundations of Logic and Scientific Method.* Dordrecht: Kluwer Academic.
———. 1989. "Varieties of Rhetoric in Science." *History of the Human Sciences* 3, no. 2, 177–93.

Firth, Raymond. 1957. *We, the Tikopia.* 1936. Reprint, London: Allen and Unwin.

Fischer, Frank. 1990. *Technocracy and the Politics of Expertise.* Newbury Park, Calif.: Sage.

Fischer, Roland. 1987. "On Fact and Fiction: The Structure of Stories That the Brain Tells to Itself about Itself." *Journal of Social Biological Structure* 10, 343–51.

Fish, Stanley. 1989. *Doing What Comes Naturally: Change, Rhetoric and the Practice of Theory in Literary and Legal Studies.* Durham, N.C.: Duke University Press.

Fisher, Sue, and Alexandra Dundas Todd, eds. 1986. *Discourse and Institutional Authority: Medicine, Education, and Law.* Norwood, N.J.: Ablex.

Fisher, Walter R. 1984. "Narration as a Human Communication Paradigm: The Case of the Public Moral Argument." *Communication Monographs* 5, no. 11, 1–22.
———. 1987. *Human Communication as Narration: Toward a Philosophy of Reason, Value, and Action.* Columbia: University of South Carolina Press.

———. "Narration, Reason, and Community." Pp. 199–218 in Richard Harvey Brown, ed. *Writing the Social Text: Poetics and Politics in Scientific Discourse.* New York: Aldine de Gruyter.

Fleck, Ludwik. 1979. *Genesis and Development of a Scientific Fact.* 1935. Reprint, Chicago: University of Chicago Press.

Ford, James E., and James F. Klumpp. 1985. "Systematic Pluralism: An Inquiry into the Bases of Communication Research." *Critical Studies in Mass Communication* 2, 407–34.

Fores, James E. 1984. "Constructed Science and the Seventeenth Century 'Revolution,'" *History of Science* 22, no. 4 (December), 217–44.

———. 1985. "Newton on a Horse: A Critique of the Historiographies of 'Technologies' and 'Modernity.'" *History of Science* 23, no. 3 (September), 351–78.

Forester, John, ed. 1985. *Critical Theory and Public Life.* Cambridge: MIT Press.

Formaini, Robert. 1990. *The Myth of Scientific Public Policy.* New Brunswick, N.J.: Transaction.

Foucault, Michel. 1970. *The Order of Things: An Archeology of the Human Sciences.* New York: Pantheon.

———. 1972. *The Archaeology of Knowledge.* A. M. Sheridan, trans. New York: Harper Colophon.

———. 1973. *Madness and Civilization: A History of Insanity in the Age of Reason.* R. Howard, trans. New York: Random House, Vintage.

———. 1977. *Discipline and Punish: The Birth of the Prison.* Alan Sheridan, trans. New York: Pantheon.

———. 1980. *Power/Knowledge: Selected Interviews and Other Writings, 1972–1977.* New York: Pantheon.

Franklin, Allan. 1986. *The Neglect of Experiment.* Cambridge: Cambridge University Press.

Freeley-Harnik, Gillian. 1978. "Divine Kingship and the Meaning of History among the Sakalava of Madagascar." *Man*, n.s., 13, no. 2, 402–17.

Freidson, Eliot. 1986. *Professional Powers: A Study of the Institutionalization of Formal Knowledge.* Chicago: University of Chicago Press.

Frentz, Thomas S. 1985. "Rhetorical Conversation, Time, and Moral Action." *Quarterly Journal of Speech* 71, no. 1, 1–18.

Freud, Sigmund. 1953. *The Interpretation of Dreams.* Pp. 1–627 in James Strachey, ed. and trans. *The Standard Edition of the Complete Psychological Works of Sigmund Freud* 4 & 5. London: Hogarth Press.

———. 1963. "Introductory Lectures on Psycho-Analysis." Pp. 57–145 in James Strachey, ed. and trans. *The Standard Edition of the Complete Psychological Works of Sigmund Freud* 21. London: Hogarth Press.

Freudenberg, Nicholas, and Carol Steinsapir. 1992. "Not in Our Backyards: The Grassroots Environmental Movement." In Riley Dunlap and Angela G. Mertig, eds. *The U.S. Environmental Movement, 1970–1990.* Washington, D.C.: Taylor and Francis.

Frye, Northrop. 1957. *Anatomy of Criticism.* Princeton, N.J.: Princeton University Press.

———. *The Secular Scripture.* Cambridge: Harvard University Press.

Fuchs, Stephan. 1986. "The Social Organization of Scientific Knowledge." *Sociological Theory* 4, 126–42.

————. 1992. *The Professional Quest for Truth: A Social Theory of Science and Knowledge.* Albany: SUNY Press.

————. 1993. "A Sociological Theory of Scientific Change." *Social Forces* 71, 933–53.

Fuller, Steve. 1988. *Social Epistemology.* Bloomington: Indiana University Press.

————. 1993. *Philosophy, Rhetoric, and the End of Knowledge: The Coming of Science and Technology Studies.* Madison: University of Wisconsin Press.

Furner, Mary O. 1975. *Advocacy and Objectivity: A Crisis in the Professionalization of American Social Sciences, 1865–1905.* Lexington: University Press of Kentucky.

Gadamer, Hans-Georg. 1975. *Truth and Method.* New York: Seabury Press.

————. 1989. "Text and Interpretation." In E. Michael Felder and Richard Palmer, eds. *Dialogue and Deconstruction: The Gadamer-Derrida Encounter.* Albany: State University Press of New York.

Gale, Richard. 1990. *Encyclopedia of Associations.* Detroit: Gale Press.

Galileo Galilei. 1989. "Considerations on the Copernican Opinion." 1615. Reprint, pp. 70–86 in Maurice A. Finocchiaro, ed. and trans. *The Galileo Affair.* Berkeley: University of California Press.

————. 1953. *Dialogue Concerning the Two Chief World Systems.* 1632. Reprint, Stillman Drake, trans. Berkeley: University of California Press.

Gamson, William. 1985. "Goffman's Legacy to Political Sociology." *Theory and Society* 14, no. 5, 605–22.

————. 1988. "Political Discourse and Collective Action." In B. Klandermans, H. Kriesi, and S. Tarrow, eds. *International Social Movement Research: From Structure to Action: Comparing Social Movement Research across Cultures* 1. Greenwich, Conn.: JAI Press.

————. 1991. "Commitment and Agency in Social Movements." *Sociological Forum* 6, no. 1, 27–50.

————. 1992. "The Social Psychology of Collective Action." In Aldon D. Morris and Carol McClurg Mueller, eds. *Frontiers in Social Movement Theory.* New Haven: Yale University Press.

Garfinkel, Harold. 1952. "The Perception of the Other: A Study in Social Order." Ph.D. dissertation, Department of Sociology, Harvard University.

————. 1967. *Studies in Ethnomethodology.* Englewood Cliffs, N.J.: Prentice-Hall.

Garfinkel, Harold, Michael Lynch, and Eric Livingston. 1981. "The Work of a Discovering Science Construed with Materials from the Optically Discovered Pulsar." *Philosophy of the Social Sciences* 11, no. 2, 131–58.

Garver, Eugene. 1987. *Machiavelli and the History of Prudence.* Madison: University of Wisconsin Press.

Garvey, C. R. 1929. "List of American Psychology Laboratories." *Psychological Bulletin* 26, no. 11 (November) 652–60.

Geertz, Clifford. 1973. *The Interpretation of Cultures.* New York: Basic Books.

————. 1981. *Negara: The Theatre State in Nineteenth-Century Bali.* Princeton: Princeton University Press.

————. 1983. *Local Knowledge.* New York: Basic Books.

Geiger, Theodore. 1973. *Tales of Two City-States.* Washington, D.C.: Washington National Planning Association.

————. 1986. *To Advance Knowledge: The Growth of American Research Universities, 1900–1940*. New York: Oxford University Press.

Geison, Gerald L. 1983. *Professions and Professional Ideologies in America*. Chapel Hill: University of North Carolina Press.

————. 1995. *The Private Science of Louis Pasteur*. Princeton: Princeton University Press.

Gellner, Ernest. 1964. *Thought and Change*. Chicago: University of Chicago Press.

————. 1979. *Legitimation of Belief*. London: Cambridge University Press.

————. 1985. *Relativism and the Social Sciences*. London: Cambridge University Press.

Genette, Gerard. 1978. "Boundaries of Narrative." *New Literary History* 8, 1.

Gergen, Kenneth J. 1982. *Toward Transformation in Social Knowledge*. New York: Springer.

————. 1990. "Metaphor, Metatheory, and the Social World." Pp. 267–99 in David E. Leary, ed. *Metaphors in the History of Psychology*. New York: Cambridge University Press.

Gergen, Kenneth J., and Mary M. Gergen. 1986. "Narrative Form and the Construction of Psychological Science." Pp. 22–44 in Theodore R. Sarbin, ed. *Narrative Psychology: The Storied Nature of Human Conduct*. New York: Praeger.

Gerhards, Jürgen, and Dieter Rucht. 1992. "Mesomobilization: Organizing and Framing in Two Protest Campaigns in West Germany." *American Journal of Sociology* 98, no. 3, 555–95.

Gibbs, Lois Marie. 1982. *Love Canal: My Story*. Albany: SUNY Press.

Gibbs, Lois Marie, and Karen J. Stults. 1988. "On Grassroots Environmentalism." In Peter Borecelli, ed. *Crossroads: Environmental Priorities for the Future*. Washington, D.C.: Island Press.

Gibson, James J. 1979. *The Ecological Approach to Visual Perception*. Boston: Houghton Mifflin.

Gide, André. 1955. *The Counterfeiters*. Dorothy Bussy, trans. New York: Knopf.

Gieryn, Thomas. 1983. "Boundary-Work and the Demarcation of Science from Non-Science: Strains and Interests in Professional Ideologies of Scientists." *American Sociological Review* 48, no. 8, 781–95.

Gilbert, G. N., and Michael Mulkay. 1984. *Opening Pandora's Box: A Sociological Analysis of Scientists' Discourse*. Cambridge: Cambridge University Press.

Gillespie, Richard. 1988. "The Hawthorne Experiments and the Politics of Experimentation." Pp. 114–37 in Jill G. Morawski, ed. *The Rise of Experimentation in American Psychology*. New Haven: Yale University Press.

Gilpin, Robert and Christopher Wright, eds. 1964. *Scientists and National Policymaking*. New York: Columbia University Press.

Gingerich, Owen. 1975. "'Crisis' versus Aesthetic in the Copernican Revolution." Pp. 85–95 in Arthur Beer and K. A. Strand, eds. *Vistas in Astronomy* 17. Oxford: Pergamon Press.

————. 1983. "Ptolemy, Copernicus, and Kepler." Pp. 138–80 in Mortimer J. Adler and John van Doren, eds. *The Great Ideas of Today*. Chicago: Encyclopedia Britannica.

Girnbaum, A. 1960. "The Duhemian Argument." *Philosophy of Science* 27, no. 1, 75–87.

Girson, Gerald L., ed. 1984. *Professions and the French State, 1700–1900*. Philadelphia: University of Pennsylvania Press.

Gittell, Marilyn. 1980. *Limits to Citizen Participation*. Beverly Hills: Sage.

Goffman, Erving. 1959. *The Presentation of the Self in Everyday Life*. Garden City, N.Y.: Doubleday.

———. 1961. *Asylums: Essays on the Social Situation of Mental Patients and Other Inmates*. Garden City, N.Y.: Anchor.

———. 1974. *Frame Analysis: An Essay on the Organization of Experience*. New York: Harper Colophon.

Goldberg, Stanley. 1976. "Max Planck's Philosophy of Nature and His Elaboration of the Special Theory of Relativity." *Historical Studies in the Physical Sciences* 7.

Golden, William T. 1994a. *Worldwide Science and Technology Advice*. New Brunswick, N.J.: Transaction.

———. 1994b. *Science Advice to the President*. New Brunswick, N.J.: Transaction.

———. 1994c. *Science and Technology Advice*. New Brunswick, N.J.: Transaction.

Goodspeed, Thomas Wakefield. 1916. *A History of the University of Chicago*. Chicago: University of Chicago Press.

Goulder, Alvin. 1968. "The Sociologist as Partisan: Sociology and the Welfare State." *American Sociologist* 3, no. 2, 103–16.

Goux, Jean-Joseph. 1973. *Economie et symbolique*. Paris: Seuil.

———. 1984. *Les monnayeurs du langage*. Paris: Galilée.

Graff, Gerald. 1982. "Textual Leftism." *Partisan Review* 49, no. 4, 558–76.

Graham, John D., and March Sadowitz. 1994. "Superfund Reform: Reducing Risk through Community Choice." *Issues in Science and Technology* (Summer), 35–40.

Gralison, Peter. 1987. *How Experiments End*. Chicago: University of Chicago Press.

Green, Bryan S. 1984. *Knowing the Poor: A Case Study in Textual Reality Construction*. Boston: Routledge and Kegan Paul.

———. 1988. *Literary Method and Sociological Theory*. Chicago: University of Chicago Press.

Greenberg, Valerie D. 1990. *Transgressive Reading: The Texts of Franz Kafka and Max Planck*. Ann Arbor: University of Michigan Press.

Greenfeld, Leah. 1987. "Science and National Greatness in the Seventeenth Century." *Minerva* 25, 107–22.

Greenwood, J. D. 1982. "On the Relation between Laboratory Experiments and Social Behavior: Causal Explanation and Generalization." *Journal for the Theory of Behavior* 12, 225–50.

Greer, Germaine. 1984. "The Sao Francisco." Pp. 113–48 in *River Journeys*. London: British Broadcasting Corporation.

Gregory, Bruce. 1988. *Inventing Reality: Physics as Language*. New York: Wiley.

Greimas, Algirdas Julien. 1987. *On Meaning: Selected Writings in Semiotic Theory*. Minneapolis: University of Minnesota Press.

Griffin, Leland M. 1969. "A Dramatistic Theory of the Rhetoric of Movements." In W. H. Rueckert, ed., *Critical Responses to Kenneth Burke, 1924–1966*. Minneapolis: University of Minnesota Press.

Grim, Patrick. 1991. *The Incomplete Universe: Totality, Knowledge, and Truth*. Cambridge: MIT Press.

Gritzer, Glenn, and Arnold Arluke. 1985. *The Making of Rehabilitation: A Political Economy of Medical Specialization, 1890–1980.* Berkeley: University of California Press.

Gronbeck, Bruce. 1978. "Celluloid Rhetoric: On Genres of Documentary." Pp. 139–61 in Karlyn Kohrs Campbell and Kathleen Hall Jamieson, eds. *Form and Genre: Shaping Rhetorical Action.* Annandale, Va.: Speech Communication Association.

Gross, Alan G. 1989. *The Rhetoric of Science.* Cambridge: Harvard University Press.

———. 1992. "Rhetoric of Science without Constraints." *Rhetorica* 9, 283–99.

Gross, Bertrand. 1980. *Friendly Facism: The New Face of Power in America.* New York: M. Evans.

Grubrich-Simitis, Ilse. 1987. "Metapsychology and Metabiology: On Sigmund Freud's Draft Overview of the Transference Neurosis." Pp. 73–107 in Ilse Grubrich-Simitis, ed. Axel Hoffer and Peter T. Hoffer, trans. *A Phylo-Genetic Fantasy: Overview of the Transference Neurosis.* Cambridge: Harvard University Press.

Gruman, Harris Lowell. 1991. *Aspects of Hope: Historical Desire and the Question of the Subject in the Novel.* Ph.D. dissertation, Program in Comparative Literature, University of Maryland, College Park.

Gurevitch, Z. D. 1988. "The Dialogic Connection and the Ethics of Dialogue." Manuscript. Department of Sociology, Hebrew University of Jerusalem.

Gusfield, Joseph. 1976. "The Literary Rhetoric of Science: Comedy and Pathos in Drinking Driver Research." *American Sociological Review* 41, no. 1 (February), 16–34.

Haber, Samuel. 1991. *The Quest for Authority and Honor in the American Professions, 1750–1900.* Chicago: University of Chicago Press.

Habermas, Jürgen. 1968. *Knowledge and Human Interests.* Boston: Beacon Press.

———. 1970a. *Toward a Rational Society.* Boston: Beacon Press.

———. 1970b. "Toward a Theory of Communicative Competence." Pp. 115–48 in Hans Peter Dreitzel, ed. *Recent Sociology, No. 2.: Patterns of Communicative Behavior.* New York: Macmillan.

———. 1979. *Communication and the Evolution of Society.* Boston: Beacon Press.

———. 1984. *The Theory of Communicative Action 1. Reason and the Rationalization of Society.* Boston: Beacon Press.

———. 1986. *Autonomy and Solidarity: Interviews with Jürgen Habermas.* Peter Dews, ed. New York: Verso.

———. 1987. *The Theory of Communicative Action 2. Lifeworld and System: A Critique of Functionalist Reason.* Boston: Beacon Press.

———. 1988. *On The Logic of the Social Sciences.* Cambridge: MIT Press.

———. 1990. *Moral Consciousness and Communicative Action.* Cambridge: MIT Press.

———. 1992. "Further Reflections on the Public Sphere." In Craig Calhoun, ed. *Habermas and the Public Sphere.* Cambridge: MIT Press.

———. 1994. *The Past as Future.* Lincoln: University of Nebraska Press.

Hagstrom, Warren O. 1965. *The Scientific Community.* New York: Basic Books.

———. 1974. "Competition in Science." *American Sociological Review* 39, no. 1, 1–18.

Hahn, Roger. 1971. *The Anatomy of a Scientific Institution: The Paris Academy of Sciences, 1666–1803.* Berkeley: University of California Press.

Halliday, M. A. K. 1978. *Language as Social Semiotic.* London: Arnold.

Halliday, Terrence C. 1988. *Beyond Monopoly: Lawyers, State Crises, and Professional Empowerment.* Chicago: University of Chicago Press.

Halloran, Michael. 1978. "Doing Public Business in Public." In Karlyn Kohrs Campbell and Kathleen Hall Jamieson, eds. *Form and Genre: Shaping Rhetorical Action.* Annandale, Va.: Speech Communication Association.

Halloran, Michael J., and Annette Norris Buford. 1984. "Figures of Speech." Pp. 179–92 in Robert J. Connor, Lisa S. Ede, and Andrea A. Lundsford, eds. *Classical Rhetoric and Modern Discourse.* Carbondale: Southern Illinois University Press.

Hallyn, Fernand. 1990. *The Poetic Structure of the World: Copernicus and Kepler.* New York: Zone.

Hanson, Norwood Russell. 1958a. *Patterns of Discovery: An Inquiry into the Conceptual Foundations of Science.* Cambridge: Cambridge University Press.

———. 1958b. "The Logic of Discovery." *Journal of Philosophy* 551, 1078–89.

———. 1961. "The Copernican Disturbance and the Keplerian Revolution." *Journal of the History of Ideas* 22.

———. 1967. "An Anatomy of Discovery." *Journal of Philosophy* 64, 321–52.

———. 1971. *Observation and Explanation: A Guide to the Philosophy of Science.* New York: Harper and Row.

Harding, Sandra. 1986. *The Science Question in Feminism.* Ithaca: Cornell University Press.

———. 1991. *Whose Science? Whose Knowledge? Thinking about Women's Lives.* Ithaca: Cornell University Press.

Harding, Sandra, ed. 1987. *Sex and Scientific Inquiry.* Chicago: University of Chicago Press.

Hariman, Robert. 1989. "The Rhetoric of Inquiry and the Professional Scholar." Pp. 210–32 in Herbert W. Simons, ed. *Rhetoric in the Human Sciences.* London, Calif.: Sage.

Harré, Rom. 1979. "Architectonic Man: On the Structuring of Lived Experience." Pp. 139–72 in Richard Harvey Brown and Stanford M. Lyman, eds. *Structure, Consciousness, and History.* New York: Cambridge University Press.

Harré, Rom, and Paul F. Secord. 1972. *The Explanation of Social Behavior.* Oxford: Blackwell.

Harrell, Jackson, and Wil A. Linkugel. 1978. "On Rhetorical Genre: An Organizing Perspective." *Philosophy and Rhetoric* 11, no. 9 (Fall), 262–79.

Harrell, Jackson, B. L. Ware, and Wil A. Linkugel. 1975. "The Failure of Apology in American Politics: Nixon on Watergate." *Speech Monographs* (November), 245–61.

Harris, Benjamin. 1988. "Key Words: A History of Debriefing in Social Psychology." Pp. 188–212 in Jill G. Morawski, ed. *The Rise of Experimentation in American Psychology.* New Haven: Yale University Press.

Harvey, David. 1989. *The Condition of Postmodernity.* Oxford: Basil Blackwell.

Hasan, S. Z. 1928. *Realism.* Cambridge: Cambridge University Press.

Haskell, Francis. 1963. *Patrons and Painters.* New York: Knopf.

Haskell, Thomas. 1977. *The Emergence of Professional Social Science: The American Social Science Association and the Nineteenth-Century Crisis of Authority.* Urbana: University of Illinois Press.

Haskell, Thomas, ed. 1984. *The Authority of Experts: Studies in History and Theory.* Bloomington: Indiana University Press.

Hays, Samuel P. 1972. *Conservation and the Gospel of Efficiency: The Progressive Conservation Movement, 1890–1920.* New York: Athenaeum.

Hegel, Georg W. F. 1967. *The Phenomenology of Mind.* 1806. Reprint, J. B. Baillie, trans. New York: Harper and Row.

———. 1977. *Hegel's Phenomenology of Spirit.* 1806. Reprint, A. V. Miller, trans. New York: Oxford University Press.

Heidegger, Martin. 1962. *Being and Time.* J. Macquarrie and E. Robinson, trans. Oxford: Blackwell.

Heider, F., and E. Simmel. 1944. "The Study of Apparent Behavior." *American Journal of Psychology* 57, 243–59.

Heinich, Nathalie. 1987. "Arts et sciences à l'âge classique: Professions et institutions culturelles." *Actes de la recherche en sciences sociales* 67–68 (March), 47–78.

Helevy, Elie. 1955. *The Growth of Philosophic Radicalism.* Boston: Beacon Press.

Helmholtz, Hermann Ludwig von. 1893. "The Aim and Progress of Physical Science (1869)." Pp. 319–48 in *Popular Lectures on Scientific Subjects,* 1st series. London.

———. 1995. *Science and Culture: Popular and Philosophic Essays.* David Cahan, ed. Chicago: University of Chicago Press.

Herman, Ellen. 1995. *The Romance of American Psychology: Political Culture in the Age of Experts.* Berkeley: University of California Press.

Herzfeld, Michael. 1985. "Converging Paths in Semiotics and Anthropology?" *Semiotica* 56, nos. 1 & 2, 153–77.

Hesse, Mary. 1980. *Revolutions and Reconstructions in the Philosophy of Science.* Bloomington: Indiana University Press.

Hikins, James W., and Kenneth S. Zagacki. 1988. "Rhetoric, Philosophy, and Objectivism: An Attenuation of the Claims of the Rhetoric of Inquiry." *Quarterly Journal of Speech* 74, 201–28.

Hirsch, E. D. 1987. *Cultural Literacy: What Every American Needs to Know.* Boston: Houghton Mifflin.

Hobbes, Thomas. 1958. *Leviathan.* 1651. Reprint, Indianapolis: Bobbs-Merrill.

Hoeveler, J. David. 1980. *James McCosh and the Scottish Intellectual Tradition: From Glasgow to Princeton.* Princeton: Princeton University Press.

Holzkamp, K. 1985. "Selbsterfahrung und wissenschaftliche Objektivitat. Unaufhebbarer Widerspruch?" Pp. 17–37 in K. H. Brown and K. Holzkamp, eds. *Subjektivitat als Problem Psychologischer Methodik.* Frankfurt: Campus.

Homer. 1978. *Homer's Odyssey.* Denison Bingham Hull, trans. Greenwich, Conn.: Hull.

Honneth, Axel. 1986. "The Fragmented World of Symbolic Forms: Reflections on Pierre Bourdieu's Sociology of Culture." *Theory, Culture, and Society* 3, no. 3, 55–66.

Hornstein, Gail. 1988. "Quantifying Psychological Phenomena: Debates, Dilemmas, and Implications." Pp. 1–34 in Jill G. Morawski, ed. *The Rise of Experimentation in American Psychology.* New Haven: Yale University Press.

Hovland, C., I. L. Janis, and H. H. Kelley. 1953. *Communication and Personality.* New Haven: Yale University Press.

Hull, Clark L. 1927–28. Idea Books. Diaries, vol. 11. Yale University Library, New Haven.

Hume, David. 1911. *A Treatise on Human Nature.* 1739. Reprint, London: Dent.

————. 1975. *An Inquiry Concerning Human Understanding.* P. H. Nidditch, ed. London: Oxford University Press.

Hunter, Michael. 1982. *Science and Society in Restoration England.* Cambridge: Cambridge University Press.

Huntington, Samuel. 1981. *American Politics: The Promise of Disharmony.* Cambridge: Harvard University Press.

Irvine, Judith T. 1987. "The Division of Labor in Language and Society." *Working Papers and Proceedings of the Center for Psychosocial Studies* paper no. 7.

Irving, C. 1969a. *Fake.* New York: McGraw Hill.

————. 1969b. *Prints and Visual Communication.* Cambridge: MIT Press.

Jablonski, Carol J. 1980. "Promoting Radical Change in the Roman Catholic Church: Rhetorical Requirements, Problems, and Strategies of the American Bishops." *Central States Speech Journal* 31, no. 4 (Winter), 282–89.

Jacob, Margaret C. 1987. *The Cultural Meaning of the Scientific Revolution.* New York: Knopf.

Jacobs, Mary-Ellen. 1989. "Textual Strategies of Claude Lévi-Strauss and Harold Garfinkel: The Rhetorical Creation of Otherness." Paper presented at the International Conference on the Rhetoric of the Social Sciences, College Park, Md., March–April.

Jacobson, Roman. 1971. "On Realism in Art." In Ladislaw Matejka and Krystyna Pomorska, eds. *Readings in Russian Poetics: Formalist and Structuralist Views.* Cambridge: MIT Press.

Jaeger, Carlo C. 1994. *Taming the Dragon: Transforming Economic Institutions in the Face of Global Change.* Philadelphia: Gordon and Breach.

Jaffee, Arnold. 1976. "Reform in Science: The Inebriety Movement and the Development of the Psychological Interpretation of Addiction, 1870–1915." In "Addiction Reform in the Progressive Age: Scientific and Social Responses to Drug Dependence in the United States, 1870–1930." Ph.D. dissertation, Department of History, University of Kentucky.

James, William. 1892. "A Plea for Psychology as a 'Natural Science.'" *Philosophical Review* 1, 146–53.

————. 1902. *The Varieties of Religious Experience: A Study of Human Nature.* New York: Longmans, Green.

————. 1981. *Principles of Psychology.* 2 vols. 1890. Reprint, Cambridge: Harvard University Press.

Jameson, Fredric. 1981. *The Political Unconscious: Narrative as a Socially Symbolic Act.* Ithaca: Cornell University Press.

Jarausch, Konrad H. 1990. *The Unfree Professions: German Lawyers, Teachers, and Engineers, 1900–1950.* New York: Oxford University Press.

Jardine, Nicholas. 1984. *The Birth of History and Philosophy of Science.* New York: Cambridge University Press.

Johnson, Michael G., and Tracy B. Henley. 1990. *Reflections on the Principles of Psychology: William James after a Century.* Hillsdale, N.J.: Lawrence Erlbaum.

Jones, James H. 1981. *Bad Blood: The Tuskegee Syphillis Experiment.* New York: Free Press.

Jost, Walter. 1991. "Review of Eugene Garver's *Machiavelli and the History of Prudence.*" *Philosophy and Rhetoric* 24, no. 1, 73–76.

Judson, Horace Freeland. 1979. *The Eighth Day of Creation: Makers of the Revolution in Biology.* New York: Simon and Schuster.

Kaberry, Phyllis. 1957. "Malinowski's Contribution to Field-Work Methods and the Writing of Ethnography." Pp. 71–91 in Raymond Firth, ed. *Man and Culture: An Evaluation of the Work of Bronislaw Malinowski.* London: Routledge and Kegan Paul.

Kafka, Franz. 1956. *The Trial.* New York: Modern Library.

Kaplan, Abraham. 1964. *The Conduct of Inquiry.* San Francisco: Chandler.

Karier, Clarence J. 1986. *Scientists of the Mind: Intellectual Foundations of Modern Psychology.* Urbana: University of Illinois Press.

Karp, Ivan. 1985. "Laughter at Marriage: Subversion in Performance." Pp. 137–54 in David Parkin, ed. *The Transformation of African Marriage.* London: International African Institute.

Katz, B., and L. Katz. 1985. *Self-Help: 1400 Best Books on Personal Growth.* New York: Bowker.

Keane, J. 1988. *Civil Society and the State: New European Perspectives.* New York: Verso.

Keat, Russell. 1981. *The Politics of Social Theory: Habermas, Freud, and the Critique of Positivism.* Chicago: University of Chicago Press.

Keith, William. 1990. "Cognitive Science on a Wing and a Prayer." *Social Epistemology* 4, 343–56.

Kelemen, Janos. 1982. "Lukács's Ideas on Language." Pp. 245–68 in Ferenc Kiefer, ed. *Hungarian Linguistics.* The Hague: Mouton.

Keller, Evelyn Fox. 1985. *Reflections on Gender and Science.* New Haven: Yale University Press.

———. 1991. "Fractured Images of Science, Language, and Power: The Postmodern Optic, or Just Bad Eyesight." *Poetics Today* 12, no. 2 (Summer), 227–44.

Kelman, Herbert. 1967. "Human Use of Human Subjects: The Problem of Deception in Social Psychological Experiments. *Psychological Bulletin* 67, 1–11.

Kennington, R. 1978. "Descartes and the Mastery of Nature." In S. F. Spicker, ed. *Organism, Medicine, and Metaphysics.* Dordrecht: D. Reidel.

———. 1987. "René Descartes." Pp. 421–39 in Leo Strauss and Joseph Cropsey, eds. *History of Political Philosophy,* 3rd ed. Chicago: University of Chicago Press.

Kepler, Johannes. 1937. *Gesammelte Werke.* Munich: C. H. Beck.

———. 1981. *Mysterium Cosmographicum: The Secret of the Universe.* A. M. Duncan, trans. New York: Arabis.

Kerby, Anthony Paul. 1991. *Narrative and the Self.* Bloomington: Indiana University Press.

Kingson, Jennifer A. 1988. "The Professors Who Make a Case." *New York Times.*

Kirk, Stuart A., and Herb Kutchins. 1992. *The Selling of DSM: The Rhetoric of Science in Psychiatry.* New York: Aldine de Gruyter.

Klandermans, Bert. 1992. "The Social Construction of Protest and Multiorganizational Fields." In Aldon D. Morris and Carol McClurg Mueller, eds. *Frontiers in Social Movement Theory.* New Haven: Yale University Press.

Klein, Martin J. 1960. "Max Planck and the Beginning of Quantum Theory." *Archive for History of the Exact Sciences* 1, no. 1, 459–79.

———. 1963. "Planck, Entropy, and Quanta, 1901–1906." *Natural Philosopher* (New York: Blaisdell) 1, 104–5.

Klumpp, James F. 1991. "The Unconsummated Flirtation in Textual Approaches to Argumentation." Pp. 54–60 in *Proceedings of the Third International Conference on Argumentation*. Amsterdam: International Centre for the Study of Argumentation.

———. 1997. "Freedom and Responsibility in Constructing Public Life: Toward a Revised Ethic of Discourse." *Argumentation* 11, no. 1 (Richard Harvey Brown, guest editor).

Klumpp, James F., and Thomas A. Hollihan. 1989. "Rhetorical Criticism as Moral Action." *Quarterly Journal of Speech* 75, 84–97.

Klumpp, James F., Patricia Riley, and Thomas A. Hollihan. 1995. "Argument in the Post-Political Age: Emerging Sites for a Democratic Lifeworld." Special Fields and Cases 4. Pp. 318–28 in Frans H. van Eemeren, Rob Grootendorst, J. Anthony Blair, and Charles A. Willard, eds., *Proceedings of the Third ISSA Conference on Argumentation*. Amsterdam: SICSAT.

Knoespel, Kenneth, and Robert Markley. 1992. *Newton and the Failure of Messianic Science: A Postdisciplinary Inquiry into the Discourses of Natural Philosophy*. Norman: University of Oklahoma Press.

Knorr-Cetina, Karin D., and Michael Mulkay. 1983. *Science Observed: Perspectives on the Social Study of Science*. London: Sage.

Koch, Sigmund. 1985. "The Nature and Limits of Psychological Knowledge: Lessons of a Century qua Science." Pp. 75–97 in Sigmund Koch and David E. Leary, eds. *A Century of Psychology as Science*. New York: McGraw-Hill.

Kolko, Gabriel. 1967. *The Triumph of Conservatism: A Reinterpretation of American History*. New York: Free Press.

Konig, René. 1987. *Soziologie in Deutschland*. Munich: Hanser.

Krauss, Celene. 1993a. "Blue Collar Women and Toxic-Waste Protests." In Richard Hofrichter, ed. *Toxic Struggles: The Theory and Practice of Environmental Justice*. Philadelphia: New Society Publishers.

———. 1993b. "Women and Toxic Waste Protests: Race, Class and Gender as Resources of Resistance." *Qualitative Sociology* 16, no. 3, 247–62.

———. 1994. "Women of Color on the Front Line." In Robert D. Bullard, ed. *Unequal Protection: Environmental Justice and Communities of Color*. San Francisco: Sierra Club Books.

Kristeva, Julia. 1973. "The System and the Speaking Subject." *Times Literary Supplement* 12, no. 3, 736, 1249–50. Reprinted in Toril Moi, ed. *The Kristeva Reader*. New York: Columbia University Press, 1986, pp. 24–33.

Kropotkin, Peter. 1993. *Fields, Factories and Workshops*. 1899. Reprint, Montreal: Black Rose Books.

Kucklick, H. 1980. "Boundary Maintenance in American Sociology: Limitations of Academic 'Professionalism.'" *Journal of the History of the Behavioral Sciences* 16.

Kuhn, Thomas. 1972. *The Structure of Scientific Revolutions*. Chicago: University of Chicago Press.

———. 1977. *The Essential Tradition: Selected Studies in Scientific Tradition and Change*. Chicago: University of Chicago Press.

———. 1981. *The Copernican Revolution: Planetary Astronomy in the Development of Western Thought*. Cambridge: Harvard University Press.

————. 1987. *Black Body Theory and the Quantum Discontinuity, 1894–1912.* Chicago: University of Chicago Press.

Kuklick, Bruce. 1977. *The Rise of American Philosophy, Cambridge, Massachusetts, 1860–1930.* New Haven: Yale University Press.

Kundera, Milan. 1984. "The Novel and Europe." *New York Review of Books* 31, no. 12 (July 19), 15–20.

Kuo, Z. Y. 1924. "A Psychology without Heredity." *Psychological Review* 31, no. 6 (November), 427–48.

Kurtz, L. R. 1983. "The Politics of Heresy." *American Journal of Sociology* 88, no. 6, 1085–115.

Lacoste, Dujardin. 1977. *Dialogue de femmes en ethnologie.* Paris.

Lakatos, Imre. 1970. "Falsification and the Methodology of Scientific Research." Pp. 91–196 in Imre Lakatos and Allan E. Musgrave, eds. *Criticism and the Growth of Knowledge.* London: Cambridge University Press.

————. 1974. "History of Science and Rational Reconstructions." Pp. 91–136 in Roger C. Buck and Robert S. Cohen, eds. *Boston Studies in the Philosophy of Science* 8. Dordrecht: D. Reidel.

————. 1978. "Newton's Effect on Scientific Standards." Pp. 193–222 in J. Worrall and G. Ciorie, eds. *Imre Lakatos, Philosophical Papers, Volume I: The Methodology of Scientific Research Programs.* Cambridge: Cambridge University Press.

Lakoff, George. 1987. *Women, Fire, and Dangerous Things: What Categories Reveal about the Mind.* Chicago: University of Chicago Press.

Landan, Larry. 1990. *Science and Relativism.* Chicago: University of Chicago Press.

Landau, Misia. 1984. "Human Evolution as Narrative." *American Scientist* 72 (May–June), 262–68.

Langellier, Kristin M., and Eric E. Peterson. 1993. "Family Storytelling as a Strategy of Social Control." Pp. 49–76 in Dennis Mumby, ed. *Narrative and Social Control.* Newbury Park, Calif.: Sage.

Langer, Susanne. 1942. *Philosophy in a New Key.* Cambridge: Harvard University Press.

Larson, M. S. 1977. *The Rise of Professionalism.* Berkeley: University of California Press.

Latour, Bruno. 1980. "Is It Possible to Reconstruct the Research Process? Sociology of a Brain Peptide." Pp. 141–70 in Karin Knorr, Roger Krohn, and Richard Whitley, eds. *The Social Process of Scientific Investigation.* Dordrecht: D. Reidel.

————. 1983. "Give Me a Laboratory and I Will Raise the World." Pp. 140–70 in Karin D. Knorr-Cetina and Michael Mulkay, eds. *Science Observed: Perspectives on the Social Study of Science.* London: Sage.

————. 1986. "The Powers of Association." In John Law, ed. *Power, Action and Belief: A New Sociology of Knowledge?* London: Routledge.

————. 1987. *Science in Action.* Cambridge: Harvard University Press.

————. 1989. "Clothing the Naked Truth." Pp. 101–28 in Hilary Lawson and Lisa Appignanesi, eds. *Dismantling the Truth: Reality in the Post-Modern World.* New York: St. Martin's.

————. 1993. *The Pasteurization of France.* Cambridge: Harvard University Press.

Latour, Bruno, and Steve Woolgar. 1986. *Laboratory Life: The Construction of Scientific Facts.* Beverly Hills, Calif.: Sage.

Laudan, Larry. 1990. *Science and Relativism.* Chicago: University of Chicago Press.

Lave, J. 1988. *Cognition in Practice.* New York: Cambridge University Press.

Lawson, Hilary. 1989. "Stories about Stories." Pp. xi–xxviii in Hilary Lawson and Lisa Appignanesi, eds. *Dismantling the Truth: Reality in the Post-Modern World.* New York: St. Martin's.

Lazlo, Erwin. 1971. "Human Dignity and the Promise of Technology." *Philosophy Forum* 9, no. 1–2 (June).

Leary, David E. 1980. "The Intentions and Heritage of Descartes and Locke: Toward a Recognition of the Moral Basis of Modern Psychology." *Journal of General Psychology* 10, no. 2, 283–310.

———. 1991a. "Metaphor, Theory, and Practice in the History of Psychology." In David E. Leary, ed. *Metaphors in the History of Psychology.* New York: Cambridge University Press.

———. 1991b. "Psyche's Muse: The Role of Metaphor in the History of Psychology." In David E. Leary, ed. *Metaphors in the History of Psychology.* New York: Cambridge University Press.

———. 1992. "Communication, Persuasion, and the Establishment of Academic Disciplines: The Case of American Psychology." Pp. 73–90 in Richard Harvey Brown, ed. *Writing the Social Text.* New York: Aldine de Gruyter.

Leinhardt, Godfrey. 1961. *Divinity and Experience: The Religion of the Dinka.* New York: Oxford University Press.

Lemert, Charles. 1979. *Sociology and the Twilight of Man: Homocentrism and Discourse in Sociological Theory.* Carbondale: Southern Illinois University Press.

———. 1992. "General Social Theory, Irony, Postmodernism." Pp. 17–46 in Steven Seidman and David Wagner, eds. *Postmodernism and Social Theory: The Debate over General Theory.* London: Basil Blackwell.

Lengerman, Patricia Madoo. 1979. "The Founding of the American Sociological Review: The Anatomy of a Rebellion." *American Sociological Review* 44, no. 2 (April), 185–98.

Levine, Donald N. 1983. "Review Essay, 'Sociology after MacIntyre.'" *American Journal of Sociology* 89, no. 3, 700–707.

———. 1985. *The Flight from Ambiguity: Essays in Social and Cultural Theory.* Chicago: University of Chicago Press.

Lévi-Strauss, Claude. 1963. *Structural Anthropology* 1. C. Jacobson and B. G. Schoept, trans. New York: Basic Books.

———. 1967. *The Savage Mind.* Chicago: University of Chicago Press.

———. 1976. *Structural Anthropology* 2. Monique Layton, trans. New York: Basic Books.

Lewis, C. S. 1947. *The Abolition of Man.* New York: Macmillan.

Lieberman, Jethro K. 1970. *The Tyranny of Experts: How Professionals Are Closing the Open Society.* New York: Walker.

Lindblom, Charles E., and David K. Cohen. 1979. *Usable Knowledge: Social Science and Social Problem Solving.* New Haven: Yale University Press.

Lippman, Walter. 1955. *Essays in the Public Philosophy.* Boston: Little Brown.

Locke, John. 1974. *Essay Concerning Human Understanding.* 1690. Reprint, New York: AMS Press.

Longino, Helen E. 1990. *Science as Social Knowledge: Values and Objectivity in Scientific Inquiry.* Princeton: Princeton University Press.

Lorrain, Jorge. 1979. *The Concept of Ideology.* London: Routledge and Kegan Paul.

Luhmann, Niklas. 1987. "The Representation of Society within Society." *Current Sociology* 35, no. 2, 101–8.

Lukács, Georg. 1971a. *The Theory of the Novel.* Anna Bostock, trans. Cambridge: MIT Press.

———. 1971b. *History and Class Consciousness: Studies in Marxist Dialectics.* Cambridge: MIT Press.

Lyman, Stanford, and Marvin Scott. 1970. "Accounts." In *A Sociology of the Absurd.* New York: Appleton Century Crafts.

Lyman, Stanford, and Arthur Vidich. 1985. *American Sociology: Worldly Rejections of Religion and Their Directions.* New Haven: Yale University Press.

Lynch, Michael. 1986. Review of Harry M. Collins, *Changing Order: Representation and Induction in Scientific Practice. Knowledge* 5, no. 4, 619–20.

———. 1994. *Scientific Practice and Ordinary Action: Ethnomethodology and Social Studies of Science.* New York: Cambridge University Press.

Lyons, Gene M. 1969. *The Uneasy Partnership.* New York: Russell Sage.

Lyons, Gene M., and Louis Morton. 1965. *Schools for Strategy.* New York: Praeger.

Lyotard, Jean-François. 1954. *La Phenomenologie.* Paris: Presses universitaires de France.

———. 1977. *Instructions païennes.* Paris: Galilée.

———. 1988. *The Postmodern Condition: A Report on Knowledge.* Minneapolis: University of Minnesota Press.

MacCannell, Dean, and Juliet Flower MacCannell. 1986. *The Time of the Sign.* Bloomington: Indiana University Press.

MacIntyre, Alasdair. 1980. "Epistemological Crises, Dramatic Narrative, and the Philosophy of Science." Pp. 54–74 in Gary Gutting, ed. *Paradigms and Revolutions: Applications and Appraisals of Thomas Kuhn's Philosophy of Science.* Notre Dame, Ind.: University of Notre Dame Press.

———. 1981. *After Virtue: A Study in Moral Theory.* Notre Dame, Ind.: University of Notre Dame Press.

Mackenzie, B. D. 1977. *Behaviorism and the Limits of Scientific Method.* Atlantic Highlands, N.J.: Humanities Press.

Macomber, William. 1968. *The Anatomy of Disillusion.* Evanston: Northwestern University Press.

Madison, G. B. 1989. "The New Philosophy of Rhetoric." *Texte: Revue de critique et de theorie littéraire* 8–9.

Mahony, Patrick J. 1987. *Freud as a Writer.* New Haven: Yale University Press.

———. 1989. *On Defining Freud's Discourse.* New Haven: Yale University Press.

Makkreel, Rudolf A. 1975. *Dilthey: Philosopher of the Human Sciences.* Princeton: Princeton University Press.

———. 1980. "Vico and Some Kantian Reflections on Historical Judgment." *Man and World* 13, 99–120.

Malinowski, Bronislaw. 1948. *Magic, Science and Religion and Other Essays.* Glencoe, Ill.: Free Press.

————. 1961. *Argonauts of the Western Pacific.* 1922. Reprint, New York: E. P. Dutton.

Manicas, Peter T. 1982. "The Human Sciences: A Radical Separation of Psychology and the Social Sciences." Pp. 155–73 in Paul F. Secord, ed. *Explaining Human Behavior: Consciousness, Action, and Social Structure.* Beverly Hills, Calif.: Sage.

————. 1987. *A History and Philosophy of the Social Sciences.* London: Basil Blackwell.

Manicas, Peter T., and Paul F. Secord. 1983. "Implications for Psychology of the New Philosophy of Science." *American Psychologist* 38, no. 4, 399–413.

Mannheim, Karl. 1936. *Ideology and Utopia.* London: Routledge and Kegan Paul.

March, James G. 1972. "Model Bias in Social Action." *Review of Educational Research* 42, no. 4 (Feburary), 413–29.

Marcus, George E. 1980. Rhetoric and the Ethnographic Genre in Anthropological Research." *Current Anthropology* 21, no. 4 (August), 507–10.

Marcus, George E., and Dick Cushman. 1982. "Ethnographies as Text." *Annual Review of Anthropology* 11, 25–69.

Marcuse, Herbert. 1972. *Counter-Revolution and Revolt.* Boston: Beacon Press.

Mariner, Dorothy Anderson. 1971. "Ideology and Rhetoric: Their Impact on an Organization and on Professional Aspirations." *Pacific Sociological Review* 14, no. 2, 197–214.

Markley, Robert. 1983. "Objectivity as Ideology: Boyle, Newton, and the Uses of Language." *Genre* 16 (Winter), 355–72.

————. 1990. "The Rise of Nothing: Revisionist Historiography and the Narrative Structure of Eighteenth-Century Studies." *Genre* 28 (Summer–Fall), 77–102.

Marsden, George M., and Bradley J. Longfield. 1992. *The Secularization of the Academy.* New York: Oxford University Press.

Marsh, G. P. 1864. *Man and Nature.* New York: Scribners.

Marx, Karl. 1946. *Capital.* New York: Everyman's Library.

————. 1971. *Marx's Grundrisse.* D. McLellan, ed. London: Macmillan.

Marx, Karl, and Frederick Engels. 1978. "The German Ideology, Part 1." Written in 1845–46; first published in 1932. Reprinted in *The Marx-Engels Reader.* R. C. Tucker, ed. New York: Norton.

Mauss, Marcel. 1967. *The Gift: Forms and Functions of Exchange in Archaic Societies.* New York: Norton.

Maynard, Douglas W., and Thomas P. Wilson. 1980. "On the Reification of Social Structure." Pp. 287–322 in S. McNall and G. Howe, eds. *Current Perspectives in Social Theory* 1. Greenwich, Conn.: JAI Press.

Mayo, Elton. 1945. *The Social Problems of an Industrial Society.* Cambridge: Harvard University Press.

McCanles, Michael. 1976. "The Literal and Metaphysical: Dialectic or Interchange." *Publications of the Modern Language Association* 91, no. 2 (March), 279–90.

McClenon, James. 1981. *Deviant Science.* Philadelphia: University of Pennsylvania Press.

McCloskey, Donald N. 1985. *The Rhetoric of Economics.* Madison: University of Wisconsin Press.

————. 1988. "Formalism in Economics and Other Social Sciences, Rhetorically Speaking." Paper presented to the American Sociological Association, Atlanta, August.

———. 1990. *If You're So Smart: The Narrative of Economic Expertise.* Chicago: University of Chicago Press.

McConnell, J. V. 1986. *Understanding Human Behavior.* New York: Holt, Rinehart and Winston.

McDougall, William. 1908. *An Introduction to Social Psychology.* London: Methuen.

McGill, Lawrence T. 1990. "Doing Science by the Numbers: The Role of Tables and Other Representational Conventions in Scientific Journal Articles." Pp. 129–41 in Albert Hunter, ed. *The Rhetoric of Social Research: Understood and Believed.* New Brunswick: Rutgers University Press.

Meadows, D. H, D. L. Meadows, and J. Randers. 1972. *The Limits to Growth.* New York: Universe Books.

———. 1992. *Beyond the Limits: Confronting Global Collapse, Envisioning a Sustainable Future.* Post Mills, Vt.: Chelsea Green Publishing.

Mehan, Hugh, and Houston Wood. 1975. *The Reality of Ethnomethodology.* New York: Wiley.

Mehlberg, Henry. 1958. *The Reach of Science.* Toronto: University of Toronto Press.

Melandri, E. 1968. *La linea e il circolo.* Bologna: Il Mulino.

Melville, Herman. 1976. *Moby Dick, or the Whale.* Harrison Hayford and Hershel Parker, eds. New York: Norton.

Menard, Henry W. 1971. *Science; Growth and Change.* Cambridge: Harvard University Press.

Mendelsohn, Everett. 1977. "The Social Construction of Scientific Knowledge." Pp. 3–26 in Everett Mendelsohn, Peter Weingart, and Richard Whitley, eds. *The Social Production of Knowledge, Sociology of the Sciences: A Yearbook* 1. Dordrecht: D. Reidel.

Merchant, Carolyn. 1992. *Radical Ecology: The Search for a Livable World.* New York: Routledge and Morgan.

Merleau-Ponty, Maurice. 1964. *Signs.* Evanston: Northwestern University Press.

Merton, Robert K. 1973. *The Sociology of Science: Theoretical and Empirical Investigations.* Chicago: University of Chicago Press.

———. 1979. *Science, Technology, and Society in Seventeenth-Century England.* 1938. Reprint, New York: Harper and Row.

Michotte, A. E. 1963. *The Perception of Causality.* London: Methuen.

Miller, Jonathan. 1995. "Going Unconscious." *New York Review of Books* 42, no. 7 (April 20), 59–65.

Miller, William Ian. 1995. *Humiliation, and Other Essays on Honor, Social Discomfort, and Violence.* Ithaca: Cornell University Press.

Mills, C. Wright. 1959. *The Sociological Imagination.* New York: Oxford University Press.

———. 1974. *Power, Politics, and People: The Collected Essays of C. Wright Mills.* Irving Louis Horowitz, ed. New York: Oxford University Press.

Mink, Louis. 1987. *Historical Understanding.* Ithaca: Cornell University Press.

Mishler, Elliott. 1986. *Research Interviewing: Context and Narrative.* Cambridge: Harvard University Press.

Mitchell, W. J. Thomas, ed. 1981. *On Narrative.* Chicago: University of Chicago Press.

Mohrmann, G. P., and Michael C. Leff. 1974. "Lincoln at Cooper Union: A Rationale for Neo-Classical Criticism." *Quarterly Journal of Sociology* 60, 459–67.

Moloch, Harvey L., and Deirdre Boden. 1985. "Talking Social Structure." *American Sociological Review* 50, no. 3, 273–87.

Morawski, Jill G. 1982. "Assessing Psychology's Moral Heritage through our Neglected Utopias." *American Psychologist* 37, no. 10 (October), 1082–95.

———. 1988. "Introduction." In *The Rise of Experimentation in American Psychology.* Jill G. Morawski, ed. New Haven: Yale University Press.

Morgan, G. 1994. "Natural Resource Management: Politically Mediated Science." *American Scientist* 82, no. 5 (September), 475–76.

Morris, Charles. 1932. *Six Theories of Mind.* Chicago: University of Chicago Press.

Moss, Jean Dietz. 1983. "Galileo's Letter to Christina: Some Rhetorical Considerations." *Renaissance Quarterly* 36, no. 4 (Winter), 547–76.

———. 1984. "Galileo's Rhetorical Strategies in Defense of Copernicanism." Pp. 95–103 in P. Galluzzi, ed. *Novita celesti e crisi del sapere: Acti del Convegno Internazionale di Studi Galileiani.* Florence: Barbera.

———. 1986. "The Rhetoric of Proof in Galileo's Writings on the Copernian Systems." Pp. 179–204 in William A. Wallace, ed. *Reinterpreting Galileo.* Washington, D.C.: Catholic University Press.

———. 1991. "Dialectic and Rhetoric: Questions and Answers in the Copernican Revolution." *Argumentation* 3, 17–37.

Mulkay, Michael, and G. N. Gilbert. 1982. "Accounting for Error: How Scientists Construct Their World When They Account for Correct and Incorrect Beliefs." *Sociology* 16, no. 2, 165–83.

Mulkay, Michael, Jonathan Potter, and Seven Yearley. 1983. "Why an Analysis of Scientific Discourse Is Important." Pp. 171–203 in Karin D. Knorr-Cetina and Michael Mulkay, eds. *Science Observed: Perspectives on the Social Study of Science.* Beverly Hills, Calif.: Sage.

Mumby, Dennis K., ed. 1993. *Narrative and Social Control.* Newbury Park, Calif.: Sage.

Munsterberg, Hugo. 1913. *Psychology and Industrial Efficiency.* Boston: Houghton Mifflin.

Murphy, Gardner. 1949. *Historical Introduction to Modern Psychology.* New York: Harcourt Brace.

Murphy, John W. 1989. *Postmodern Social Analysis and Criticism.* New York: Greenwood.

Musser, Joseph F. 1984. "The Perils of Relying on Thomas Kuhn." *Eighteenth Century Studies* 18, no. 2 (Winter), 215–26.

Myers, Gerald E. 1986. *William James, His Life and Thought.* New Haven: Yale University Press.

Nagel, Ernest. 1961. *The Structure of Science.* New York: Harcourt, Brace, World.

Namboodiri, Krishnan. 1987. Review of Stephen M. Stigler, *The History of Statistics: The Measurement of Uncertainty before 1900.* In *Contemporary Sociology* 16, no. 5 (September), 762.

Nandy, Ashis. 1988. "Introduction: Science as a Reason of State." Pp. 1–23 in Ashis Nandy, ed. *Science, Hegemony and Violence: A Requium for Modernity.* Delhi: Oxford University Press.

Napoli, D. S. 1981. *The Architects of Adjustment: A History of the Psychological Profession in the United States.* Port Washington, N.Y.: Kennikat Press.

Narveson, Jan. 1967. *Morality and Utility.* Baltimore: Johns Hopkins University Press.

Nash, Dennison, and Ronald Weintraub. 1972. "The Emergence of Self-Consciousness in Ethnography." *Current Anthropology* 13, no. 5 (December), 527–42.

Nash, June. 1979. *We Eat the Mines, the Mines Eat Us.* New York: Columbia University Press.

Neale, Stephen. 1980. *Genre.* London: British Film Institute.

Nelkin, Dorothy. 1979. "Scientific Knowledge, Public Policy, and Democracy." *Knowledge: Creation, Diffusion, Utilization* 1, no. 1, 106–22.

———. 1984. *Science as Intellectual Property: Who Controls Scientific Research?* AAAS Series on Science and Technology. New York: Macmillan.

———. 1987. *Selling Science: How the Press Covers Science and Technology.* New York: W. H. Freeman.

Nelson, John. 1990. "Political Foundations of the Rhetoric of Inquiry." Pp. 258–91 in Herbert W. Simons, ed. *The Rhetorical Turn: Invention and Persuasion in the Conduct of Inquiry.* Chicago: University of Chicago Press.

Nersessian, Nancy, ed. 1987. *Process of Science: Contemporary Philosophical Approaches to Understanding Scientific Practice.* Dordrecht: Martimes Nijhoff.

Neugebauer. 1968. "On the Planetary Theory of Copernicus." *Vistas in Astronomy* 10, 89–113.

Newton, Isaac. 1952. *Opticks.* New York: Dover.

———. 1966. *Mathematical Principle of Natural Philosophy and His System of the World.* Florian Cajori, trans. Berkeley: University of California Press.

Newton-Smith, W. H. 1989. "Rationality, Truth, and the New Fuzzies." Pp. 23–42 in Hilary Lawson and Lisa Appignansi, eds. *Dismantling Truth: Reality in the Post-Modern World.* Madison: University of Wisconsin Press.

Nickles, Thomas. 1980. *Scientific Discovery: Case Studies.* Boston: D. Reidel.

Nussbaum, Martha. 1992. "Human Functioning and Social Justice: In Defense of Aristotelian Essentialism." *Political Theory* 20, 202–46.

———. 1993. "Non-Relative Virtues: An Aristotelian Approach." In Martha Nussbaum and Amarta Sen, eds. *The Quality of Life.* Oxford: Clarendon Press.

O'Donnell, John M. 1979. "The Crisis of Experimentation in the 1900s: E. G. Boring and His Uses of History." *American Psychologist* 34, no. 4, 289–95.

———. 1985. *The Origins of Behaviorism: American Psychology, 1870–1920.* New York: New York University Press.

Oelschlaeger, Max. 1991. *The Idea of Wilderness: From Prehistory to the Age of Ecology.* New Haven: Yale University Press.

Offe, Claus. 1983. "Competitive Democracy and the Keynesian Welfare State: Factors of Stability and Disorganization." *Policy Sciences* 15, 225–46.

———. 1990. "Reflections on the Institutional Self-Transformation of Movement Politics: A Tentative Stage Model." In Rullel J. Dalton and Manfred Kuechler, eds. *Challenging the Political Order: New Social and Political Movements in Western Democracies.* New York: Oxford University Press.

Okrent, Mark. 1988. *Heidegger's Pragmatism: Understanding, Being, and the Critique of Metaphysics.* Ithaca: Cornell University Press.

Olby, Robert. 1974. *The Path to the Double Helix.* Seattle: University of Washington Press.

Olson, A., and J. Voss, ed. 1979. *The Organization of Knowledge in Modern America, 1860–1920.* Baltimore: Johns Hopkins University Press.

Ornstein, Allen C. 1985. *An Introduction to the Foundations of Education.* Boston: Houghton Mifflin.

Osborn, Michael. 1967. "Archetypal Metaphor in Rhetoric: The Light-Dark Family." *Quarterly Journal of Speech* (April), 115–25.

Overington, Michael. 1977. "The Scientific Community as Audience: Towards a Rhetorical Analysis of Science." *Philosophy and Rhetoric* 10, no. 3, 143–63.

———. 1979. "Doing the What Comes Rationally: Some Developments in Metatheory." *American Sociologist* 14, no. 1, 2–11.

Parsons, Talcott. 1951. *The Social System.* Glencoe, Ill.: Free Press.

———. 1968. "Professions." *International Encyclopedia of the Social Sciences* 12. New York: Macmillan, Free Press.

Pascal, Blaise. 1969. "Treatise on Geometrical Demonstration." In *Oeuvres.* Jacques Chevalier, trans. Paris: Gallimard.

Pavlov, Ivan. 1928. *Lectures on Conditional Reflexes: Twenty-Five Years of Objective Study of the Higher Nervous Activity (Behavior) of Animals.* W. H. Grant, ed. and trans. New York: International.

Paz, Octavio. 1987. "Who Won the Spanish Civil War? The Barricades and Beyond." *New Republic* (November 9), 26–30.

Pearce, W. Barnett, and Victoria Chen. 1989. "Ethnography as Sermonics: The Rhetorics of Clifford Geertz and James Clifford." Pp. 109–32 in Herbert W. Simons, ed. *Rhetoric of the Human Sciences.* Newbury Park, Calif.: Sage.

Peirce, Charles Sanders. 1986. *Collected Papers.* Charles Hartshorne and Paul Weiss, eds. Cambridge: Harvard University Press.

Pels, Dick. 1985. "Rivaliteit en relativisme. Een kritische beschouwing over Pierre Bourdieu's kennissociologie." *Kennis & Methode* 9, 2.

———. 1991. "Values, Facts, and the Social Theory of Knowledge." *Kennis & Methode* 15, 3.

———. 1995. "Intellectual Autonomy: Toward a Political Ethics of Knowledge." In Daniel Schubert, Joan Vecchia, and Richard Harvey Brown, eds. Special issue, *American Behavioral Scientist* 38, no. 7 (June–July), 1018–41.

Penniman, Thomas Kenneth. 1974. *A Hundred Years of Anthropology.* New York: Morrow.

Pepper, Stephen. 1965. *World Hypotheses; A Study in Evidence.* Berkeley: University of California Press.

Perelman, Chaim, and Lucie Olbrechts-Tyteca. 1969. *The New Rhetoric: A Treatise on Argumentation.* Notre Dame, Ind.: University of Notre Dame Press.

Perinbanayagam, R. S. 1985. *Signifying Acts: Structure and Meaning in Everyday Life.* Carbondale: Southern Illinois University Press.

Perutz, M. F. 1995. "The Pioneer Defended." *New York Review of Books* (December 21), 54–58.

Peters, J. P., and J. R. Lyme. 1991. Review of Alasdair MacIntyre's *Whose Justice? Which Rationality? Quarterly Journal of Speech* 77, no. 1, 82.

Pfohl, Stephen. 1977. "The 'Discovery' of Child Abuse." *Social Problems* 24, no. 3, 310–24.

Pickering, Andrew. 1984a. *Constructing Quarks: A Sociological History of Particle Physics.* Chicago: University of Chicago Press.

———. 1984b. "Against Putting the Phenomena First: The Discovery of the Weak Neutral Current." *Studies in History and Philosophy of Science* 15, no. 2, 85–117.

Pickering, Andrew, ed. 1992. *Science as Practice and Culture.* Chicago: University of Chicago Press.

Pillemer, David. 1992. "Remembering Personal Circumstances: A Functional Analysis." Pp. 236–63 in E. Winograd and U. Neisser, eds. *Affect and Accuracy in Recall: Studies of "Flashbulb Memories."* New York: Cambridge University Press.

Pinch, Trevor, and Trevor Pinch. 1987. "Reservations about Reflexivity and New Literary Forms: Or Why Let the Devil Have All the Good Tunes." In Steve Woolgar, ed. *Knowledge and Reflexivity.* London: Sage.

Pinnick, Cassandra L. 1994. "Remarks on Robert Boyle and Thomas Hobbes in Seventh-Century Science." Manuscript. University of Hawaii.

Piroe, Emanual. 1990. *Science and Academic Life in Transition.* New Brunswick, N.J.: Transaction.

Piven, Frances, and Richard A. Cloward. 1977. *Poor People's Movements.* New York: Pantheon.

Planck, Max. 1959. *The Philosophy of Physics.* In *The New Science.* James Murphy and W. H. Johnston, trans. New York: Meridian.

———. 1972. *Planck's Original Papers in Quantum Physics.* D. ter Haar and Stephen G. Brush, trans. Hans Kangro, ed. London: Taylor and Francis.

Platt, Jerald. 1983. "The Development of the Participant-Observation Method in Sociology." *Journal of the History of the Behavioral Sciences* 19, no. 4 (October), 379–93.

Pointing, Clive. 1991. *A Green History of the World.* New York: St. Martin's.

Polanyi, Michael. 1958. *Personal Knowledge: Toward a Post-Critical Philosophy.* Chicago: University of Chicago Press.

Polkinghorne, Donald E. 1991. *Narrative Knowing in the Human Sciences.* Albany: SUNY Press.

Pomian, Krzysztof. 1978. "Entre l'invisible et le visible: La collection." In *Encyclopedie Einaudi* 3. Milan: Editions Einaudi.

Popper, Karl. 1959. *The Logic of Scientific Discovery.* New York: Basic Books.

———. 1963. *Conjectures and Refutations: The Growth of Scientific Knowledge.* London: Routledge.

———. 1966. *The Open Society and Its Enemies* 2. London: Routledge and Kegan Paul.

———. 1977. *Objective Knowledge: An Evolutionary Approach.* New York: Oxford University Press.

Porter, Theodor. 1989. "Objectivity and Authority: How French Engineers Reduced Public Utility to Numbers." Manuscript. Department of History, University of Virginia.

Prelli, Lawrence J. 1989. *A Rhetoric of Science: Inventing Scientific Discourse.* Columbia: University of South Carolina Press.

Pribram, Karl H. 1990. "From Metaphors to Models: The Use of Analogy in Neuropsychology." Pp. 79–103 in David E. Leary, ed. *Metaphors in the History of Psychology.* Cambridge: Cambridge University Press.

Price, Don. 1967. *The Scientific Estate.* Cambridge: Harvard University Press.

Prince, Derek J. 1969. "Contra-Copernicus." In M. Clagett, ed. *Critical Problems in the History of Science.* Madison: University of Wisconsin Press.

Proctor, Robert. 1991. *Value-Free Science?* Cambridge: Harvard University Press.

Quine, Willard Van Orman. 1953. *From a Logical Point of View.* New York: Columbia University Press.

————. 1960. *Word and Object.* Cambridge: MIT Press.

————. 1969. *Ontological Relativity and Other Essays.* New York: Columbia University Press.

Rabinow, Paul. 1982. "Masked I Go Forward: Reflections on the Modern Subject." Pp. 173–85 in Jay Ruby, ed. *A Crack in the Mirror: Reflective Perspectives in Anthropology.* Philadelphia: University of Pennsylvania Press.

Radcliffe-Brown, A. R. 1958. "The Method of Ethnology and Social Anthropology." Pp. 3–38 in M. N. Srinivas, ed. *Method in Social Anthropology.* Chicago: University of Chicago Press.

Radnitzky, G. 1973. *Contemporary Schools of Metaphysics.* Chicago: Henry Regnery.

Rancière, Jacques. 1994. *The Names of History: On the Poetics of Knowledge.* Minneapolis: University of Minnesota Press.

Rappoport, Anatol. 1964. *Strategy and Conscience.* New York: Schocken Books.

Ravetz, Jerome R. 1971. *Scientific Knowledge and Its Social Problems.* Oxford: Clarendon Press.

Rawls-Warfield, Anne. 1987. "The Interaction Order Sui Generis: Goffman's Contribution to Social Theory." *Sociological Theory* 5, no. 2, 136–49.

Reagan, Michael. 1969. *Science and the Federal Patron.* New York: Oxford University Press.

Reed, Edward, and Rebecca Jones, eds. 1982. *Reasons for Realism: Selected Essays of James J. Gibsons.* Hillsdale, N.J.: Lawrence Erlbaum.

Reichenback, Hans. 1949. *Einstein: Philosopher-Scientist.* Evanston: Northwestern University Press.

Reingold, Nathan. 1980. "Through Paradigm-Land to a Normal History of Science." *Social Studies of Science* 10, no. 4, 475–96.

Reissman, Catherine Kohler. 1993. *Narrative Analysis.* Newbury Park, Calif.: Sage.

Rheticus, Joachim. 1982. *Narratio Prima.* Henri Hugonnard-Roche and Jean-Pierre Verdet, eds. and trans. Studio Copernica 20. Wroclaw: Maison d'edition de l'Académie polonaise des sciences.

Ricci, David M. 1984. *The Tragedy of Political Science: Politics, Scholarship, and Democracy.* New Haven: Yale University Press.

Richardson, Laurel. 1991. "Value Constituting Practices, Rhetoric, and Metaphors in Sociology." *Current Perspectives in Social Theory* 11, 1–5.

Ricoeur, Paul. 1970. *Freud and Philosophy: An Essay on Interpretation.* D. Savage, trans. New Haven: Yale University Press.

————. 1980. "Existence and Hermeneutics." Pp. 236–56 in Joseph Bleicher, *Contemporary Hermeneutics: Hermeneutics as Method, Philosophy, and Critique.* London: Routledge and Kegan Paul.

————. 1981. *The Rule of Metaphor: Multidisciplinary Studies of the Creation of Meaning in Language.* Robert Czerny, trans. Toronto: University of Toronto Press.

————. 1984. *Time and Narrative* 1. Kathleen McLaughlin and David Pellauer, trans. Chicago: University of Chicago Press.

Rieber, R. W. 1980. *Wilhelm Wundt and the Making of a Scientific Psychology.* New York: Plenum.

Riffaterre, Michel. 1984. "Intertextual Representation: On Mimesis as Interpretive Discourse." *Critical Inquiry* 11 (September), 141–62.

Rilling, R. 1975. *Theorie und Soziologie der Wissenschaft.* Frankfurt: Fischer.

Ritzer, George. 1975. *Sociology, Multiple Paradigm Science.* Boston: Allyn and Bacon.

————. 1988. "Sociological Metatheory: A Defense of a Subfield by a Delineation of Its Parameters." *Sociological Theory* 6, no. 2 (Fall), 187–200.

————. 1991. "Metatheorizing in Sociology." *Sociological Forum* 5, 3–15.

Rochbert-Halton, Eugene. 1986. *Meaning and Modernity: Social Theory in the Pragmatic Attitude.* Chicago: University of Chicago Press.

Roche, Maurice. 1973. "Class Analysis and the Showing of Dichotomy." In Paul Filmer, Michael Phillipson, Maurice Roche, Barry Sandywell, and David Silverman, eds. "Stratifying Practices." Manuscript. Goldsmith's College, London.

Rock, Paul Elliot. 1979. *The Making of Symbolic Interactionism.* Totowa, N.J.: Rowman and Littlefield.

Rogers, Raymond S. 1982. "Generic Tendencies in Majority and Non-Majority Supreme Court Opinions: The Case of Justice Douglas." *Communication Quarterly* 30, 232–36.

Root-Bernstein, Michele. 1984. *Boulevard Theatre and Revolution in Eighteenth Century Paris.* Ann Arbor: UMI Research Press.

Rorty, Amelie Oksenberg. 1987. "Persons as a Rhetorical Category." *Social Research* 54, no. 1 (Spring), 55–72.

Rorty, Richard. 1979. *Philosophy and the Mirror of Nature.* Princeton: Princeton University Press.

————. 1982. *Consequences of Pragmatism.* Minneapolis: University of Minnesota Press.

————. 1988. "The Propriety of Democracy to Philosophy." In M. D. Peterson and R. C. Vaughn, eds. *The Virginia Statute for Religious Freedom: Its Evolution and Consequences in American History.* Cambridge: Cambridge University Press.

————. 1989. *Contingency, Irony, Solidarity.* Cambridge: Cambridge University Press.

Rosaldo, Renato. 1987. "Where Objectivity Lies: The Rhetoric of Anthropology." Pp. 87–110 in John S. Nelson, Allan Megrill, and Donald N. McCloskey, eds. *The Rhetoric of the Human Sciences: Language and Argument in Scholarship and Public Affairs.* Madison: University of Wisconsin Press.

Rose, Hilary, and Steven Rose. 1979a. "The Incorporation of Science." Pp. 16–33 in Hilary Rose and Steven Rose, eds. *Ideology of/in the Natural Sciences.* Cambridge, Mass.: Schenkman.

Rose, Hilary, and Steven Rose, eds. 1979b. *Ideology of/in the Natural Sciences.* Cambridge, Mass.: Schenkman.

Rose, Nikolas. 1985. *The Psychological Complex: Psychology, Politics, and Society in England, 1869–1939.* London: Routledge and Kegan Paul.

Ross, Andrew. 1995. "Science Backlash on Techno-Skeptics." *Nation* (October 2), 346–50.

Ross, Dorothy. 1979. "The Development of the Social Sciences." Pp. 107–38 in Alexandra

Oleson and John Voss, eds. *The Organization of Knowledge in Modern America, 1860–1920.* Baltimore: Johns Hopkins University Press.

Ross, W. D., ed. 1927. *Aristotle Selections.* New York: Charles Scribner's Sons.

Rossi, Ino. 1983. *From the Sociology of Symbols to the Sociology of Signs: Toward a Dialectical Sociology.* New York: Columbia University Press.

Rossi-Landi, Ferruccio. 1975. *Linguistics and Economics.* The Hague: Mouton.

———. 1983. *Language as Work and Trade.* South Hadley, Mass.: Bergin and Garvey.

Rouse, Joseph. 1987. *Knowledge and Power: Toward a Political Philosophy of Science.* Ithaca: Cornell University Press.

———. 1988. "The Narrative Reconstruction of Science." Paper delivered at the Center for the Humanities, Wesleyan University, Fall.

———. 1996. *Engaging Science: How to Understand Its Practices Philosophically.* Ithaca: Cornell University Press.

Rubin, J., ed. 1995. *Remembering Our Past: Studies in Autobiographical Memory.* New York: Cambridge University Press.

Rueschemeyer, Dietrich. 1986. *Power and the Division of Labour.* Stanford: Stanford University Press.

———. 1996. *States, Social Knowledge, and the Origins of Modern Social Policies.* Princeton: Princeton University Press.

Sahlins, Marshall. 1985. *Islands of History.* Chicago: University of Chicago Press.

Saloman, Jean-Jacques. 1977. "Science Policy Studies and the Development of Science Policy." In Ina Spiegel-Rösing and Derek Price, eds. *Science, Technology, and Society.* London: Sage.

Samelson, Franz. 1979. "Putting Psychology on the Map: Ideology and Intelligence Testing." Pp. 103–68 in Allan R. Buss, ed. *Psychology in Social Context.* New York: Irvington.

Sampson, E. E. 1977. "Psychology and the American Ideal." *Journal of Personality and Social Psychology* 35, 767–82.

———. 1983. "Deconstructing Psychology's Subject." *Journal of Mind and Behavior* 4, 135–64.

Sandbach, Francis. 1980. *Environmental Ideology and Policy.* Montclair, N.J.: Allanheld, Osmun.

Sanford, E. C. 1892. "A Laboratory Course in Physiological Psychology," *American Journal of Psychology* 4.

Sarbin, Theodore R., ed. 1986. *Narrative Psychology: The Storied Nature of Human Conduct.* New York: Praeger.

Saunders, John. 1987. "Power, Discourse, and Discourse of Power." Manuscript. Department of Sociology, University of Maryland, College Park.

Saussure, Ferdinand de. 1982. *Course in General Linguistics.* Wade Baskin, trans. New York: McGraw-Hill.

Scheibe, Karl E. 1988. "Metamorphoses in the Psychologist's Advantage." Pp. 53–71 in Jill G. Morawski, ed. *The Rise of Experimentation in American Psychology.* New Haven: Yale University Press.

Scheman, Naomi. 1991. "Who Wants To Know? The Epistemological Value of Values." In Joan E. Hartman and Ellen Messer-Davidow, eds. *(En)Gendering Knowledge: Feminists in Academe.* Knoxville: University of Tennessee Press.

Schiebinger, Londa. 1989. *The Mind Has No Sex? Women in the Origins of Modern Science.* Cambridge: Harvard University Press.

Schlick, Moritz. 1959. "The Foundation of Knowledge." Pp. 199–227 in A. J. Ayer, ed. *Logical Positivism.* New York: Free Press.

Schneider, Mark A. 1991. "Boundary Problems in Seventh-Century Natural Philosophy." Paper presented to the American Sociological Association, Cincinnati, Ohio, August.

Schollmeier, P. 1984. "A Classical Rhetoric of Modern Science." *Philosophy and Rhetoric* 17, 209–20.

Schon, David A. 1979. "Generative Metaphor: A Perspective on Problem Setting in Social Policy." Pp. 254–83 in Andrew Ortony, ed. *Metaphor and Thought.* New York: Cambridge University Press.

Schrag, Calvin O. 1986. *Communication Praxis and the Space of Subjectivity.* Bloomington: Indiana University Press.

Schrum, Wesley. 1988. "Review Essay: The Labyrinth of Science." *American Journal of Sociology* 2, no. 1 (September), 386–403.

Schudson, Michael, and Paul Crellanin. 1984. "Embarrassment and Erving Goffman's Idea of Human Nature." *Theory and Society* 13, no. 5, 633–48.

Schuon, Karl. 1972. *Wissenschaft, Politik, und Wissenschaftliche Politik.* Cologne: Pahl-Rugenstein.

Schuppe, James S. 1991. "Formism Re-Formed? A Meta-Theoretical Investigation of Generic Criticism." Manuscript. Department of Speech Communication, University of Maryland, College Park.

Schutz, Alfred. 1964. "The Well Informed Citizen: An Essay in the Social Distribution of Knowledge." In *Collected Papers* 2. The Hague: M. Nijhoff.

———. 1970. *On Phenomenology and Social Relations.* Chicago: University of Chicago Press.

Schwab, Jim. 1994. *Deeper Shades of Green: The Rise of Blue-Collar and Minority Environmentalism in America.* San Francisco: Sierra Club Books.

Scult, Allen. 1988. "What Is Friendship?: A Hermeneutical Quibble." Manuscript. Department of Rhetoric, Drake University, Des Moines, Iowa.

———. 1991. "Beyond Narrative." Manuscript. Department of Rhetoric, Drake University, Des Moines, Iowa.

Seghers, Anna. 1981. "Letters to Georg Lukács," June 28, 1938, and February 1939. In Georg Lukács, *Essays on Realism.* Rodney Livingstone, ed. Cambridge: MIT Press.

Seltzer, Mark. 1984. "Reading Foucault: Cells, Corridors, Novels." *Diacritics* (Spring), 78–89.

Shapere, Dudley. 1984. *Reason and the Search for Knowledge: Investigations in the Philosophy of Science.* Boston: D. Reidel.

Shapin, Steven. 1990. "Science and the Public." In R. C. Olby, et al., eds. *Companion to the History of Modern Science.* London: Routledge.

Shapin, Steven, and Simon Schaffer. 1986. *Leviathan and the Air-Pump: Hobbes, Boyle, and the Experimental Way of Life.* Princeton: Princeton University Press.

Shapiro, Ian, and Alexander Wendt. 1992. "The Difference That Realism Makes: Social Science and the Politics of Consent." *Politics and Society* 20, no. 2 (June), 197–223.

Shapiro, Michael J. 1988. *The Politics of Representation: Writing Practices in Biography, Photography, and Policy Analysis.* Madison: University of Wisconsin Press.

Shawcross, William. 1984. "The Mekong." Pp. 77–112 in *River Journeys.* London: British Broadcasting Corporation.

Shinn, Terry. 1980. *Savoir scientifique et pouvoir social: L'Ecole Polytechnique, 1794–1914.* Paris: Presses de la fondation nationale des sciences politique.

Shostak, Marjorie. 1981. *Nisa: The Life and Words of a !Kung Woman.* Cambridge: Harvard University Press.

Shotter, John. 1997. "Academic Discourse and Civil Society." In Richard Harvey Brown, ed. *New Roles for Rhetoric: From Academic Criticism to Civic Affirmation.* A special issue of *Argumentation* 11, no. 1 (February), 95–112.

Shumway, David, and Ellen Messer-Davidow. 1991. "Disciplinarity: An Introduction," *Poetics Today* 12, no. 2, 201–25.

Simmel, Georg. 1978. *The Philosophy of Money.* Tom Bottomore and David Frisby, trans. London: Routledge and Kegan Paul.

Simons, Herbert W. 1978. " 'Genrealizing' about Rhetoric: A Scientific Approach." Pp. 33–50 in Karlyn Kohrs Campbell and Kathleen Hall Jamieson, eds. *Form and Genre: Shaping Rhetorical Action.* Annandale, Va.: Speech Communication Association.

———. 1990. "Introduction: The Rhetoric of Inquiry as an Intellectual Movement." Pp. 1–34 in Herbert W. Simons, ed. *The Rhetorical Turn: Invention and Persuasion in the Conduct of Inquiry.* Chicago: University of Chicago Press.

Simons, Herbert W., ed. 1989. *Rhetoric in the Human Sciences.* London: Sage.

Simpson, Christopher. 1994. *Science of Coercion: Communication Research and Psychological Warfare, 1945–1960.* New York: Oxford University Press.

Sims, George Robert. 1984. *How the Poor Live; and Horrible London.* 1889, London: Chatto and Winders. Reprint, New York: Garland.

Skipper, J. M., Jr., A. L. Guenther, and G. Nass. 1967. "The Sacredness of .05." *American Sociologist* 2, no. 1 (February), 16–18.

Smith, Dorothy E. 1990. *The Conceptual Practices of Power: A Feminist Sociology of Knowledge.* Boston: Northeastern University Press.

Smith, Laurence D. 1986. *Behaviorism and Logical Positivism: A Reassessment of the Alliance.* Stanford: Stanford University Press.

———. 1990. "Metaphors of Knowledge and Behavior in the Behaviorist Tradition." Pp. 239–66 in David E. Leary, ed. *Metaphors in the History of Psychology.* New York: Cambridge University Press.

Snow, David A., and R. D. Benford. 1988. "Ideology, Frame Resonance and Participant Mobilization." in B. Klandermans, H. Kriesi, and S. Tarrow, eds. *International Social Movement Research: From Structure to Action: Comparing Social Movement Research across Cultures* 1. Greenwich, Conn.: JAI Press.

———. 1992. "Master Frames and Cycles of Protest." In Aldon D. Morris and Carol McClurg Mueller, eds. *Frontiers in Social Movement Theory.* New Haven: Yale University Press.

Snow, David A., and Richard Machalek. 1984. "The Sociology of Conversation." *Annual Review of Sociology* 10, 167–90.

Snow, David A., E. Burke Rochford, Jr., Steven K. Worden, and Robert D. Benford. 1986. "Frame Alignment Processes, Micromobilization, and Movement Participation." *American Sociological Review* 51, no. 4, 464–81.

Sola, Giorgio. 1985. "Sviluppi e scenari dilla sociologia italiana: 1861–1890." Pp. 75–180 in Filippo Barbano and Giorgio Sola, eds. *Sociolgia e scienze sociale en Italia*. Milan: Angeli.

Soley, Lawrence C. 1995. *Leasing the Ivory Tower: The Corporate Takeover of Academia*. Boston: South End Press.

Sorokin, Pitirim. 1976. *Fads and Foibles in Modern Sociology and Related Sciences*. Westport, Conn.: Greenwood Press.

Soyland, John. 1994. *Psychology as Metaphor*. Newbury Park, Calif.: Sage.

Spairosu, Mihai. 1989. *Dionysius Reborn: Play and the Aesthetic Dimension in Modern Philosophical and Scientific Discourse*. Ithaca: Cornell University Press.

Spence, Donald P. 1982. *Narrative Truth and Historical Truth: Meaning and Interpretation in Psychoanalysis*. New York: Norton.

———. 1987. *The Freudian Metaphor: Toward Paradigm Change in Psychoanalysis*. New York: Norton.

———. 1990. "The Rhetorical View of Psychoanalysis." *Journal of the American Psychoanalytical Association* 38, no. 3, 579–603.

Stack, Carol. 1974. *All Our Kin*. New York: Harper and Row.

Stam, Henderikus J. 1987. "The Psychology of Control: A Textual Critique." Pp. 131–56 in Henderikus J. Stam, T. B. Robers, and Kenneth J. Gergen, eds. *The Analysis of Psychological Theory: Metapsychological Perspectives*. Washington, D.C.: Hemisphere.

Stanley, Manfred. 1981. *The Technological Conscience: Survival and Dignity in an Age of Expertise*. 1978. Reprint, Chicago: University of Chicago Press.

———. 1983. "The Mystery of the Commons: On the Indispensability of Civic Rhetoric." *Social Research* 50, no. 4 (Winter), 851–83.

———. 1986. "Can American Pluralism Tolerate Civic Education? An Examination of the Status of Civic Rhetoric in America." Paper presented at the conference on Case Studies in the Human Sciences. Temple University, Philadelphia, April.

———. 1990. "The Rhetoric of the Commons: Forum Discourse in Politics and Society." Pp. 238–57 in Herbert W. Simons, ed. *The Rhetorical Turn: Invention and Persuasion in the Conduct of Inquiry*. Chicago: University of Chicago Press.

Stauder, Jack. 1986. "The 'Relevance' of Anthropology to Colonialism and Imperialism." Pp. 38–61 in Lew Levidow, ed. *Radical Science Essays*. London: Free Association Books.

Stein, M. 1988. "Writing about Psychoanalysis: I. Analysts Who Write and Those Who Do Not." *Journal of the American Psychoanalytic Association* 36, 105–24.

Sterne, Laurence. 1940. *The Life and Opinions of Tristram Shandy*. New York: Odyssey.

Stewart, Charles J. 1980. "A Functional Approach to the Rhetoric of Social Movements." *Central States Speech Journal* 31, no. 4 (Winter), 298–305.

Stewart, Charles J., Craig Allen Smith, and Robert E. Denton. 1989. *Persuasion and Social Movements*. Prospect Heights, Ill.: Waveland Press.

Stigler, Stephen M. 1986. *The History of Statistics: The Measurement of Uncertainty before 1900*. Cambridge: Harvard University Press.

Stocking, George W., Jr. 1987. *Victorian Anthropology*. New York: Free Press.

Stoller, Paul. 1989. "The Reconstruction of Ethnography." Pp. 51–74 in *Taste of Ethnographic Things: The Sense in Anthropology.* Philadelphia: University of Pennsylvania Press.

Storr, Richard J. 1966. *Harper's University: The Beginnings.* Chicago: University of Chicago Press.

Strasser, Stephan. 1963. *Phenomenology and the Human Sciences.* Pittsburgh: Dusquesne University Press.

Sulliman, Susan Rubin. 1980. "Redundancy and the 'Readable' Text." *Poetics Today* 1, no. 3, 119–42.

Sullivan, R. J. 1977. *Morality and the Good Life.* Memphis: Memphis State University.

Swatez, Gerald U. 1970. "The Social Organization of a University Laboratory." *Minerva* 8 (January), 36–58.

Tambiah, Stanley J. A. 1989. *Magic, Science, and Religion and the Scope of Rationality.* New York: Cambridge University Press.

Taylor, Bob Pepperman. 1992. *Our Limits Transgressed: Environmental Political Thought in America.* Lawrence: University of Kansas Press.

Taylor, Serge. 1984. *Making Bureaucracies Think.* Stanford: Stanford University Press.

Theocharis, T., and M. Psimopoulos. 1987. "Where Science Has Gone Wrong." *Nature* 329, no. 15 (October), 595–98.

Thernstrom, Stephan. 1969. *Poverty, Planning, and Politics in the New Boston.* New York: Basic Books.

Thomas, William I., and Florian Znaniecki. 1958. *The Polish Peasant in Europe and America.* 5 vols. New York: Dover.

Thompson, Grahame. 1989. "Homo Rhetoricus: Economics and the Social Sciences Discover the Linguistic Model and Postmodernism, or Do They?" Manuscript. Faculty of Social Sciences, Open University, England.

Thompson, John B. 1984. *Studies in the Theory of Ideology.* Berkeley: University of California Press.

Thorndike, E. L. 1923. "Measurement in Education." In G. M. Whipple, ed. *Twenty-First Yearbook of the National Society for the Study of Education.* Bloomington, Ind.: Public School Publishing Company.

Todd, Alexandra Dundas. 1988. *Gender and Discourse: The Power of Talk.* Norwood, N.J.: Ablex.

———. 1989. *Intimate Adversaries: Cultural Conflict between Doctors and Women Patients.* Philadelphia: University of Pennsylvania Press.

Todorov, Tzvetan. 1975a. *The Poetics of Prose.* Ithaca: Cornell University Press.

———. 1975b. *The Fantastic: A Structural Approach to a Literary Genre.* Ithaca: Cornell University Press.

Tolman, E. C. 1926. "A Behavioristic Theory of Ideas." *Psychological Review* 33, no. 5, 352–69.

———. 1932. *Purposive Behavior in Animals and Men.* New York: Century.

Tomlinson, Hugh. 1989. "After Truth: Post-Modernism and the Rhetoric of Science." Pp. 43–57 in Hilary Lawson and Lisa Appignanesi, eds. *Dismantling the Truth: Reality in the Post-Modern World.* New York: St. Martin's.

Toulmin, Stephen. 1972. *Human Understanding.* Princeton: Princeton University Press.

Toulmin, Stephen, and David E. Leary. 1979. "The Cult of Empiricism in Psychology, and

Beyond." Pp. 594–617 in Sigmund Koch and David E. Leary, eds. *A Century of Psychology as Science.* New York: McGraw-Hill.

Touraine, Alain. 1985. "An Introduction to the Study of Social Movements." *Social Research* 52, no. 4, 749–88.

Trilateral Report. 1975. *The Crisis of Democracy: Report on the Governability of Democracies to the Trilateral Commission.* New York: New York University Press.

Turner, Stephen P. n.d.a. "Forms of Patronage." Manuscript. Center for Interdisciplinary Studies of Culture and Society, University of South Florida, St. Petersburg.

———. n.d.b. "Depoliticizing Power." Review of Joseph Rouse, *Knowledge and Power,* and Barry Barnes, *The Nature of Power.* Manuscript. University of South Florida, St. Petersburg.

Tyler, Stephen. 1985. "Ethnography, Intertextuality, and the End of Description." *American Journal of Semiotics* 3, no. 4, 83–98.

Unger, Roberto M. 1975. *Knowledge and Politics.* New York: Free Press.

Valesio, Paolo. 1980. *Novartiqua: Rhetorics as a Contemporary Theory.* Bloomington: Indiana University Press.

Van den Daele, Wolfgang, and Wolfgang Krohn. 1983. "Science in a Crisis of Legitimation." Pp. 237–50 in Wolf Schäfer, ed. *Finalization in Science: The Social Orientation of Scientific Progress.* Dordrecht: D. Reidel.

Van Maanen, John. 1988. *Tales of the Field: On Writing Ethnography.* Chicago: University of Chicago Press.

———. 1995. "Trade Secrets: On Writing Ethnography." Pp. 60–79 in Richard Harvey Brown, ed. *Postmodern Representations: Truth, Power, and Mimesis in the Human Sciences and Public Culture.* Urbana: University of Illinois Press.

Veblen, Thorstein B. 1965. *The Higher Learning in America: A Memorandum on the Conduct of Universities by Business Men.* New York: Augustus M. Kelley.

Venn, C. 1984. "The Subject of Psychology." Pp. 119–52 in J. Henriques, W. Hollway, C. Urwin, C. Venn, and V. Walkerdine, eds. *Changing the Subject.* London: Methuen.

Veysey, Laurence R. 1965. *The Emergence of the American University.* Chicago: University of Chicago Press.

Vickers, Brian. 1983. "Epideictic Rhetoric in Galileo's *Dialogue.*" *Annali dell'Instituto e Museo di Storia della Scienze di Firenze* 8, 69–102.

———. 1985. "Restoration Prose Style: A Reassessment." Pp. 1–76 in *Rhetoric and the Pursuit of Truth.* Los Angeles: Clark Library.

Vico, Giambattista. 1965. *On the Study Methods of Our Time.* Elio Gianturco, trans. Indianapolis, Ind.: Bobbs-Merrill.

———. 1972. *The New Science of Giambattista Vico.* Thomas Goddard Bergin and Max Harold Frisch, trans. Ithaca: Cornell University Press.

Vidich, Arthur J. 1989. Review of Robert G. Bannister, *Sociology and Scientism. Contemporary Sociology* 18, no. 3 (May), 405–8.

Vidich, Arthur J., and Stanford M. Lyman. 1985. *American Sociology: Worldly Rejections of Religion and Their Directions.* New Haven: Yale University Press.

Wagley, Charles. 1977. *Welcome of Tears.* New York: Oxford University Press.

Wagner, Peter. 1989. "Social Science and the State in Continental Western Europe: The

Political Structuration of Disciplinary Discourse." *International Social Science Journal* 41, no. 122, 509–28.

Wagner, Peter, Carol Weiss, Björn Wittrock, and Hellmut Wollmann, eds. 1990. *Social Sciences and Modern States: National Experiences in Comparative Perspective.* Cambridge: Cambridge University Press.

Wagner, Peter, and Björn Wittrock. 1990. "Analyzing Social Science: On the Possibility of a Sociology of the Social Sciences." Pp. 3–21 in Peter Wagner, Björn Wittrock, and Richard Whitley, eds. *Discourses on Society: The Shaping of the Social Sciences Disciplines.* Dordrecht: Kluwer.

Wagner, Roy. 1980. *The Invention of Culture.* Chicago: University of Chicago Press.

Waitzkin, Howard. 1968. "Truth's Search for Power: The Dilemmas of the Social Sciences." *Social Problems* 15, no. 4, 408–19.

Walker, James. 1982a. *Lakota Belief and Ritual.* Raymond J. DeMallie and Elaine A. Jahnes, eds. Lincoln: University of Nebraska Press.

———. 1982b. *Lakota Society.* Raymond J. DeMallie, ed. Lincoln: University of Nebraska Press.

———. 1983. *Lakota Myth.* Elaine A. Jahnes, ed. Lincoln: University of Nebraska Press.

Wallace, Robert M. 1987. "Translator's Introduction." Pp. ix–xviii in Hans Blumenberg, *The Genesis of the Copernican World.* Cambridge: MIT Press.

Walter, Emil. 1989. *Das Ange der Firma.* N.p.

Ward, J. P. 1979. "The Poem's Defiance of Sociology." *Sociology* 8, no. 1 (January), 89–102.

———. 1986. "Poetry and Sociology." *Human Studies* 9, no. 4, 323–45.

Ware, B. L., and Wil A. Linkugel. 1973. "They Spoke in Defense of Themselves: On the Generic Criticism of Apologia." *Quarterly Journal of Speech* 59 (October), 273–83.

Watson, James D. 1968. *The Double Helix.* New York: Atheneum.

Watt, Ian. 1957. *The Rise of the Novel: Studies in Defoe, Richardson and Fielding.* Berkeley: University of California Press.

Wax, Murray L. 1982. Review of Alasdair MacIntyre's *After Virtue: A Study. Moral Theory in Contemporary Sociology* 3 (May 11), 346–48.

Weber, Max. 1949. *The Methodology of the Social Sciences.* E. A. Shils and H. A. Finch, eds. Glencoe, Ill.: Free Press.

———. 1978a. *Economy and Society.* 1922. Reprint, Berkeley: University of California Press.

———. 1978b. "Science as a Vocation." Pp. 77–156 in H. Gerth and C. W. Mills, eds. *From Max Weber: Essays in Sociology.* New York: Oxford.

Webler, Thomas. 1992. "Habermas Put Into Practice: A Democratic Discourse for Environmental Problem Solving." Paper presented at the sixth annual meeting of the Society for Human Ecology, Snowbird, Utah, October 2–4.

Webler, Thomas, Hans Kastenholtz, and Ortwin Renn. 1994. "Can Public Participation in Impact Assessment Enable Social Learning?" Paper presented at the seventh meeting of the Society for Human Ecology, April 22.

Weibe, Robert H. 1967. *The Search for Order, 1877–1920.* New York: Hill and Wang.

Weinsheimer, Joel C. 1985. *Gadamer's Hermeneutics: A Reading of "Truth and Method."* New Haven: Yale University Press.

Weiss, Carol H. 1977. *Using Social Research in Public Policy-Making*. Lexington, Mass.: Lexington Books.

Weiss, Carol H., with M. J. Bucuvalas. 1980. *Social Science Research and Decision-Making*. New York: Columbia University Press.

Weisz, George. 1979. "L'idéologie républicaine et les sciences sociales." *Revue française de sociologie* 20, 83–112.

Wendt, Alexander, and Ian Shapiro. 1993. "The Misunderstood Promise of 'Realist Social Theory.'" Paper presented at the meetings of the American Political Science Association, Washington, D.C.

Wessely, Anna. 1991. "Transposing 'Style' from the History of Art to the History of Science." *Science in Context* 4, no. 2, 265–78.

Westman, Robert S. 1975. "The Wittenberg Interpretation of the Copernican Theory." Pp. 7–30 in O. Gingrich, ed. *The Nature of Scientific Discovery: A Symposium Commemorating the Five Hundredth Anniversary of the Birth of Nicolas Copernicus*. Washington, D.C.: Smithsonian Institute Press.

Wexler, P. 1983. *Critical Social Psychology*. Boston: Routledge and Kegan Paul.

White, Hayden. 1973. *Metahistory: The Historical Imagination in the Nineteenth Century*. Baltimore: Johns Hopkins University Press.

———. 1978. *Tropics of Discourse*. Baltimore: Johns Hopkins University Press.

———. 1987. *The Content of the Form: Narrative Discourse and Historical Representation*. Baltimore: Johns Hopkins University Press.

Whitley, Richard. 1984. *The Intellectual and Social Organization of the Sciences*. Oxford: Clarendon Press.

———. 1987. "The Structure and Context of Economics as a Scientific Field." *Research in the History of Economic Thought and Methodology* 4, 179–209. Greenwich, Conn.: JAI Press.

Whyte, William Foote. 1969. *Street Corner Society: The Social Structure of an Italian Slum*. Chicago: University of Chicago Press.

Wigdor, A. K., and W. R. Garner, eds. 1982. *Ability Testing: Uses, Consequences, and Controversies*. Washington, D.C.: National Academy Press.

Wilkie, Richard W. 1976. "Karl Marx on Rhetoric." *Philosophy and Rhetoric* 9, no. 3, 232–46.

Willard, Charles. 1991. "Authority." *Informal Logic* 12, 11–22.

Willey, Basil. 1942. *Seventeenth Century Background: Studies in the Thought of the Age in Relation to Poetry and Religion*. New York: Columbia University Press.

Williams, Patricia. 1991. *The Alchemy of Race and Rights*. Cambridge: Harvard University Press.

Wilson, Daniel J. 1990. *Science, Community, and the Transformation of American Philosophy, 1860–1930*. Chicago: University of Chicago Press.

Windt, Theodore Otto, Jr. 1972. "The Diatribe: Last Report for Protest." *Quarterly Journal of Speech* 58 (February), 1–14.

Witten, Marsha. 1993. "Narrative and the Culture of Obedience in the Workplace." Pp. 97–120 in Dennis Mumby, ed. *Narrative and Social Control*. Newbury Park, Calif.: Sage.

Wittgenstein, Ludwig. 1963. *Philosophic Investigations*. G. E. M. Anscombe, trans. Oxford: Basil Blackwell.

Wittrock, Björn, Peter Wagner, and Richard Whitely. 1991. *Discourses on Society: The Shaping of the Social Science Disciplines.* Dordrecht: Kluwer.

Wittrock, Björn, Peter Wagner, and Hellmut Wollmann. 1991. "Social Science and the Modern State: Policy Knowledge and Political Institutions in Western Europe and the United States." Pp. 28–85 in Peter Wagner, Carol Hirschorn Weiss, Björn Wittrock, and Hellmut Wollman, eds. *Social Science and Modern States: National Experiences and Theoretical Crossroads.* Cambridge: Cambridge University Press.

Wolff, Kurt H. 1986. "Exploring Relations between Surrender-and-Catch and Poetry, Sociology, Evil." *Human Studies* 9, no. 4, 347–64.

Wood, Elizabeth. 1988. "Nautical Metaphors as Markers of Discourse Shifts in Western Literature." Manuscript. Program in Comparative Literature, University of Maryland, College Park.

Wood, Michael. 1984. "The Congo." Pp. 11–44 in *River Journeys.* London: British Broadcasting Corporation.

Woolgar, Steve. 1988. *Science: The Very Idea.* London: Tavistock.

Woolgar, Steve, and Dorothy Pawluch. 1985. "Ontological Gerrymandering: The Anatomy of Social Problems Explanations." *Social Problems* 32, no. 3, 214–27.

Woollett, E. L. 1980. "Physics and Modern Warfare: The Awkward Silence." *American Journal of Physics* 48, no. 2, 104–11.

Wundt, Wilhelm. 1908. *Grundzüge der Physiologischen Psychologie* 1. 6th ed. Leipzig.

Zajonc, R. B. 1980. "Copresence." Pp. 35–60 in P. B. Paulus, ed. *Psychology of Group Influence.* Hillsdale, N.J.: Lawrence Erlbaum.

———. 1965. "Social Facilitation." *Science* 149, 269–74.

Zijderveld, Anton. 1970. *The Abstract Society: A Cultural Analysis of Our Time.* New York: Doubleday.

Ziman, John. 1968. *Public Knowledge: An Essay Concerning the Social Dimension of Science.* London: Cambridge University Press.

Zuckerman, Harriet. 1977. *Scientific Elite: Nobel Laureates in the United States.* New York: Free Press.

Zyskind, Harold. 1950. "A Rhetorical Analysis of the Gettysburg Address." *Journal of General Education* (April), 202–12.

Index